To Michy + ...

CW00766438

With Best wishes

Theodore Norman

+with love from

Joe Neville (The Sorcerer's
Apprentice)

AN OUTSTRETCHED ARM

1 Baron Maurice de Hirsch

AN OUTSTRETCHED ARM

A History of the
Jewish Colonization Association

THEODORE NORMAN

. . . I will bring you out from under the burdens of the
Egyptians, and I will deliver you from their bondage,
and I will redeem you with an outstretched arm. . . .

Exodus VI:6

Routledge & Kegan Paul
London, Boston, Melbourne and Henley

First published in 1985
by Routledge & Kegan Paul plc

14 Leicester Square, London WC2H 7PH, England,

9 Park Street, Boston, Mass. 02108, USA,

464 St Kilda Road, Melbourne,
Victoria 3004, Australia, and

Broadway House, Newtown Road,
Henley-on-Thames, Oxon RG9 1EN, England

Set in Linotron Bembo
by Input Typesetting Ltd., London
and printed in Great Britain
by Hartnoll Print
Bodmin, Cornwall

© Jewish Colonization Association 1985

No part of this book may be reproduced in
any form without permission from the publisher,
except for the quotation of brief passages
in criticism

Library of Congress Cataloging in Publication Data

Norman, Theodore, 1910–
   An outstretched arm.
   Includes bibliographical references and index.
   1. Jewish Colonization Association.   2. Jews—Coloni-
zation.   3. Farmers, Jewish.   I. Title.
DS143.N66   1985   909'.04924'006   84–9901
British Library CIP data available

ISBN 0–7102–0253–9

Dedicated to the memory of

Sir Henry d'Avigdor Goldsmid, Bart., DSO, MC, TD,

President of JCA from 1951 to 1976
and shaper of its policy after the Second World War,

and of Mordechai Paran,

JCA's Manager in Israel from 1966 to 1978

CONTENTS

Plates

Frontispiece
1   Baron Maurice de Hirsch

Between pages 88 and 89
2a   Moisesville, Argentina, early twentieth century. Settlers from Eastern Europe in the synagogue
2b   Lipton Colony, Canada. Early settlers

Between pages 120 and 121
3a   Saskatchewan, Canada, 1919. Jewish farm workers
3b   Saskatchewan, Canada, 1919. Farm machinery purchased with JCA funds
4a   USSR, between the wars. Improved farming methods in the Jewish rural communities helped by JCA
4b   Ukraine, pre-1925. Loan kassa

Between pages 152 and 153
5a   Beer Tuvia, Israel. Farmer's house before the 1929 disturbances
5b   Beer Tuvia, Israel, 1930. The settlement in ruins
6a   Beer Tuvia, Israel. The settlement after reconstruction
6b   Israel, 1937. Surveying the Huleh swamps

Between pages 184 and 185
7a   Kishinev, Bessarabia, 1920s. Trade school
7b   Poland, 1925. Trade school
8a   Petrovka, Bessarabia, 1920s. Jewish farmer and son
8b   Petrovka, Bessarabia, 1924. Wine-making

Between pages 216 and 217
9a   Petrovka, Bessarabia, 1924. Milking sheep and goats
9b   Lvov, Galicia, 1924. Separating cream
10a Colony Clara, Argentina, 1948. Grain elevator
10b Colony Clara, Argentina, 1964. Vegetable oil extraction plant

Maps

FOREWORD

by the Hon. L. H. L. Cohen, President of JCA

I am deeply grateful to Ted Norman for his work in writing this history of the first 90 years of the Jewish Colonization Association (JCA). As Director of the Baron de Hirsch Fund, New York, he has a wealth of knowledge on the background of Baron Maurice de Hirsch's charitable enterprises, and for him this has been a labour of love.

This history is in one sense an act of memorial to Baron Maurice de Hirsch, JCA's founder, who was born 152 years ago and died in 1896. A claim might be made that he was the greatest Jewish philanthropist of the nineteenth century, and certainly JCA was the recipient of the greatest of his philanthropies. The 14th edition of the *Encyclopaedia Britannica*, published in 1929, still referred to JCA as probably the greatest charitable trust in the world.

As the Association approaches the centenary of its foundation it is not inappropriate to look back and see how the great wealth with which the Baron entrusted JCA in his lifetime and by his will has been used to carry out his wishes for the resettlement of Jews on the land or for their relief in other ways from poverty, persecution and misery.

JCA was only one of many recipients of the Baron's charitable outlay. The Alliance Israélite Universelle of Paris, the Baron de Hirsch Fund of New York and the Baron de Hirsch Stiftung of Vienna were likewise beneficiaries. He set up a personal charitable service to relieve the victims of the Russo-Turkish War of 1877. The winnings of his horse-racing in England – £40,000 in 1892 alone – went to the London hospitals. Kurt Grunwald, writing in *Türkenhirsch*, calculated that he made charitable donations in his lifetime and by will in excess of US$100 million (which today might have a purchasing power of $2,500 million).

These charitable activities were largely concentrated into the last ten years of the Baron's life, and his wife was associated with them. Even if he was not faithful as a husband, he was singularly happy in his marriage, and his wife Clara showed sufficient largeness of heart to refer in her will to his two illegitimate children as her 'adopted children' and to make provision for them on top of what he had given them in his lifetime. It may be regarded as a human vanity on his part that he cultivated royalty and nobility with assiduity and that, having achieved success, he applied himself with enthusiasm to owning a horse-racing stable, to shooting and to other activities which gave him a social background that went with his fortune. During his working life he had made his homes at different times in Munich, Brussels and Paris and had also had to spend much time in Constantinople. After his retirement he divided his time between his residence in Paris, his estate at Beauregard near Versailles, his large shooting estate, Schloss St Johann in Hungary, and his properties in Moravia. In England he would rent a house in London and a shooting lodge in East Anglia.

When the Baron founded JCA, it was natural that the seven signatories of the original Memorandum of Association should include, apart from himself, so many of the 'grand dukes' of British and French Jewry. They were in fact Lord Rothschild, Sir Julian Goldsmid, Bt, Sir Benjamin Cohen, Bt, Sir Ernest Cassel, Bt, Monsieur S. H. Goldschmidt (President of AIU), Monsieur Salomon Reinach of Paris and Mr F. D. Mocatta. Of the original 20,000 shares in JCA, Maurice de Hirsch was allotted 19,991, and he devoted much of his time in the last four years of his life to the direction of the Association's affairs. His shareholding, by his direction, was distributed to the Alliance Israélite Universelle, the Anglo-Jewish Association and the Jewish Communities of Brussels, Berlin and Frankfurt.

By its constitution the government of JCA is vested in a Council of Administration whose membership over the years can be seen in Appendix A. Originally drawn entirely from Jewry of England, France, Belgium and Germany, it is now composed of members from England, France, Belgium, Israel and the United States.

Much of the day-to-day administration of JCA is dealt with on a delegated basis by the President (the names of the Presidents over the years are set out in Appendix B). World Jewry owes a great debt, however, to those who have over more than 90 years administered the affairs of the Association, and here I am referring to its staff. JCA has operated in the past on a world scale, and with its agricultural settlement work, its activity in vocational schools and in loan kassas and the many other aspects of its mission of helping poor and needy Jews, has employed many hundreds, perhaps thousands, of staff members in different countries. Some of those people paid with their lives for their loyalty to the Jewish community. I have in mind particularly those working in the USSR right up to 1938, when the Soviet authorities clamped down on the activities of JCA and its staff in that country disappeared without a trace. I am also thinking of the staff members in Germany and Eastern Europe at the start of the Second World War who were victims of the Holocaust along with the Jewish communities whom they served.

Among the staff of JCA were many men of distinction and of devotion to their vocation of relieving poor Jews who were the victims of man's inhumanity to man. The first Director of JCA, who served from the time of its incorporation until 1911, was Dr Sigismond Sonnenfeld, previously the Baron's 'General Agent'. Monsieur Louis Oungre, Director for many years, is referred to frequently in this book; he left his mark on the activities of JCA today, not least by reviving the Association's presence in Palestine in the 1930s. Other past Directors were Mr Emile Meyerson and Mr Victor Girmounsky (happily still alive), to whom JCA owes a special debt of gratitude. Vice-Directors included Monsieur Edouard Oungre, Mr Schmoll and Mr Mirkin, all life-long servants of JCA.

Up to the outbreak of the Second World War the JCA Head Office was in Paris, notwithstanding that the Association is in form an English company. There, a staff of some 20 people were employed. There were also employees in Russia, where there was a Head Office in Moscow, under the supervision first of Mr J. Blum and later Mr Sachs, as well as offices in Poland under Mr Knobelman, in Romania (Bessarabia) under Mr Trachtman, in Argentina under the direction successively of Messrs Starkmeth, Weil and Calius, in Brazil under Messrs Raffalovich, Leitchic, Schall and Eisenberg, in Canada under Messrs Belkin and Lister, and in Palestine/Israel where the names of Mr Chaim Kalvarisky and Mr Charles Passman will long be remembered as pioneers of JCA's work in that country. Mention should also be made of Mr Aronstein, who was for a time co-Director with Mr Girmounsky of JCA's world-wide activities and had also served in Argentina.

I give this catalogue of names without apology; for without its staff JCA would have been nothing, and without the ability and dedication of its senior executives the quality of its work would have been gravely depreciated.

After Paris was overrun in 1940 the management was located in New York. In 1949 the Head Office was removed to London, where it has remained. The Association's affairs are run from there with the greatest economy by a staff of four, and by a staff in Israel of seven.

JCA was not founded by Baron de Hirsch with an obligation to be a perpetual charity. There is nothing in its constitution which requires it to maintain its capital intact and spend only its

income. Over the years much of the Baron's magnificent foundation has been spent in doing those things which he wished to be
done. Confiscations, inflation and recession have also taken their
toll, so that, although the capital is still of approximately the same
nominal value, its real value is sadly eroded. If JCA can operate
now only on a much reduced scale, it can look back on its past
with pride and to its future with a determination to apply in the
best possible way what resources are left to it. The Association
has never appealed to the Jewish public for money, but if it is to
maintain a meaningful presence among the Jewish philanthropic
bodies of the world it now needs to do so.

In a retrospect of JCA's labours over 90 years, one cannot fail
to be impressed by the grandeur of Baron Maurice de Hirsch's
concept of what should be done to help 'poor and needy Jews';
saddened by the shortfall between concept and achievement; and
grateful for what has nevertheless been achieved on a world-wide
scale through his philanthropy.

December 1983

I am grateful to the Jewish Colonization Association (JCA) for its help to me in connection with the preparation and publication of this book. In addition, the Association has borne some of the publishing costs. Mr Joseph Neville, Director of JCA from 1971 to 1979 and on its staff for many years before, and the Hon. L. H. L. Cohen, President of JCA, read the manuscript and made many useful corrections.

The book, good or bad as it may be, is my own, which is not to imply I was not helped. I am glad now to acknowledge the assistance of a number of people. First, I have to pay tribute to Mrs Bertha Spector, who was able to read and transcribe what seemed to me an interminable and illegible manuscript, written (and overwritten) with a thick black pencil on legal pads. I thank Mr Nicholson Smith, who assisted with the organisation and language of Chapter 10 on Poland and Eastern Europe. Mr Joseph Neville afforded inestimable help by searching through thousands of pages of JCA records to extract needed information, and as I have indicated, he read and edited the entire manuscript with the greatest care. He also contributed to the Preface and Appendices and the preparation of the maps and photographs. Suffice it to say that this book would probably never have seen the light of day without his unfailing and cheerfully rendered assistance. Any errors that remain are, of course, my responsibility.

I wish to thank Mr Victor Girmounsky, for many years Director-General of JCA, and Mr Jacques Rosemblum, retired staff member, for the time they spent in interviews. Dr Maurice Hexter, a member of the JCA Council since 1952, was most generous and helpful in sharing his many memories.

I also would like to express gratitude to the members of JCA's London staff – Mr Charles Rappaport, the Director, Mr Julian Kay, his assistant, Mr Leslie Dayan, the accountant, and Miss Elaine Garwood, secretary – for their unflagging courtesy and solicitude.

I have deliberately omitted any bibliography as, apart from the works referred to in the Notes, it would have listed almost exclusively JCA-generated materials – the Annual Reports, which began in 1891; many staff reports, such as those written by Louis Oungre, Director-General from 1910 to 1949, Georges Aronstein, D. Mirkin and others; memoranda and minutes of meetings; and the unpublished history of JCA's activities in Argentina by Lazaro Schallman, a JCA staff member. Incidentally, matters not noted but attributed to a particular year are described in the Annual Report for that year. There are however notes for non-JCA sources and, when it seemed appropriate, for JCA sources as well.

As Mr Cohen points out in the Foreword, JCA was in its time, as stated in the *Encyclopaedia Britannica* (vol. XIII, 1910, p. 525), 'probably the greatest charitable trust in the world'. How this enormous Fund was deployed and how usefully will become clear, I hope, in the pages that follow.

August 1983   T. N.

The Jewish Colonization Association (JCA) was one of the first highly organised, well endowed and long enduring of charitable institutions. Its history presents a great many differing, but interconnected, facets.

1 The most obvious way of looking at it is to regard it as a great philanthropic enterprise, as it assuredly was and still is. But it was a philanthropic enterprise with a new look. As the Baron de Hirsch, its founder, said:

> I contend against the old system of alms-giving which only makes so many more beggars; and I consider the greatest problem in philanthropy is to make human beings who are capable of work, who would otherwise become paupers, into useful members of society.

In other words, he was opposed to the nineteenth-century or older concept of charity as a dole, a hand-out to 'the deserving poor'. He wanted instead to employ his bounty to make its recipients self-supporting citizens. In fact, his original concept was that the Association's colonists in Argentina should repay its costs in full. In the event this proved to be impossible, but thousands of the Jewish settlers did pay very substantial sums to JCA for the property transferred to them.

2 JCA carried out one of the first experiments in planned migration on a large scale. It is hard to think of any comparable programme that was not implemented by a governmental or international agency. Questions can certainly be raised as to the degree of JCA's success, as so many of the families placed on farms in Argentina, Brazil and Canada moved on elsewhere, but there is no doubt that the Association's efforts helped to open these countries to Jewish immigrants; for, in addition to those whom it placed initially on farms, there was a much larger number whom it helped to cross the Atlantic – tens of thousands from Russia and Romania before the First World War – through its network of committees in those countries and in the countries of transit. Likewise, after the Second World War, JCA, on its

1

own or in conjunction with other agencies, helped refugees from Russia, emigrants from Poland and victims of Nazism to move from Europe to locations overseas. Thus JCA's activities constitute an important chapter in the endless history of Jewish migration from one country to another.

3   In many ways JCA was an important innovator. The system of loan *kassas* (*caisse* in French – a small savings and loan association) that it built up in Russian Poland and Bessarabia before the First World War, and which afterwards was expanded in collaboration with the Joint Distribution Committee (JDC), was a major instrument of rehabilitation and relief for the depressed Jewish populations in Eastern Europe during the inter-war period. And again after the Second World War, pursuing the same objects and methods, JDC established a network of kassas in Eastern Europe.

4   JCA's work can be viewed as the culmination, or at least the most extensive example geographically and vocationally speaking, of the so-called 'productivisation' movement which had great influence among Jews in the nineteenth century. This was based on the notion that anti-Semitism would decline, or even disappear, if Jews were to become engaged in manual labour, producing tangible goods instead of being traders and money-lenders or, even worse, '*luftmentschen*' with no visible means of sustenance. Thus they would become indistinguishable from the people among whom they lived and not be denigrated and persecuted by xenophobic neighbours. (One ironic aspect of the 'productivisation' theory was that, while there were doubtless many Jewish tradesmen, money-lenders and even *luftmentschen* in Eastern Europe, a large proportion of the artisans in that area were also Jewish. They were known as *schlusslers*, 'locksmiths', a word that covered a variety of other occupations.) Also, from the latter part of the eighteenth century, there came the belief that farming was the most honourable of all occupations. Thomas Jefferson, who frequently extolled the benefits of rural life as contrasted with the evil influence of cities, was the great American exemplar of this ideology, which he shared with the eighteenth-century French physiocrats. The Baron de Hirsch, with his almost compulsive feeling that Jews should become farmers, was obviously a fervent believer in this particular form of 'productivisation'.

5   It is often said that all Jews are brothers, or at least that all Jews feel responsible for one another. Certainly JCA exemplifies this maxim; for it was administered by a Council composed of wealthy, highly placed Western European Jews who manifested by word and deed their concern for their co-religionists in Eastern

Europe. These co-religionists were in many respects – their fervent orthodoxy, their education, which was restricted to the Talmud and the Torah, their language (Yiddish) and their whole view of the world – utterly alien to the members of the JCA Council. Despite this, the Council were more than accessible to their pleas for help, for the Association not infrequently went to the succour of needy Jews before being asked.

6 'An institution is but the lengthened shadow of a man' is a cliché that can certainly be applied to JCA, especially in its first years when the Baron de Hirsch ran it almost single-handed. Its emphasis on planting immigrants on farms rather than opting for any other vocation resulted from the Baron's physiocratic views, which dominated the Association's policy during his lifetime and greatly influenced it afterwards. For example, in 1897, after the Baron's death, one of the Argentine colonies sent a deputation to the Paris headquarters of JCA to urge that clothing be manufactured in the colony to occupy its members, especially the women and children, during the winter season when farming tasks were light. In turning down this seemingly reasonable request the JCA office emphasised its intention to maintain the agricultural nature of its settlements.

7 Lastly, the story of JCA can be regarded as a wild, romantic adventure without precedent. In fact, it was an adventurous, gambling streak in the Baron's character that accounted for his plunging his wealth into the hazardous enterprise of building railways in Turkey a hundred years ago. When this project made him a millionaire many times over, it was equally bold and venturesome of him to pluck up thousands of ill-prepared Russian Jews and fling them down on the raw, uncultivated pampas, where the only human inhabitants were gauchos who spoke only a sort of Spanish and whose occupation was to guard roaming herds of half-wild cattle. This venture, and the others that followed it, is now related in the history of the Jewish Colonization Association.

PART I

1891–1914

In the 1880s and 1890s the situation of Russian Jewry, miserable at best and punctuated by pogroms at worst, was the major concern of the world Jewish community. The reaction of the Baron de Hirsch was to attempt to move large numbers of Jews out of Russia and establish them as farmers in a free country. The Jewish Colonization Association, which the Baron formally established in 1891, carried out his policy by transporting thousands of Russian Jewish families and settling them on farms in Argentina. Later the work of agricultural settlement was extended to Brazil, Canada and the United States, and even on a small scale to Turkey and Cyprus. Concomitant with this activity up to the First World War was the organisation of the orderly emigration of Jews from Russia and Eastern Europe, while the larger numbers who remained behind in those countries were assisted through education, vocational training, loans schemes for artisans and help of various kinds for farmers. After the Baron's death in 1896, the Association started helping some settlements in Palestine which had been set up in the 1880s, and eventually took over the administration of the colonies established by the Baron Edmond de Rothschild. In all of these efforts, JCA was concerned not only with the economic interests of the people affected but also with their social, cultural, physical and spiritual well-being.

CHAPTER 1

The Baron de Hirsch and Russian Jewry

In 1891, 900 Russian Jews intending to settle in Palestine arrived in Constantinople. At this stage of their journey they were informed by the Turkish authorities (Palestine then was part of the Ottoman Empire) that they would not be given permission to emigrate to that country.

The travellers were in an agonising dilemma. Having already sold their homes and belongings, they could not face the thought of returning to Russia; neither could they remain in Turkey; and they did not have the money to pay for a journey to settle elsewhere – and indeed, where would that 'elsewhere' be? The members of Constantinople's Jewish community were almost equally agonised, for they had already begun making contributions to take care of some of the 900, but this was too large a group to be supported for any length of time by the small indigenous Jewish population. Not knowing what better to do they cabled the Baron de Hirsch in Paris, telling him of the desperate circumstances of the Russians. In short order the Baron replied, authorising their transport to France, whence they would be sent to Argentina, where the Jewish Colonization Association (JCA), just created by the Baron, had initiated the settlement of Jews on the empty pampas. The 900 were duly shipped to Argentina, where they had further misadventures before their eventual arrival at JCA's farm colonies. But the point was that at this time of acute emergency the Baron was called upon to help his fellow Jews – and he responded.

Again, in July 1893 a sizeable group of Jewish refugees reached the Baltic port of Libau – and were caught there with no means of living or leaving. In this extremity they sent a telegram to David Feinberg, who was the Secretary of JCA's Russian committee in St Petersburg. Feinberg immediately communicated with the Baron de Hirsch, and without delay the Baron sent a draft for 200,000 marks to the Libau group. When he was apprised of this, Feinberg grumbled that the people in Libau had received more money than they needed. But, again, the Baron's response was almost automatic; the information that a group of Jews was in trouble was enough to evoke instant action.

A similar situation arose as Jewish emigration from Russia to Canada (as to the USA and elsewhere) increased through the 1880s. The Young Men's Hebrew Benevolent Society of Montreal (YMHBS) took upon itself the task of meeting the incoming ships and caring for the new arrivals, but as emigration grew so did expenditures, and so did the need for additional funds. The creation of the Baron de Hirsch Fund in New York in 1890 (it was not formally incorporated until February 1891) inspired the Canadians to appeal for help to the Baron in May 1890. They were surprised by the promptness and generosity of his reply: he said he might assist them in the future (he did), but for the present was enclosing a cheque for $20,000.

Of all the appeals that were made to the Baron's generosity, however, the most important was that by Dr Wilhelm Löwenthal in 1890.

In July 1889 some 120 families of Russian Jews (numbering about 800 individuals) landed in Buenos Aires, under the impression that they had title deeds to plots of land in up-country Argentina. The transaction had been consummated through the mediation of an office in Paris maintained by the Argentine government to encourage immigration into that vast, underpopulated land. When the weary travellers disembarked from their ship, they were horrified to learn that their contracts were invalid, that the papers they had received were worthless. Their situation was serious in the extreme – strangers in a strange city, where the language was incomprehensible to them, and with such money as they had melting away to pay for maintaining themselves. Public-spirited members of the small Jewish community in Buenos Aires came to the rescue of the miserable 'Podolians' (so named because they came from Podolia in Russian Poland) and arranged for them to buy a tract of land from a large land owner, Dr Pedro Palacios. It was located in Santa Fe province, on the railway some hundreds of miles northwest of the Argentine capital. Palacios promised that, in addition to the land, he would provide housing, equipment and provisions until such time as the Podolians could grow their own crops. When they arrived at Palacios station (the railway station and the estate were also called Palacios), the immigrants were thunderstruck for a second time; there was no housing, only a couple of old empty freight cars and an abandoned warehouse for shelter; there was no food and no tools.

The Podolians lived – if that is the appropriate word – some out in the open (and this was in the middle of the rainy season), without food, which they had to beg from passing travellers or scavenge from the leavings of the dining cars of the trains that went through Palacios. It was hardly surprising that under these conditions 50–60 children died. Fortunately, one of the travellers who passed through the station and was deeply affected by their situation was a Dr Wilhelm Löwenthal. He was a Romanian Jew who had attended medical school in Germany, had made a reputation as a sociologist in that country, and had been engaged by the Argentine government to make a survey. Löwenthal was horrifed by what he saw, and as soon as he got to Buenos Aires he told the Argentine authorities about the plight of the Podolians. Pressure was brought on Palacios to supply the unhappy settlers with some of the things that had been promised.

In addition, and in the long run more important, this incident caused Löwenthal to think about the whole question of how best to help masses of Russian Jews leave their oppressive homeland. He concluded that a planned migration to Argentina to settle Jews as farmers on the empty pampas offered a reasonable means of escape for thousands of them. When he returned to Europe he formulated a plan along these lines. It was obvious to him where to present it. Through the mediation of the Alliance Israélite Universelle,[1] he put his proposal to the Baron de Hirsch, whose name was already widely known throughout the Jewish world because of his vast benefactions and his efforts to help the beleaguered Russian Jews.

The Baron de Hirsch

Who was this great, rich and generous Baron whom Jews turned to a hundred years ago when they were in trouble – and who seemingly could be counted on for a helpful and open-handed response?

Moritz von Hirsch was born in 1831 in Bavaria. That the Jewish family into which he was born had a 'von' in its name signifies how far his grandparents had come in distinguishing themselves as bankers to the Bavarian royal court and as successful businessmen; Jews did not obtain official honours in Germany, either then or later, without manifesting exceptional ability and a fair amount of aggression. The patent of nobility was granted to Jacob Hirsch, the grandfather of Moritz, in 1818, enabling him to place 'von' before his name, because his banking skill had been of great use to the reigning family of Bavaria. His ennoblement was in fact the end result of the purchase of an estate that carried with it judicial powers. Only members of the nobility 'were entitled to administer justice'; so Jacob petitioned to be ennobled, producing a very impressive list of assets as proof of his qualifications.

The Hirsches – Joseph, the father of Moritz, as well as Jacob – were involved in many other legal proceedings to establish their rights as citizens. Many of these cases were being actively pursued during Moritz's youth, so that, though born to wealth, he was early on made acutely aware of the disabilities that even rich Jews attached to the Court could suffer. He also was exposed to other, more agreeable, aspects of Judaism, for the family home contained a small synagogue and he received a thorough grounding in Jewish history and religious practice.

Moritz von Hirsch (or Maurice de Hirsch, as we shall call him[2]) must have been a very lively and adventuresome young man, but he also had a precocious business sense. In his fourteenth year he was sent to Brussels to study, and three years later he went to work in the Bischoffsheim and Goldschmidt bank in that city. This was one of the most important banking institutions in Belgium, with branches in Paris and London. In 1855, at the age of 24, he married Clara Bischoffsheim, daughter of his senior partner. She brought with her an appropriately handsome dowry, as well as a noble and generous spirit and a knowledge of business practices, for she had served as her father's secretary for some years. She also brought an understanding of the Jewish situation, for her father, in addition to being a leading banker, was much involved in Jewish affairs – among other things he was a member of the Central Committee of the Alliance Israélite Universelle.

After his marriage Hirsch worked in his father-in-law's firm for a while, but he soon launched into banking on his own, particularly involving himself in railway finance. Of this period in his life Grunwald, his biographer, says:

> Between 1848, when as a lad of seventeen Hirsch began to interest himself in railway ventures, and 1869, when he obtained the concession from the Ottoman government which was to turn him into one of the tycoons of the century, he apparently had acquired widespread railway interests, of which, however, only a few are known.[3]

These interests included railway construction in Russia, Hungary and Austria.

Of Hirsch's many business relationships, most interesting was that with one Langrand-Dumonceau, financier, entrepreneur and adventurer, whose ambition was to 'christianise capital' by putting Catholic enterprises on a par with Protestant and Jewish ones, an aim that had great appeal to the priesthood. In the course of initiating 'Christian' financial, railway and insurance companies, he found it necessary as a practical matter at times to collaborate with Jewish firms or individuals. Alas, neither his piety nor his collaboration could prevent Langrand's bubble from bursting. In 1870, his numerous companies in collapse, he fled to Brazil. Out of the wreckage of Langrand's bankrupt empire, Hirsch was able to obtain one valuable asset, or more accurately what could become a valuable asset; namely, a concession to build railways in Turkey, linking up with the European network through Austria. There are several versions of how Hirsch acquired the concession; according to one, he 'bought' Daoud Pasha, the Turkish Minister of Public Works, who then resigned and never went back to Turkey.[4]

The idea of a connection between the European railway system and Constantinople, and perhaps going even farther east (the Berlin-to-Baghdad line was a treasured aim of German diplomacy before the First World War), had been entertained by many statesmen, particularly in Austria. Hirsch himself had apparently long had in mind a plan for a rail link between Vienna and Constantinople. Once he had the Turkish concession, he tried to interest the Austrian railways in extending their lines to meet his projected Turkish ones. Although at first the South Austrian Railway seemed willing to fall in with his plans, in the summer of 1869 'negotiations failed . . . owing to the resistance of the Viennese House of Rothschild'.[5]

Hirsch therefore evolved an alternative means of obtaining capital, through Turkish government bonds. While such securities were a drug on the European market, those issued to pay for the construction of the railway had a special feature, for their holders could participate in a two-monthly lottery offering several prizes. Hirsch acquired the bonds from the Turkish government at a large discount on their face value and marketed them through a syndicate at a substantial profit in two issues in 1870 and 1872. In 1875 the Turkish government, in even more stringent financial straits than usual, stopped payment on the bonds until 1881, when Turkey's debts were reorganised. One of the most bizarre aspects of the whole affair was the failure of some of the lottery winners, who had gained prizes of 300,000 and even 600,000 francs, to claim their prizes.

The financial issue having been more or less settled, Hirsch set up a construction company and an operating company. So rapidly did work proceed that by 1872 some of the track was already in operation. In 1871 a new Turkish *vizier* (premier) had been appointed; in contrast to his predecessor, under whom the original arrangements for Hirsch's railways had been negotiated, this one was anti-German and anti-Austrian but pro-Russian. He tried to have the concession cancelled, but Hirsch fought back, with gratuities judiciously distributed,[6] and in the end a compromise was reached, reducing his concession from 2,500 to 1,179 kilometres. This reduction may not have been entirely to Hirsch's displeasure, for it absolved him of the task of building railways over some very rough, hilly Balkan country. By 1874 the work on the reduced concession was completed. The Turkish government itself undertook to build the uncompleted parts of the line but proved unable to do so, and it was not until 1883 that Austria-Hungary, Bulgaria, Serbia and Turkey were able to sign an agreement that led to the completion of a link between Vienna and Constantinople.

Hirsch's profit on the bond sale was variously estimated at between 255 and 285 million francs. Grunwald estimates the cost of construction at about 180 million, leaving a net figure of 75–105 million. To this must be added 50 million francs of operating profits over ten years, making a grand total of 125–155 million francs in profit. From the estimate below it can be seen what this sum, equivalent at the time to £5 million to £6 million sterling, would be worth at present, even reduced, as it had to be, by immense overhead expenses, including baksheesh. Whatever the profit was, as Grunwald says,

> it was hard earned. It would be unjust to forget the greatness of the conception, the tremendous hard work, diligence and intelligence, and particularly the most remarkable persistence, shown by this little banker from Brussels in order to plan, direct and almost single-handed complete such an important and useful enterprise, in the midst of bitter hostilities and most serious difficulties in a semi-barbarian country such as Turkey then was.[7]

Hirsch had never intended to operate the railway he had built, but had been forced to do so by the lack of any alternative. When in 1890 the arrangements had been made for it to become part of a larger entity and the accounts with the Turkish government had been settled, he transferred the control of the company, through the sale of the shares he held, to the Deutsche Bank.

Not only had Hirsch acquired a vast amount of cash in all these transactions; he was also by this time the owner of many businesses and of great houses and estates in France, England and Austria-Hungary. His fortune was estimated to be between £16 million and £30 million sterling, or $80 to $150 million, which in today's terms would be worth between £1,940 million and £3,630 million.[8]

The Baron had also become a member of the social circle of

the Prince of Wales (Queen Victoria's son, later King Edward VII). He had, in fact, bought his way in; he loaned Prince Rudolf of Austria 100,000 gulden to introduce him to the English prince, and apparently won his way into the latter's good graces by lending him very handsome sums and never thinking of, let alone asking for, repayment. The pinnacle of social acceptance was however denied him: Queen Victoria would not receive him.[9] He was refused membership of a certain French club also; so he bought its premises and forced the club to vacate. According to one legend, it was the French Jockey Club that blackballed Hirsch, and after he acquired their building he used it to stable his horses. As befitted a man who moved in high society, he owned a successful string of racehorses, but significantly he donated all his winnings to charity.

The Baron and Baroness had two children, a daughter who died in infancy, and a son, Lucien, born in 1856, who died of pneumonia in 1887 at the age of 31. While Lucien had not shown any inclination for business, having been interested in books, manuscripts and coins and not in making money, it may well be that his death deprived the Baron of any lingering hope that his heir might be persuaded to undertake a business career, and that this influenced him to sell his Turkish railway shares in 1890. In any case, Lucien's death did seem to stimulate his already manifest interest in performing good works. His standard reply to persons commiserating with him on the loss of his son was: 'I have lost my son but not my heir; all humanity is my heir.'

It is quite likely that it was the beneficent Clara who persuaded the Baron to look into the situation of the poor Jews in Turkey and the Balkans,[10] and this, in turn, had some influence on his decision to join the Alliance Israélite. In December 1873 he donated 1 million francs for the Alliance's educational programme in Turkey. He was elected to its Central Committee in 1876, and then, to quote another of his biographers,

From 1879 onwards he contributed an annual 50,000 francs for the Artisans' Training Scheme of the Alliance. After 1882 he undertook to meet the considerable annual deficit of the AIU which over the years ran into several hundred thousand francs, thus safeguarding the independence of the organisation. In 1889 he replaced these annual contributions by setting up a Fund which secured the Alliance an annual income of 400,000 francs. In 1882 he contributed another million francs to an Emergency Fund for refugees who had been victims of the Russian pogroms. It is estimated that up to his death in 1896 Baron de Hirsch had donated a minimum of 12 million francs to the Alliance alone. [11]

In addition to these great gifts to the Alliance, which devoted much of its effort to educating and otherwise helping Jews in the Middle East, the Baron was assisting the Israelitische Allianz of Vienna in its educational work. His own acquaintance with Austria and Hungary and the influence of the Chief Rabbi of Vienna led him to establish a foundation, the Baron de Hirsch Stiftung, to provide funds for building schools, primarily vocational, in Galicia and Bukovina (then the northeast segment of the Hapsburg Empire), to teach Jewish artisans and farmers their trade and to make loans to such persons. This foundation was set up with a grant of 12 million kronen in 1888, but the anti-Semitic Austrian government delayed its formal incorporation until 1891. The Baron also opened welfare agencies in Vienna, Budapest, Lemberg and Cracow which he provided with an annual budget of 120,000 florins to assist poor people and to make interest-free loans.[12]

However, his great benefactions to the Alliance and in Austria were eclipsed in the end by the magnitude of his gifts for the benefit of the 5 million Russian Jews who constituted the largest mass of suffering Jews in the world. The task of trying to alleviate this suffering proved to be of sufficient interest for the Baron to engage his full attention on it, and the full exercise of his administrative and negotiating skills, for the rest of his life.

Jews in nineteenth-century Russia

During the Middle Ages some Jews had migrated to the northern shores of the Black Sea because they had been the subjects of oppression by the Byzantine emperors. When this area became part of Russia in about the fifteenth century, the Jews, being comparatively few in number, were left undisturbed but were forbidden to reside in Russia proper. At the end of the eighteenth century, however, when Poland was partitioned, with Russia getting the lion's share, upwards of 3 million Jews in Poland, Lithuania, the western Ukraine and Bessarabia became subjects of the Czar. These areas were constituted the 'Pale of Settlement' within which Jews were obliged to live. The centre of Russia, including St Petersburg and Moscow, was forbidden to them, except under the most stringent conditions. Czar Alexander I (1801-25) made some gestures toward liberalising the regulations affecting Jews but was disappointed when these did not result in any great rush to convert to Christianity. His brother and successor, Nicholas I (1825–55), was a flagrant anti-Semite who made oppression of the Jewish population one of the major themes of his administration, promulgating a number of anti-Semitic *ukases*, against the opposition of his own ministers who pointed to the economic harm that would result. In 1836 a plan to settle Jewish families in Siberia was approved, and thousands of people started to move there. But while they were *en route* Nicholas changed his mind, ordered them seized and moved back, destitute, to the Pale of Settlement. In 1843 Jews were ordered out of the area along Russia's western border, and at the same time the army draft, which called for twenty-five years of service, was ordered to be enforced against Jews, even though they were required to pay the fees that ordinarily sufficed to procure exemption. In 1855 Alexander II became Czar and, in accordance with his more liberal tendencies (it was he who freed the serfs), eased the restrictions upon Jews. But he was assassinated in 1881 and his successor, Alexander III, reverted to the attitudes of Nicholas. His government sought to turn opposition away from itself by encouraging, or at the very least permitting, a wave of pogroms which swept across southern Russia in 1881–2. Thousands of Jews fled in fear, and many of them arrived at the Austrian border town of Brody with no means of sustaining themselves. Their plight stirred western Jewry to action. The Alliance Israélite sent emissaries to give help; in London, the Mansion House Committee was formed which raised considerable sums to alleviate the condition of the poor migrants.

The Russian government, however, showed no mercy. Its commission of inquiry found that 'Jewish exploitation' was at the root of the pogroms. Therefore the 'May' Laws (of 1882) were instituted, which among other things prohibited Jews from living in villages, thus depriving them of the businesses by which they earned their living. Shortly afterwards the *numerus clausus*, limiting the access of Jews to secondary and higher schools, was put into effect. One of the most outrageous of all these anti-Semitic actions was the expulsion of thousands of Jewish artisan families from Moscow in 1891. Without warning, police and soldiers invaded their homes and dragged them out. But, indeed, 'the expulsion of Jews from towns and villages where they had lived peacefully during the reign of Alexander II . . . became a daily occurrence'.[13] Pobiedonostsev, the head of the governing body of the Russian Orthodox Church, summed up official policy by declaring that, hopefully, 'one-third of the Jews will die, one-third will convert, and one-third will flee the country'. And flee the country they did: it is estimated that 2 million Jews left Russia between 1881 and 1914.

However, this vast exodus had little effect in reducing the Jewish population. There had been about 2½ million Jews in Russia in 1800; there were about twice as many in 1900 and, in spite of emigration, about the same number in 1914. The natural increase that brought about these results was indeed one of the causes of Jewish misery; for, confined to the Pale, unable to buy land and prevented from entry into professions, the effect of an increasing population was to intensify competition among Jewish traders and merchants and to reduce their already minuscule incomes.

In 1894 a new Czar, Nicholas II, succeeded to the throne. There had been hopes that he would be more liberal than his predecessor, but in the event his reign turned out to be no better. The notorious Kishinev pogrom took place in 1903, and this was followed by several others in which the police and army units actively participated. This wave of anti-Jewish riots and killing subsided in 1906, but the government managed to devise further restrictive regulations and in 1913 to institute a blood libel trial in Kiev.[14] The czarist regime maintained its anti-Jewish stance until its very end. During the First World War, in 1915 and 1916, Jews were deported from the war zones and forced to give hostages for their good behaviour.

The revolution of 1917 reversed this history. Jews were freed of all restrictions and became citizens equally with all other Russians. In the civil wars that followed, however, Jews, especially in the Ukraine, were again the victims of pogroms, and hundreds of thousands fled Russia. And anti-Semitic discrimination reappeared in the last years of Stalin's rule, to continue until now.

The Baron and Russian Jewry

We have listed the great gifts that the Baron made to the Alliance Israélite and his almost equal gifts to the Stiftung and other organisations in Austria-Hungary. However, it was the plight of the Jews in Russia, which intensified after the events of 1881, that gave the Baron the incentive to donate money on a scale never seen before. In 1881 he gave 1 million francs to the Emergency Fund. In that same year he sent two representatives, Charles Netter and Emile Veneziani, both of the Alliance, to Brody, the stopping place for the Jews fleeing from Russia; Veneziani is reputed to have distributed no less than 5 million francs on behalf of the Baron to the penniless Jews marooned there.

The Baron, in conjunction with his friends in the Alliance, then focused on means of ameliorating the condition of the great mass of Jews remaining in Russia. He first came to believe that proper education was the best means of achieving this end. A plan was formulated whereby the Baron was to donate 50 million francs to the Russian government for the establishment of elementary and agricultural schools in the Pale. Not only would Jews receive education, but those who did would be placed on a 'basis of equality with Russian citizens'.[15] In order to ease the transaction, the Baron gave 1 million francs to Pobiedonostsev, the leading (after the Czar) anti-Semite in Russia. That holy man was pleased to accept this *pourboire*; but the negotiations, pursued over a year, broke down because the Baron would not yield control over his proposed gift to the Russian government. Bold and adventurous he may have been, but he certainly would not take the risk of putting 50 million francs into the hands of the Czar's minions.

This experience convinced the Baron that emigration was the only solution for the Russian Jews. (And, of course, a million of them had already come to the same conclusion – and left.) Some years after, the Baron wrote:

> The government of the Czar means to get rid of the five million Jews who inhabit Russian territory. Let it allow the many who, like himself, are interested in the fate of these victims of persecution and who certainly will be prepared to make the greatest sacrifices on their behalf, to save them. . . . Let a period of twenty years – let us say – be fixed; let it be agreed that every year a certain number of Jews will leave the country; but let them be left in peace until the hour of their departure arrives. If the Czar will order a measure of this character to be adopted, those who are interested in the fate of the Russian Jews will do what is necessary to provide funds for conveying to their new country the number of emigrants ordered to leave early.[16]

After the collapse of negotiations with the Czar's government, the Baron's next effort on behalf of Russian Jews took place, curiously enough, in the United States. Oscar Straus, who had been US Ambassador to Turkey and had become well acquainted with Hirsch during the course of the latter's activity there, presented the Baron with a letter written by Michael Heilprin (1823–88). Heilprin, a Polish-Hungarian Jew, had come to the United States in 1856 and had been very active in trying to persuade Russian Jews to settle on farm colonies. His document was a brief in support of the idea that immigrant Jews should be placed in agricultural or industrial settlements. He expected by this means to 'productivise' the incoming Jews, as he did not believe in unproductive charity. Neither did the Baron, who was so taken by Heilprin's arguments that in May 1889 he had the Secretary of the Alliance Israélite let a group of prominent American Jews know that he was prepared to set up an agency to help Russian and Romanian Jews emigrating to the United States. The Americans were somewhat hesitant to accept the Baron's offer, fearing to increase the influx of Russian Jews into the country, but in the end an agreement was reached to set up the Baron de Hirsch Fund in New York. It was formally incorporated in February 1891, with a grant of $2.4 million from the Baron. The Fund had a large number of purposes, the overriding one being 'the education and relief of Hebrew emigrants from Russia and Romania' and their children. More specifically, the money was to be used for loans to farmers; for transport from the ports of arrival to a place where the immigrants could find employment; for training in mechanics, handicrafts and trades; and for 'instruction in the English language and in the duties and obligations of life and citizenship in the United States, the establishment of schools if necessary for such training, and instruction in agriculture'.

The Fund is, to this day, engaged in helping Jewish immigrants to the United States and Israel. This brief account of the American Fund would not be complete without noting that, for two years before it was legally incorporated, the Baron sent the Committee in New York $10,000 per month which it used to help immigrants.

CHAPTER 2

The Beginning of the Jewish Colonization Association

The Baron's offer of 50 million francs to the Czar's government and the breakdown of negotiations thereafter was well publicised in the European press. In addition, it was known through magazine and newspaper articles and interviews that the Baron was a physiocrat who believed in the regenerative powers of the soil, and that he had his own quite individualistic view of how philanthropy should be dispensed. He had written: 'I contend against the old system of alms-giving, which only makes so many more beggars; and I consider the greatest problem in philanthropy is to make human beings who are capable of work, who would otherwise become paupers, into useful members of society.'[1] Clearly, by philanthropy the Baron meant providing poor people with the training and tools necessary to make them self-supporting, and, even better, able to earn enough to repay their benefactor.

When Löwenthal returned to Europe in 1890, after his experience with the 'Podolians', and started to compose a memorandum intended for the Baron proposing relief measures for the Jews of Russia, he stressed the good climate, the good soil, the availability of land and the democratic nature of the government in Argentina, which he depicted as a haven where Russian Jews could become independent farmers.

He also pointed out that the 50 million francs that presumably were burning a hole in the Baron's pocket could earn (with interest at 10 per cent) 5 million francs a year, and that 500 families at a cost of 10,000 francs each could be settled annually in Argentina by use of the interest alone. He made it clear that his plan called for eventual repayment by the settlers, and suggested further that, because of his own interest in Eastern Jews and his background, he might be appointed head of the enterprise he was outlining.

Löwenthal did not use his time in Europe only in writing to the Baron; he also solicited a gift from a rich German Jew to help the miserable 'Podolians', who by this time (December 1890) had moved from their wretched quarters at the railway station to the lands they were supposed to be buying. They named this settlement Moisesville, in honour not of Maurice (Moses) de Hirsch, as has sometimes been asserted, but of the biblical Moses, the 'father of us all'.

While some of his associates at the Alliance had their doubts, the Baron was taken with Löwenthal's proposal. The idea of 'productivising' poor Jews through employment in agriculture was both familiar and agreeable to him; agreeable also was the notion that the cost of transport and installation on farms could in the end be repaid. Settlement in Argentina was a new thought, but on consideration it seemed reasonable.[2]

Argentina had a small population, about 3 million, and a great deal of land to which the government was eager to bring immigrants. The Baron even toyed with the idea of buying an entire province in which an autonomous Jewish state could be established. As a preliminary he sent out an exploratory expedition, consisting of Löwenthal himself, a Belgian army colonel, Vanvinckeroy, and an English engineer, Cullen. Early in 1891 the emissaries returned with a favourable report, which strengthened the Baron's original impulse to proceed.

He realised however that a decision about a destination for Russian Jews was not sufficient; he also had to make arrangements to get them out of Russia, because that country officially forbade emigration (though obviously thousands of Jews and others had succeeded in leaving). As his representative for this purpose the Baron chose Arnold White, an English Member of Parliament and journalist. Everyone who has written about this episode comments on the curious nature of the Baron's choice, for White was a well known anti-Semite. Yet the Baron knew what he was doing: he said that it was for this very reason that an affirmative report from White would carry weight. White turned out to be an excellent choice. With David Feinberg he toured the areas in southern Russia where Jews had been established in agricultural colonies in the early nineteenth century and brought back enthusiastic reports about their character in general and their adaptability to agriculture in particular. More important, on a second visit to Moscow he induced the Czar's government, which at that very moment was considering further restrictions on Jews, and had recently expelled the Jewish artisans from Moscow, to make three concessions. The government agreed (1) to permit the Baron to establish local committees in Russia to assist would-be emigrants; (2) to grant passports without charge to the emigrants and exempt them from the army draft; (3) to provide free, or at least especially cheap, transport. When one considers the hermetic nature of the Russian regime at that time (not so different from now), they really were acting with remarkable liberality, according to their lights. The attitude adopted by the Russians may have been the result of the utterly illusory magnitude of the estimates that White submitted concerning the projected rate of emigration – 20,000 per annum in the first few years, then 100,000 per year. In twenty-five years it was expected that over 3 million Jews, a majority of those then living in Russia, would leave the country.

The Baron's proposals were officially approved in May 1892 and a Committee headed by Baron Horace de Günzburg, a wealthy banker and the best known Jew in Russia at the time, was established, with David Feinberg as executive secretary. One of its members was J. Poliakoff, a major railway builder in Russia, one of whose relatives later married a relative of the Baron. In 1891, while White was negotiating in Russia, the Baron took another giant step towards realising his dream. He established the Jewish Colonization Association, which was formally incorporated in London on 10 September 1891. He chose the form of an English corporation because the English Companies Acts required a minimum of formality and imposed a minimum of restrictions on a company's actions. Thus the Baron assured to his instrument perpetual life and the freedom to do what he wanted. The Memorandum of Association was signed by the Baron, Lord Rothschild, Sir Julian Goldsmid, Sir Ernest Cassel, Frederick Mocatta, S. H. Goldschmidt, Salomon Reinach and Sir Benjamin L. Cohen. All of these men were prominent members of the London or Paris Jewish communities. The authorised capital of JCA was £2 million divided into 20,000 shares of £100 each. The Baron subscribed for 19,991 shares, the others one each.

To complete the story of the Baron's benefactions to JCA, he bequeathed a further £7,100,602 to the Association. After payment of death duties JCA was left with £5,872,104 (in addition to the initial paid-up capital of £2 million). The purchasing power of these gifts in 1982 terms might be some £200 million.[3] In addition, JCA is the trustee for the benefit of the Alliance Israélite Universelle of a legacy under the will of the Baroness of £425,000.

The principal objects of the Association were stated to be:

1 to assist and promote the emigration of Jews from any part of Europe or Asia, and principally from countries in which they were being subjected to special taxes or political or other disabilities, to any other parts of the world, and to form and establish colonies in various parts of North and South America and other countries for agricultural, commercial and other purposes;
2 to purchase in any part of the world lands that could be colonised;

3 to accept gifts for the benefit of Jewish communities or individuals;
4 to establish commercial or agricultural settlements on the lands acquired.

The first General Meeting of the Company, attended by most of the signatories of the Memorandum of Association in person or by proxy, was held in London on 14 October 1891. They appointed the Association's governing body, its Council – what would ordinarily be called its Board of Directors – and outlined its chief functions. The first members of the Council were the Baron de Hirsch, S. H. Goldschmidt and Isidore Loeb.

The Council m et on 30 October; among other things they approved the arrangement entered into between the Baron and Wilhelm Löwenthal; ratified the purchase of land in Argentina at a place that later became the colony of Mauricio; ordered the refund of £16,911 to the Baron for expenditures incurred prior to incorporation, especially in Argentina; and appointed S. Sonnenfeld as general director and N. M. Rothschild & Sons as bankers (an interesting choice, in view of the recurring reports that the Baron and the Rothschild family were frequently at odds).

JCA in Argentina

While occupied in 1891 in negotiating with the Russian government and getting JCA legally established, the Baron had not neglected the main object of the exercise – preparation for emigration to and settlement in Argentina. In April 1891 he had sent Dr Löwenthal back to that country with the power to buy land. As we have just seen, Löwenthal did buy a tract at what was to become Mauricio, 300 km southwest of Buenos Aires, and also redeemed the land at Moisesville where the original 'Podolians' had made down payments. He entered into complex negotiations with the Argentine government and private persons to buy more land, but he was unsuccessful for various reasons, partly because the Baron would not approve some of the deals on the grounds that the price was too high. While engaged in efforts to purchase land on a large scale, Löwenthal also had the duty of seeing to it that houses were erected on lands already bought and equipment and animals provided (oxen and horses to furnish power, cattle and poultry to furnish meat, milk and eggs). Immigrants had already started to arrive from Russia. By July 1891 about 775 were *en route* and 4,000 more were expected to set out in the near future. Löwenthal sent representations to the Baron to halt this influx, which in part was due to his own over-optimistic reports about his ability to handle a large number of immigrants. Unfortunately his messages were misunderstood, and newcomers kept arriving. To add to the confusion of immigrants landing before JCA was able to take care of them, word came that the 900 Jews who had been stranded in Constantinople were also now on their way to Argentina.

Before this latter group arrived, however, two ships bringing 571 Russian Jews docked at Buenos Aires. What happened to them was symptomatic of the difficulties and confusion that attended the beginnings of the JCA-sponsored immigration. Certain members of the local Jewish community[4] who were antagonistic towards JCA started disturbing rumours (some were even spread by disaffected returnees from the settlements) that the provisions given to the new arrivals on disembarking contained horse meat[5] (which is not kosher), that they would be sold into slavery, and such like. A tremendous fuss ensued, until the immigrants could be reassured that they *could* eat the meat and would not be enslaved. Then the group entrained for the station nearest to Mauricio, where they were to settle. After a journey of twelve hours they were met at the destination by one L. Gerbel, who was to be the administrator of Mauricio. They were by this time tired, hungry and thirsty. Unfortunately Gerbel, an Italian Jew who had converted to Christianity, knew little or no Yiddish or Russian, and the resulting difficulty in communication made for great frustration on both sides. What was clear, however, was that there was no water or food for the group except for some dry biscuits. Mauricio was several kilometres away, so some wagons and carriages were provided, but too few. Therefore the women and children rode and the weary and disgruntled men walked. On the way they were struck by a savage, overwhelming thunderstorm. Finally arriving at Mauricio, they found that nothing had been prepared for them – no houses, implements or livestock, nothing but an old warehouse, which provided shelter for the women and their younger offspring.[6]

Although tents and a bakery were later provided, it is hardly surprising that not long afterwards the unhappy settlers rioted and the police had to be called in to restore order.

One of the major sources of unrest could scarcely be blamed on the JCA administration in Argentina. In their hasty departure from Europe many settlers had been separated from their baggage and arrived with no effects except the clothes on their backs and no means of replacement thereof; more serious, a number of husbands came without their wives and children, who were to follow later. For whatever reason, JCA did not succeed – or else took years – in reuniting many of these divided families, whose men were an element readily stirred to complaint and even action against the administration.

Nor did nature help. We have seen that a violent thunderstorm was unleashed on the poor travellers at the precise moment when they were out in the open, trudging from the railway station to Mauricio. Worse, the first crop that the 'Podolians' were able to raise was destroyed by locusts.

There was another cause for disaffection. Because of a lack of implements the colonists were not able to work the soil, and neighbouring Italian and other Christian farmers were hired to put in the first crop. This caused considerable concern among the colonists and real disturbance to the Baron.[7] When the news trickled back to him in garbled form he flew into a rage, under the impression that the colonists were living in idleness. He announced that he had made a success in business by taking quick decisions and, utterly unmindful of the quite undeveloped nature of the area, he peremptorily ordered Löwenthal to have houses built, which was an impossibility as material and men were lacking in the empty pampas. He also ordered Löwenthal to make sure that all the colonists worked 15 hours a day, seven days a week; and further commanded that Löwenthal expel all those who could not stand the pace.

Philanthropic as he was, the Baron was obviously determined to be philanthropic in *his* way, and sometimes his way was not consistent. The case of the 'Pampistas' (this from the name of the ship they came on) from Constantinople, who were dumped on Löwenthal with little warning, was wholly at variance with his earlier instructions that full preparations had to be made before emigrants were sent out.

Löwenthal, on the spot, knew that expelling families who had just arrived in Argentina would be unfair to them and would have a very bad effect on public opinion. Further, under the terms of the Baron's arrangement with the Russian government an indemnity had to be paid for each immigrant who returned.

When the Baron first appointed Dr Löwenthal he had complete confidence in him and gave him what appeared to be full power. In actual fact, Löwenthal did not have clear authority to buy land; for, as noted, many deals that he negotiated were countermanded by the Baron before they could be concluded, thus wasting the effort and time Löwenthal had put in. Beyond that, Löwenthal spread himself too thin, trying simultaneously to handle large real estate transactions and attend to the multitudinous details of preparing dwellings and buying equipment for the settlers, who were not only strangers in a strange land but often had no farm experience, or else had experience only on the small, much cultivated farms of south Russia and not on great stretches of virgin territory. One of his major problems was the near impossibility of finding suitable assistants. Many of the men who worked for him spoke neither Yiddish nor Russian and some even looked down on the Russian Jews. Beyond this, he came to lose the Baron's trust by asserting that he could successfully settle many more immigrants than in reality he could. Lastly, he was not strict enough to satisfy Hirsch. All this led the Baron to change his mind completely about Löwenthal, who was dismissed in November 1891. He died in 1894, a frustrated and broken man, at the age of forty-four. A great part of the credit for the Argentine enterprise must be given to him, for he was both its inspirer and its initiator.

If the broken-hearted Löwenthal could only have been aware that his term of less than a year as manager of JCA's affairs in Argentina was to be about the norm, it might have been some consolation to him. Between the time of his dismissal and the Baron's death less than five years later no fewer than six men (on occasion two served simultaneously) headed JCA's office in Buenos Aires. The Baron was quite conscious that this was a highly excessive rate of turnover, and he complained bitterly that his greatest handicap was his inability to find adequate personnel. Still, to his credit it must be said that, as the rapidity of change demonstrates, he never stopped trying.

Löwenthal was succeeded by Adolfo Roth, an Argentinian, and the English engineer Cullen, who had been a member of the Baron's original three-man exploratory expedition. Cullen soon disgraced himself by supplying the Baron, who was still looking for new lands to purchase, with a very enthusiastic report on the Chaco, the area lying between Bolivia, Argentina and Paraguay. Cullen must have made the report without setting foot there, because the Chaco is a notoriously pestiferous, marshy, hot and distressingly humid area, which has not been settled to this day. Luckily, before the Baron made any offers he received a cable from another English engineer whom he trusted, telling him not to touch the Chaco.

As for Roth, Cullen's co-director, he succeeded in doing what poor Löwenthal never quite managed to, that is buying immense tracts of land. Rumours that Roth benefited personally from his purchases on behalf of JCA had a good deal to do with his dismissal, but a very intensive search by an agent of the Baron turned up no evidence of any defalcation on Roth's part.

By 1892, if not before, the news of the Baron's plans had

percolated throughout the Russian Jewish community. Already frightened by the expulsion of the Jews from Moscow and other punitive measures taken by the czarist regime the year before, they felt under great pressure to take advantage of the opportunity to emigrate. The Baron then felt impelled to issue a proclamation to Russian Jewry, telling his co-religionists that he was trying to help them but that they must be patient and not flee headlong, and that committees were to be set up in Russia (with the consent and under the supervision of the imperial government) for the purpose of selecting emigrants and seeing to it that the exodus would be accomplished in a business-like way. Furthermore, he pointed out, at the beginning the 'number of emigrants cannot be large' for necessary preparations had to be made for their reception. The Baron had learned something, obviously, from the misadventures of 1891 in Argentina. Therefore he called upon the Russian Jews to exercise patience 'as the heirs of their fathers who for centuries suffered so much'.

Ironically, these admonitory words were hardly needed, for by 1893 the rush was over. What with the bad reports coming back from Argentina and the deliberation with which the newer groups of expectant colonists were treated by JCA, the numbers desiring and able to go receded to a manageable level.

Before relating the later history of the settlements, we might pause to glance over what had been accomplished so far. We can do it by reference to the first annual report of JCA,[8] covering the year beginning 1 September 1891. As such things go, this report spoke with considerable candour. It acknowledged that there were still great difficulties to be overcome, as might be expected at the inception of 'any enterprise of this character'; that the 'first persons who were placed at the head of it were not equal to the task'; that this 'painful position' had been created by the

> eruption of emigrants towards the Russian frontiers and the precipitation with which the local Committees were obliged to act, and the haste with which the choice of colonists took place. It will be readily understood that many emigrants have been introduced into the colonies who are new to agriculture, and thus detrimental to organisation, and that these seriously increased the initial difficulties of the work. Of course this is precisely the opposite to what should have happened if it had been possible for us to have selected people used to agricultural labour, and offering the requisite guarantees of stability, discipline, morality.

The report further revealed that land had been purchased as follows:

	(Acres)	(Hectares)
Mauricio (Buenos Aires Province)	72,500	29,000
Moisesville (Santa Fe Province)	25,000	10,000
Entre-Rios Province	232,500	93,000
	330,000	132,000

The number of families settled had been about 1,000 (a JCA report published 50 years later indicates that there were only 500 colonist families actually in the settlements at the end of 1892), with over 150 acres each, and the total land area so far occupied and partly ploughed was about 180,000 acres. It was noted that for the moment the 'forwarding of emigrants' was being suspended because of a cholera epidemic in Russia and the need to reorganise the existing colonies. The report calls attention to the difficulty of finding suitable staff and expresses the hope that JCA will be able to find 'instructors amongst the colonists themselves'.

The report made it very clear that, in accordance with the Baron's principles, the lands were not given 'gratuitously to the colonists'. They were expected to repay all costs plus interest in ten annual payments. Lastly, the report indicated that £330,000 of the original capital had been spent: of this, £160,000 had been employed in the purchase of land at about 10 shillings per acre, and the remainder had been used mostly for the installation of colonists. The report also carried the information that, in order to avoid a too large agglomeration of Jewish colonists in Argentina, 'JCA had formed a colony in Western Canada with 100 families'.[9]

Though the report failed to mention it, an important event that had occurred in 1892 was the recognition of JCA by the Argentine government as a charitable institution.

Events in Argentina had been followed by an attentive press throughout the Americas and Europe. The Hebrew and Yiddish press especially in Russia was avidly interested in what was going on in distant South America. The most prominent Hebrew language paper in Russia, *Hamelitz* of St Petersburg, was extremely and consistently critical. And while its attitude may have been coloured by its Argentine correspondent, who was JCA's enemy because friends of his, it was alleged, had proposed a self-serving scheme to JCA and been rebuffed, there were enough blunders, mishaps and misunderstandings in JCA's early efforts to justify severe criticism, and not only in the Jewish press. Theodore Herzl, the correspondent of the Vienna *Neue Freie Presse*, also wrote a dispatch about JCA's difficulties.

It was not only at Mauricio that the administration was unprepared for newcomers. When the 'Pampistas' from Constantinople reached a new colony, San Antonio, there was in effect a re-enactment of the Mauricio incident. There was no living accommodation, no meat, no fuel, a general lack of food; the new arrivals had to sleep on the ground or in ditches, or at best, in wagons and wrecks of old buildings; the administrator did not speak or understand Russian or Yiddish; when food finally was provided, there was a question as to whether it was kosher. It was no wonder that here too there was a riot against the administration and the police had to be called in. However, after all this, when the 'Pampistas' were finally provided with building materials, they set to work energetically erecting houses and barns.

In a sense, the adventures of the 'Pampistas' epitomised the story of all the first Argentine colonies. Conditions at the start were terrible, but when the proper materials and supplies were made available at least some of the settlers were able to get on their feet and begin to make order out of chaos. A contributor to this improvement was the next chief administrator in Buenos Aires, the successor to Roth, Colonel A. E. W. Goldsmid.

Goldsmid, a regular officer of the British Army, was a unique individual. His father was a converted Jew, a member of the Indian Civil Service. The younger Goldsmid entered the British Army in India a Christian, read and learnt about his Jewish heritage, decided he wanted to become a Jew, and converted back. He was a very active member of the early Zionist movement in England.

The Baron had great hopes of the Colonel, who seemed to be blessed with the most desirable qualities: a successful military administrator, with just those traits of decisiveness and severity that the Baron felt had been lacking in his predecessors, yet a Jew, interested in Jewish problems, and devoted to his fellow Jews – at least in the abstract. Also, what doubtless appealed to the Baron's snobbish side, Goldsmid had been recommended if not by the Prince of Wales personally, then by an important member of his entourage. The Baron expected that the Colonel would correct past errors and would set up an effective organisation, one that would provide, in good time, houses, tools and animals and would impose discipline. This, indeed, was a major point in the Baron's instructions. He told Goldsmid to send back any colonists who did not work hard and were not content with a minimum of food, and suggested that in cases of mass insubordination the Colonel should have recourse to mass repatriation. In his desire to bring order to the unruly colonies the Baron seemed to forget that the unrest of the settlers may have had a reasonable basis.

Goldsmid began with a tour of the colonies. He travelled to

Moisesville, northwest of Buenos Aires, to Clara, directly to the north, and to Mauricio to the west. Throughout, he was received most respectfully, like a visiting potentate. And he did make certain reforms; for example, instead of supplying provisions and materials to the incoming settlers he arranged for JCA to pay them subsidies which left them the responsibility and freedom to obtain what they needed themselves. He also carried out the Baron's injunction to be strict. At Mauricio he told the colonists who wanted to leave to do so, with JCA paying their fare even to the USA – and some did. At Clara he expelled four families who had demonstrated a complete incapacity to do any work, though the settlement as a whole seemed to be faring well. Here implements and animals had been provided, although the latter included some untrained horses and oxen, which had to be broken in by the newcomers who had very little experience of such esoteric skills. At Moisesville the Colonel arranged for a definitive distribution of land, parcelled out tools and cattle to the settlers, and got houses built; not surprisingly, there was a great reduction in the volume of complaints. He also reduced the JCA staff, which had grown intolerably. But not everything in Goldsmid's administration was plain sailing. He wanted to expel some families from Moisesville,[10] but members of a mission of inspection sent by Hirsch himself sided with the settlers. Even after his reforms there was still trouble in Moisesville as many colonists had not received tools or cattle.

Goldsmid's worst troubles came from his relationship with the Baron de Hirsch. Apparently Goldsmid wanted the Buenos Aires office, rather than Paris (which meant the Baron), to have the authority to make decisions. Not succeeding in obtaining as much freedom of action as he wanted, the Colonel resigned in May 1893 after having served 15 months. He was succeeded by a Russian-Jewish engineer, Kogan, the first administrator who was a compatriot of the colonists. He believed that the unrest and unruliness of the settlers was due to the previous administrators' lack of understanding. But it did not take long for Kogan, who was an arrogant, self-confident and self-willed individual, to get into hot water himself.

JCA had formed nine groups in Russia, each consisting of about 50 families expecting to emigrate to Argentina. Each of the groups sent one or two representatives to Argentina to inspect the colonies before the bulk of the would-be emigrants embarked. Kogan quarrelled bitterly with the representatives. Their differences arose because the Russians wanted to live in villages, as they had at home, with their farms lying outside, while Kogan favoured the North American system of having each house on its own land; even under such an arrangement, by placing the houses near where the four corners of separate properties touched, as many as four houses could be near each other, and some neighbourly propinquity was a necessity for these newcomers on the empty, unfriendly pampas. The argument for the village arrangement was that it was the customary one in Russia (and throughout much of Europe also); the argument against it was that with farms of 100 acres or more, much larger than in Russia, a villager might have to walk 15 km a day just to get to and from his property. This controversy over the plans for new settlements delayed the departure of the nine groups for months. The intention had been to finish the houses and other buildings for 350 families by October 1893, but these were still not quite complete by August 1894. The families in the meantime had wound up their affairs and then remained marooned in Russia for a year longer than they had expected. In the middle of 1894 they finally managed to sail, but true to the JCA tradition of misfortune they had to wait several days in Genoa to transfer to the ships for Argentina, suffering illness and hunger because of the difficulty in obtaining kosher food. Most of them arrived in the midst of the Argentine winter. Many contracted typhus on account of the cold. Finally, because of their arrival late in the year they were not able to work the virgin land assigned to them until 1895, only then making preparations for a wheat crop to be harvested in 1896.

By that time Kogan, who had been largely responsible for delaying their voyage, was long gone. In fact, he had lasted only six months, until November 1893. He had not exactly been dismissed by the Baron, but the latter had appointed two new directors at the end of 1893 and Kogan, a proud man, took this as a rather too obvious hint. Further, the new administrators, though they did not agree with the Russian delegates, had given way to them in order to settle the housing controversy which had gone on far too long.

These new administrators were Samuel Hirsch (no relation of the Baron) and David Cazès, both of whom had been responsible officials in the Alliance Israélite's school system. It is remarkable that there appears no record of any disagreement between them, although they served together for about 15 years. Perhaps equally remarkable was the fact that they were not dismissed by the Baron. This was partly because he had little opportunity, as he lived for only two years after their appointment, and partly because he had apparently given up hope of finding a perfect head for the Argentine enterprise. Though he was often heard referring to Cazès and Hirsch contemptuously as 'Melamedim' – poor schoolteachers – he was careful not to berate them. When he

differed with them he expressed himself carefully and circum-
spectly so as not to offend.

Thus, when the great 'contract' revolt broke out in the colonies
and the Baron made extravagant statements that *all* the settlers
should be sent back to Russia, despite the costs, penalties and
logistical difficulties that would be entailed, he allowed himself
to be persuaded not to take so self-destructive a course. Hirsch
and Cazès not only had the advantage over the previous directors
in that the Baron gave them more latitude; they also had a fairly
secure base from which to operate. Roth, as we have said, had
been a great purchaser of land, and the next two administrators,
Goldsmid and Kogan, also added to JCA's holdings, which
amounted to 444,780 acres by the end of 1894. Four colonies –
Moisesville, Mauricio, Clara and San Antonio – had been established on a fairly sound footing, and some if not all of the local
managers could communicate with the colonists. The slowing
down of the rate of arrivals and the end of emergency shipments
of immigrants made it possible for adequate preparations to be
made for their reception. No longer were there disastrous, long-
lasting waits in the open by hungry and thirsty newcomers. Now,
on the whole, accommodation was ready in advance of the arrival
of the occupants.

The contracts[11]

Samuel Hirsch and Cazès, however, had their share of difficult
times, especially at the beginning of their service; for they were
soon confronted by the affair of the contracts.

By 1894 the Baron had decided that the development of the
settlements had proceeded so far that it was time to enter into
definitive agreements with the colonists. In fact, a lack of any
contract indicating what the settlers might expect had allowed the
enemies of JCA to spread the rumour that the Russian Jews
working JCA lands were slaves, as they had no definite promise
of what goods and property they might receive or when. The
contracts were intended to resolve these doubts. In working out
what was owed, *all* JCA's costs were taken into account – transport, maintenance, subventions, houses, animals, equipment. The
average cost per family for these items came to £150–£180. The
cost of the land added £120, making the typical family's debt
£270–£300. In addition, the putative contracts imposed a 5 per
cent charge for interest. Even these figures did not cover JCA's
total expenditure because, reasonably enough, the charges against
the farmers did not include the amounts JCA had spent mistakenly

or because of errors by its staff; these sums, which amounted to £180,000, had been written off.

JCA proposed that the debt of each farmer be paid in 12 equal annual instalments. Furthermore, the contracts provided that some of the land involved might have to be given up by the purchaser if it were needed by the community for roads etc. Also, the land could not be used for any but agricultural purposes – in some cases not even for cattle raising – and could not be farmed by a third party. Lastly, if any of the regulations were broken the property would revert to JCA.

Most of the colonists reacted with shock and dismay to the Baron's proffered contracts; the reaction of many was exacerbated because the contract was read to them rapidly in Spanish, which they did not understand. The settlers in Moisesville, who had been in Argentina the longest, were not so antagonistic to the idea of signing, because they were familiar with the agreements offered by private colonization companies which did not differ greatly from JCA's. On the other hand the organisers of these other companies did not claim to be philanthropists, a point the opponents of the contract were quick to make.

The agitation stirred up by the contracts was compounded by the fact that, at the same time as they were proffered, JCA ordered that the wheat harvested by its colonists was to be delivered to its own warehouses to be sold by its agents, and only the surplus, if any, over the annual payment due was to be remitted to the growers. The latter claimed, not without justice, that this measure left them no wherewithal to pay immediate debts or to live until the next harvest. And besides, since the grain was to be sold at JCA's discretion, what assurance did the growers have that the best price would be obtained?

The protests regarding the grain deliveries were reasonable enough to cause the Buenos Aires office to retreat; settlers were allowed to retain some of the grain for sale for their own account. But the matter of the contracts was not so easily concluded. The 1894–5 harvest, which had aroused great hope, in the event came to grief. Frost killed much of the crop at Mauricio; then a heat-wave scorched the grain that was left. In the northern colonies prolonged rains flattened the wheat so that the crop was both small and expensive to harvest. The 1894–5 maize crop at Clara had been ruined by drought, and the high prices expected did not materialise.

With consummate lack of tact and judgment, Hirsch and Cazès chose this time to let the farmers know that they would be expected to pay for the harvesting costs without help from JCA. Real rebellions broke out in Clara and Mauricio, and the colonists called on the police and provincial governments to protect them against the administration. Hirsch and Cazès visited the villages and adopted a generally conciliatory policy, suspending payments and promising material and financial aid. The Baron in Paris fumed. He wanted the instigators punished, but Hirsch and Cazès stood up to him, and the Baron himself, on reflection and learning more about the details of the situation, became more sympathetic.

As we have indicated, some of the uproar about the contracts was due literally to lack of understanding; in time matters were clarified. The administration made new agricultural machinery available to contract-signers, and the Baron was quoted as saying that he would take 25 per cent off the purchase price for worthy settlers. Also, Hirsch and Cazès made concessions. They would extend the repayment period, make more land available for cattle raising, allow the farmers to hire labour and compensate them for land taken for railways. All this led to many contracts being signed, though a large proportion of the colonists still held out.

The reaction to the contracts had not gone unnoticed in the world outside. Some of the Argentine papers had commented to the effect that the contracts were overly onerous; enemies of JCA saw to it that the story reached and was carried by a notoriously anti-Semitic paper in Russia; but other periodicals, like the London *Jewish Chronicle*, took a more tolerant view.

As for the Baron himself, despite the doubts and despairs he admitted to in private in view of the continuing setbacks resulting from the weather and the conflicts between the settlers and the administration, he put on a brave front in public. In interviews with the *Jewish Chronicle*[12] he boldly continued to predict that the Argentine colonies would yet be the home of hundreds of thousands of Russian Jews.

Life in the settlements

The private and public Baron here contradicted themselves. But he was often nothing if not contradictory. He was open-handed in the extreme; yet in the matter of the contracts he was very strict initially with the settlers in Argentina. This paradox might be explained by saying that he had not set up JCA as a charitable enterprise; his original idea was that the sums invested would be repaid, so that the money could be applied in relieving others in a similar way. On another matter, however, it is more difficult to reconcile the seeming paradox. In the 1880s the Baron had been willing to spend 50 million francs on the education of Russian Jews; yet he was opposed to vocational education for the

Jews he had brought to Argentina, feeling that they should have already learnt the practice of agriculture and also being opposed to educating them in general. His conception apparently was that the Russo-Jewish immigrants should be farmers at the low level of Turkish or Hungarian peasants and not in the much more expansive English or American sense. At times he expressed his dislike of Jewish intellectuals, asserting that Jews' troubles arose from over-emphasis on intellectual skills. However, he had no objection to the provision of religious, historical and Hebrew teaching by the colonists for their children. As early as 1891 there was a *cheder* in a tent in Moisesville, and not long afterwards there were similar schools at the other three colonies. Soon proper schools were built in all the colonies with the assistance of the Alliance Israélite and staffed with teachers trained by it. A small library was established in Mauricio in 1892, the first of many.

Nor did JCA neglect the physical well-being of the colonists. By 1894 there were 'hospitals' (more properly called clinics) at Clara and Mauricio, and doctors to serve in them – in Clara, indeed, the doctor had four assistants – and the doctors had to be rather exceptional. In the words of the 1894 Report,

> It was necessary to find doctors furnished with diplomas recognised by the Argentine Government and who, besides having a knowledge of Spanish, were also acquainted with the customs of our Colonists and with their peculiar language.[13] They had also to be men of sufficient physical vigour to frequently travel day and night over very great distances.

Many of the doctors were Russian Jews who distinguished themselves by their devotion to the needs of their patients. One of these, Dr Noe Yarcho, who came to Clara in 1893, was esteemed by the settlers not only for his self-sacrifice on behalf of their health but also because he took their side in their frequent battles with the administration.[14]

The population of the colonies increased considerably in 1894 and 1895, when 14 groups that had been recruited in Russia arrived in Argentina. Most were placed in small villages in the Clara area, where by 1896 there were 20 sub-villages, and some at Moisesville. There were on the average 40 families in each group. Several of the incoming groups were settled in traditional European style, in villages of 40–50 houses close together. Four others were established on a mixture of village and isolated-farm systems, with the 40–50 dwellings arranged in units of 2 to 12 so that the pasturage and cultivated lands should not be too far away. Yet others were divided into two units of 25 houses each. So the controversy over the plan of the villages was decided by adopting both forms that had been proposed and adding a new and different one.

By this time each family had a small but substantial two-room house of brick, with a galvanised iron roof, a kitchen (and windows, some of the historians are careful to add). In addition, many had a stable for their complement of draught animals. (This early in the history of the JCA colonies, milk production was not important as it became later.) Also, each family had on the average an allocation of 185 acres.

By 1895 there were 1,222 colonist families, but by 1896 this figure had been materially reduced to 910, comprising 6,757 persons. The reduction was due to the administration's sporadic purges from the settlements of the unwilling and incapable settlers. In fact, the 1895 Report of JCA had clearly stated that up to 10 per cent of the settlers were poor human material and must be 'got rid of, root and branch'. It should not be forgotten that JCA was willing to pay the travelling expenses of the expelled families, even to the United States. In addition to those expelled by JCA, a large number left the colonies out of discouragement. The crops in most of the years at the beginning of JCA's activities had been poor because of rain or drought; the weather had been dry at normally rainy seasons, and then in 1894–5, when a good crop was expected and was about ready for harvesting, very heavy rains smashed the wheat to the ground so that it could not be reaped. The crop of 1895 was remembered as especially poor precisely because expectations had been high. In addition to the bad weather there were periodic attacks by swarms of locusts which were difficult to combat.

We have noted previously that the Baron had disapproved of some deals for land that Löwenthal had made, on the ground that the prices were too high; the Baron calculated that on the basis of such prices the settlers would never be able to repay JCA. This land that he refused to acquire was located on the *pampa humeda*, a broad band of good soil several hundreds of miles wide covering most of Buenos Aires province and extending into the south of the provinces of Entre-Rios and Santa Fe. But JCA's land purchases were made at the margin of the *pampa humeda*, or even beyond its borders, where the land was distinctly inferior. Consequently the JCA colonies in these areas were more exposed to plagues of locusts, drought and floods than farms in the better-quality area.

In spite of the poor results in 1895, the administration cut off subsidies in that year to all colonists except the very newly arrived groups and some of the older families who were in an especially parlous situation. However, the poor crops in 1896, exacerbated by three separate waves of devouring locusts, made necessary a resumption of subsidy payments in the northern colonies of Moisesville, San Antonio and Clara. Mauricio, in the central part of the country, escaped the plague, and its residents were not subsidised. Another factor that contributed to the colonists' dissatisfaction was the low level of wheat prices in these years, for wheat was their major crop. In 1896 a total area of 37,385 hectares (approximately 93,000 acres) was planted. Wheat amounted to 68 per cent of this total, flax to 21 per cent, maize to about 6 per cent, and the rest was kitchen gardens and alfalfa (lucerne). In view of this preponderance of low-priced wheat, the head office in Buenos Aires instructed its corps of agronomists to try to persuade the farmers to diversify into more intensive crops. But diversification into such things as fruit or vegetables was inexpedient because the colonies were so far from the urban centres that would be the natural markets for such produce. JCA was, however, successful in introducing the settlers to the production of milk, cheese and butter.

One contradictory feature of the situation was that, despite all the wheat they produced, the colonies had to pay high prices for flour because this was brought in from elsewhere in the country. To eliminate this anomaly, steam-powered mills for grinding wheat were installed in Clara in 1895 and in Mauricio a year later.

Perhaps because he had been troubled by the exodus from the colonies (although JCA claimed that their loss of population was much less than in other newly developed parts of Argentina), perhaps because he wanted witnesses to refute the usual spate of anti-JCA articles in certain sectors of the Jewish press, and perhaps for a third reason which we shall mention in a moment, at the end of 1895 the Baron sent Dr Sonnenfeld, the head of the Paris office of JCA, and David Feinberg, secretary of the St Petersburg Committee, to Argentina on a tour of inspection. Feinberg, though castigated in some colonies by the individuals he had selected to migrate from Russia – some of them told him they would have been better off if they had never left – took a favourable view of the Argentine settlements, at least in his public statements. He wrote:

My general impression is most favourable to our colonists. It was with joy that, when I passed from one colony to another, I was able to convince myself of the marvellous aptitude of our co-religionists for the hard work of the fields. It was I who selected the colonists in Russia. They were for the most part small merchants, shop-keepers, subordinate employees, and in general people who had never been engaged in agricultural pursuits. But evidently the fault, if fault there was, was not theirs. And the proof is that, when they have been given the means of cultivating the soil, they have shown a zeal and ardour which in less than two years have made them suitable agriculturists.[15]

Nevertheless, Feinberg and Sonnenfeld recommended that immigration should be held up until those farmers already in Argentina were on a really firm footing.

The third reason the Baron may have had for sending his two emissaries to South America was that he wanted a first-hand report. There is some evidence that he was planning to visit the Americas himself – he had never been across the Atlantic – bringing with him a large entourage of journalists who could look into the results of JCA's labours. However, while Feinberg and Sonnenfeld were still in Argentina, on 21 April 1896, Baron Maurice de Hirsch died quite suddenly, presumably of a massive heart attack, while at the country house of a friend near his own recently purchased estate of O'Gyalla in Hungary.

What had the Baron accomplished?

So the Baron did not live to see with his own eyes what he had wrought in America. 'What he had wrought' is in this context an accurate statement; for, though JCA had a Council of three, the Baron was obviously the dominant member. Indeed, by virtue of a resolution passed at the first meeting in October 1891, he legally had complete power; this resolution, which was re-adopted annually for some years thereafter, vested the President with all the powers of the Council. And the Baron acted in conformity with this authorisation. S. H. Goldschmidt and Isidore Loeb attended the meeting in October 1891, but subsequently, until April 1894, only the Baron and Goldschmidt were present. Loeb was apparently ill, and he died in July 1892. Then H. G. Lousada, the solicitor, was elected in Loeb's place, but he did not come to the Council meetings that Hirsch and Goldschmidt regularly held.[16] In 1894 Salomon Reinach was elected to the Council and made a third member at the meetings until the Baron's death in 1896. JCA's address, 2 rue de l'Elysée, Paris (the Baron's home), was further testimony to the complete identification of JCA in its first five years with its founder. The statement in the 1896 Annual Report, 'He was during his lifetime not only the President but the soul of the Jewish Colonization Association' (translated), is succinct – and true.

Chaim Avni, an Israeli historian whose detailed account of JCA's first five years in Argentina has been a valuable source for this chapter, is of the opinion that the Baron's choice of Argentina as a place of settlement was based on inadequate information and misconceptions, though he had the benefit of reports by observers whom he himself had dispatched there. Hirsch had hoped that he could obtain control of an autonomous region, which he was unable to do. He had no idea of the strength of anti-Semitism in Argentina, as manifested in the press and legislature, and he did not know how strongly the Argentines felt that all immigrants should be integrated into the local society. He overestimated the amount of good land available and overestimated the ability of Russian Jewish farmers, who had worked small plots intensively with primitive implements and had had alternate occupations, to accustom themselves to cultivating the virgin expanses of the pampas.

The committees that chose the colonists for emigration had no understanding of conditions in Argentina. Worse, the delays, stretching to years, which were not the fault of the colonists, discouraged many. The Baron, says Avni, had the rather naïve notion that the immigrants were born either 'good or bad', and did not seem to understand that unwarranted delays and resentment against what seemed to be an unfair contract might turn a 'good' settler into a 'bad' one. The blunders of the administration – the placing of non-Jews on the staff and their aloofness – contributed to the discontent. The result was that, of every two families brought to Argentina, only one stayed on the farm. By 1901, 1,550 families had been settled in the colonies of Clara and San Antonio in Entre-Rios province. Of these, 841 left and 709 stayed. And yet, Avni is careful to point out that Jews who signed contracts with *private* colonization companies in Argentina and failed to fulfil them were also expelled. Further, the Argentine government attempted a similar settlement venture at a place called Yehia, which failed dismally. Therefore the setbacks, disappointments and failure of JCA's enterprise were not due entirely to the mistakes of the Baron and the JCA staff. They were in large part the result of the inherent difficulty of transferring individuals *en masse* to a strange land where language, customs and working conditions were utterly different from what they had been used to. And indeed, the goals that JCA had set for itself in 1892 were impossible to accomplish.

There was another and very potent reason the settlers did not remain on the farm. The intellectual apostles of 'productivising' Jews, of which the Baron was one, believed that, if enough of their brethren became 'productive' workers, making and growing things by manual labour, anti-Semitism would be alleviated. But the object of this 'productivisation' – the settler himself – may have had different ideas. If he could better himself by abandoning the farm with its back-breaking labour and improve his material situation by becoming a tradesman, doctor or engineer in a town or city, why shouldn't he? And that is just what the Jews who came as colonists, or their children, did. A disproportionate number of the professional class in Argentina came to be children of JCA settlers who attended lower schools in the colonies and then went on to university. One Argentine colonist pithily summed up this tendency by saying, 'We have sown wheat and harvested doctors.'

Dr Avni makes it clear, without perhaps saying so explicitly, that he regards the great JCA venture into Argentina as a failure, and for a multitude of reasons besides the fact that the colonies were planted on poorish land, outside the *pampa humeda*: (1) the lack of any kind of ideology like that which has inspired farming in Israel; (2) the enforced resort to mono-culture; (3) the problems of marketing with the cities so far away; (4) the Argentine tendency to favour urban dwellers, giving them superior status as compared with the farming class; and (5) the rigid and hierarchical nature of the JCA administration. There is some truth in all this, but we would nevertheless enter a strong demurrer to the conclusion. While admitting that at present Jewish agriculture in Argentina has practically come to an end, and that at no time did JCA come anywhere near fulfilling the large and impossible aims of its sponsors, in a larger perspective – that of European Jewry on the one hand and the Argentine nation on the other – claims can be made as to the beneficial effect of the Baron's bold venture. At the end of Chapter 13 we describe some of the contributions made by the Jews to Argentina's agriculture. Also, while JCA-sponsored immigration was responsible for Argentina's obtaining a large accretion to its stock of professionals, Jews as a whole also benefited, because of the introduction of a new destination for the great numbers who wanted to leave Europe, especially Russia. All observers agree that JCA's colonization drive opened up the country to large-scale Jewish immigration. The 1895 census counted only 6,085 Jews in Argentina; a JCA survey in 1909 estimated a population of 55,000 Jews in that country, of whom 15,771 were in the JCA colonies; in 1919 the corresponding figures were 125,000 and 26,500. There are no firm figures on the present number of Jews in Argentina, but in the 1982 *American Jewish Yearbook* (p. 284) an estimate is given for 1980 of 242,000.

The Baron's work, as we have said, lived after him and indeed lives still. As Narcisse Leven, who was elected President of JCA a few months after the Baron died, said in the 1896 Report:

> We have first of all a duty to fulfil, that is to render homage to the memory of the founder of our organisation, the Baron de Hirsch, who died on 21 April 1896. He had the generous idea of coming to the help of his coreligionists living in countries where they suffered under discriminatory laws by improving their lot, both materially and morally. Not only did he provide without limit the means of accomplishing this great work, but he put at its service his intelligence and his efforts. The outlines of the work were traced by his hand. Fate, unfortunately, only granted him time to begin it. . . .

The Baron's death had, perhaps unexpectedly, a profound effect on the Argentine colonists. In their interminable quarrels with the JCA administration they had always regarded the Baron as distinct from his subordinates. The news of his decease inspired spontaneous and universal expressions of loss and mourning throughout the settlements. Some of the colonists went so far as to say that grief arising from the incessant difficulties with and recriminations by them had contributed to his fatal attack. Not only were memorial services held in every synagogue in Argentina, but resolutions were passed urging that all male children born during the first year after his death be named after him. At the end of that year, again, the *Kaddish* prayer was recited in all the country's synagogues in his memory.[17]

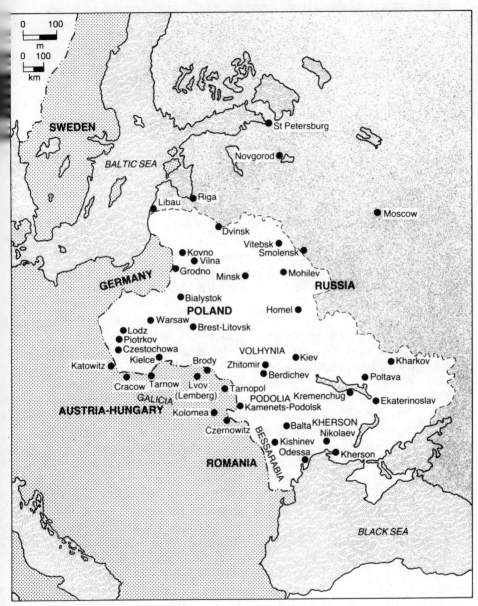

Map 1   The Pale of Settlement

CHAPTER 3

Activities in Russia

The Annual Reports of JCA for the years from 1892 to 1900 were at first fairly succinct, but by the end of that period they ran to about 100 pages and went into considerable detail concerning the settling of Russian Jews in Argentina, which was indeed JCA's most important theatre of operation. Only the briefest of paragraphs were devoted to its activities in Russia. However, after 1900 the Annual Reports became even more detailed, and JCA's work in Russia began to be described as fully and meticulously as its interests elsewhere.

What was the reason for this brevity in the early reports? The rationale that best suggests itself is that JCA, knowing that every step it took in Russia came under the scrutiny of that country's arbitrary and unpredictable bureaucracy, believed that by keeping a low and inconspicuous profile it would avoid arousing attention. Then, when there were no adverse repercussions after the first few years, a fuller coverage was felt to be possible. Brief as the early reports were, there is enough material in them, and in an interview that the Baron gave to the London *Daily Graphic* of 7 July 1894, for us to form a fair idea of what JCA was doing in Russia in the last decade of the nineteenth century.

It will be remembered that Arnold White, the Baron's emissary, on his second visit in 1892 had obtained permission for JCA to establish a Central Committee in St Petersburg with subordinate committees in provincial capitals. Their function was to select the settlers for the Argentine colonies. In the course of 1892 these committees were duly set up, and David Feinberg was appointed Secretary of the Central Committee. He did not confine himself to the capital, but travelled widely, working with local groups who chose the emigrants. These were assembled into groups of 40–50 families, generally originating from one locality. It was hoped that these groups would be self-governing, and as a first step in this direction two delegates from each were chosen as an advance party of inspection to Argentina. By 1893 these delegates had gone there, but the emigration of the groups themselves was held up because of an outbreak of cholera in Russia and also by

42

the inability of the JCA administration in Buenos Aires to make a decision as to the mode of settlement. Finally, however, by 1894, 3,000 Russian Jews had been 'forwarded' to Argentina.

In 1896 there was an interesting change in policy: JCA decided that young Russian Jews should be given an agricultural education (something the Baron had been opposed to, and it is significant that this was undertaken only after the Baron's death). Therefore a small number were sent to two agricultural schools operated by the Alliance Israélite – Mikveh-Israel outside Jaffa, and Djedeida in Tunisia. An even more significant departure from past practice was a declaration on JCA's part of a desire to help Jewish schools and other establishments to produce arts and crafts objects within Russia itself. Many of the members of JCA's Russian Committee, including Baron Günzburg, the Chairman, had basically favoured a policy of improving the situation of Jews within Russia rather than encouraging emigration.

And then, David Feinberg made a point which he had intended to convey to the Baron after his return from his trip to Argentina, but had been forestalled by Hirsch's death. Feinberg's visit had convinced him that the colonies could not absorb more than a couple of hundred families per year, and that therefore immigration should be held up for some years to permit consolidation. In the meantime, he felt, more funds could be usefully expended in Russia itself. Although it was too late to tell this to the Baron, Feinberg did talk to the Council, who agreed with him and, as we shall see, expanded the scope of JCA's activity in both Russia proper and Russian Poland.[1]

In the following six years the scope of JCA's activities in Russia was quite firmly established. These activities were:

1 help to Jewish farmers working individually or in colonies with loans for the purchase of high-quality seed, modern implements and good breeding stock, and by using itinerant instructors to teach and demonstrate current techniques;
2 help to a number of agricultural schools;
3 help with the financing and supervision of what came to be an extensive network of hundreds of *loan kassas* (a form of savings and loan society), with hundreds of thousands of members, which were the sole source of credit for small Jewish businessmen, artisans and farmers;
4 assistance, financial and otherwise, to a widespread group of vocational schools for both boys and girls, which had in total some thousands of pupils, and, ancillary thereto, to a number of evening classes for artisans – *ateliers* where they could perfect their skills, and a small number of sales agencies;

5 through the Society for Primary Education, support of nearly a hundred primary schools with some 10,000 pupils;
6 the financing of a number of diverse enterprises like the Société des Logements Hygiéniques or the weaving factory at Dubrovna;
7 the establishment of what grew to be hundreds of bureaux of information on the means and methods of emigration from Russia. This operation, commenced in 1904, became properly effective in 1905, a year of which the normally unemotional and restrained JCA report remarked that a mainspring of Russian political policy seemed to be the destruction of the Jewish population.

This of course was the year of the abortive revolution that followed Russia's defeat in its war with Japan. Though the Czar retained his throne, the uprising was sufficiently threatening to cause him to accede to the establishment of the Duma, the first elected Russian legislature. Although liberal members of the Duma introduced bills to ease restrictions on Jews, these proposals were blocked by the later and more reactionary assemblies, and the government's anti-Semitic policy continued unchanged. Despite the terrifying alarums, the expulsions and the pogroms that pervaded the life of the Jews in Russia and Russian Poland during these years, JCA maintained its many functions; indeed, in the case of the kassas and the local information bureaux for would-be emigrants, it expanded their scope.

To exemplify the wide range of JCA's operations during the period 1900–14, we will take the year 1913 as a sample (we may refer occasionally to other years to fill the picture out).

Agriculture

True to its ideological origins, JCA laid great emphasis on its work for the benefit of Jewish farmers in Russia. In 1913 the JCA Council voted special credits for the kassas in the Kherson and Ekaterinoslav provinces in the Ukraine so that the loans made by the kassas should be also a means of improving agricultural practices. Using both their own funds and those borrowed from JCA, the kassas enabled the farmers to buy good seed or cattle of superior breeds, or to rent lots that had been left idle because their lessees had emigrated. Also, in Lithuania and northern Poland, where loans had hitherto been made through the agronomists employed by JCA, farm credit was now made available through kassas, for fertilisers, farm implements and the culture of strawberries, a new crop on which the agronomists gave instruction. In Bessarabia-Podolia on the Romanian border (before 1914 Bessarabia was part of Russia; after 1918 it belonged to Romania; after the Second World War it reverted to Russia), JCA made loans to five kassas to be re-lent to tobacco farmers. The Association also made advances through kassas for the purchase of cows, but cut down on loans for viticulture, which did not do well enough in this area.

Despite the general prohibition on Jews owning land, it seems that it was possible for them to buy small plots, and JCA lent individuals almost 7,000 roubles for this purpose. And so it went on – loans for the purchase of beehives, for the rental of pasturage, for the purchase of cows. Wherever there was a Jewish farm colony or farmer, whatever branch of agriculture he practised, the tireless JCA agronomists sought him out, made him loans or arranged for the local kassa to do it, and gave him instruction, performed demonstrations, even subsidised libraries so that the farmers could purchase material concerning agriculture.

JCA was not only concerned with the welfare of practising Jewish farmers; it also looked to the instruction of young people who might become farmers. As we have seen, it had for many years subsidised the running expenses of a small number of agricultural schools, helped out with their building programmes, and supervised the curricula. In 1913 the institutions so helped were in Minsk in White Russia, Novopoltava near Kherson, and Czenstoniev and Czestochowa in Poland. The student complement of all four together was 149, so obviously JCA's farm school activity was relatively modest. In addition to the teaching of agriculture, courses were given in religion, Hebrew, Polish and Russian.

There was also a tree nursery at Soroki, in Bessarabia. This nursery was a source of thousands of apple, pear, cherry and other fruit trees, vines, and other plants for Jewish farmers. In 1912 it had been attacked by a plague of parasites. Apparently there had been a tendency to grow some stock for show rather than for purely commercial considerations. In 1913 the nursery was reorganised to produce plants and trees strictly of marketable nature.

JCA's statistical report on the economic condition of Russian Jewry tells us that 13,059 families, comprising 75,887 people, had agriculture as their main occupation. As we have seen, thousands of these families benefited directly or indirectly from JCA's activities.

The report in question, *La Situation Economique des Israélites de Russie*, which is a vast storehouse of historical information, was one of the truly great accomplishments of JCA in Russia. This work, originally produced in Russian, was translated into French and published in Paris. The first volume, containing 437 pages, appeared in 1906 (Felix Alcan, editor) and the second, of 373 pages plus an appendix containing 68 statistical tables, in 1908. More than 1,000 individuals, including businessmen, teachers, rabbis and prominent members of the community, responded to letters of inquiry from St Petersburg, often more than once. The staff there collated these replies into hundreds of statistical tables and wrote an extensive expository text. No topic bearing even remotely on the Jews' economic situation was neglected, and hardly any community, no matter how small and remote, remained unprobed and unmentioned; 1,302 localities were covered. As an example, the sixth and final part, which is a survey of educational facilities available to the Jews in Russia, lists all the schools and *cheders* wherever they were, the number of pupils in each, the costs of operation and the subjects taught. It then goes on with the same thoroughness to cover the vocational schools. Other sections of the study treat in the same complete fashion Jewish misery and good works and the part played by Jews in manufacturing, with special attention to the textile industry – spinning, weaving, knitting, clothes production etc. – both in former Poland and in the Pale generally. All this occupied the second volume; the first volume contained an extensive review of Jewish farmers, with separate chapters for the *gubernias* of Kherson and Ekaterinoslav in the Ukraine, Bessarabia, Poland and other provinces. The remainder of the first volume is devoted to a survey of Jewish artisans, handworkers and small private industry.

The kassa movement

The kassa movement, which JCA had begun 11 years before, was still flourishing in 1913 despite poor commercial conditions in consequence of the Balkan Wars, which had particular effect in the southern and southeastern regions of Russia, and despite the poor circumstances of the Jewish population of this area, which was subjected to mass expulsion from the villages where they lived and worked. In fact, many kassas had extended their field of operations beyond credit and begun to act for their members as purchasing agents for machinery and raw materials, and likewise as sellers of their members' products. The rapidity and extent of the spread of the kassas is not a matter for surprise; until they came into being, there was no source of credit for the small Jewish businessman, artisan or farmer, or for a family confronted by an emergency.

More generally, the services of the kassas were intended for the poorest groups in the population – principally small tradesmen faced with an urgent problem, where a 100-rouble loan might be of critical importance, or artisans who lacked the funds to buy the tools of their trade or were in temporary distress because of illness or a strike. Without the kassas, such people could only resort to usurers, to their frequent ruin. By providing loans at reasonable rates of interest, the kassas rendered 'invaluable service to these poor, hard-working classes who constituted the majority of Russian Jews' (1908 Report, p. 224).

By 1913 there were 680 kassas in Russia: 42 had been started in that year, of which 33 were in operation by December. Altogether, the kassas had about 450,000 members. As, presumably, not more than one person in a family belonged to a kassa, it is clear that a high proportion of all the Jewish families in Russia had a representative in a kassa. These institutions had at their disposal 40 million roubles (about £4.2 million) available for lending, of which two-thirds arose from members' deposits.

As evidence of the good financial health of the kassas, JCA reports (with, alas, unconscious irony, just before the outbreak of the First World War) that many were reaching the point where their deposits would be sufficient for their needs without further advances from JCA. Indeed, more than a third of those presenting accounts were already in this position. The scale of operations can be envisaged from the size of the loans issued. In 1913, of the 373 reporting associations, 32 had a 100 rouble (£10) limit on loans, 183 imposed varying limits between 100 and 250 roubles, 151 made loans up to 300 roubles, and 7 even went beyond 300. To become a member in most of the kassas required a deposit of 10 roubles (which could be paid in instalments); others had larger requirements, up to 50 roubles.

Vocational schools

While the agricultural schools had relatively few pupils, that was not the case with the JCA network of vocational schools in general. They were located in the principal centres of Jewish population like Bialystok in Poland, Dvinsk, Grodno, Odessa, Riga, Vilna, Warsaw and many others. In 1913 there were 18 such institutions for boys, with 1,892 pupils (as compared with 1,415 in 1912). For girls there were 13 schools, with 1,135 pupils. For the boys, the principal skill taught was that of locksmith-mechanic, which covered metalworking in general. About 75 per cent of all male students were in this field, because it was the one that offered the best job opportunities. The other major courses were for electricians, woodworkers and weavers. For the girls dressmaking was even more predominant than metalworking among the boys – 88 per cent – and the other major courses were related to it, e.g., sewing lingerie and making layettes. These skills were in demand, and employment was therefore relatively easy to obtain. The Central Committee in Petrograd (on the eve of the First World War the name of the capital was changed to a Russian form to rebut charges of undue German influence at the Court) was very much concerned with girls' education and made special efforts to ensure that the teachers became acquainted with up-to-date styles by visiting the salons where the latest fashions were displayed. JCA also contributed to three special primary schools for girls – in Dvinsk (Latvia) and Zhitomir and Poltava (Ukraine) – where, as well as the customary curriculum, pattern cutting and dress design were taught.

In addition to regular vocational schools, JCA supported evening classes and established model workshops, where artisans could not only perfect their skills but also learn mathematics and design. There were 1,050 artisans attending 18 such institutions, half of which were in Vilna.

Primary schools

Another great JCA educational enterprise was its programme of subventions for Jewish primary schools. Through 'The Society for the Propagation of Instruction', JCA was contributing in 1913 to the running expenses of no fewer than 66 institutions (25 for boys, 25 for girls, 8 mixed and 8 night-schools) with 11,134 pupils (6,829 girls and 4,305 boys), who received the elements of a modern education although, interestingly enough, a large number of the boys' schools were connected with Talmud-Torahs. A little more than half the pupils paid some tuition fees; the others were admitted free. JCA contributed not only towards running expenses but also in a number of cases towards the cost of buildings and equipment.

The local Jewish communities often raised money for the schools by means of special events like dances or theatrical performances. In Odessa the local authorities, with special malevolence, prohibited such activities. Nevertheless, the 'Society for Instruction' operated 17 schools there, with 2,335 pupils who were not included in the totals quoted in the previous paragraph. Also not included were the figures for Russian Poland. In that area, through the medium of the Society 'Daath' (knowledge), JCA helped 15 schools with 2,139 regular pupils and 452 who attended evening classes. Counting all these categories together, over 16,000 children were at schools helped by JCA in 1913. It is interesting that only one or two of these schools were founded before 1890, that is before JCA came to Russia, and only a handful before 1900, when JCA began to operate there on a major scale. In other words, it was the encouragement and funds provided by JCA that were responsible for the existence of almost all of these primary schools.

As in the case of the vocational schools, JCA was careful to upgrade the quality of the teaching. For this purpose a summer course was operated in Odessa, attended by 240 teachers from about 150 localities. In addition to discussions of educational theory, lessons were given in zoology, botany, physics and design. More formally, 54 teachers attended courses in Grodno, studying particularly the teaching of Hebrew.

Bureaux of information

Through its Central Committee in St Petersburg, JCA had launched yet another enterprise in Russia involving tens of thousands of Jews, the Bureau of Information for Emigrants. This was initiated in 1904, which as we have seen was a time when recruiting for the Argentine settlements had greatly declined. The Central Committee set up this Bureau of Information to help the many Jews who wanted to leave Russia for any destination, especially the United States. By 1908 there were no fewer than 360 local committees, offshoots of the Central Bureau, that had official governmental recognition. These, as might be expected, were concentrated in the areas where there was a preponderance of Jews – the so-called Northwest (Russian Poland and the Baltic region) and the Southwest (Ukraine and Bessarabia). By 1913 the number of local committees had grown to 507, grouped under 18 regional committees.

The Bureau was careful to establish committees in towns near the Austrian and German borders and to put them in touch with emigration aid groups just across the frontier in these two countries, making for a most useful collaboration. The frontier committees established good relations with the border-control officials, and the local committees in the interior also dealt with local border-crossing problems. The chief exit points from Russia where these committees operated were Thorn, Myslowitz, Eydt-kuhnen and the Baltic port of Libau.

The work of the Bureau and its hundreds of local committees was far from being merely informational. Among their principal functions was to help would-be emigrants through the procedures for obtaining passports and railway and steamship tickets and to represent them in the event of a dispute with the navigation companies. The bureaux got cheap steamship tickets for the emigrants, secured fare reductions on the Russian railways and also, through the Israelitische Allianz in Vienna, on the Austro-Hungarian railways. At times they were able to form some of the emigrants into groups and shepherd them to the points of embarkation. A major objective was to protect the departing Jewish families against unscrupulous agents who were ready to take advantage of the ignorant and frightened travellers, for most of whom the journey overseas meant a plunge into the unknown.

The bureaux did not sit back and wait for inquiries. They printed placards in Yiddish telling how to obtain visas and passports and posted them in synagogues. They published a bi-monthly newsletter, *Der Jüdischer Emigrant*, which furnished news on current government policy and regulations. They published a Manual of Emigration with separate sections on Australia, New Zealand and Argentina, and information sheets on the United States, describing living conditions and job opportunities. They also printed pamphlets giving instructions on the procedures for medical examinations.

A particular concern was the health of the emigrants. Medical examinations were provided to ensure that they were not suffering from any disease that would bar them from entering their country of destination. Special attention was paid to the condition of the eyes, for any manifestation of eye trouble would make it impossible to enter the United States. For this reason a special eye clinic was established in the town of Homel. In 1913 the Committees in Kiev, Minsk, Warsaw, Kovno and other cities received special JCA subsidies to enable them to organise medical services. Thousands received examinations, and also treatment, often free.

In this year there was an increase in emigration from the North-western area because of the widespread expulsion of Jews from rural localities on the pretext that they had been doing business illegally. The 153 committees functioning in this region received 19,825 requests for information. In the Southwest, Jews were also subjected to mass expulsion and extreme harassment in consequence of anti-Semitic agitation. Economic conditions were poor in general, so that non-Jews also left the area, but in addition Jewish shopkeepers suffered from the competition of consumer co-operatives. In this region 197 committees received 26,619 inquiries. In the South the story was broadly the same. Jewish farmers and tobacco planters were expelled *en masse*, and the Jewish population in Kherson and Bessarabia was very apprehensive of physical attack. From this part of the Empire there were 7,470 requests for help and information, including 3,595 addressed to the Odessa office and 1,183 to the one in Kishinev, Bessarabia. The situation was no different in Russian Poland. Here Jewish merchants were subjected to a boycott and Jews were expelled from the countryside as they were forbidden to engage in farming on land owned by Polish nationals. Sixty local bureaux received 10,596 inquiries.

Totalling these figures, it appears that in all 63,340 inquiries concerning emigration were made to the Bureaux for Emigration Information in 1913. As each inquiry usually involved two persons, a total of at least 126,000 would-be emigrants received information from the bureaux. This number is roughly equal to the figure for Russian Jewish arrivals overseas in 1913; 94,120 went to the United States, 10,049 to Argentina, 9,882 to Canada, and a few thousand elsewhere – nearly 120,000 in all.

Other activities

The preceding pages have outlined the major enterprises conducted by JCA in Russia. There were also some minor ones, which are worth mentioning if only to demonstrate the depth and range of the work. Buildings in Vilna were erected with JCA's help by the Société des Logements Hygiéniques. In 1913 these 200 apartments were all let, but JCA was operating them at a loss. In addition, in ten towns scattered through the country JCA had made loans to help build housing for two or three families in each that had been displaced by fires. In the summer of 1913 the Société participated in an exhibition in Petrograd organised by the Interior Ministry and was awarded a silver medal on the basis of photographic brochures about the Vilna installation.

JCA also experimented, though on a small scale, with establishing selling co-operatives for Jewish artisans. Thus it promoted a store in Vilna to sell furniture and cabinets produced by an *atelier-modèle* and twelve workshops belonging to Jewish cabinet-makers. In 1913 total sales amounted to 33,184 roubles. However, in order to dispose of its merchandise the store had to engage an agent to make sales to merchants in other cities; this ran up expenses and created a deficit. There was a similar furniture store in Bobruisk which operated without a deficit, and another in Homel for the sale of shoes made by 75 artisans. The weaving mill at Dubrovna continued to operate, giving a livelihood to 500 workers.

All of this gave JCA hope for the future. That future came all too soon. Eight months into 1914, the First World War was raging. Since the Jewish Pale ran roughly along the Russian border with Germany and Austria-Hungary, much of the fighting took place in areas where the Jewish population was concentrated, as indeed did the civil wars after the Bolshevik Revolution as well as the Russo-Polish War of 1920–1. The devastation consequent on these conflicts and the disturbances and pogroms that accompanied them wiped out the elaborate networks of institutions that the Jewish community, with the help of the Central Committee of JCA in Petrograd (now Leningrad), had developed. After the war, when the Communist government had re-established some sort of order, JCA re-entered the country and embarked on a programme to help the surviving Jewish farmers and others in the Ukraine. We shall talk about this in a later chapter. But the bulk of its enterprises in Russia were destroyed by the war, the revolution and their aftermath.

The czarist regime was dictatorial, rigid and suspicious of innovation. Nevertheless, it apparently never raised serious objection to the widespread range of JCA's activities before the First World War. A primary school system, a group of vocational schools, conventions and colloquia for the teachers freely attended by those who wished to go, hundreds of small savings and loan agencies with hundreds of thousands of members, and hundreds of bureaux distributing information on how to emigrate – all this considerable apparatus directed and subsidised by a foreign organisation could have been snuffed out in an instant if the government had so decreed. So if, as the preceding pages have shown, czarist Russia was an utterly miserable place for Jews, it was also a place which for a time granted them latitude to create elaborate self-help institutions and, more notably, allowed these institutions to receive assistance from outside the country.

JCA's activities in Russia were also notable for what they indicated about JCA itself. Many if not most of these activities were far removed from any connection with agriculture, demonstrating that, despite the Baron's almost mystical feeling that 'salvation' for Jews would be found in their becoming farmers, the Council recognised that, as a practical matter (and indeed as the statutes of the Association provided), a multi-faceted approach was required even to begin to address the infinitely complex problem of helping the Jewish population in Russia and elsewhere.

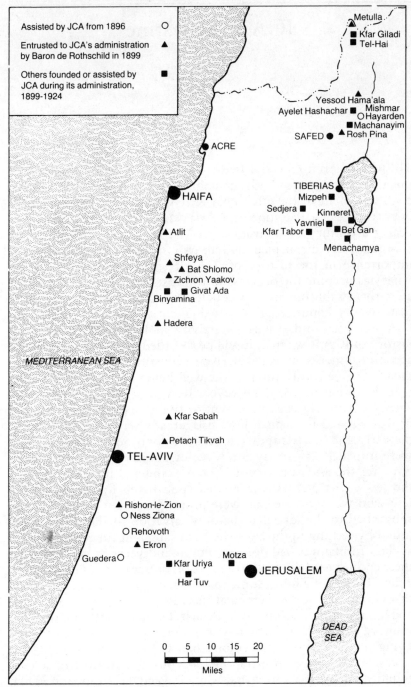

Assisted by JCA from 1896 ○

Entrusted to JCA's administration ▲
by Baron de Rothschild in 1899

Others founded or assisted by ■
JCA during its administration,
1899-1924

Metulla ▲
■ Kfar Giladi
■ Tel-Hai

Yessod Hama'ala
Ayelet Hashachar ■ Mishmar
○ Hayarden
■ Machanayim
SAFED ● ▲ Rosh Pina

ACRE

HAIFA

TIBERIAS
Mizpeh ■
Sedjera ■ Kinneret
▲ Atlit Yavniel ■ ■
Kfar Tabor ■ ■ Bet Gan
Menachamya

▲ Shfeya
▲ Bat Shlomo
▲ Zichron Yaakov
■ ■ Givat Ada
Binyamina

▲ Hadera

MEDITERRANEAN SEA

▲ Kfar Sabah

▲ Petach Tikvah

TEL-AVIV

▲ Rishon-le-Zion
○ Ness Ziona

○ Rehovoth
▲ Ekron
Motza
Guedera ○ ■ Kfar Uriya ● JERUSALEM
■
Har Tuv

DEAD
SEA

0   5   10   15   20
Miles

Map 2   Palestine: Settlements associated with JCA, 1896–1924

CHAPTER 4

JCA in Palestine

The JCA report for the year 1896, which opened with the announcement of the Baron's death, contained, a few pages further on, a brief statement to the effect that JCA was looking for settlement opportunities in Palestine and Asia Minor. With the benefit of nearly a century of hindsight, we can now appreciate that this comparatively inconspicuous reference marked a matter of great importance in the history of JCA. It signified the initiation of what has become the organisation's most important mission; for, after the establishment and conclusion of programmes in more than twenty countries, the most influential and vital function of JCA has been and still is its activity in Israel. When the final history of JCA is written, it will be recorded that the Association's accomplishments in Palestine/Israel constituted its greatest and most effective contribution to the well-being of the Jewish people.

In Palestine in 1896, however, JCA was not the pioneering agency that it had been in Argentina five years before. A number of Russian and Romanian Jews had already settled in Palestine in the early 1880s, attempting to make a living on the land. They were impelled in part by the wave of pogroms that had broken out after the assassination of Czar Alexander II in 1882. Most of the Jews who fled Russia at this time made for America; the few who went to Palestine were proto-Zionists who had already subscribed to the idea that the only salvation for Jews was to be found by settling in the ancestral homeland and cultivating its soil as their forefathers had done two thousand years before. Some of these enthusiasts belonged to a loose organisation called 'Chovevei Zion' (Lovers of Zion)[1], some to local groups in cities like Warsaw or Odessa, and some were unaffiliated.

The first 'new' colony was Petach Tikvah, northeast of Jaffa, founded as early as 1878 by Jews from Hungary and others already living in Jerusalem. This colony had been abandoned, but was restarted by a Russian group in 1883. In 1882 Romanian settlers founded Zichron-Yaakov, halfway between Tel-Aviv and Haifa, and Rosh Pinna in the interior of the country to the northeast. In 1883 the area of Rishon-le-Zion, also near Jaffa, was purchased by a contingent of Russian Jews who had landed in that port. Native-born Palestinian Jews from Safed established the agricultural village of Mishmar Hayarden in Galilee in 1884. By 1886 another set of immigrants had bought land at Waad-el-Hanine (now Ness Ziona) bordering Rehovoth on the west. In 1890 a Warsaw society purchased the area of Rehovoth itself, and groups from Vilna, Riga and Kovno acquired Hedera, near the coast between Jaffa and Haifa.[2]

All these settlements suffered common, and nearly fatal, trials. The immigrant founders generally expended all their capital in getting to Palestine and buying land; they had little or no money left for the purchase of seed, animals and implements. Though they were eager to till the soil, they had no experience or knowledge of agriculture, and the soil itself was sandy or rocky or both. In addition, while water was lacking, the areas intended for farming were often near marshes, which were excellent breeding grounds for malaria-spreading mosquitoes. Then the colonists had to deal with the capricious Turkish administration, which forbade foreigners to buy land in one town and permitted land purchases somewhere else but prohibited houses from being built thereon. With so many obstacles to overcome, the fragile new colonies came close to collapse within months of their founding.

Petach Tikvah, Zichron-Yaakov, Rishon-le-Zion, Rosh Pinna and other pioneer colonies were saved by the intercession of a fabulously wealthy Jewish baron. This saviour baron was not Maurice de Hirsch but Edmond de Rothschild, a scion of the French branch of that most famous Jewish family who shared many similarities of both temperament and attitude with Hirsch. Rothschild was dictatorial and paternalistic and would not brook opposition. He believed that it was important as a defence against anti-Semitism to prove that Jews could be successful farmers, and he therefore would not permit industrial work of any kind to be performed in 'his' colonies.

Baron Edmond de Rothschild

Edmond de Rothschild differed from Maurice de Hirsch in being more religious; and though not a Zionist in the nationalistic sense, he had an appreciation for the spiritual appeal of Palestine to Jewry in the Diaspora, a sentiment that was wholly alien to Hirsch. In 1882 Rothschild had had an emotional meeting with a charismatic rabbi, Reb Mohilever, who pressed him to sponsor Jewish settlement in Palestine. When this was followed by a visit from an emissary from Rishon-le-Zion with the same plea,

Rothschild responded favourably and took immediate action to establish an organisation to advise and assist the colonists. In a fairly short time he was supporting an elaborate bureaucracy, with horticulturists trained in Versailles and wine experts who tried to teach the settlers to grow fine French grapes on the intractable Palestinian soil. Arrangements were made to pay very high prices for the grapes (which, of course, helped support the growers) and elaborate and expensive wine-pressing and storage facilities were built in Rishon-le-Zion and Zichron-Yaakov.

It was not for lack of opportunity that Hirsch had been neither the founder nor the saviour of the original Jewish farm colonies. Early in the 1880s he had sent an agent, Veneziani, to Palestine accompanied by competent surveyors. Veneziani's report was quite discouraging; it noted the failure of the Jewish colonies already established to achieve any degree of self-sufficiency and emphasised the bad effect of the Palestinian environment on the health of the European settlers and especially of the children. Some years later Hirsch explained his feelings concerning settlement in Palestine in a long memorandum to a meeting convened in Paris in 1891 for the express purpose of bringing the two barons together to foster emigration to Syria and Palestine.[3] Hirsch explained that it was not so much that he was against Palestine, which he thought might be investigated further, but because Argentina was so superior, with its large, fertile and unpopulated areas and its sound government, he had decided to concentrate his efforts there. (While this was true enough, settlement in Argentina presented plenty of difficulties, as he was to find out.) So Hirsch felt at the time; at other times and in other places he raised other objections. Palestine was in an area that might be seized by Russia; there was no point in moving Jews out from under the Czar's thumb only to have the Czar come after them, as it were. More serious, settlement in Palestine required dealing with the Turkish government; this, as Hirsch well knew from his own experience, would be difficult, expensive and fraught with uncertainty. Above all, what deterred him, or at least gave him an excellent pretext for inaction, was the fact that Edmond de Rothschild was already deeply committed to helping the nascent Jewish colonies in Palestine, and Hirsch had no wish to compete with him.

What Hirsch did not appreciate was the power of an idea, in this case the idea of the return to the ancestral homeland. Indeed, Herzl, after his famous interview with Hirsch, in a letter to him said just that: 'It is with a flag that people are led whithersoever one desires, even to the Promised Land. For a flag men live and die.'

Hirsch and Herzl

In June 1895, Theodor Herzl met the Baron de Hirsch in the latter's home in Paris. The notion of Zionism, of the return of the Jews to their ancient homeland, as a means of resolving the 'Jewish problem' was simmering in Herzl's mind. It was while he had as yet no firm plan for an organisation, or even for the kind of book he wanted to write to publicise his ideas, that he was moved to approach the Baron, so well known for his interest in his co-religionists. Herzl wrote, 'You have hitherto been only a philanthropist. . . . I want to show you the way to become something more.' Hirsch was willing to be shown and made an appointment. At the meeting Herzl put forward some visionary schemes for Hirsch to implement, such as awarding prizes for notable achievements, apparently with the idea that publicising great accomplishments by Jews would dispel anti-Semitism. The Promised Land was hardly mentioned.

Herzl also spoke of raising the 'general moral level'. Hirsch broke in, 'No, no, no. I do not want to raise the general level. All our misfortunes come from the fact that the Jews want to climb too high. We have too much brains. My intention is to restrain the Jews from pushing ahead. All of the hatred against us stems from this.'

Perhaps because the Baron, who had promised not to interrupt him, spoke up after he had covered only six of his twenty-two pages of notes, Herzl broke off the interview, but not before the Baron had said, 'This is not our last conversation.'

In the next couple of weeks Herzl wrote two long letters to the Baron, containing some of his ideas about raising money to finance the exodus of Jews to the Promised Land. Among other points, he called attention to the power of an ideal, as mentioned above. The Baron replied briefly from London that he would be glad to see Herzl again but that this could be only after his return to Paris some months later. The sensitive Herzl interpreted this as a polite dismissal and fired off yet a third letter to the Baron, saying that there was little point in further communication; but in his diary he wrote, 'If this man goes along with me, we may really change our times.'[4]

In the few months remaining before the Baron's death Herzl made no attempt to communicate with him, but on 21 April 1896 he wrote to his associate Nordau suggesting that the latter sound out the Baron for a donation – too late, alas, for this was the day the Baron died. Herzl then wrote in his diary, 'His death is a loss to the Jewish cause. Among the rich Jews he was the only one who wanted to do something big for the poor ones. Today I have the feeling that our cause has grown poorer. For I always believed I would still win Hirsch over to the plan.'[5] This may be an instance of over-optimism on the part of Herzl, who to sustain his drive for Zionism needed to be an optimist. Hirsch's general inclination was against enterprises in Palestine, though there was a certain ambiguity in his attitude.

JCA's first steps in Palestine

At the Council meeting held on 15 October 1896, six months after the Baron's death, Zadoc Kahn, the Chief Rabbi of France, proposed that the Association should grant loans to colonies in Palestine established by emigrants from Russia. This suggestion provoked more controversy than was usual at Council meetings. Herbert Lousada, the solicitor, took particular exception to it, pointing out that JCA's function was to move Jews out of Asia as well as Europe and that, moreover, the Baron himself had been opposed to settlement in Palestine. The Rabbi replied that he was concerned not to have JCA set up colonies but merely to help individuals in trouble. As for the Baron not wishing to act in Palestine, that was because someone else (Edmond de Rothschild) was already doing this; furthermore, in Hirsch's memorandum to the Paris meeting in 1891 he had indicated that he had a positive interest in settlement in Palestine (this seems to have been a rather strained interpretation on the part of the Rabbi). Mr Plotke, the German member, poured oil on troubled waters by the customary device of proposing a committee to study the question and if necessary send an emissary to the area to prepare a detailed report to the Council. In the meantime, might not the Council, without commitment, vote loans for settlers in two or three colonies? The Council then agreed to make advances to three colonies to a maximum of 157,000 francs.

The Council, however, at the same meeting refused requests for assistance from certain charitable organisations operating in Palestine, wishing to maintain the principle that JCA's own philanthropic activities should be given preference over the subventioning of other charities.

JCA's policy on this beginning of its work in Palestine was thus not to establish its own new colonies, as it had done in Argentina and Canada, but to come to the assistance of settlements that were not being helped by Baron Rothschild. Such were the first three that received credits in 1896: Mishmar Hayarden in Galilee, and Ness Ziona and Guedera in Judea. The next year JCA – not without some opposition in the Council – extended its operations to Rehovoth, the biggest colony in Judea, and Hedera in Samaria. As in the first three settlements, JCA in general made loans to individual families for particular projects. In Mishmar 13 families had received such loans in 1896, and more advances were then made to install 12 new families. In Ness Ziona 9 families received credits to buy vines, plant orange trees, buy animals and tools and repair houses. JCA also hired a graduate of Mikveh-Israel, the agricultural school near Jaffa founded by the Alliance Israélite in 1870, to provide instruction and advice. In Hedera JCA was concerned about miasmas arising from marshes nearby, but when assured that these would be drained it was willing to make loans to 35 families to buy cattle, tools and seed and to construct houses and stables. In Rehovoth it made advances for the purchase of vines and cattle and for the repair of houses. It also made loans collectively for the construction of a mill to grind the locally produced wheat and barley, the digging of a reservoir and the purchase of a pump. It is obvious from this long list of actions taken that, once having decided to work in Palestine, JCA did not hesitate to go full steam ahead.

The next year saw more of the same. Of the 20 settlers in Ness Ziona, 15 received loans for the purchase of cattle and vines and for house construction. The Turkish government made difficulties before building permits were granted, but finally 12 small houses and stables were put up, each in a court enclosed by walls. Irrigation ditches were also dug, and, in listing the crops here, JCA called attention to the excellent grove of young orange trees, which gave great hope for the future. And indeed, to this day Ness Ziona is an important producer of oranges. In Rehovoth further loans were made for the building of dwellings and to enable the settlers, all of whom now had both horses and cows, to buy the implements they lacked. In Guedera (Katra), established by young Russian Jews in 1884, collective loans were again made, to install a pump and a mill. The JCA and Rothschild colonies were not aloof from each other; for example, Ness Ziona and Rehovoth sent their grapes to Rishon-le-Zion to be pressed.

The year 1898 saw two important new developments. First, JCA purchased land near Sedjera, in the Tiberias area, with the intention of founding a new colony. Land purchases by JCA and by Baron Rothschild, and also, as we shall see later, by both jointly, were an important part of the process of enlarging the territory owned by Jews in Palestine. Later history showed that these purchases were a vital contribution to the basis for what eventually became the Jewish State.

JCA's other new departure was its attempt to help the poor Jews in Jerusalem. From time immemorial the great majority of

Jews in that city had lived on *Chaluka*, donations by the Jews of the Diaspora, in return for which the Jerusalemites prayed for the souls of their benefactors. The Alliance Israélite had established a vocational school in the city to teach useful trades, and its graduates, who had settled in Damascus, Salonika and elsewhere, were reported to be doing well. For its part, in 1898 JCA started a weaving *atelier* which employed 26 workers and distributed a number of knitting machines. The Association was to do more along these lines in subsequent years.

The Rothschild colonies

While JCA had moved wholeheartedly into Palestine and had for the most part expanded its initial operations there, the number of 'its' colonies and their population were much smaller than the Baron de Rothschild's. But by this time that Baron was beginning to have, not doubts, for his faith in his great Palestinian enterprise seems never to have diminished, but second thoughts about the way in which it was being conducted. A series of reports written towards the end of the decade by D. Apfelbaum, a horticultural expert, raised some pertinent and troubling questions. For example, it was pointed out that, in its 16 years of existence, Zichron-Yaakov had cost Rothschild no less than 11 million gold francs and there seemed no prospect of reducing this outflow. In fact, the whole basis of Rothschild's efforts was questioned by Apfelbaum, who noted that there were in effect two classes of farmers in the Rothschild colonies. The first class enjoyed a passable standard of living, because they were paid much more for their produce than its market value – to Rothschild's loss. The second class consisted of those who came outside the administration's purview and who made a minimal living as labourers. Apfelbaum proposed to cure this anomalous situation by establishing co-operative settlements akin to the present-day Israeli moshavim, to be made viable by investing heavily in modern implements. Furthermore, such a co-operative development among the Jewish settlers would make unnecessary the use of Arab labour, which was increasing – a situation that greatly distressed Rothschild who was most anxious to have it demonstrated that Jews could be successful farm workers as well as operators.

It must be noted that the accumulation of losses was due in part to Rothschild's stubborn preconceptions. He insisted that his colonies grow wine grapes of high quality, though the soil and climate were not appropriate, and to encourage such culture he paid extravagant prices for the grapes produced and constructed very expensive wine cellars. As Schama says, Rothschild felt that the Jewish farmers should live like the native *fellahin*; yet he wanted them to produce 'fancy' crops – such as silk, or geraniums for perfume – rather than the plebeian coarse grains and chick-peas grown by the indigenous population.[6] Another factor affecting Rothschild's state of mind was a long siege of bad health, which continued in some degree until he underwent major surgery in 1918. (He died in 1934, aged 89.) Also, he may have discerned that he was not in a good position to impose the economies in administration that were so patently required. Finally, the Chovevei Zion and the noted essayist Achad Ha'am had severely criticised the Rothschild administration for its dictatorial attitude, which fostered a spirit of extreme dependency among the settlers.[7]

The Commission Palestinienne

Many factors, then, contributed to Rothschild's decision in 1899 to turn the control of his colonies over to JCA. However, he was far from being left out of the picture. The agreement for the transfer of the administration laid down that the future policy of the Rothschild colonies would be established by a 'Commission Palestinienne', to consist of three members selected by JCA and two selected by Rothschild, with the sixth member and President for life being Baron Edmond himself, who immediately provided the Commission with 15 million francs. So while JCA might administer, the Baron still held the purse strings. From 1900 to 1924, when JCA gave up the administration of the Rothschild colonies, its reports on its Palestinian activities were carefully divided between accounts of the Baron's settlements and those of its own, plus its activities in Jerusalem.

Having agreed to the arrangement (not without some reservations on the part of Council members, who considered that this added burden would be too much for Council and staff), JCA set about converting the Rothschild administration into a facsimile of its own. It reduced the staff, put an end to the system of subsidies that the Baron had instituted (though it was ready to make loans in time of necessity), and tried to eliminate or cut down on all non-productive expenses. One step towards achieving this end was to make the colonists themselves responsible for sanitation, control of water supplies and communal activities, including the establishment of co-operatives, notably the Société Coopérative Vigneronne. As Emile Meyerson, then Joint Director of JCA, put it rather delicately, Rothschild, while emphasising

61

technical accomplishments, had been neglectful of economic reality – to wit, costs as well as means of marketing the crops produced.[8]

JCA attacked the first of these problems by cutting the prices paid for grapes. This inspired a near revolt among the settlers, who sent a deputation to Paris. Actually, this delegation's proposals were in agreement with many of JCA's actions: it favoured a reduced administrative overhead and asked for more land for the colonies and the elimination of Arab labour; the delegates also wanted more autonomy, doing away with the necessity of referring all important decisions to Paris. This last demand infuriated Rothschild (whose choler was easily aroused). He told the delegation off roundly, asserting that JCA should be firm, even harsh, with the colonists. And JCA did indeed remove some families it considered unsuitable, but, following the precedent set in similar cases in Argentina, it paid them compensation.

As a further step in improving the economic situation, JCA tried to wean the colonists away from dependence on a single crop, usually grapes (it managed to reduce the number of vines even at Zichron-Yaakov), and not only to diversify, but to diversify in the direction of growing oriental crops like chick-peas and sesame, and – always a favourite ploy of JCA – to introduce grande culture, the growing of the basics, like wheat and other grains, rather than try to practise horticulture in the manner of Versailles.

This attempt to prune Palestinian agriculture of all esoterica, however, was not altogether successful. Under Rothschild, attempts had been made in Rosh Pinna and elsewhere to grow mulberry bushes and develop silk culture, one argument being that women could be employed in the spinning and weaving. Even after JCA took over, efforts to produce silk continued for some years, until its manifest unadaptability to conditions in the Holy Land finally forced its abandonment.

Other activities

JCA continued to help the poor inhabitants of Jerusalem. In 1901 it inaugurated a loan kassa, which made 89 loans to small shopkeepers, workers and artisans. It also began a programme of building houses for workers, rather grandiloquently labelled cités ouvrières, though no more than 50–100 houses were built altogether, and not all in 1901. It also distributed a number of knitting machines, as it continued to do for many years thereafter. It supported a small weaving establishment, the products of which were sold in Damascus and Cairo. None of these programmes was very important in itself. However, they were interesting in that, together with similar and contemporaneous projects in Russia, they mark the commencement of JCA's assistance to Jews who were not somehow connected with agriculture.

Expansion of Jewish settlement

From 1903 to 1914 the population of Jews in Palestine doubled, from 40,000 to 80,000. The population of the Rothschild and JCA colonies followed this trend. In 1903 there were 4,900 individuals under the jurisdiction of the Commission Palestinienne and a few hundred more in the JCA colonies, half in Rehovoth. By 1911 there were 7,417 living in these farm settlements and by 1913 about 9,000. Clearly, progress was being made in the basic task of building up the population of Jews within Palestine in general and on the land in particular.

Not only did the number of farmers increase, but so did the amount of land at their disposal. Almost every year important land acquisitions were made – in the Tiberias area, other places in Galilee, near Rishon, near Petach Tikvah and elsewhere. These purchases were made by the Commission Palestinienne, by JCA and at times by the settlers themselves (notably at Sarafand, between Jaffa and Jerusalem) with the aid of JCA loans. Especially active in this sphere was Chaim Kalvarisky, an agent of JCA, who was a bold, swashbuckling corner-cutter, not above greasing an outstretched palm or neglecting a legal nicety. But if the agreements that Kalvarisky made were not completely watertight, JCA's very capable lawyers saw to it that all leaks were plugged by the time the deeds were put into final form. Kalvarisky is to be remembered not only for his large and important land purchases but because, earlier than most, he understood the benefits that would accrue from Jewish–Arab co-operation, a highly desirable end which now appears impossible to attain, but which perhaps might have been attainable if more people had shared Kalvarisky's foresight.

The bland statement that the Jewish population in Palestine doubled in the ten years before the First World War and that Jewish landholdings concomitantly increased should not be interpreted to imply that these developments came about easily or without interruption. The earlier years of this period were marked by severe droughts, widespread epidemics that resulted in the death of a large proportion of the cattle, and depredations by field mice, who made up for their small size by huge numbers which

devastated the grain crops. Nor were the settlers' troubles all due
to natural causes. Some were man-made.

Their Arab neighbours, and sometimes the nomadic Bedouin,
occasionally raided Jewish fields and warehouses. There were not
many instances of attacks on individuals, but these did happen,
and some Jews were killed. The colony that was most affected
by difficulties with the native population was the isolated
northernmost one of Metulla, which was in perpetual conflict
with a neighbouring Druze village. A situation like this was a
patent call to the Jewish settlers to embark on organised self-
defence.

Nor were all the man-made troubles due to action by Arabs.
The year 1909–10 was one of *shemita*, the sabbatical year enjoined
by the Bible when lands were supposed to lie fallow, unworked.
In 1895–6, during the Rothschild regime, there had been efforts
by some settlers to observe the year of *shemita*, but in 1902–3,
after JCA took over, no colonist paid any attention to the biblical
injunction. In 1907, however, the farmers in two Galilee villages,
Yesud Hal'va'da and Mishmar Hayarden, declared their intention
to carry out the letter of the law and abstain from planting. It
must be stated that this decision was not the result of a sudden
spate of religious zeal[9] but was due to the fact that a rabbi in Safed
had promised these farmers a generous gift if they would not
plant. Kalvarisky and Frank, the JCA officials in charge, were
taken utterly by surprise because the previous *shemita* period had
passed without incident, but they recovered quickly and warned
the newly observant farmers that JCA would lease their lands to
Arabs for the season and confiscate their cattle. As Schama points
out, 'such a measure was in accordance with religious precepts,
being in effect a "Gentile sale" '. In the event, the JCA administration carried out their threat and went ahead with leasing the lands
to Arabs. Fortunately, at the end of the year the leased areas
reverted to the Jewish settlers without incident, and JCA
'ploughed back the rental into the running of the two colonies'.

The improvement in the situation of the Jewish farm colonies
over the first ten years of the twentieth century was not due
altogether to the fact that weather conditions in the latter part of
the decade were much better than in the former. The tightened
and realistic administration of JCA also had something to do with
it, although, interestingly enough, at the end of the decade, at the
1912 annual meeting, JCA's President, Narcisse Leven, solemnly
intoned a pessimistic forecast concerning the future. Palestine was
different from and more difficult than other loci of JCA activity
like Canada, Brazil and Argentina, he said, echoing a plaint first
uttered in 1905. Palestine did not inspire much hope as a place of

mass settlement for Jews because it was already thickly settled, unlike these other countries. Monsieur Leven was belied in part by the contemporary rural population figures that we have just seen (let alone by what has happened since then). Though the figures did not add up to great masses, they were not much smaller than those for the JCA colonies in Argentina.

JCA's special contribution

We can point to a number of specific JCA policies that were particularly useful in improving farming conditions and thus helping to attract immigrants. One was the encouragement of citriculture, which was favoured by the climate, did not then require a huge investment and was well suited to family farming. In particular, D. Bril, the JCA agent in Petach Tikvah, himself a large orange grower, encouraged the farmers there to put in new orange varieties, to irrigate their orchards by the use of motor pumps and to employ insecticides. These were options open to the Jewish farmers because they could obtain JCA financing, an advantage their Arab neighbours did not enjoy. Not surprisingly, citrus output increased enormously in the Jewish settlements, notably Petach Tikvah and Ness Ziona.

Perhaps because of the success of the selling co-operatives, which had sprung up early in the JCA's Argentine colonies, JCA was assiduous in sponsoring similar developments in Palestine and assisting co-operatives there with advice and loans. Two orange-selling co-operatives were formed, and the grape growers were united in the Société Coopérative Vigneronne (SCV), which was given control of the wine-pressing and storing facilities at Rishon-le-Zion and Zichron-Yaakov and was also assigned the responsibility of disposing of the product. In some years, as in 1906, the SCV, which was not aiming at a quality product as had been the case in Rothschild's day, was able to sell wine for the mass market quite successfully. However, the Palestinian production now had to compete with that of other mass producers like North Africa, Spain or Italy, and this competition in many later years was difficult to contend with.[10]

Another contribution of JCA was to improve ancillary services, such as the water supply, and see to it that medical attention was available on a regular basis. JCA also brought about a reform in the educational apparatus of the colonies, which under the Rothschild regime had consisted of a group of traditional *chederim* staffed by equally traditional *melamdim*. JCA introduced teachers trained by the Alliance Israélite in contemporary pedagogical methods and culture.

The Association also contributed to the advancement of Jewish agriculture in Palestine by its operation in Sedjera, located southwest of the Sea of Galilee, where the land had been purchased in 1899. The settlement contained 18,000 dunams (4,500 acres), half of which was cultivable. The land, instead of being leased or sold to settlers, was operated by workers under JCA supervision with the intention of training them as practical agriculturists. For a time the redoubtable Kalvarisky was in charge. He laid out a programme for the employment of 60–70 workers for a year or two; they would then move on to farms elsewhere in Palestine while a new group of trainees replaced them. Given the fact that a large proportion of agricultural school graduates customarily found work in other occupations whereas the majority of those who worked in Sedjera remained in agriculture, the experiment can be termed a success.[11]

Arab opposition

In 1908 the Young Turk Revolution took place in European Turkey, forcing the Sultan to grant a constitution. The excitement generated by this event seemed to exacerbate the feelings of the local *fellahin* against the Jewish settlers in Sedjera. Scuffles and attacks ensued, in the course of which three settlers were killed and a fourth, David Grien by name (later David Ben Gurion), was wounded.

This conflict with their neighbours prompted the residents of Sedjera to form the first unit of Hashomer, the Jewish self-defence force in Palestine before the First World War, the ancestor of the Haganah. The fighting died down after 1908 and Sedjera returned to normal. The settlement proved in the long run not to be viable, however, because of a lack of water, and it was more or less abandoned in the 1930s. But in the earlier years of its existence it performed a useful educational function for hundreds of Jewish farm settlers.

Jerusalem

While the main focus of JCA's work in Palestine was the farming settlements, it continued its activity in Jerusalem. In 1909 the Association reported that the loan kassa there, in the ten years since its founding, had made 1,060 advances; and 359 accounts were still open. In that same year one knitting machine was turned over to a user, bringing the total distributed to 125. In the *cité ouvrière* of Nahalat-Zion 53 houses had been completed and all were occupied. There is no mention of the weaving establishment after 1903 in the JCA reports, so it must be inferred that it was discontinued, but the other activities went on as before. In 1912 the kassa made 121 loans and was owed 87,465 francs on 429 outstanding debts; 5 knitting machines were distributed; and 64 families lived in the *cité ouvrière*. In the following year all payments due on the kassa's loans, on the knitting machines and the rents on the workers' houses were paid on time. Such was the situation in Jerusalem on the eve of the First World War, which was to disrupt Jewish life in both the towns and the farms of Palestine and to bring about a complete overturn in the government of the area. We must mention one more facet of JCA's activity in Jerusalem, which was its financing of the departure of Jewish families who had given up hope in Palestine and wanted to leave the country. In almost every year under review, JCA helped a small number (12–15) of families to depart.

Summary

Turning back to the farm settlements, what was their status just before the First World War broke out? Due credit has to be given for difficulties overcome or at least combated, for it must be confessed that the previous pages have not stressed sufficiently the heavy obstacles and handicaps faced by the pioneering settlers; to have listed all the droughts and other unfortunate vagaries of the weather, the epidemics that afflicted both humans and cattle, the losses caused by insects and field mice, the hostile actions of the natives (which in 1912 made necessary large expenditures for guarding the fields against predatory nomads and Bedouin) would weary the reader with repetition. Nevertheless, these economic, physical and psychological factors must be remembered and taken into account in trying to appraise what had been accomplished up to 1914 by Baron Edmond, the Commission Palestinienne and JCA. We should like to quote Simon Schama's assessment:

What had been achieved on the eve of the war? It is tempting, given subsequent developments, to see the period as one in which the Jewish settlement put down firm roots in Palestine, but its growth was as yet very limited and expensively maintained. Of the 30,000–40,000 Jewish immigrants since 1882, barely a quarter were on the land and most of those concentrated in the colonies of the south. The ideal of the self-reliant cultivator, whether a yeoman peasant or comrade of the soil, had been realised in only a handful of farms in Galilee. Their finances were always a headache for the JCA administration, and their security already seriously imperilled. Yet, arguably, some sort of beginning had been made. The JCA stewardship had brought the settlements from a period of feverish oscillation between financial cosseting and threatened bankruptcy towards a cooler and more realistic appreciation of their potential and their limitations. The wine and citrus industries seemed to be established on a reasonably sound basis and the co-operatives producing and marketing them certainly marked an important step forward in the economic independence of the 'Yishuv'. But they were still terribly vulnerable to sharp changes in world commodity prices. That was even more the case for the cereal farming, which provided the major part of the income of the Galilean settlements. Their major achievement was, in any case, unquantifiable. By simply surviving they demonstrated that Jewish agriculture could succeed without depending on Arab labour and without being spoon-fed by enormous subsidies. To that extent, the JCA principle that the paternalistic 'tutelle' of the earlier period had not only not helped the viability of the colonies, but had actually hindered it, seemed to have been borne out.[12]

Beyond demonstrating that Jews could farm successfully in Palestine, the JCA and Rothschild settlements were, as we have said, important participants in the laying of the foundation of the future Jewish State. Baron de Rothschild at the beginning, JCA and the Commission Palestinienne afterwards, acquired hundreds of thousands of dunams in Galilee and in Judea. Not only did they buy land directly but, as we have seen, they made loans to individual farmers for land purchase and also lent large sums to the Palestine Land Development Company (PLDC), a Zionist agency, to enable it to acquire territory. A look at a map showing the holdings of JCA and the Commission superimposed on the proposed Jewish areas in British-sponsored partition plans of the 1930s will show that much of the latter consisted of land originally owned by JCA and Baron Edmond, who himself possessed about half a million dunams when he died in 1934. Nor was JCA content just to buy land. It peopled the areas it acquired, founding settlements like Yavneel, Bet Gan, Mesha and many others in Galilee.[13] In asserting Jewish claims later, the presence of people was probably even more important than ownership of the land.

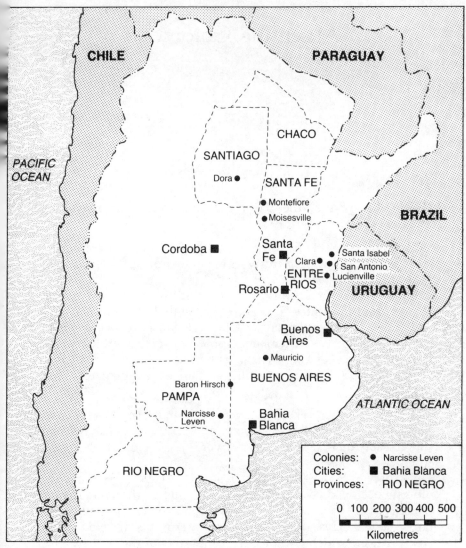

Map 3   JCA colonies in Argentina

CHAPTER 5

Argentine Colonies

At the turn of the century

In 1896, the year of the Baron's death, there were four JCA settlements in Argentina:

1 Moisesville in Santa Fe province, with 91 families of 'colonists', that is, settlers who were working tracts of land which they would ultimately own;
2 Mauricio in Buenos Aires province, with 187 colonist families;
3 San Antonio in Entre-Rios province, with 44 families;
4 the much larger settlement of Clara, also in Entre-Rios, which comprised 18 sub-settlements, some of which were occupied by the groups of fifty which had been organised in Russia. There were 588 colonist families in the Clara aggregate.

Altogether, there were 910 families in the four colonies. There were also Jewish storekeepers and health and farm workers and their families. With the inclusion of the service personnel and workers and their families, there were 6,757 individuals in the settlements.

JCA owned 200,000 hectares of land (500,000 acres), and the colonists occupied about half this area. Thus on the average each farming family had about 275 acres at its disposal. They cultivated about 100,000 acres, the most important crop by far being grain, mostly wheat, which occupied three-quarters of the planted area. Flax and maize were the other important crops. There were considerable plantings of alfalfa (lucerne) in Moisesville and small amounts in some of the Clara settlements, and also some vegetable plots.

At the beginning of 1896 the administration felt that the colonists had made sufficient progress to enable the payment of subsidies to them to be discontinued, except for the newly arrived and the elderly poor; but a bad crop in 1896, following a similarly inadequate one in 1895, forced the Buenos Aires office to resume payments. However, says the 1896 Annual Report, despite the two successive poor crop years, and despite 'the plague of locusts and tempestuous rains, the colonists approach their work with ardour'. More tangible evidence of development was the presence of two steam mills in the Clara complex which were operating successfully, and the opening of two new schools there, albeit quite primitive ones. At the Baron's death, in accordance with a wish he had expressed, the colonists' debts were reduced by 25 per cent. Small amounts on account of these debts were in fact repaid to JCA in 1896. Another telling sign that the colonists felt they were in Argentina to stay was the creation of a fire insurance company in 1899.

In one respect, however, no advance was made during the remaining years of the nineteenth century. In 1896 the number of colonist families was 910, in 1900 only 906, and the count had fallen lower in the intervening years. There was much movement in and out of the colonies. JCA consoled itself by asserting that the people who went were unsuited to agriculture and congratulated itself on the purge of inadequate individuals. To balance the losses and to add a young, spirited element to the colony the administration installed 115 families of sons and sons-in-law who had previously been considered part of the fathers' families and who had not enjoyed a sufficient share in the crops that they had helped to produce. And the next year JCA installed 200 immigrants who had come from Russia at their own risk and expense.

Another evidence of progress, or at least of the Association's visibility on the Argentine scene, was the governmental decree in 1899 freeing JCA from taxes because of its 'charitable purpose'.

The chaos and lack of planning that had marked the settlement efforts in 1891 and 1892 were, by the end of the century, things of the past. The greatly reduced number of immigrants and sufficient notice of their arrival made adequate preparation possible. The 1900 Report notes proudly that the members of a group of 50 families that came to Moisesville in that year were installed in their assigned homes and at work in the fields within twenty-four hours of arrival. These new families, as well as the older ones, now lived in small but substantial two-room brick houses (with the kitchen outside) and each had a stable for work animals and milk cows. The settlers were beginning to be able to buy farm implements, especially reaping and threshing machines. The two oldest colonies, Mauricio and Moisesville, had taken charge of their own affairs to some extent, coping with health services, education and ritual slaughtering.

In the older colonies the dwellings were clustered; in the newer ones they were scattered in small groups of two to twelve, next to the cultivated fields. In addition to the villages where the farmers lived, which were beginning to assume a settled look – some had by now groves of trees which had reached heights conspicuous on the flat pampas – little towns had begun to grow up, usually around the railway stations. Here were the communal buildings, stores, clinics, schools and a synagogue (sometimes the school buildings were used for religious services). Also large and prominent was the residence of the local JCA manager, or administrator, as he was called. Schools were, as we have noticed, an important concern of the settlers, who did not fail to manifest the characteristic Jewish interest in learning by providing each settlement with at least one school and sometimes more. The schools had begun to enlarge their curricula to include the Spanish language and Argentine history as well as Hebrew and Jewish ritual. By 1900 there were twenty schools in the colonies, attended by 1,200 pupils, 667 boys and 533 girls.

By this time also Argentina had developed a very extensive network of railways radiating from Buenos Aires, and all the JCA's settlements included a station within their boundaries or were close to one. Some, like Mauricio, were served by several railway lines. The large warehouses or elevators that JCA built adjacent to the railways were prominent features on the flat landscapes which caught the eyes of contemporary travellers. Access to the railways and to the little towns in or near the settlements was provided by roads which the colonists built at their own expense.

Another sign of the settlements' progress in the closing years of the nineteenth century was the founding of a new colony in 1898, in Entre-Rios province. This was Lucienville, named after the Baron's deceased son. The land for it had been purchased in 1894 and set aside for children of the settlers. JCA, which had been embarrassed in Löwenthal's time by the scarcity of its supply of land, obviously had no intention of being in that kind of situation again; in every year between 1896 and 1912 it bought land in quantity, sometimes adjoining its existing colonies, sometimes, if a favourable opportunity offered, in an area quite distant from any of its previously acquired holdings. One such area was Zeballas, a tract of 9,236 hectares (about 23,000 acres, or 36 square miles) purchased in 1898 in the district of La Paz, northwest of Entre-Rios, in the extreme north of Argentina. Since this land did not seem fit for colonization, JCA operated it as a cattle and sheep ranch; it was equipped with corrals and shelters for the animals, and even a 'hospital' for the sheep. In 1900 there were approximately 2,500 milking cows here, out of a total of 5,455 animals including 1,150 sheep and 189 horses. By that year Zeballas was able to return a profit of some 9,000 pesos to the administration derived from the sale of cattle, a sum that permitted Buenos Aires 'to be reimbursed for the advances it had made that year and to cover its general expenses there'.

But Zeballas, for all its 9,236 hectares, was a relatively small part of the acreage JCA purchased in the years just before and after 1900. By 1902 the Association owned 359,314 hectares, of which 109,500 were occupied by colonists, to whom ultimate sale was promised. Even this amount did not satisfy JCA's aims and ambitions. In 1904 a domain of 100,000 hectares named Leloir, partly in Buenos Aires province and partly in the adjoining territory of La Pampa, was acquired. Here the administration planned to install 500–600 families, which it did eventually in two colonies named respectively Baron Hirsch, founded in 1904, and Narcisse Leven, founded in 1908. By 1912 JCA owned a total of 586,473 hectares. The bulk, 363,959 hectares, was occupied by settlers who had been promised title; 391 hectares had been sold to colonists; and the remaining 222,123 hectares was held in reserve for future colonization. The total remained unchanged throughout the First World War, until the late 1920s when JCA purchased some more land.

In its search for sufficient land for settling anticipated immigrants, JCA did not confine itself to purchases in Argentina. In 1901 Mr Cazes, one of the co-heads of the Buenos Aires office, and Mr Lepine, on the administrative staff, went on an exploratory expedition through Brazil's southernmost state, Rio Grande do Sul, and were favourably impressed. As a result, JCA bought a large acreage there and soon afterwards planted a colony on it, the story of which will be told in chapter 6.

Further evidence of the growing maturity of the colonies was the willingness of the settlers to go beyond the original basic crops of cereal and flax. By 1900 cattle raising and fattening had become an important occupation, especially in Mauricio, close to large meat packing establishments. Here and elsewhere poultry raising, vegetable plots, milk production in sufficient amount to make necessary the building of creameries and even beekeeping were undertaken.

The progress of the settlers, their satisfaction with their lot, and their intention to continue farming in Argentina were further evidenced by the fact that many of them paid the fares to bring their relatives from Russia and have them settle in the colonies.

The Baron's dream and desire had been to establish an independent, self-sufficient, self-supporting and self-governing community of Jewish farmers in Argentina. We have cited a number of developments that took place in 1900 which indicated that at least a beginning had been made in giving concrete form to his vision. The Baron's conception of independence and self-sufficiency included the idea that 'his' farmers would be able to repay the costs of establishing them on the land (remember that he had written that he 'contended against the old idea of philanthropy' – the mere giving of doles or alms). His feeling about repayment was embodied in the original contracts that JCA had offered the settlers in 1894, the form of which he had himself approved. His departed spirit must then have noted with satisfaction that in 1898 half the settlers in Moisesville, despite a mediocre crop and mediocre prices, made repayments to JCA.

But the Baron's concept of these communities, or at least the JCA Council's interpretation of it, had been rather narrow. In 1897 the residents of Moisesville sent a delegation to Paris to ask that the Council permit the establishment of clothing factories, to operate during the winter, the slack farming season, and to authorise the building of vocational schools to teach skills not related to farming, and for these or other schools to teach Spanish and arithmetic. The Council snubbed the petitioners, telling them that they and their children were to work the land and indulge in no distractions. In fact, as we have seen, the schools in the colonies did give courses in Spanish, which was a simple necessity for citizens of Argentina, and in arithmetic as well. Also, as time went on almost all the girls' schools gave courses in dressmaking.

JCA's original concept of what was meant by 'agriculture' was so strict that it excluded cattle-raising from the canon. In a later JCA review of the situation in Argentina, it was noted with an air of some surprise that experience had shown that the colonists could not live on the proceeds of agriculture alone, and in order to make a living had to resort to cattle-raising on a large scale – thus indicating that in its view cattle-raising was not quite completely 'agricultural'.

Jewish peasants?

The Baron, and the Council after him, entertained manifestly contradictory notions of what would constitute a successful outcome of the great settlement effort in Argentina. On the one hand, as the colonies made progress in population and income through the first decade of the twentieth century, the annual reports repeatedly and proudly pointed out that they gave proof that Jews could till the soil successfully once they were allowed to own land, and that the scoffings of anti-Semites who said Jews could never be farmers were obviously without foundation. But curiously, that great capitalist, the Baron de Hirsch, did not envisage the possibility that, if Jews proved to be good farmers who made virgin soil fruitful, the value of the land would thereby be increased, and some owners might be prompted to take advantage of that increase. His concept seemed to have been that the Jews in Argentina would become European-type peasants, with father leaving the ancestral homestead to the son, from generation to generation, and that the family would never contemplate moving from it. As for the Council, they apparently believed that in a world of private ownership, with open communications, they could fence off an enclave and somehow insulate the Jewish farmers in Argentina from the commercial currents flowing all about, and through, the settlements.

Therefore the contracts provided for penalties or cancellation if the colonist let his land or did not work it himself and, moreover, did not permit the contract-purchaser to pay the amount due in advance in order to take title and thus be enabled to sell the land he was cultivating before the expiration of the contract. Such an action was regarded as reprehensible speculation. Interestingly enough, this position of JCA was upheld by an Argentine court in 1910. The court took the view that, because a Jewish colonist had agreed to become part of a special homogeneous farm colony and had received many benefits from this membership, he could not opt out at any time he chose. JCA's enforcement of the time-scale of the contract was obviously at best a delaying action. The profit potential of the land, or the cultural and commercial attractions of urban life and its amenities, or both, were bound eventually to overcome JCA's attempt to maintain a 'peasant' class. And indeed, JCA recognised (1910 Report, p. 39) that there was a vast difference between a French peasant and the Russian Jewish colonist in Argentina. But this did not prevent a raising of eyebrows when it was reported that some of the settlers had purchased sulkies, a more comfortable and speedier form of transport than the usual heavy farm wagon, that some had gone so far as to install indoor WCs and that – in a few very rare cases – some families even possessed pianos.

The lawsuit referred to had been brought by residents of Mauricio. This colony was a centre of 'anti-contract' agitation, because it was well established and prosperous; land values there had risen very noticeably, and therefore discontent with the strict contract provisions was most keenly felt. This discontent was made manifest not only in the lawsuit but in the 'Jazanovich incident'.[1]

Leon Jazanovich was a Jewish journalist who had come to Argentina in 1909 as a propagandist for the Poale-Zion (Labour Zionist) movement and perhaps also with the idea of establishing a periodical. He toured all the colonies and happened on Mauricio at a time of agitation by the settlers who were unable to obtain title from JCA. Jazanovich was deeply touched by the grievances of these colonists and set off on a whirlwind tour of all the settlements, stirring up anti-JCA sentiment. (According to Schallman, this action coincided with, and perhaps was intensified by, the first manifestations of a trade union movement in the country.[2]) Jazanovich's campaign came to an abrupt end early in 1910, when he was expelled from the country.

Jazanovich believed, although Schallman, a partisan of JCA, asserts there is no evidence, that he had been denounced to the Argentine authorities as a 'dangerous anarchist' and a 'revolutionary' by agents of JCA. At any rate, on his return to Europe he published a book, *The Crisis of Jewish Colonization in Argentina and the Moral Bankruptcy of the JCA Administration*. He also went on a speaking tour through France, Germany, Poland, Lithuania and elsewhere. Schallman claims that Jazanovich, despite his publications and his oratory, did not arouse any special attention in the Jewish community at large. Schallman himself, however, was sufficiently aroused, 50 years later, to cite Jazanovich's three major complaints – and refute them. These were: (1) the failure of the villages and towns near the settlements to provide sufficient cultural and social activity, so that the colonists lived in an ambience of isolation; (2) what Jazanovich labelled 'philanthropic feudalism', by which he meant JCA's contract procedure; and (3) the inflated presumption of some JCA staff members.

In addition to these major points, Jazanovich made some rather extravagant – and untrue – allegations that tend to weaken his credibility. In rebutting Jazanovich, Schallman asserts that the villages of colonies Moisesville, Mauricio and Clara did provide ample cultural opportunities. The sufficiency of such opportunities is a matter of opinion, but whatever the older colonies provided, the newer ones like Baron Hirsch or Narcisse Leven offered none. On the other hand, persons who volunteered to undertake pioneering in the Argentine back-country could not really have expected to enjoy much in the way of cultural amenities.

Schallman also pointed to the co-operatives as a means of social contact. As for the 'philanthropic feudalism', there is no question but that JCA exercised a considerable degree of control over the economic affairs of the colonists; but on the main bone of contention in this area, the matter of the contracts, there was a clash of values. The colonists, or at least some of them, wanted to make what profits they could when they could: JCA tried to prevent this in the name of maintaining a viable Jewish farm population.

One can sympathise with JCA's objectives, while recognising, as the outcome eventually proved, that they were impossible to attain in the circumstances. As for the colonists, they would have to have been superhumanly altruistic to refuse, without making at least an attempt to obtain them, the riches that seemed to be almost within their grasp. The Argentine court ruled that JCA was in the right in these circumstances, and if a court has so ruled perhaps we should accept its judgment. As for the third charge, that the JCA staff were presumptuous, this was undoubtedly true of at least some of them.

While Schallman refuted Jazanovich's accusations and JCA won the lawsuit, JCA nevertheless liberalised the terms of its contracts in 1912. It now decreed that a colonist who had been installed 22 years and had made 12 annual payments of the 22 due could attain ownership by paying in full the amount remaining due. The contracts were further liberalised in 1917 and again later.

Further progress

The eagerness of the settlers to obtain full possession of their land was evidence of their success. The general advance of the Argentine economy was also an important factor in the rise of land values. JCA itself, as we have seen, was far from reluctant to point out that by the first years of the twentieth century the settlers had achieved a solid economic and social base. In addition to these assertions and the evidence of prosperity provided by the sulkies, WCs and pianos, there are numerous attestations by witnesses to the progress of the colonies. Various Argentine officials, provincial or federal, spoke of the well-being of the JCA colonies; and as for Jewish farm workers, an Argentine observer remarked that they were better than those of other ethnic origins because they were not given to drink.

A government commission set up to formulate large land settlement schemes consulted the JCA administration on how to go about it. But while the Argentine witnesses may have been influenced by the wish to win the favour of a large new constituent group, the same cannot be said of a visitor who travelled through the colonies in 1904. This was one Krukoff, on the staff of the Russian Ministry of Agriculture, who had been sent by his government to study farming practices in the United States, Australia and Argentina. Krukoff was favourably impressed by what he saw, by the transformation of merchants and artisans into successful farmers (he had never seen a Jewish farmer in Russia). He mentioned several individuals who had large farms with many animals and ample equipment and who had left Russia penniless.

Another point that struck Krukoff was the rapidity of assimil-
ation of the Jewish settlers. He said:

> The Jews when they land at Buenos Aires surprise the natives
> because of their miserable aspect. Their coats are long, dirty
> and torn. Their hats are bizarre. They have 'payis' on their
> temples. Their faces are haggard and lugubrious. But in
> Argentina they are quickly transformed. Their dress becomes
> similar to that of the other Argentines, and one sees with
> satisfaction that they have an open physiognomy and a bold
> look. The younger generation especially, which has gone
> through school and speaks Spanish, is quite indistinguishable
> from the 'true' Argentinians. [translated from the French,
> JCA Report for 1904]

Krukoff also recorded that, although the colonists had been
desperately poor in Russia and without any prospect of bettering
their lot, they nevertheless felt that Russia was their homeland –
after all, they had been born there. And despite the fact that they
had the 'manners and customs' of the Argentines, some at least
felt that they were still strangers in the country.

Money talks. When the Argentine settlers had reached the stage
where they had begun making repayments on their debts to JCA,
that was an eloquent indication that they had passed beyond the
subsistence stage; they were beginning to earn a good deal more
than their bare keep. Indeed, as we have seen, many were able to
pay for their relatives' passage to the colonies, and many were
able to contribute to their poor relations back in Russia. In 1905,
for example, 126,084 francs were transmitted to Russia as gifts
through JCA, which set up an office to handle transfers of money
in Europe. More may have been sent direct.

Immigration

The number of colonists and other settlers grew, especially after
1905. If we remember that the colonists' families tended to
average six persons, the addition of 850 colonists, as took place
between 1905 and 1910, meant an accretion of 5,000 or more
people. Also, as the number of farmers increased, so did the
number of merchants and service personnel living in the colonies.
Table 5.1, drawn from the relevant Annual Reports, gives a
picture of the growth of the colonies between 1900 and 1913.

Jewish emigration from Russia was spurred by the Kishinev
pogrom of 1903.[3] Disturbances associated with the disastrous
Russo-Japanese war of 1904–5 were an added stimulus, as Russian

Table 5.1 *Growth of the Argentine colonies, 1900–13*

	1900	1905	1910	1911	1912	1913
Jewish population in colonies	6,782	11,422	21,115	20,038	24,040	26,648
Number of colonists	906	1,251	2,103	2,265	2,527	2,655
Area sown (hectares)	54,358	80,452	187,322	224,501	183,038	197,010
Number of cattle	19,645	73,094	98,335	60,746	59,415	60,445

policy was left with one object, as was bitterly remarked: 'to kill Jews'. Besides these violent expressions of the czarist government's 'policy', another incentive to Jewish emigration was the generally poor economic situation of Russia's Jews, and in particular of the Jewish farmers in the Ukrainian provinces of Kherson and Ekaterinoslav, as well as Bessarabia, who could scarcely eke out a living on tiny land holdings they could not enlarge.

This situation made these areas fertile recruiting grounds for JCA. Other families came to Argentina on their own, or with tickets paid for by relatives already there. By this time, because of the well established JCA settlements, Argentina had become a recognised destination for Jews departing from Russia. In 1904 the immigration was about 4,500, of whom 508 went direct to the colonies (these included couples with children, men who had temporarily left their families behind, and bachelors); in 1905 it had increased to 7,516. In the following six years it continued at approximately the same level, and then in 1912 it almost doubled, to 13,416, but in 1913 it fell back to the previous average of 7,000-plus – not large numbers compared with the more than 100,000 going annually to the United States, but still substantial. As in 1904, so in each of the subsequent years, some 10 per cent or more of the thousands who came to Argentina went to the settlements.

JCA estimated that in 1910 there were 43,000 Jews in the country in addition to the 21,115 in the colonies, 64,000 in all. JCA had a high regard for those it called 'spontaneous' colonists, who came across the Atlantic at their own expense and risk to farm in Argentina. It also favoured individuals who had spent two or three years as farm labourers, selecting those it considered most able and installing them on its lands. As we have seen, it continued to do some recruiting in Russia, but not on the scale of the 1890s, and it chose as candidates for settlement only those who really had some farming experience. Many of these new-comers were able to contribute something towards the settlement costs. Helping to swell the immigration statistics were the relatives of previously established settlers.

Another group that added to the Jewish farm population were

the sons and sons-in-law of the settlers, who were generally installed in the same colonies as their parents. By 1905, fifteen years after the initial Argentine settlement, there was a sufficient number of children to constitute an appreciable proportion of the new colonists installed that year and subsequently.

Social organisations

There is an old saying that if three Jews are stranded on a desert island they will build four synagogues, a tribute to their tendency to establish and join a multitude of organisations. The settlers in Argentina conformed to this image. Once they felt they were on a solid footing in their new home, they started to set up various types of social, religious and economic institutions which strengthened the fabric of their society and contributed to its growing prosperity. Thus, for example, in 1904 JCA reported that in Mauricio there were three philanthropic societies of which two were to help poor widows and orphans and the third to relieve the sick; in Lucienville there was a co-operative society, occupied with the general interests of its members; in Clara a loan society had just been created, as well as an insurance association to pay crop losses caused by fire and another to cover medical expenses. In Mauricio and Moisesville the medical care was under the settlers' direction and they also paid the costs. JCA intervened only to cover the fees for new settlers. In Clara JCA still bore the greater part of the medical expenses but the administration of the health programme was in the hands of the colonists. The doctors were usually of Russian origin, and following Russian custom the medical personnel included *feldshers* (something like barber-surgeons), who could render first aid or diagnose and treat minor illnesses.

JCA encouraged these co-operative efforts by the settlers, hoping thereby to create a spirit of solidarity and concern with the common good. With the same intent, in 1904 JCA added to its Argentine staff Rabbi Halphon, a young man of Russian birth who had been trained in the rabbinical seminary in Paris. Halphon was to act as rabbi-in-general for the colonists, who it will be remembered had built synagogues (or used other buildings for services) in each settlement and had also built *mikvahs* (ritual baths) in most. Part of Halphon's time was to be spent in organising religious services, addressing the colonists in the sacred tongue, Hebrew, and giving them consolation at times of bereavement. His other task was to be inspector of the colonies' schools, to oversee religious instruction and to encourage the parents to have their children attend school regularly.

In the same way as the colonists set up synagogues in each settlement, they also built schools; but the schools lacked direction. This it was Halphon's duty to provide. A meeting of teachers, held in Buenos Aires in 1905 with Halphon presiding, laid out a programme of studies to be put into effect throughout the school system in the colonies, which by then comprised 26 schools with 1,817 pupils. Because of the great distances involved (from Mauricio, the southernmost colony, to Moisesville, the northernmost, was 600 kilometres), no single person, even one as energetic as Halphon, could supervise all the schools. Therefore a senior principal in each of the four chief villages was assigned the task of inspecting the schools in his own area, as well as continuing in charge of his own. This was especially necessary to ensure that the agreed reforms were carried out. By 1910, in step with the increase in population, there were 50 schools in eight colonies, with 3,538 pupils.

In addition to being energetic, Halphon was evidently also a man of address and learning, for after some years in JCA's service he was offered and accepted the rabbinate of the chief congregation in Buenos Aires.

At about this same time, in 1909, JCA received reports that, while the material situation of the Jews living outside its colonies was satisfactory, the same could not be said for this population's religious instruction. JCA felt it incumbent on itself to fill this gap. In April 1911 religious courses were begun and by 1,913 there were 23 such courses, 5 in the provinces, the rest in Buenos Aires and the surrounding area. Attendance had risen to 1,392, and about 2,700 pupils had taken these courses during the three years they had been offered. Hebrew language primers, compilations of prayers with Spanish translation and Bible anthologies were also distributed.

Reasonably enough, because of the distances involved, many of the pupils in the colonies went to and from school on horseback, which certainly for Jews in general was a fairly unusual means of transport. That young Jews should ride horses was not only a necessity, but part of the process of absorbing Argentine mores, which Krukoff had noted. In fact, this process had gone so far that the most prominent of Argentine Jewish writers, Alberto Gerchunoff, called his sketches of Jewish life in the settlements, published in 1912, *Los Gauchos Judíos* (The Jewish Gauchos).

Discussion of communal activity in the JCA colonies would be incomplete if it did not include an account of the co-operative movement, which began with the founding of the Sociedad Agricola of Lucienville in 1900, almost as soon as that colony itself had been set up. A pamphlet (*75 Años de Colonización Judía en la Argentina* – no author, no date, but presumably published in Buenos Aires in 1966 or 1967) says of this organisation (translated) 'It is considered the true dean of the farm co-operatives in Argentina', being of the multi-purpose type, of which it was the first example, and a form that was adopted by the majority of agricultural co-operatives established subsequently. The second co-operative, 'Fondo Comunal', was set up in Domínguez, part of the Clara complex, in 1904 and was of the same character. To continue with the account in *75 Años de Colonización*: 'The great majority of those established later adopted the same criteria, setting forth as basic objectives: the purchase for its associates of the materials needed for consumption and work, the sale of their products and obtaining credit for the development of productive facilities.' The full flowering of the co-operative movement in the colonies took place in the 1920s and 1930s, but the foundation was laid by these two co-operatives plus four more that were started before 1910. By that year there was a co-operative in every colony. These associations were not entirely the creations of the colonists, but owed a good deal to the active intervention of JCA. Dr Sonnenfeld, the Director of the Association in Paris, wrote a report stressing the need for such institutions. Not only did JCA provide them with finance, but JCA staff took a large part in creating and setting them up and also served on their governing bodies.

JCA's interest in the movement was not only to build up a spirit of solidarity among the colonists; the co-operatives could relieve the Association of certain administrative functions and lead the colonists to assume a greater share in the management of their affairs. A first step was to use the co-operatives as agents of JCA in making short-term loans. The JCA office in Buenos Aires, which previously had passed all applications for such loans, could now save itself the detailed work involved by advancing a lump sum to a co-operative, which would scrutinise the applications and itself take care of the credit needs of its settlement.

The co-operatives also took over the financing and control of the colonies' medical services. One hospital had been long established at Domínguez, and another was built at Lucienville. JCA made a loan towards it but reported proudly that it was a small loan, accounting for only one-fifth of the expense, the major part coming from the colonists or their organisations.

The co-operatives' assumption of medical costs was only a beginning. The colonists had almost from the start paid the expenses of putting in local roads and maintaining them. Now the co-operatives did this. Under the same heading of municipal service came their contributions to the cost of policing the settlements.

One gets the impression that the settlers were a rather quarrelsome lot, for JCA reported with considerable satisfaction that the co-operatives, by establishing panels to mediate differences about property boundaries, saved the JCA administrators a great deal of time previously consumed in dealing with trivial disputes.

The purpose of the co-operatives, it will be remembered, was to provide moral as well as material benefits, and they did carry out this part of JCA's intention. They helped, for example, to maintain libraries, some of which had originally been subsidised by JCA; they built auditoriums and arranged lecture series. Two co-operatives joined to publish a bi-weekly paper of news and agricultural information, the *Juedischer Colonist*. They helped immigrants find jobs and organised charitable works for the indigent. In these many ways they performed much more than the strictly economic functions that are generally regarded as the proper duties of a buying and selling co-operative, and helped the colonists achieve what JCA so often said was its aim, self-government.

Zenith?

Scattered through JCA's annual reports for the first decade of the twentieth century are a number of self-congratulatory remarks to the effect that the colonists had proved themselves as farmers in Argentina – how well developed and prosperous the colonies had become; how ardently the transplanted Jews loved cultivating the soil; how attached they were to the pastoral way of life; etc. The sentiments that had given rise to these statements seem to have been especially strong in 1911–12, when they found concentrated and outspoken expression in the presidential address to the Annual General Meeting of 7 July 1912, which reviewed the events of 1911. The address was delivered by the Vice-President, Franz Philippson, as the President, Narcisse Leven, was ill. In the course of his allocution Philippson proclaimed (translated from the French):

> In Argentina truly we have realised the dream of our founder in bringing to work on the soil thousands of Jewish families who left the ghettos of Poland and Russia. All these people have become true agriculturists, a little more refined by the suffering they have endured than European peasants, but like

these last suffused with a love of the soil. . . . I am proud
to be able to say that they remain faithful to their race and
their religion. . . . At Basavilbaso [the railroad town serving
the southern part of the Clara settlements] it is market-
day. . . . all along the main street the farmers come and go,
talking about their business affairs, looking at the baskets
where the smaller cultivators display for sale the products of
their gardens. Is one in a Jewish colony or a French
village?. . . . The travellers go down the main road which
passes between the neat and bright cottages of the country-
folk. In the fields to the right and left, the workers are at
their tasks. It is evening and the school is empty, the children
are returning to the farms. One sees them passing in light
carriages or mounted two or three on their big horses which
they guide like accomplished equestrians. One cannot
prevent a surge of emotion contemplating this engaging
picture. Our founder, who undertook to bring the Jews to
work on the soil, would have been fully recompensed if he
had lived long enough to have seen the realisation of his
dream. Is it necessary, after this, to enumerate the riches which
our colonies now possess?

And then, after the habit of speakers who say it is unnecessary
to enumerate and then proceed to do so, Philippson enumerated.
He listed the 569,000 hectares owned by JCA, the 205,000 hectares
under cultivation, the more than 23,000 cows and 53,000 horses,
the wagons, the reapers, the innumerable other machines owned
by the colonists. Earlier in his speech he had mentioned the fact
that there were over 2,000 families of colonists in the nine colonies
– Mauricio, Moisesville, Clara, Lucienville, San Antonio, Santa
Isabel, Baron Hirsch, Narcisse Leven and Dora – comprising
15,501 persons. In addition, there were 800 families of farm
workers and artisans, making the total Jewish population 20,038.
From every point of view, the contrast with twenty years before,
when the first settlers, unfed, unhoused and unequipped, had
struggled into Moisesville and Mauricio, was a high noon to dark
midnight.

Philippson's pride in the accomplishments of JCA and the
settlers had considerable justification; for, as some of the reports
noted, in undertaking its Argentine enterprise JCA was setting
forth on a absolutely untrodden path, with no experience of its
own or others to guide it. Now a point had been reached where
sufficient numbers of Russian Jews were well established on the
land for it to be proclaimed that the Baron's hopes had been
fulfilled, except in one respect. The millions, or at least tens of

thousands, that he had hoped to pull out of Russia were still there. In fact, a good deal of the success of JCA's colonies was due to the strict limitations it had put on additional settlement after the initial phase, attempting the establishment of small groups only, rather than masses of people, and accepting only candidates who had agricultural experience and some resources of their own.[4]

In 1912 and 1913, 14 colonists in Mauricio received the title deeds to their farms. They were among the first to obtain ownership of the lands they had worked. A remarkable aspect of the process of handing over ownership to the colonists was the very name that JCA applied to it, at its beginning in 1912 and ever afterwards. The 1912 report, after remarking that the first property titles had been transferred in Mauricio, goes on to say that there would be seen in a few years a Jewish colony entirely emancipated (*émancipé* in the French), and when in later years statistics on the number of colonists obtaining title are presented, the heading is 'Number emancipated'. Now 'emancipated' is a word generally used in a quite precise way, meaning 'freed from bondage'. That JCA itself used this word gives rise to speculation concerning its conception of its role in Argentina and lends some credence to the oft-expressed criticism that it was, especially in the early days, excessively paternalistic and even dictatorial in dealing with the colonists. As the old symbolic myth about JCA had it, if a cow in one of the settlements fell down a well, authorisation had to be obtained from Paris before the farmers could do anything about pulling up the unfortunate animal.

Nadir?

Despite JCA's large land purchases in earlier years, prompted by visions of increasing colonization, the Association continued to acquire parcels of land. Thus in 1910 it purchased 3,000 hectares at a place called Dora, in the province of Santiago del Estero, about 300 kilometres north of Moisesville and 850 kilometres from Buenos Aires. This area was purchased only after careful inspection and approval by JCA agronomists and an irrigation expert, whose opinion was solicited because it was clear that the land needed watering to be productive. By this time JCA felt that to provide 150 hectares per colonist, as it had sometimes done in the past, was too costly and would soon encroach on the acreage it had in reserve. For this reason, and also because intensive cultivation would be practised, 30 hectares were assigned to each of the 83 settling families, carefully selected as hard and tenacious workers, who came from the older colonies to Dora in 1911 and 1912.

Dora, despite all the careful inspections that had preceded its purchase, was in difficulties from the start. Water was available from a tributary of the Paraná River, but there were insufficient dikes to retain it in the area to be planted and allow it to soak in, so only a small part could be irrigated effectively. By 1912 it was clear that disaster impended. The fields were saline, and infertile; in the whole area the settlers were able to dig only four or five wells that gave potable water. The alfalfa crop was entirely lost. Yet the colonists hung on. JCA decided to regard Dora as an experimental farm and tried various methods of improving the saline soil. The cultivation of vegetables and fruits was also attempted. But by 1916 exceptional drought and lack of water had nullified these efforts. The situation was aggravated in February 1917 by a fearful invasion of locusts which ate what was left of the crop. Some of the colonists left, finding work in nearby forests. Even drinking water failed, and in June 1917 the remaining colonists telegraphed Buenos Aires, calling attention to the imminent bankruptcy of the colony and asking that their lands be exchanged for others that would be productive. Receiving no answer, a few days later the enraged colonists rushed the Administrator's quarters and forced him to send another telegram to Buenos Aires asking for the intervention of the Directorate. The Administrator did not suffer this invasion lightly and called the police, who maltreated and arrested some of the protestors. Peace was restored by the intervention of the Argentine Socialist Party, which sent as its representative Dr Dickman, a deputy in the National Assembly, from Clara Colony. Dickman's visit led to the creation of an investigating commission, whose conclusions bore out the complaints of the colonists concerning the lack of water and infertility of the soil. By 1919 only 33 of the original 83 families remained. JCA, with its customary obduracy, continued to work with the remaining settlers. It reduced the price of the lots and gave generous terms for the repayment of the colonists' debts. These measures served to keep the place alive, but only just. In 1941, the thirtieth anniversary of Dora's founding was celebrated by the 20 or 25 families who were still there.[5]

In its quest for more land, as the Dora experience indicates, JCA was perhaps not as cautious in making acquisitions as it should have been. Half the colony of Baron Hirsch was underlain by a chalky formation very close to the surface,[6] which made cultivation difficult; and another new colony, Montefiore, where the land had also been carefully examined before it was purchased in 1912, turned out to be afflicted by ravenous mosquitos and subject to flooding by tempestuous rains. Montefiore was located in Santa Fé province, a short distance north of Moisesville and 670 kilometres from Buenos Aires. In 1912 it was settled by 208 families, mostly drawn from the older colonies. Each received 75 hectares of land. Even in their very first year the settlers suffered from a plague of mosquitos, but worse was to come. In 1913 there was a drought and plagues of locusts, and in 1914, overwhelming rains. The colonists, moreover, were unable to deliver what crops they had harvested because their draught animals were so troubled by mosquitos. JCA had to grant a special credit because of the settlers' lack of income. In the next year, 1915, the rains were even worse. It is not surprising that by 1919 only 140 colonists remained. It is interesting that many of the farmers who left Montefiore formed an independent Jewish colony in the Chaco area, where they raised cotton. As for Montefiore, while it continued to exist, it did not grow. In 1941 there were 105 colonists there, chiefly producing alfalfa, raising cattle and selling milk.[7]

Somewhere in between

Franz Philippson, when he spoke with such pride of JCA's achievements in Argentina in his 1912 address, had been prescient. Generally speaking, the position of the colonists improved through the first decade of the twentieth century, and reached a peak in 1911–12. The most informative index of the colonists' prosperity was the extent of the repayments they made to JCA. While the amounts due were fixed by contract, the colonists knew that if they failed to pay in any one year for good reason, or even a shadow of one, they would not be penalised. Therefore the amount returned to JCA was a fair measure of their ability to pay. Anyhow, 1911 was a banner year for repayments, as Table 5.2, compiled from the relevant Annual Reports, shows.

The 1911–12 harvest was also the most abundant crop up to that time for the Jewish farmers. They produced 852,164 quintals (a quintal in Argentina is 101.3 lb) of cereals and flax, compared with 501,398 in the previous year and 635,895 in the following year when there was an invasion of locusts in the northern colonies and not only locusts but a drought as well in the south. Nor did the Jewish settlers suffer alone. The conditions of Argentine agriculturists in general at that time were so difficult that the government found it necessary to come to the aid of farmers in the southwest territory of La Pampa, where the JCA colonies

Table 5.2   Debt repayments to JCA

Year	Pesos
1896	1,724
1899	21,625
1901	113,858
1905	211,261
1909	499,348
1910	534,429
1911	687,201
1912	443,665
1913	413,089

Baron Hirsch and Narcisse Leven were located. The government distributed money for the purchase of seed, in which aid the Jewish farmers shared.

In its account of the colonists' troubles in 1913, JCA noted that in part these were due to their failure to follow JCA's advice, which was that they should turn from a reliance on cereals and flax and diversify by cultivating more vegetables and fruit and raising more poultry. But even in the midst of its rather querulous observations about the colonists' deafness to its well intentioned admonitions, JCA's 1913 report (p. 9) remarked on the basically improving situation of the Jewish farming centres in Argentina:

> Their prosperity manifests itself from the first in the growth of the population and by the increase and improvement of the inventory [of animals and tools]. It appears even more interesting to us that the immigrants and the colonists continue to buy lands from us in the villages that are close by the settlements, where they construct dwellings or commercial buildings, creating centres of attraction where small industry can develop spontaneously.

The report goes on to mention as examples of this kind of growth the villages at the railway stations near or within Lucienville, Dominguez (close to Clara), Clara itself, San Antonio, Moisesville and Mauricio.

It may be remarked parenthetically that JCA in the first years of the twentieth century had been criticised by Argentine political figures and periodicals for being reluctant to sell lots in these villages. It had adopted this policy originally for fear of diluting the agricultural character of the colonies. Under the pressure of this criticism JCA changed its attitude, and by 1907 and 1908 began to sell lots in the villages to tradesmen such as tailors, cobblers and purveyors of food. This led to the considerable expansion of these places to which, by 1913, JCA was pointing with pride.

2a Moisesville, Argentina, early twentieth century. Settlers from Eastern Europe in the synagogue

2b Lipton Colony, Canada. Early settlers

Thus, despite the poorness of the 1912–13 harvests as compared with the year before, and despite the difficulties or even failures encountered in the new colonies, Dora and Montefiore, on the eve of the First World War, JCA surveyed its works in Argentina and found them good. Or even too good – in 1911 Louis Oungre, in his survey of the Argentine settlements, remarked that the colonists possessed an over-abundance of machinery. He complained that they behaved like *estancieros* rather than *paysans*!

For the sake of consistency we shall close this chapter in our account of JCA's enterprise in Argentina at this point, though the change in its programme in that country, untouched by the war, was minimal as compared with what happened in Europe or even in Palestine. One major effect of the war, however, was the complete cessation of immigration from Eastern Europe, which had been the source of the settlers in the colonies and the fountain-head of their growth.

\

CHAPTER 6

JCA Elsewhere

We have described the activities of JCA in Argentina, Palestine and Russia up to the outbreak of the First World War. While the Association's major efforts were devoted to these countries, however, its activities were by no means confined to them. Its interests were global. It undertook colonization enterprises of varying magnitude in Brazil, where hundreds of individuals were involved; in Canada, where a few thousand were helped to settle; and in Cyprus, where the Jewish settlers were numbered in tens. In Romania, though on a much smaller scale, its activities resembled those in Russia, comprising assistance, especially for educational programmes, to the Jews who were unfortunate enough to live in that country. It also started a network of loan kassas in Galicia, then part of Austria. Its reach extended even to the United States, where it did not carry out a programme of its own but assisted its smaller and poorer cousin, the Baron de Hirsch Fund, with advice and substantial subventions. And beyond all this, JCA made contributions to a number of other charitable organisations in whose work it had an interest, particularly the Alliance Israélite Universelle, which had been a favourite beneficiary of the Baron de Hirsch himself.

Brazil

In Chapter 5 we noted that Cazes and Lepine had gone on an exploring expedition to Rio Grande do Sul, the southernmost province in Brazil, and had found land which they considered suitable for Jewish settlement. In consequence in 1902, after having a careful survey made by an agronomist from Paris, JCA purchased an estate of 4,472 hectares, later enlarged to 5,500. JCA named the place Philippson, after its vice-president, and in 1904 settled 37 families (267 persons) on twenty-five hectares each, having built small houses for them and provided livestock and tools. The land was part forest and part pasture, but JCA forbade the settlers to clear the forest, perhaps because this was regarded as a non-agricultural activity.

Alas, the same fate befell the settlers here as had befallen the colonists of Montefiore and Dora. In spite of the careful inspection, the Philippson land was

> uneven and stones can be found at a slight depth below the surface; there is only a light layer of humus. . . . Manure was not used at that time, and as the soil, without humus, is stony, and as there was a drought during the first two years, the results were disastrous, in spite of the settlers' great efforts.

These are the words of Isidore Eisenberg, JCA's administrator in Brazil after 1934.[1] To compound their difficulties, Eisenberg notes, the first settlers had no 'knowledge of the soil of Rio Grande do Sul, or any idea of its conditions or the method required to work it'.

It is rather disheartening to see repeated in Philippson, after more than a decade of experience in Argentina, some of the blunders and miscalculations that had plagued JCA's efforts in that country – the settling of people who had no notion of how to farm under South American conditions, and in a location that, despite 'careful investigation' by an agronomist, proved to have infertile soil, was difficult to cultivate, and was subject to drought and other drawbacks. Why JCA's inspectors made such unfortunate choices of land here and in Argentina is not a question on which the Association's records cast any light. And in Brazil in 1902, JCA did not have the excuse it had in Argentina in 1891 – that refugees were already on the ships *en route* and had to be settled quickly.

Not surprisingly after the almost complete nullity of reward for their efforts in their first years, the settlers wanted to leave Philippson. JCA kept them there by paying subsidies. Then in 1908 the administration of the colony was reorganised. More land was given to each colonist, and they were allowed to clear the forest and rear cattle. Also, they were given more cows, and a butter factory was established to which they could sell their milk. The added income from this source plus the returns from the sale of the timber produced in clearing their lots provided enough revenue to enable JCA to end the subsidies. In addition to producing beef, milk and timber, the colonists grew maize, potatoes, peanuts, cassava, oranges and vegetables. By 1910 JCA felt sufficiently heartened by the turn-around at Philippson to settle 40 more families there, some of them children of the original settlers, some of them from Europe. More importantly, it bought a huge property of 93,000 hectares (360 square miles) in the northern part of Rio Grande do Sul, called Quatro-Irmãos.

But JCA's hopes for Philippson were not fulfilled. To be a successful farmer there required, in the words of Isidore Eisenberg, 'working methods [that] were very different from and much harder than those the colonists had known in Europe'. This was due to the necessity of clearing the forest, which before the day of the chain saw was very arduous labour. Also, the colonists could make more money in the towns with easier work. Third, land values rose, so that the Philippson settlers, having paid their debts to JCA and received title, and thus in JCA's phraseology having become emancipated, were able to sell their lands at a profit, leave the colony and find more lucrative employment elsewhere. By 1926 JCA had closed its office at Philippson. A large part of the area sold by the settlers came into the hands of two Jewish farmers who at that time were working their holdings successfully. The rest of the land that had belonged to the colony came to be farmed by non-Jews.

The immense tract of 360 square miles called Quatro-Irmãos, most of it covered by timber, was first colonized in 1912, one year after its purchase, by more than forty families. Most were recruited among farm workers in the agricultural settlements in Argentina, but there were also some who had recently arrived from Russia.[2]

Apparently rumours about a great new settlement scheme in Brazil had been rife both in Europe and in Argentina. This was partly because JCA's enterprise at Quatro-Irmãos was confused with a Brazilian government settlement project on adjoining land. Anyway, many more immigrants came than JCA was prepared to handle. To quote Eisenberg again, 'Moreover, neither had the plans nor the preparations for the colonists recruited by JCA been studied or executed with sufficient care, and the number was excessive.' Not only were there too many settlers, but those whom JCA had brought there did not know how to farm in southern Brazil, especially in a heavily wooded area. Since the settlers were unable to earn their living, JCA again had to resort to subsidies. By 1913 there were at Quatro-Irmãos 150 colonists, who with their families numbered 837 people. In an effort to provide them with the means to support themselves, JCA had begun the construction of a railroad spur 19 kilometres long which connected with the main line from Rio de Janeiro to Montevideo, Uruguay. This would not only provide easy access to the colony but would also make the shipment of its produce, especially timber, economical. Before any effect could be felt, however, the First World War broke out. Paris found it impossible to send money to Brazil; so the subsidies could no longer be paid. The situation at Quatro-Irmãos became so difficult that JCA had to transfer a number of families to Argentina, leaving only 516 persons in the colony.

After the end of the war the colonists began to earn money and the population started to grow again. In 1919 there were 716 inhabitants, but only half of them were Jews. Prosperity, such as it was, did not endure for long. In 1923 a revolution broke out in Rio Grande do Sul and the insurgents occupied Quatro-Irmãos. They were driven out by federal troops, but in the next year there were more political disturbances and the colony was invaded by thieves and outlaws, who called themselves revolutionaries so as to have an excuse to pillage. In these circumstances it was impossible to farm, and again there was a considerable exodus. To build up the population for self-defence, JCA sold some hundreds of plots to German and Italian settlers whose relations with the Jews, Eisenberg tells us, were harmonious. After the incursions and invasions ceased, JCA again started to bring in new Jewish settlers. It settled eighty families from Poland and Lithuania in 1926, and in the years following they and the older colonists worked hard, with favourable results. But not for long. In 1930 there was yet another revolution; and the violent decline in prices incident to the Great Depression began in 1931 and continued for years. Again many colonists left, and those who remained had to be subsidised all over again.

Unfortunately, in 1930 the Brazilian government, to protect the domestic labour market during the Depression, in effect closed the country's doors to further immigration. Thus, while conditions at Quatro-Irmãos improved, particularly after 1934 when Eisenberg, a qualified agronomist, was appointed administrator, the Jewish population continued to decline as there were no more immigrants coming into the country to replenish it. In view of this, JCA turned to a different style of colonization at a place called Rezende in the province of Rio de Janeiro.

The difficulties experienced in Philippson and Quatro-Irmãos had been due in large part to their remoteness, as both were distant from any considerable urban centre. Therefore, when JCA made its third purchase in Brazil – Rezende – in 1936, it chose a site on a railway line, only 190 kilometres from Rio and even nearer other large cities, such as São Paulo, where produce could be sold. As new immigrants from Germany could not be brought into the country as JCA had hoped, 15 families already in Brazil were settled on plots of 20 hectares each.

In both Philippson and Quatro-Irmãos JCA built schools and synagogues, but its major contribution to Jewish culture in Brazil was made in the cities and towns. As the Association became conscious of the lack of organised Jewish life and even of religious congregations in Rio, São Paulo and other cities, it felt it necessary to remedy this situation. Therefore in 1923 it commissioned a survey of the Jewish communities in Brazil by a European rabbi, I. Raffalovich, who was instructed not only to inspect but also to awaken and institutionalise Jewish sentiment in these communities. By the end of 1924 five schools had been established in as many cities with help from JCA, and three or four others were in the process of formation. Hebrew and biblical lore were taught in addition to basic education in Portuguese. JCA had to work from the ground up because textbooks of Jewish history in Portuguese did not exist and had to be written. Also, teachers who had the requisite language skills were hard to find. By 1925 there were 12 schools with which JCA was involved and Rabbi Raffalovich had inspired the communities in Rio and São Paulo to plan the erection of synagogues and other communal buildings; he had also arranged for the translation of a book on Judaism into Portuguese. In 1926 the number of schools had reached 18, with 820 pupils, and the JCA report for that year noted that the rabbi had been able to establish Jewish communal organisations in towns where none had existed before. Later JCA expressed pride in the fact that its office in Rio was the centre to which the Jewish organisations in Brazil turned for encouragement in their moral and cultural efforts. In the later 1920s this work continued to expand. By 1928 there were 19 schools with 1,064 pupils. The notion of organisation had become so acceptable to the Jewish community that in 1929 a levy for charitable purposes was imposed on its members without a murmur of opposition. By this time there were 30,000–40,000 Jews in the country.

The next decade began auspiciously. The admission of 3,500 Jewish immigrants was secured without difficulty in 1930, partly because of the strong presssure brought by the Jewish community that JCA had helped to build. The school system grew to cover 1,600 pupils in twenty-five locations. By 1931, as the Depression deepened, the picture began to darken; only 1,940 Jews were admitted to the country (of whom more than half were helped by committees formed by JCA) and the school population remained more or less static. In 1934 JCA was subsidising 27 out of a total of 40 Jewish schools, but by 1939, on the eve of the Second World War, the number of schools subsidised had fallen to 21, as the local communities themselves were better able to bear the expense of education. Though Jewish immigration was almost shut off during the later 1930s, those who did manage to enter the country needed help, and JCA participated in the organisation of loan kassas for this purpose.

So, albeit on a smaller scale, the effect of JCA's activity in Brazil was not unlike that in Argentina. The people brought in to be farmers, or their children, migrated to urban centres where they helped to build up organised Jewish life and, to the extent permitted by the government restrictions, paved the way for more Jewish immigrants. And the build-up of Jewish communal life owed much not only to the immigrants brought in by JCA but also to JCA's direct efforts to establish and strengthen that communal life.

Canada

When Jewish emigration from Russia began in earnest in the 1880s, the vast, empty lands of western Canada seemed to some a desirable destination. Canada enjoyed a democratic government and had a system favouring smallholders similar to that in the United States; the government was furthermore on record as being willing to encourage immigrants. The Mansion House Committee, which had been formed in London in 1881 to help Jews fleeing from Russian pogroms, and which did finance travel for some of them, declared its intention of sending 'agriculturists and able-bodied labourers' to the United States and Canada. A movement of Russian Jews to Canada began, but it was not of any great magnitude. In 1881 there were only 2,445 Jews in the country as a whole, and by 1891 the total was no more than 6,501. Among these immigrants were small groups who tried to farm in western Canada. One such aggregation of twenty-seven families who received very small loans from the Mansion House Committee settled in Moosomin, Saskatchewan, in 1884. But the very severe climate, lack of transport and difficulty in cultivating the virgin soil were too much for them and the colony disintegrated. Another colony was established in 1888–9 near Wapella, also in Saskatchewan; this one lasted long enough to be taken under the wing of JCA when the Association began operations in Canada. (One of the members of the Wapella colony was Ezekiel Bronfman, the progenitor of the famous Canadian Jewish family.)

In a certain sense the JCA activity commenced in Canada before the Association itself came into legal existence in September 1891. As we have seen, early in May of that year the Baron de Hirsch sent a $20,000 cheque to the Young Men's Hebrew Benevolent Society (YMHBS) in Montreal. With this money YMHBS bought a building which it named the Baron de Hirsch Institute;

the Society used it for administrative purposes and to house a school for immigrants. It also set up a committee to look into the possibility of creating farm settlements in western Canada for Jewish newcomers.

These uses of the Baron's gift foreshadowed JCA's two major activities in Canada – helping immigrants settle in the country and, within that general framework, attempting to establish some of them on farm colonies. Shortly after JCA's incorporation, the Canadians sent a delegation to Paris who told the Baron that Moosomin was past saving but that a colony should be started near Oxbow, about 75 miles from Regina, the capital of Saskatchewan, where a few Jewish farmers had arrived on their own. This suggestion was accepted. The Canadian government made a grant of land to the colony, which was given the name of Hirsch; and 49 families were brought in by JCA and the Alliance Israélite in May 1892 and more came later in the year. These colonists suffered almost overwhelming hardship owing to harsh weather, the obduracy of the hard-packed virgin soil and plagues of grasshoppers; so a large proportion left. But a few hung on, the weather improved, so did the crop results, and by 1897 there was a sufficient population to require the existence of two schools, the expenses of which were covered by JCA.

Undaunted by the at best ambiguous results at Hirsch, in 1900 JCA came to an agreement with the Canadian government whereby the Canadian immigration agent in London would select a number of Romanian Jewish families, for whose settlement all expenses would be paid by JCA. An area 75 miles northeast of Regina, 25 miles from the railway station of Qu'Appelle, was chosen. According to Simon Belkin, JCA's Canadian manager for many years and historian of Jewish immigration into Canada, the land was suitable for mixed farming but 'subject to early frost and too cut up. . . to be suitable for wheat growing'.[3] Early in 1901, 49 families comprising 100 people arrived at Qu'Appelle. With the ill-luck that seemed to attend the initiation of so many JCA enterprises, however, they were struck by an epidemic of diphtheria and had to wait weeks until they could proceed to their land, erect log houses under the instruction of 'some Indian half-breeds from the nearby reservation', plant some potatoes and seed some land for hay. In JCA's agreement with the Canadian government it was provided that the latter would furnish guidance and instruction for the settlers. Unfortunately, the local residents chosen for this function could not communicate with the immigrants, who spoke only Yiddish, German or Romanian. In any case, the local people 'despised the newcomers and looked upon the entire scheme as a costly joke doomed to failure'. A deposit of $200,000 by JCA, which was intended for the purchase of equipment and livestock, went to buy food, leaving no funds for tools or animals to work the land. In consequence many settlers left.

At this juncture JCA asked the Jewish Agricultural Society (JAS) of New York to take over the supervision. Agents of JAS, by weeding out the less capable settlers, stopping the dole and making further advances for the purchase of implements and draft animals, succeeded by 1904 in getting the colony at Qu'Appelle on its feet. In 1907 JAS withdrew and JCA's Canadian Committee took on the management of the colonies. In the subsequent years these colonies and two additional ones started by JCA managed, if not to prosper, at least to maintain themselves. Although there was a considerable movement out, sufficient replacements were found to keep the population stable.

One reason for the departures was the harshness of the living and working conditions in these colonies, especially at the beginning. A descendant of one of the early Canadian pioneers writes:

> The colony [Edenbridge, founded 1906] became a monument to the courage, enterprise and adaptability of the Jew. Out of the dense poplar, pack pine and willow, with the axe and plough, they won their little clearings acre by acre from the surrounding forest, and built their log houses and stables, chinked with clay and coated with white-wash. The scrub was so thick that one settler got lost for a full day on his own homestead.[4]

Within a surprisingly short time, however, those settlers who remained did well enough to be able to enjoy some of life's amenities. By 1917 there was an active theatrical group in Edenbridge, numbering more than a dozen.

Through its Canadian Committee, JCA continued its close relationship with the colonies, making advances for seed and equipment and dispatching instructors. In 1915 there were 225 Jewish farm families, 966 people in all, in the five principal JCA colonies: Hirsch, Lipton (Qu'Appelle), Sonnenfeld and Edenbridge in Saskatchewan and Rumsey in Alberta. The total number of Jews then living on Canadian farms was about 3,000, counting minor JCA colonies and individuals not connected with JCA. Among these individual farmers was a group some 300 strong near Winnipeg, who rented or owned 20–30 acres each. They produced eggs, milk, butter and vegetables, which they brought into town for sale each day.

With the coming of the First World War the government urged all farmers to expand their operations. The farmers complied.

They borrowed to enlarge their planting, often on unsuitable land, and increase their livestock; this also made more land necessary, which was purchased with more borrowed money. The sharp decline in prices in 1919–20 then forced many out of business. Instead of building up the colonies further, JCA had to 'engage in rescue operations to save farmers from bankruptcy'.[5] And even if they did not go bankrupt, many farmers left the land; war prosperity and jobs in munition factories had already provided many with the means and incentive to do so. Young people of marriageable age were under particular pressure to go to areas of more concentrated Jewish population because of the difficulty of finding suitable mates in the scattered, sparsely populated colonies. The result of these economic and social influences was a reduction in the number of Jews in agriculture.

In 1925 there were 142 farmers, 620 persons, in the five settlements, a clear reduction from the 1915 figures of 225 and 966 respectively. In that year (1925) there were altogether 132,000 Jews in Canada[6], so the farmers constituted a very small proportion of the Jewish population. Nevertheless, Belkin sums up as follows:

> It is clear that Jewish land settlement in Canada made a contribution to the growth of the Jewish community in several ways. It attracted many Jewish immigrants from Eastern Europe and even from the United States to come to Canada and settle on homesteads. It provided many immigrants who arrived in Canada with a profitable occupation of their own choice. It helped disillusioned factory workers or other city Jews unable to find occupations for their manual labor in the cities to establish themselves in independent enterprises. Jewish farming also served the Jewish community well from a public relations point of view. With the exception of the Mennonites, Jews were the first immigrants from Central and Eastern Europe to make a contribution to the agricultural development of what was then known as the North-West Territories. They proved that Jews can be pioneers even if not motivated by national or religious ideals. They also proved that Jews accustomed to city living can, with adequate financial support, become. . . as good farmers as any ethnic group.[7]

From a numerical point of view, the immigration work of YMHBS in Montreal affected many more people than went to the western colonies. By 1901 the total number of Jews in the country had increased to 16,401, about 10,000 having come during the previous decade. In 1899 alone 2,202 Romanian Jews arrived in Canada, many of whom had been sent from that country by JCA. Later, in the years 1901–6, 4,304 Romanian Jews arrived in Canada with the direct or indirect assistance of JCA.[8]

After the Kishinev pogrom of 1903, and the pogroms in 1905 inspired by the unsatisfactory conclusion of the Russo-Japanese War, the bulk of the Jewish immigrants to Canada – 40,000 in the period 1906–10 – came from Russia. YMHBS provided the customary services: reception at the port, housing, instruction in English through the Baron de Hirsch Institute, the finding of employment and the provision of legal representation where necessary. In 1910 the most interesting placement was that of a dozen graduates of JCA's European farm schools on Canadian farms.

Immigration work had grown to such an extent that JCA felt that this should be separated from the local activities of YMHBS. The Association therefore established its own Canadian Committee in 1907 to take charge of its immigration and farm settlement programmes. When in the depression of 1907–8 a Jewish soup kitchen was set up in Montreal, JCA paid its expenses.

Jewish immigration into Canada, which had followed a rising course in the first years of the twentieth century, reached a peak of 24,000 in 1913–14. The First World War brought about an almost complete cessation of this movement, which, however, resumed after 1919, but not at the same high level. The figure for 1921–2 was 8,404. In 1920 the Jewish Immigrant Aid Society of Canada (JIAS) was formed, just in time to deal with the migrations of European Jews displaced in the war. JCA's Canadian Committee was a member of JIAS and for many years contributed largely to its support. Ironically, no sooner had JIAS been set up than the Canadian government in 1920 and 1922 promulgated regulations that made mass Jewish immigration impossible. The decade 1922–31 saw Jewish immigration fall to about 3,000 a year, and in some years more Jews left Canada for the United States than came into the country.

In 1923 JIAS did persuade the Canadian authorities to permit 5,000 Russian Jewish refugees, from a much greater number stranded in Europe, to come to Canada at the rate of one hundred a week; but only 3,000 people selected by JCA came in under this arrangement and there was an infinity of bureaucratic hair-splitting, ending in the government's cancellation of the unused permits.[9] In the next decade, 1931–41, when Jews' need for a haven was most acute because of Hitler's rise to power, Jewish immigration to Canada was cut to about 600 or 700 a year, which was equalled by the movement of Jews from Canada to the United States.

A recent book published in Toronto[10] asserts that Canada, in comparison with its size, had the worst record of any Western nation for admitting Jewish immigrants during the Hitler period. The book says that between 1933 and 1945 the United States admitted '200,000 Jewish refugees, Palestine 120,000, embattled Britain 70,000, penurious Brazil 27,000, distant China 25,000, tiny Bolivia and Chile 14,000 each'. All this while Canada admitted only the trickle just mentioned. The reason, the book makes clear, was plain and simple anti-Semitism, which ran from the highest level, the Prime Minister (Mackenzie King), and the High Commissioner in London (Vincent Massey) down to and through the operating levels of the bureaucracy. Unfortunately, the position of these officials reflected a basic attitude of the Canadian people at large.[11] This policy of exclusion continued after the war. 'Fully three years after some death camps had been liberated. . . almost no Jewish refugees had yet entered Canada.'[12] It is true that, just before the Second World War broke out, about 200 Jewish farm families, mostly from Czechoslovakia, who had means of their own, did manage, with enormous tribulations and the help of the Canadian Jewish community, to settle; and in 1941 Canadian Jewish Congress was able to obtain residence permits for about 1,000 German refugees who had been sent to Canada from England. But these were small palliatives which did little to lighten the black record.

The history of JCA in Canada after the First World War is centred on the same two main concerns as in the years before – the support of the Jewish farm colonies, and the facilitation of Jewish immigration and assistance to the immigrants. Unfortunately, the Association was doomed to disappointment in both these endeavours. In a sense, Jewish farming in Canada never recovered from the 1919–20 slump. JCA kept manfully sending small groups of new arrivals out to the western colonies, providing them with guidance by capable agronomists, buying more land for eventual sale to the farmers, and above all making loans to them; but the number of Jewish farmers in Canada just did not increase. As new ones settled, older ones departed.

We have seen how low the population figures for 1925 were in the five chief colonies. This was not for want of effort. In 1922 JCA recorded that over the previous 15 years it had made 1567 loans for a total of $520,000 (of which half had been repaid). JCA's provision of credit in western Canada was more important than elsewhere because of the lack of other sources of financing. The Association also helped by supporting synagogues, schools and ritual baths. In 1923, 251 loans were made, totalling $52,051, but repayments were only $13,864 because in that year agriculture did not prosper and all the Canadian settlements lost population. In 1925, when crops were much better, only 12 loans were made, and collections were the best in five years. The Canadian Committee was thus emboldened to settle 100 people in the following year. By that time JCA owned 149 farms that had been abandoned by previous settlers, of which 100 were let to tenants pending their occupation by newcomers. In spite of owning all this land, JCA was optimistic enough to buy 10,000 acres near Hirsch and Sonnenfeld and to provide houses and barns for prospective new settlers. Although 1927 was a year of mixed results owing to unseasonably cold weather and the prevalence of wheat rust, and in 1929 the weather so deteriorated that the Jewish farmers produced practically no crops, JCA nevertheless installed thirty-four new families.

With the onset of the Great Depression, agricultural prices fell and stayed down; in one sense, however, this did not matter to the Jewish farmers, because from 1929 onwards disaster befell almost every crop. These were the years of the great droughts, especially severe from 1933 to 1937. And if there was not drought, there was excessive heat; if not heat, there were locusts; and if not locusts, stem rust ruined the wheat. In 1934 JCA reported the worst crop in ten years, and in 1937 it reported that crops were worse than ever.

This multiplication of woes, however, did not destroy the western colonies entirely. About 80 farmers – 235 persons – hung on. JCA continued to dispense loans, which from the inception of the Canadian Committee in 1907 until 1946 totalled $726,664. And despite all the hardships the western farmers suffered, JCA received back from them over this same period a total of $694,762 – $474,829 in repayments of principal and $219,933 in rentals and reimbursement of tax payments.

Romania

If any country in the period before the First World War could have claimed the dubious honour of being a close second to Russia in the intensity of its anti-Semitic actions and attitudes, it was probably Romania. In 1900 its population included 250,000 Jews.

Before the war the country consisted of the two provinces of Wallachia and Moldavia, which had broken away from Turkey and had had its independence recognised by the Congress of Berlin in 1878. One condition of this recognition was the grant of civil rights to the Jews.[13] The Romanian government paid no attention to this condition however and managed to win recognition from many of the Great Powers, for example Germany, by a simple process – bribery.[14] By government decree, then, Jews were forbidden to be lawyers, teachers, chemists or stockbrokers, or to sell commodities that were the subject of government monopolies (tobacco, salt, alcohol).

It was also very difficult for Jewish youngsters to attend public schools: they were treated as foreigners and were allowed to register in school only if there were vacancies, an unlikely occurrence because of the insufficiency of places; furthermore, if a Jewish child was fortunate enough to be admitted, a high tuition fee was demanded; finally, in 1893, a law was passed expelling Jews from school entirely. In these circumstances the Jewish communities organised their own schools, defraying expenses out of gifts, subscriptions and the proceeds of social events such as plays and fêtes. The Jewish schools followed the government's curricula and in addition taught Hebrew and German. As time passed, however, the Jewish organisations found the task of financing the school system more and more onerous. It was especially hard to raise the funds for erecting new buildings. Towards the end of the century an economic crisis began to manifest itself, and the Romanian Jews appealed to JCA for help. JCA despatched an emissary to Romania and in 1899 undertook to help ten schools in Bucharest, the capital, and Jassy, the second city. These were the chief locations of the Jewish population. Jassy, though a centre of Jewish learning, was also the centre of anti-Semitic activity in the country.

The economic crisis deepened as the nineteenth century ended, and this led to the persecution of the Jews as a sort of relief valve for the discontent of the populace. While JCA continued to help schools, it also focused its attention on helping Jews to leave Romania. As we have already seen, the movement of 'walkers' out of Romania began in 1900. In 1901 JCA stationed an emigration agent there, who set up a network of offices to help migrants in all places with a large Jewish population and enlisted the help of prominent Jews, usually the heads of the local B'nai Brith societies. By this time the economic decline had become so serious that JCA was distributing food to the poor.

In 1901, 3,187 Romanian Jews were helped to emigrate. The Israelitische Allianz in Vienna and the Montefiore Society in Rotterdam, both recipients of JCA subventions, furnished advice, travel information, documents and sometimes lodging to the travellers. It is interesting, in view of the Canadian government's attitude towards Jewish immigrants after the First World War, that in the first decade of the century some hundreds received governmental assistance to get to Canada. By 1903 the number of Romanian emigrants helped by JCA and the transit societies had risen to 6,826. Disturbances in 1905 and the peasant revolt of 1907, in the course of which Jewish shops and homes were pillaged, plus a decree expelling Jews from villages, caused a further exodus from the country.

In the meantime the JCA involvement with the Jewish school system expanded, from 24 schools in 1900 to 35 in 1905, including a vocational school where the boys were taught carpentry and metalwork and the girls sewing and other skills related to dressmaking. JCA was proud of the fact that it overcame conservative opposition to schools mixing boys and girls.

In 1908 the Jewish minority was further disadvantaged by legislation that made it very difficult for its members to obtain factory jobs and almost impossible for them to work in agriculture. At the same time the public schools were closed to Jews entirely, and attendance at the JCA-assisted schools went up to 7,121. The next year JCA helped four more schools, bringing the total number of pupils involved to 7,772. Also in that year, clothes, shoes and books were distributed to the poorer pupils. From this time until the outbreak of the First World War, JCA's support for the Jewish schools in Romania increased, as the economic difficulties owing to the Balkan Wars of 1912–13 reduced local school revenues. By 1913 JCA was aiding 45 schools and had contributed to the construction or rehabilitation of 30 school buildings. Besides this support, JCA had influenced 'its' schools, attended now by 10,534 boys and girls, to introduce modern curricula, including mathematics and European languages.

Galicia and Bukovina

Of the great Austro-Hungarian Empire before the First World War, Galicia was the northeasternmost province. Largely populated by Poles (it became part of Poland after the war), it also contained a sizeable number of Jews – about 900,000 out of a total population of 8 million. Even among the generally poor Jews of Eastern Europe, the Galitzianer had the reputation of being the poorest of the poor. The Baron de Hirsch himself, in the course of his travels through the territory on his railway-building enterprises, had noticed how exceptionally poverty-stricken the Jews were in that province. One of the major purposes of his Austrian Stiftung was to provide schooling for Jewish children there. Before the First World War the Stiftung operated 48 schools with 7,800 pupils.[15] The Stiftung had also created an apprenticeship programme but was having trouble in finding employment for its graduates. In 1899 JCA agreed to give it a subvention to help place 100 students over a three-year period.

JCA had in that year sent agents to Galicia in order to start an assistance programme; this began with the purchase of a domain called Slobodka-Lesna, on which JCA intended to establish a farm school and to raise crops on its own account.

In the course of the next few years, as the Slobodka farm became operational, it produced grain, beet and peas and raised some cows. Forty men, among them a number of Jews, worked the place. The chief crop, however, was potatoes, which were converted into alcohol by a distillery on the property. The farm school there was also functioning, with about seventy-five students. A number of graduates of Slobodka-Lesna migrated to Canada and settled in the JCA colonies in the West.

Later, JCA widened its educational activity to start a carpentry school in Stanislavov, Galicia's principal city, the pupils of which included some graduates of the Stiftung system. This place, however, was not successful and by 1912 it was decided to close it. The farm school continued to operate and even expanded somewhat; in 1913, in addition to teaching carpentry and agriculture, it provided courses in metal forging, and that year sent ten graduates overseas and ten to jobs in Austria. Although 1913 was a poor crop year, the farm at Slobodka-Lesna had increased its planted area to about 860 acres.

However, the outstanding accomplishment of the JCA mission of 1899 was the initiation of a network of loan kassas in Galicia. In that year the JCA agents set up kassas in three of the principal cities, Kolomea, Stanislavov and Tarnow, to serve workers and small businessmen. In 1900 a fourth was added in Brody, famous as the stopping place for refugees from the Russian pogroms of the 1880s. These institutions filled an obvious need of Galicia's Jewry; by 1903 there were six, with 4,427 members.

As time went on, the kassa movement continued to expand. By 1905 there were 11, with branches in smaller cities, covering communities with a total of about 150,000 Jewish inhabitants. These kassas had 14,515 members, which meant that half the Jewish families belonged, on the assumption of one member per family. This major JCA activity in Galicia continued to grow at a high rate until the outbreak of the First World War. In 1913, when there was a depression owing to fear of a war with Russia, the enterprise proved its worth by extending credit to Jewish clients when all other sources dried up. By then Galicia had 27 kassas, mostly in the eastern part of the province, with 39,000 members. These associations had made over 20,000 loans amounting to 4,675,000 Austrian kroner (worth about £195,000 in 1913).

Bukovina, the province to the south of Galicia, was of less interest to JCA because its Jewish population was much smaller – 102,000 out of a total of 800,000. However, in 1912 JCA helped a kassa to open in Czernovitz, the principal city. After the First World War, Galicia became the southern part of the new Poland and Bukovina was joined to Romania.

Cyprus

One characteristic of JCA in its early years was courage, not to say foolhardiness. JCA did not forbear to rush in where others had not thought to tread. Fortunately, in view of their unfruitful outcomes, the efforts in Cyprus and Turkey were on a very small scale in comparison with the Argentine or even Canadian colonization.

In 1897 a group of Russian Jewish families who had reached London and formed a society called Ahavat Zion (Love of Zion) asked JCA for a loan to purchase land in Cyprus on which they would settle and farm. (Why these lovers of Zion wanted to go to Cyprus is not clear from the record.) On the basis of an investigator's favourable report, JCA granted the loan. Ahavat Zion bought an estate of 1,110 hectares called Margo-Tchiflik, about 14 kilometres from Nicosia, the principal city on the island. Some 15 families who claimed (with little justification) to be farmers settled there. They were provided with houses, stables, animals, tools and seed. A school for the children was set up. Three of the first families, who had left good jobs in London, promptly returned to England.

This episode in a sense epitomised the history of JCA in Cyprus. The settlers there, because they had trouble making a living, because they could not tolerate the island's extreme heat, because of the lack of Jewish life (the colony was so small) and because Palestine was so close, were constantly leaving, though it must be said the leavers were replaced – often by Jews from Palestine.

By 1899 only five of the original families remained; the others had been replaced by Palestinian Jews who had attended the Mikveh-Israel agricultural school near Jaffa. Included in the Jewish population were a teacher, a storekeeper and some artisans. More important, perhaps, JCA became the owner of Margo-Tchiflik instead of just being a lender. By the turn of the century it was apparent that numerous obstacles had to be overcome: much of the land, uncultivated for many years, had to be cleared, and some of the equipment used was primitive; many of the departing families sold their livestock before leaving Cyprus, so that only six cows were left in the colony. Also, young unmarried men from Mikveh-Israel had replaced families with children; there were so few youngsters now that the school was closed.

At Margo-Tchiflik in 1902, in addition to the five families of Jewish settlers, there were four farm workers, former Mikveh-Israel students. The only sign of progress was an increase in the number of sheep. By 1908 the number of families was built up to 16, but in the course of that year nine families departed, for the reasons we have mentioned earlier and for the added reason that a number of those newly come from Russia suffered from marsh fever, to which the old inhabitants were immune.

There was no essential change in the nature of the Cyprus situation from this time to the start of the First World War. No sooner had JCA brought in new settlers to fill the vacancies than there were further departures. In 1912 the Jewish population fell to 155 (the peak had been 189), but in its report for that year JCA still hoped to stabilise the colony.

Turkey

In 1896 JCA had come to the assistance of Rehovoth and other Jewish colonies in Palestine, and in 1897, when it had helped in the purchase of the estate on Cyprus, the Council had felt the need to take additional action on behalf of Jews in the Orient. They voted a credit to establish sixteen graduates of the Jerusalem vocational school of the Alliance Israélite in business in either Palestine or Asia Minor – then, as now, part of Turkey. In 1898 JCA took the further step of determining to buy a domain of about 2,600 hectares on a railway line 107 kilometres from Smyrna (now Izmir), the principal port in Asia Minor. Its intention was to use most of this tract, which it named Or Yehuda (Light of Judah), for settling Jewish farmers, and to reserve part of it for an agricultural school. By 1900 the operation was under way. JCA farmed 193 hectares itself, mostly under vines, but it also had a herd of almost 1,000 sheep, as the place seemed especially well suited for oviculture. As a workforce it employed ten former students of Mikveh-Israel and three Russian settlers.

Another 178 hectares were cultivated by share-croppers whose principal crop was grain; 151 hectares were let. The latter were used for grain, tobacco and opium poppies. The 1900 report innocently says (p. 62, translated): 'the land for opium and tobacco is particularly scarce and can be let under excellent conditions. Or Yehuda contains sufficiently large areas which can be adapted to these crops.' Actually, opium was not an important product of Or Yehuda. In subsequent reports the references thereto are of the briefest, while considerable space is devoted to other products like grapes, olives, wool, etc. Altogether there were 94 people on the domain (not counting the students), of whom 76 were Jewish, the rest Greek. (At that time the west coast of Asia Minor, though part of Turkey, was largely inhabited by Greeks.)

As for the agricultural school, a temporary building had been put up to accommodate 30 students – four young men from Mikveh who were to complete their studies and also work on the farm, ten from Alliance Israélite schools, and 16 Romanians who had to learn French before they could study because instruction was in that language.

In 1903 JCA undertook a new responsibility in Turkey. Dr Warburg of Berlin, a scion of the famous banking and philanthropic family, had earlier helped a group of Romanian Jews to settle in two localities in Turkish Anatolia. There were 45 families, 250 people, at a place called Karaya and 35 families, 140 people, at a location named Salizar. Warburg began to find it impossible to finance and manage these colonies and appealed to JCA for help. JCA responded by taking charge and extending credit to help the settlers build houses and obtain equipment. In 1905 the harvest was very poor and many families left Salizar. JCA consoled itself by remarking that they were not well suited to be farmers, a note it had sounded so often on similar occasions that it was beginning to sound hollow. In 1907 the crops were poor again owing to excessively cold and dry weather, and more settlers left both places. JCA tried to retrieve the situation by shifting the emphasis from grain to sheep. The following year the Association removed its administrator from the settlements and put the management in the hands of committees of the farmers, retaining an agronomist to instruct them. In 1910 matters improved somewhat as 15 new Russian families, largely self-financed, took over the lots that others had abandoned. But these colonies were not fated to enjoy success for long. In 1912, with the outbreak of the Balkan Wars, the Jewish immigrants left Karaya (which had been renamed Mamouré) in a body and only 12 families hung on at Salizar.

Despite the setbacks it suffered at these two places, JCA was sufficiently confident of prospects in Turkey to open an office in Constantinople (Istanbul) in 1910 for the guidance of Russian Jewish immigrants interested in farming in the Sultan's empire. After all, the results at Or Yehuda, where JCA farmed for its own account, and where about a dozen Jewish share-croppers were working, were relatively favourable. Or Yehuda was producing a very wide variety of crops – grain, fruits, vegetables, tobacco, in addition to the wool, olives and grapes we have mentioned. The school was also continuing to function with about fifty pupils. Beyond this, two groups of Russian would-be immigrants were negotiating for the purchase of lands near Constantinople, and JCA made a loan to one of these. As soon as the Balkan Wars came to an end in 1913 the two groups took possession of their lands where they intended to raise cattle for sale in the city but where timber cut on the estates turned out to be more profitable.

While farming operations at Or Yehuda were relatively successful, apart from occasional crop failures owing to bad weather, JCA was discovering that it was very difficult to place the graduates of the agricultural school, though some had gone as far as Canada to find jobs. Mikveh-Israel apparently was able to furnish all the Jewish agronomists and farm managers that were required in the Middle East.

As the previous record amply demonstrates, JCA was nothing if not persistent. In Cyprus it hung on for years after it was manifest that Jews just did not want to stay there. Likewise, it kept the school going at Or Yehuda after it was clear that this too was superfluous. But in nothing was JCA more persistent than in its never-ceasing search for suitable destinations for Russian Jews. In furtherance of this quest, in 1909 and 1910 it sent investigators into Cilicia, part of Turkish Asia Minor, and to Mesopotamia, then also part of the Turkish Empire, to assess the possibilities these places offered for Jewish settlers. Both areas were at that time relatively uninhabited, but Cilicia needed extensive drainage and Mesopotamia needed great irrigation works, and since JCA had no confidence in the capacity of the Ottoman government to carry out such enterprises, it decided not to look further into these locations. It gave up its hopes for Mesopotamia with regret, because Baghdad, the principal city, had a sizeable Jewish population. With the wisdom of hindsight, we can today be thankful that JCA forbore to try to plant a colony of Russian Jewish farmers in what is now the country of Iraq.

The United States – Baron de Hirsch Fund and Jewish Agricultural Society

The year 1891, on paper at least, marked the culmination of the Baron's philanthropic efforts. For it happened that the three great foundations he established all came into legal existence in that year: the Jewish Colonization Association in London, the Baron de Hirsch Fund in New York and the Baron de Hirsch Stiftung in Austria. The Fund in New York received a starting capital gift of $2.4 million (later increased by gifts from the Baroness); this was much less than JCA's initial capital, but then its intended field of operation was much smaller. The Baron's Deed of Trust for the Fund, and its articles of incorporation, laid down that it was to confine its activities to the United States (in 1970 its constitution was altered to permit it to act in any country), while there were no territorial limitations on JCA.

The Fund was charged with the duty of educating and relieving 'Hebrew emigrants from Europe' and their children. It was to accomplish this by granting loans to agriculturists, by transporting immigrants from the port of arrival to their place of employment, by training them in mechanics and handicrafts, and by instruction in English and in agriculture. On its inception the Fund purchased a tract of eight square miles in southern New Jersey, later incorporated as the town of Woodbine, on which it built houses with the intention of having settlers cultivate farms during the spring and summer, and in the winter work in factories, a number of which the Fund erected. This agro-industrial experiment turned out to be unsuccessful,[16] but early in its history the Fund devoted a section of the Woodbine property to the buildings and grounds of the newly established Baron de Hirsch Agricultural School. This institution's student body in some years numbered 120, but the immense growth of public schools of agriculture and the drop in attendance during the First World War influenced the Fund's trustees to close it in 1917. In the course of its existence, representatives of JCA visited the school and prepared reports on its activities for the information not only of their own head office but also of the Fund. JCA did more than inspect; in 1901, when a fire destroyed a Woodbine factory, which was apparently not insured, JCA contributed toward its rebuilding.

The Fund had already asked for and received other material aid from JCA. Very early on, the Fund had attempted to provide immigrants with vocational training and soon decided that it would have to construct its own building to offer effective teaching. Therefore in 1899 it put up the Baron de Hirsch Trade School in Manhattan, helped by large contributions from Baroness Clara and JCA. This institution gave practical short courses in painting, carpentry, plumbing, sheet metalwork, printing and other skills. The Trade School, which did not charge tuition fees, operated until 1935. It was then closed, partly because

109

the city school system was offering vocational training and partly because the Fund's resources had been depleted in the Great Depression; moreover, JCA in 1926 stopped its annual subventions to the Trade School because it also was financially hard-pressed. In the course of its useful life, about 10,000 young men attended this institution.

The trustees were well aware of the Baron's conviction that the best defence against anti-Semitism would be the existence of a large and successful Jewish farming class. Therefore, one of the Fund's first acts was to help Jewish farmers, immigrants from Russia, who had in the 1880s settled near Vineland, New Jersey. But this was a relatively minor enterprise. Later, in view of the many other activities carried on by the Fund, such as the financing of port work in half a dozen cities, the support of English and Americanisation classes and the agricultural and trade schools, the trustees decided that it would be advisable to create a separate entity to work with Jewish farmers. In 1900 the Jewish Agricultural and Industrial Aid Society was incorporated. Its financial base was provided by an annual subsidy of about $68,000 from the Fund, which at times of necessity was increased, and by a pledge of $80,000 a year from JCA, which was paid until 1914, when the losses suffered by the Association's investments incident to the outbreak of the war forced it to suspend its payments. The expenses of one branch of the Society, which bore the un-euphonious name of 'Industrial Removal Office', were wholly paid by JCA. Its function was to keep Jewish immigrants from concentrating in New York; for the well established American Jews – those who themselves or whose fathers had come to the country before the big influx of Russians began – feared an upsurge of anti-Jewish sentiment if 'too many' uncouth, Yiddish-speaking 'greenhorns' collected in New York's Lower East Side. These feelings were shared by the JCA Council, and some time later by 'established' Jewish families in Buenos Aires and Montreal, who were also worried lest too many new arrivals should stay in their cities. The Industrial Removal Office operated from 1900 to 1917, dispersing Jewish immigrants from New York, the chief port of disembarkation. It did this by paying the fare for the immigrant and his family to some interior city such as Detroit or Cincinnati, where its agents, usually local B'nai Brith officials, had found a job opening. In its seventeen years the Industrial Removal Office dealt with no fewer than 79,000 individuals.

The other branches of the Jewish Agricultural Society (the words 'Industrial Aid' were dropped in 1921) over these years developed a technique for helping Jewish would-be farmers. This technique, which remained relatively unchanged for about 60 years, was to provide such farmers with subordinate loans after they had borrowed as much as they could from conventional banking or government sources. Before the Federal Extension Service commenced its work in 1914, the Society operated a small extension service of its own, having itinerant agents travelling through states such as New York, New Jersey and Connecticut which had numbers of Jewish farmers, giving them instruction and advice. From 1907 to 1957 the Society published a monthly magazine in Yiddish and English. At the beginning of the twentieth century, the Society, as we have seen, provided management services for the JCA colonies in western Canada. From 1900, when JCA started publishing comprehensive annual reports, until 1937, long after it had ceased making contributions to the American organisations, these reports included a section devoted to the Baron de Hirsch Fund and the Jewish Agricultural Society. It must be confessed that the latter's rather modest accomplishments were described by JCA in adulatory terms that they did not quite deserve.

In 1946, after the Second World War, the Fund turned $128,000 over to JCA, with the intention that the Joint Distribution Committee, in agreement with JCA, distribute this sum to needy 'Jews overseas'. The money was used to help some Jews depart from Europe and for emergency relief needs there.

The movement of so-called 'displaced persons' from Europe to the United States from 1946 to 1952 created a period of great activity for JAS, as 2,500 to 3,000 Jewish immigrant families settled on farms in those years or soon thereafter. These newcomers mostly bought or built small poultry farms in New Jersey, helped by second, third or fourth mortgages from JAS. In 1951 about a thousand immigrant farmers joined a self-help organisation, the South Jersey Poultry Farmers Association, which made interest-free loans to its members. The demand for loans outran the resources, and JAS, feeling that the $1 million it had then outstanding in loans in the area was enough, requested help from JCA. The Association, always ready to hasten to the assistance of Jewish farmers in trouble, agreed to provide $35,000. The mid-1950s marked the peak years of prosperity for New Jersey egg and poultry producers. When, later, this trade ceased to be profitable, almost all of them were forced out of business, their Association disintegrated and the lenders lost nearly half their investment.[17]

Grants to organisations

The Alliance Israélite Universelle was founded in 1860 in Paris as a Jewish defence organisation, the first such institution in Jewish history. Its purpose was to help protect Jews subject to attack because of accusations of ritual murder, conspiracies against Gentiles and other such timeworn or newly invented anti-Semitic fabrications. It was created in specific response to a number of incidents such as the notorious Mortara case in Italy in 1858, when a Jewish child was abducted by Catholic conversionists.

Besides defence, a second and subsidiary object of the Alliance was 'to encourage the pursuit of useful handicrafts'.[18] Accordingly, it built up a network of schools, mostly vocational, for Jewish young people in the countries of the Levant. Among these were agricultural schools at Djedeida in Tunis and Mikveh-Israel in Palestine. It is interesting that, although the Alliance was far from being Zionist (in fact, at the Versailles Peace Conference the Alliance's representative took an anti-Zionist position), it chose Palestine as the site of the second of these institutions.

Another branch of the Alliance's activity was to provide relief for Jews in trouble. The Alliance raised money for those fleeing the Russian pogroms of 1881 and helped a number of them on their way to America, including, as we have seen, the Jewish settlers in Moosomin in western Canada.

As we also saw earlier, the Baron de Hirsch's first substantial philanthropic gift of 1 million francs in 1873 went for the benefit of the Alliance schools in Turkey. He also made large gifts to the organisation annually, notably another million francs in 1882 for a fund for refugees from Russian pogroms. His beneficence to the Alliance culminated in 1889, when he set up an endowment the income from which was intended to cover the organisation's annual 400,000-franc deficit. Besides making gifts to it, the Baron relied on advice from its members in his philanthropic activities. Narcisse Leven, a member of the JCA Council and its President after the Baron's death, was also President of the Alliance from 1898 to his own death in 1915. Hirsch and Cazes, the joint heads of JCA's Buenos Aires administration for many years, had previously been administrators of Alliance schools. They were only two of many JCA staff members and teachers who had come from this source.

It is not surprising then that, after the Baron's death, JCA made grants to the Alliance and in fact has continued to make such grants every year from that time to the present. When the Baroness died in 1899 she left £425,995 to JCA with the proviso that the income from this legacy be paid over to the Alliance.

This sum was sadly reduced to £118,261 by the ravages in the German and other European securities caused by the First World War.

At the end of the nineteeth century and at the beginning of the twentieth, JCA's grants were intended to help the Alliance schools, like the Ecole Normale at Auteuil in France, the vocational schools in Jerusalem and elsewhere, the primary schools in Arab areas then part of the Turkish Empire, and the agricultural schools in Tunis and Jaffa (Mikveh-Israel). Many alumni of this last migrated to JCA colonies in America, Cyprus and Turkey, and many became agronomists on JCA's staff in those places.

But JCA's grants-in-aid went far beyond the Alliance. Jewish organisations of many varieties and in many locations have benefited from JCA's generosity. For example, a horticultural school at Ahlem, near Hamburg, to which JCA sent dozens of students from Russia, was one; another was a teachers' training establishment in Frankfurt-am-Main where Russians were sent to study prior to employment in JCA's Russian school network; another was a horticultural school in Budapest. We have already mentioned that JCA subsidised the Montefiore Society of Rotterdam and the Ezra Society in Antwerp because they assisted emigrants *en route* overseas. Likewise, associations in Germany and Austria that helped Jews in transit received JCA subventions, as did, in 1913, a committee in Basle performing the same services. The London Board of Guardians for the Relief of the Jewish Poor, which was interested in sending Jewish *émigrés* to overseas destinations outside the Americas, received support for many years beginning in 1905. This Board helped hundreds of clients in this way each year; in 1907 it sent 665 people overseas, to Canada (breaking its own general rule), South Africa, New Zealand and Australia. Because JCA was so much concerned with the possibility that Jewish women travelling alone might be the prey of white slavers, it contributed to the Jewish Association for the Protection of Girls and Women in London, which in the year 1906 alone inspected 782 ships and 37,982 passengers in England and Argentina. Similarly, JCA in 1910 helped the Association pour la Répression de la Traite des Blanches, which maintained agents at the railway stations in Paris, and the Association pour la Protection de la Jeune Fille Israélite, which had committees in Cherbourg and Boulogne.

Nor did all this exhaust the list of beneficiaries. For several years before the First World War there was a loan kassa in Prague, with hundreds of members, that received help from JCA.

The general pattern into which these benefactions fell was largely within the two major fields of JCA's interest: support of

113

educational institutions, and help to Jews leaving Europe for overseas destinations.

PART II

THE INTER-WAR YEARS

During the First World War the difficulties of communication between Paris and South America made transfers of money nearly impossible. Curiously, however, sending funds to the Near East and Poland seems to have been possible. At various times between 1915 and 1918 when Turkey was an active ally of Germany, JCA transferred funds to the German Consul-General in Smyrna for the JCA farm at Or Yehuda and to Constantinople for the relief of poor Jews in that city and in Asiatic Turkey. To Palestine, which until the victories of General Allenby in 1917 and 1918 was under Turkish rule, JCA managed to transmit considerable sums for the use of the orange growers, for the relief of the poor and for the JCA administration. Most surprising was the dispatch of money for the benefit of vocational schools in Warsaw and other cities in what had been Russian Poland, an area conquered and occupied by the German Army within a year or so after the outbreak of war in August 1914.

In general, however, the 1914–18 period was one of virtual hibernation for JCA. The settlements in Argentina and Canada maintained themselves. The Brazilian colony, Quatro-Irmãos, as we have seen, lost a large part of its population. In Palestine there was a severe economic depression, and the situation varied from place to place. Jews were often subjected to arrest and harassment by the Turkish military because of a probably justified suspicion that they were pro-Allies at heart. (The Turks did uncover an active Jewish spy-ring serving the British – the Nili Conspiracy.) The Jews in Palestine were also under pressure to adopt Turkish citizenship, which carried the obligation of military service. In consequence, almost 40 per cent of the 80,000 Jews who were in Palestine in 1914 left, some JCA/Rothschild colonists among them. However, certain areas, notably Galilee, survived the war with little bad effect. The same can unfortunately not be said of the networks of committees, elementary and vocational schools and loan kassas that JCA had established in western Russia and Romania. These institutions lay athwart the path of the advancing German armies and were, for all practical purposes, wiped out.

After the war, the nature of JCA activities and thereby the history of JCA entered a new phase. The following pages relate the variety of JCA programmes and the countries in which they were carried out during the inter-war years.

CHAPTER 7

Argentina after the First World War

On 31 December 1913 JCA counted 26,648 Jewish people living in its Argentine colonies, of whom 18,900 were members of colonists' families.[1] At the end of 1918 the comparable figures were 26,698 and 18,763 respectively. Thus, during these five years the population of the settlements had maintained itself with remarkable stability. At the same time, in response to wartime conditions, there had been some change in farming practices, and notably a shift to wheat from other cereals. Hectares planted to wheat had expanded from about 90,000 in 1913 to 125,000 in 1918, while flax had been halved to 25,000. Both the total area under cultivation and the average cultivated area per colonist had decreased. On the other hand, the cattle stock had grown from 60,000 to 85,000 and sheep from 4,000 to 14,000, all this in response to strong export demand.

The relationship between the colonists and JCA

If the essential pattern of production had not changed much during the war, the same could not be said of the spirit of the colonists. They were more ready and better prepared than they had been in the past to manifest their feelings of opposition to and dislike of JCA. Not that some had been reluctant as early as 1900 to battle fiercely with JCA over the form of the contracts and to criticise it in the press. Again, in 1910 the Mauricio settlers had brought lawsuits against JCA to win freedom to sell their holdings at their own, not JCA's, pleasure, and applauded Jazanovich on his anti-JCA 'crusade'. But there was not a concerted, organised effort to oppose JCA until after the First World War. In 1910 an association of all the co-operatives in the JCA colonies had been formed, but this was not noticeably militant. In 1923, however, the co-operatives established what eventually came to be called the Fraternidad Agraria, whose avowed purpose, said one of its founders, Marcos Wortman of Clara colony, was to fight JCA and uphold the dignity of the colonists in opposition

117

to it.[2] The relationship between JCA and the settlers was inherently one that could very easily give rise to conflict.

We shall examine the built-in divisive factors in a moment, but first we would like to mention certain extraneous influences which helped to strengthen the atmosphere of opposition. In 1917 there took place an attempt to unionise Argentine agricultural workers in which some members of the governing body of Fondo Comunal, the big co-operative in Clara colony, were prominent. This incipient movement to organise the workers was soon crushed by a wave of arrests. The movement, or at least the participation of the Jewish co-operative leaders in it, had been inspired in part by the Russian Revolution, the course of which the colonists followed with great interest, and which kindled in some of them, socialists or children of socialists in Russia, primordial feelings of class war. In fact, as some of the colonists saw the antagonism between themselves and JCA, they were the proletariat, the providers of labour, while JCA was the provider of capital. As Judith Elkin, a leading student of Latin-American Jewry, puts it,[3] 'To the settlers the JCA was the patron', the traditionally familiar Latin American figure who protected the farmers working for him but also exercised 'control over their lives. They left with an attitude of resentment against JCA that persists to this day.' An added irritant was the personality of the head of JCA's Buenos Aires office during and after the First World War, Isaac Starkmeth. A man of Russian origin, his rigidity and strict adherence to the letter of the law alienated even his principal subordinates.

Notwithstanding the attempts to unionise the farm workers, and notwithstanding some settlers' Marxist ideology or the personality of the JCA director, the objective situation was such that conflict between JCA and the colonists was inevitable. When the colonies were first established JCA had been an all-providing foster parent, furnishing food, housing, land to be worked and the animals and implements for working it. That JCA, providing the colonists with the means of existence, stood to some extent *in loco parentis* was clearly recognised by the colonists themselves. In the history of the Fondo Comunal co-operative in Clara colony it is written:

The new inhabitants encountered in the New World,
especially in the first years, complete economic and social
disorientation. . . . The logical result was that JCA supplied
whatever was necessary: schools, synagogues, health
institutions, credit, representation with the police and the
government and all other necessities of social and cultural

life. In this way the JCA administration concentrated in itself all the development of the social, cultural and economic life of the colony.[4]

So pervasive was the influence of JCA in the early years that the book goes on to say: 'it appeared quite natural that a couple desirous of getting married would approach the JCA administration to inquire whether they possessed the constancy to make it sensible for them to enter into the marriage contract.' Indeed, JCA had more power over the lives and fate of the colonists than many a parent has over a grown child – certainly more over their economic lives.

At least four perennial bones of contention should be mentioned, to list only the more important. These were the terms of the contract of sale of land to the colonists, the area to be allowed each colonist family, the allocation of farms to sons and sons-in-law, and the provision of credit. All these issues, except perhaps for that involving sons, were starkly economic. The price and the time at which a farmer could take title were obviously matters of the first importance, and control was in JCA's hands; likewise the acreage he could acquire; likewise the amount and terms of the credit he could obtain. No one facing an entity with power over such fundamental questions could feel comfortable in the situation, even if there were perfect harmony between the parties in attitude and expectation. Certainly when their aims and objects differed widely, as was the case, friction was bound to result. In addition to the economic conflict, Judith Elkin points to the issue of acculturation dividing the settlers from JCA.[5] JCA attached high priority to the matter of their integration, but the settlers themselves found little of value to integrate with.

> Argentina lacked the great nationalizing institutions – schools, adult education, especially, and a homogenizing industrial plant – that might have served to integrate the immigrants into national life. The absorption of immigrants was retarded by the absence of social structures with the capacity to integrate them into the intellectual, economic, or patriotic life of the republic.

In 1917 JCA eased its terms for the transfer of their farms to the colonists by permitting those who had been on their farms for five years to start anticipating payments. In 1923 this provision was further liberalised: a five-year settler was now permitted to take title, subject to a mortgage to JCA, whereas previously an eight-year occupancy had been required. However, the so-called 'moral' clauses of the contracts still remained – the requirements that the colonist till his land with his own and his family's labour, that he live on the property, and that he should not alienate any of it. The most irksome of the provisions was that which gave JCA the right, up to three years after the date of sale, to re-acquire property at the colonist's original purchase price. This was intended to enable JCA to rid a colony of an undesirable resident. Colonists complained bitterly that such a provision made it very difficult for them to sell, but in fact JCA does not seem to have made much, if any, use of this 'buy-back' right.

With the value of the land having increased to some hundreds of pesos a hectare, while the contract, drawn up years before, set a price that had been deliberately fixed below the then market – perhaps 50 pesos a hectare – it would have taken a very strong character, committed to the point of self-abnegation to the ideal of maintaining a viable Jewish farm population in Argentina, to resist trying to take advantage of such a profitable margin.[6] So the colonists went to law to abrogate the contracts or tried to devise other stratagems to obtain the profit that a sale could bring long before the expiration of the contract. The courts, as the JCA staff noted with some bitterness, were inclined to disregard the 'moral' clauses and pay heed only to evidence as to whether the monetary payments had been made. In this way, as we have seen, some of the colonists in Mauricio had been able to obtain title to their farms. This attitude of the courts made it difficult for JCA to win the many lawsuits it brought to expel farmers who had completely neglected to observe the provisions in question.[7] On the other hand, in 1921 and again in 1946, the Argentine legislature enacted laws that might have been written to please JCA, for they were designed to encourage farmers to cultivate their soil with their own hands and not break up their patrimony.

As time passed, the controversy over the form of contract tended to become less acute, as more and more colonists became *émancipés*, land-owners in fee simple, and thus free of JCA's restrictions. In 1922 so many colonists in Mauricio had attained this status that JCA withdrew its administrator from the colony. By 1934 almost exactly 50 per cent of the 3,144 colonists then on farms in Argentina had acquired ownership. This ratio grew with time: in 1948 it was 86 per cent of a total of 2,600 colonists.

While the dispute over the contracts petered out in time, two other subjects of dissension – the proper area to be allotted to a colonist and the question of how JCA should treat the sons – continued to excite lively controversy. One factor that influenced the pressure for an enlargement of the holdings was the beginning of the shift from horses and oxen to motors as the source of motive and other kinds of power on the farm. The provision of

3a Saskatchewan, Canada, 1919. Jewish farm workers

3b Saskatchewan, Canada, 1919. Farm machinery purchased with JCA funds

4a USSR, between the wars. Improved farming methods in the Jewish rural communities helped by JCA

4b Ukraine, pre-1925. Loan kassa

feed for draught animals had occupied no less than 25 per cent of the total farm area. Now a large area was being freed to produce crops for sale. This movement began in the 1920s in the older, better-off colonies like Moisesville but was not completed in the poorer, more remote colonies like Baron Hirsch until the 1950s.[8] A farmer who has invested thousands of dollars or pesos in buying a motor-driven harvester-thresher, for example, feels great inducement to spread this overhead expense over as large an acreage as possible. In any case the original grants of 150 hectares or so in certain marginal areas, like colony Baron Hirsch, were simply too small to be economic. As late as 1960 the Jewish farms in this colony, though they ran to 245 hectares, were less than half the size of the average holding in the region.[9] Why JCA resisted the pressure for more acreage for so long – it acceded finally and officially in 1950 – is not clear. The reason put forward was that it had to maintain reserves of land for new immigrants (it retained about 250,000 hectares, most of it of poorer quality than the already settled areas). Perhaps JCA's attitude was inspired by the events of the Löwenthal era back in 1891, when at times it appeared that there would be insufficient space for a horde of arrivals. But this argument seemed specious in the 1930s, because after the First World War not many Jewish immigrants came to Argentina. In the 1920s there were 5,000–6,000 a year on average, and of these only a few hundred went to the settlements. By the 1930s Jewish immigration was practically nil.

JCA used the same argument – the need to maintain large reserves – in the unending quarrel over the question of allocations for sons. The Association also invoked other and better reasons on this issue, which seemed to come up at every meeting between staff and colonists. One was that JCA had been committed to rescuing Jews from Russia, and once the family had been settled in Argentina JCA had no further obligation. Second, in the populist political climate that prevailed in Argentina in the first quarter of the twentieth century, it was necessary to avoid making it appear that Jewish farmers were building up latifundia. Therefore, JCA made it a rule that at least 10 kilometres (later reduced to 5) must separate the sons' or sons-in-law's holdings from the fathers'. Many other conditions were originally imposed on the sons – that they be married, that there be other brothers remaining at home to help the fathers with the farm work – conditions that were softened or eliminated as time passed, until in 1950 they were dropped altogether.

Even though JCA had a modicum of reason on its side, its stance in this matter seems indicative of a rather frozen attitude. A position had been taken early in the twentieth century that the colonists should not appear to be land-grabbers; and JCA maintained this position until the middle of the century, though by that time the settlers, or rather their children or grandchildren, had long been citizens of Argentina and were mature enough and knew the country well enough for it to be presumed that their judgment about Argentine reactions should be respected. Perhaps more strangely, JCA, in making the settlement of sons difficult, was putting obstacles in the way of reaching one of its chief objectives, the building up of a permanent Jewish farming class in Argentina. It was also flying in the face of reality. In the decade after 1918, 40 per cent of new installations (they averaged about sixty-five a year) were of sons and sons-in-law. In the period 1930–5 they accounted for 50 per cent.

The matter of credit was also a perennial subject of discussion and argument. This is not surprising, for if a farmer needs anything he needs to be able to borrow. Here JCA followed a judicious course of yea-and-nay, acceding to some requests and refusing those it considered unnecessary. However, in the too-frequent cases of natural disaster that afflicted the settlements it was invariably willing to extend a helping hand. For example, Montefiore colony suffered great hardship in the 1924–5 season when its crops were devastated by insect infestations and early frosts and many families left. JCA hastened to bring aid to those who stayed; it supplied each family with 10–12 cows, bulls, stallions and a complete set of equipment; the settlement's co-operative was reorganised with the help of the other Jewish co-operatives; and JCA made the renewed institution a sizeable advance.

Just as helpful as JCA's readiness to extend credit was its willingness, not to say alacrity, to cancel debts when colonists were in difficulties and sometimes, indeed, even when they were not. We have seen that the amounts due from the settlers were reduced by 25 per cent at the time of the Baron's death in 1896. In 1914–15 Moisesville, the most firmly established of the colonies, was severely affected by floods, followed by intensely damaging locust infestations the following year. Many settlers left. In order to induce the remainder to stay, JCA sharply reduced their debts. Again, during the Great Depression of the 1930s JCA deferred the payment of debts and cancelled or reduced the interest due.

The capability of granting, withholding or altering the terms of credit is tantamount to the power to permit a struggling group of farmers to breathe freely, inhale with difficulty, or not breathe at all. Thus JCA's generally lax policy in the matter of collection of debts made life easier for the colonists. At times JCA had spasms of conscience and decided to tighten things up – or at least to update its records. It therefore resolved, in 1919, to have all its accounts paid up to date, but whether it took any further positive action is not clear. Some years later, in 1922, it made an effort to expel those colonists who had not made payments of at least 2,000 pesos or had neglected their annual obligations for a long time.[10]

On the whole, however, the colonists' requests for loans were turned down often enough for them to feel justified in complaining about the Association's severity. The history of Fondo Comunal[11] contains a record of 40 years of requests for credit, most of which were not granted. By the 1920s the colonists individually and their co-operatives collectively were well enough established for JCA to be no longer their sole source of credit; they were able to borrow not only from the National Bank, but from local agricultural and other banks, some of which they themselves had helped to establish.

Enough has been said to indicate that the relationship between JCA and the colonists was complex and ambiguous. If JCA was, especially for the early colonists, a surrogate parent, modern psychologists know that the feelings between many parents and children partake of the emotions of both love and hate – especially when the children are grown and begin to feel themselves individuals in their own right. Like many natural parents, JCA had a hard time appreciating that its 'children' had attained maturity. It could not recognise that the time of tutelage might be over.[12]

One of the major objectives of the establishment of the Fraternidad Agraria was to force JCA to accord the colonists proper respect by requiring it to consult with their representatives. Such an infringement of its liberty of action JCA would not tolerate, and when the first assembly of the Fraternidad was convened in Buenos Aires in 1925 the JCA directorate refused to meet its officers. In 1926 the JCA staff relented and did meet the farmers' delegates; but a year later it was the Fraternidad's turn to be angry and, far from meeting with JCA, it spent its 1927 convention denouncing the Association. These contentions may have been in part matters of personality rather than substance. Wortman's fervent socialism and Starkmeth's rigidity made an explosive mixture. JCA and the Fraternidad had no relationship to speak of until the Great Depression of the 1930s forced them to collaborate.

The colonies, 1920–30, and the 'quintas'

After the drop in prices incident to the world-wide commodity crash of 1919–21, Argentine agriculture recovered and enjoyed reasonable stability and even prosperity until the 1930s. The Jewish farmers shared in the general prosperity. There were then 120,000 farmers in Argentina, of whom 3,100 (2.6 per cent) were Jewish.[13] In Entre-Rios province, which Oungre claimed had been opened for agriculture by Jews, 1,390 out of 15,314 farmers, nearly 10 per cent, were Jewish. (The number of Jews then in Argentina was 200,000, 2 per cent of the total population of 10 million.)

The state of well-being that the Argentine farmers enjoyed in this period was due not only to better incomes but to the gradual introduction of the internal combustion engine. Not only did the technological system of the Jewish farmers change, but so did their life-style – and its acceptance by JCA. Pianos and good furniture no longer caused raised eyebrows. However, JCA was still concerned enough to record with disapproval that settlers coming from Bessarabia were free-spenders who used their income to support a relatively expensive mode of living, while the Russians were frugal and thrifty.

The number of Jews in the farm areas increased somewhat in the first three post-war years. By 1922 there were 29,781 Jews living in the settlements, of whom about two-thirds consisted of colonist families. The number remained almost static through to 1930 when it was 29,606. These figures, however, should not be interpreted as evidence of immobility. There was a continual drift out of the colonies, for the reasons we have cited and for one other – the often-remarked-on Jewish interest in advanced education. In 1920 the JCA report noted that the younger generation who were sent to urban institutions to study tended not to return to the colonies, which offered a limited field of activity to an ambitious young man who wanted to be a lawyer, accountant or university teacher. But the exodus was balanced by an influx of about 500 or 600 Jewish immigrants each year.

In the 1920s another demographic tendency manifested itself which had grave portents for the future, particularly with reference to the Baron's dream of a permanent large Jewish farming settlement in Argentina. At that time the number of non-Jewish inhabitants of the colonies became noticeable. In the ensuing decades more and more non-Jews drifted in while, as we shall see, the Jews tended to leave, so that by the 1950s non-Jews became the majority. Considering, on the one hand, the attractions of city life, and, on the other, the almost complete cessation of Jewish immigration after 1930, this was hardly a surprising development.

JCA had decided, as early as 1913, that it would not actively recruit new colonists but would accept those who came voluntarily and who had some resources of their own to invest. In order to encourage such spontaneous settlement, what was called the *quinta* system was instituted. From newcomers who had gained some experience in farm work in Argentina, those who seemed most promising were selected and placed on *quintas*, i.e. comparatively small lots of 15–25 hectares. The idea was that the husband would derive income from working for colonists in the vicinity and produce, say, vegetables on his own land, while his wife and children would tend a poultry flock and help with the vegetables. The *quinteros* were provided with small houses, fenced lots, animals and implements.

A great advantage of the *quintas* was that they were cheaper to establish than a conventional farm. Each year, beginning in 1923, 50 or 60 *quinteros* were settled, and of these a number were chosen to be given the opportunity to become fully fledged colonists. These selections were made on the basis of a searching scrutiny on the part of the JCA staff, a scrutiny that did not cease when the *quintero* became a colonist. As late as 1935, even though maintenance of the Jewish farm population was becoming difficult, 18 colonist families (who may not have been *quinteros*) were expelled as 'bad elements, behind on their payments and not personally working their lots'. So, *quinteros* or not, those given the status of colonist remained under JCA's watchful eye. The *quinta* system appeared so promising that Louis Oungre, reporting on his inspection of the Argentine colonies in 1928, recommended that all new settlers start as *quinteros*. Unfortunately, not long thereafter, the steep decline in farm prices resulting from the Great Depression was under way, the deleterious effect of which on farmers' income in Argentina, as in North America, was intensified by many years of drought; in consequence, newcomers lost all ambition to become *quinteros*, and the settlers already on *quintas* neglected their lands, having to find other ways of making a living.

Argentine government takes over the schools

An important organisational change took place in the periods just before and after the First World War. It has been noted how concerned JCA was with the education of the children of its colonists. By 1914 there was a well developed network of about 100 schools in the colonies, the curricula and standards of which were supervised by JCA. However, an education law had been passed which made it impossible for a private school system like JCA's to continue. The Association therefore decided on the generous gesture of transferring its schools and their quite elaborate appurtenances, without any charge, to the national Ministry of Education. These appurtenances included notably the many houses for teachers that JCA had built in order to induce them to come and stay in the comparatively remote rural provinces. The only compensation JCA asked and received was that the school buildings be available for religious instruction at the end of the regular sessions. The transfer of the buildings was effected in stages and was largely completed by 1919, though a few schools remained with JCA until 1923. In that year about 7,000 pupils were receiving post-school religious instruction.

JCA's and the colonists' expenditure may have been reduced by the government's take-over of the schools in the settlements, but not for long; the Education Ministry, it soon appeared, was neglecting maintenance. JCA found it necessary to protest to the Ministry regarding the condition of the buildings, but the Association was more concerned about this matter than the Ministry, for in 1924 the former agreed to spend 105,000 pesos on repairs, and there is no record that the government paid anything. The JCA Council further agreed that in subsequent years it would appropriate annually enough money to cover one-third of the costs of necessary repairs.

JCA continued to maintain its interest in the religious instruction it had initiated for the Jewish residents of Buenos Aires and other cities. In 1925 it provided eighty-seven such courses attended by 3,815 pupils. Later, when JCA began to feel the pinch of the Depression on its income, it decided to ask the Argentine Jews who were benefiting to pay the costs themselves. It was found that they were well able to do this, so that by 1930 JCA's contributions for this purpose could be reduced to almost nil.[14]

Oungre's Report – and Aronstein's

In 1928 Louis Oungre, the redoubtable Director-General of JCA, paid a long visit to Argentina, spending time at every colony and, as was his custom, writing afterwards a comprehensive, confidential report for the Council. On the whole, Oungre was pleased with what he saw. He had to admit that the question of the settlement of sons was controversial, but he felt that JCA's position on this issue and on the issues of settler participation in decisions and on contracts was well taken, though he did let slip his impression that JCA's stance was perhaps a little too rigid. In 1934–5 Georges Aronstein, a sub-director in the Paris office, paid an equally long visit to Argentina and wrote an even longer report. While Aronstein also wrote elegantly, his style was not so pithy as Oungre's. The important difference between these reports, however, was in the substance, not the style. While Aronstein covered much the same ground – the seemingly eternal questions of land for the sons, the status of the contracts, the position of the *quinteros* – the real issue that concerned him was the 'stagnation' of the colonies, an expression that, despite his tendency to circumlocution, he used plainly and openly.

The difference between these two reporters was partly a difference in time; Oungre's visit took place after a period of general prosperity, Aronstein's took place six years later, years marked by the deepest depression in capitalist history, which in Argentina had been aggravated by drought and insect infestation. By the end of Aronstein's visit a small measure of recovery had been felt in Argentine agriculture, but in essence his overview was bleak.

The co-operatives, which JCA never forbore to praise notwithstanding their bitter criticisms of their surrogate parent, and which Oungre in the main found to be prospering, were declared by Aronstein to be on the edge of bankruptcy. Some of the smaller ones indeed had already gone over the brink, but had been reorganised and set going again by JCA. Even the strongest of them, reported Aronstein – those at Moisesville (Mutua Agrícola) and Clara (Fondo Comunal) – were technically bankrupt, but because their largest creditor was the National Bank, which was lenient for political reasons, they were permitted to continue operations. The reason for this general collapse was that during the years of prosperity the co-operatives had been willing to extend credit freely to the farmers, without any provision for amortisation; now that hard times had come, the co-operatives' assets consisted of the farmers' paper, which with the decline of prices to fractions of their pre-Depression levels was worthless. The Fondo Comunal had been bold enough – it was the only co-operative to do so – to build a huge grain elevator that dominated the level landscape. When this structure was completed, however, the co-operative was unable to pay for it; but because the builder, who remained the owner, had no alternative use for it, Fondo Comunal was able to rent it for a very reasonable fee. JCA was forced into the position of taking possession of the grain delivered to the co-operatives by their members, so that the produce could not be seized by the creditors, and the farmers were thus deprived of what little they had earned for their labour in those parlous years.

JCA, in collaboration with its former enemy, the Fraternidad, strove to preserve the co-operative structure because of its importance to the colonists. Not only did the co-operatives provide a sales outlet for the farmers that was in their own control; but on the buying side, where the colonists had been pretty well at the mercy of such traders as happened to be in the neighbourhood, the co-operatives provided competition which lowered the cost of seed, barbed wire, farm equipment, etc. They also tried to upgrade the farmers' livestock by supplying them with superior animals. They were largely responsible for social and cultural events, such as lectures, concerts and dramatic performances. In addition, they provided advocacy for the colonists in confrontations with banks, civil authorities and, not least, JCA. Oungre summed up the situation in somewhat flowery terms. The co-operatives, he said, are 'l'émanation des colonies, leur représentation, leur protection, leur banque'.[15]

As for the *quintas* in which Oungre had placed such high hopes for the future growth of the colonies, Aronstein reported that in the years since 1931 they had not increased, that the hundred or so that still existed in 1934 were utterly uncared for, being used not for farming but as suburban residences by their holders, who, if they were lucky, had been able to resort to their previous occupations, for example shoemaking. Aronstein noted with regret that only a handful of Germans had gone to the settlements (Hitler had been in power for two years when Aronstein wrote). However willing they might be, he declared, the essentially urbanised German Jews were just not fit for the rough and isolated life of the pampas. In making this observation, he was somewhat hasty. As we shall see, two or three years later some hundreds of families from Germany were settled in the colonies.

Immigration situation

Aronstein's report sounds a distinct and unmistakable note of melancholy and resignation. Oungre used the word 'stagnation', but Aronstein really meant it. He suggested various schemes to revive the colonies, but his proposals had little force or conviction. The great lack was new settlers. In part this was due to the general paucity of Jewish newcomers in the country. Except for the outstanding year of 1923, when 12,000 arrived, Jewish immigration ran below the figures for the pre-First World War period. This was at a time when there were more than 100,000 homeless Jewish refugees from Russia spread over the European continent and whom the Jewish migration agencies were most anxious to place somewhere, anywhere, overseas. This also was a time when Polish Jews, 3 million strong, were eager to leave that country which, itself freed from the oppression of the Russian Czars, nevertheless fastened the bonds of anti-Semitism tighter and tighter around its hated minority. The Polish Sejm, if it could do little else, could always pass a law making it harder for Jewish inn-keepers, liquor-dealers or artisans to carry on business, and easier for Polish co-operative organisations to compete with Jewish retailers. Polish Jews did go to Palestine in tens of thousands, and would have gone to the United States but for the restrictive American immigration laws passed in 1924; but they did not go to Argentina.

JCA was inclined to blame adverse publicity about the settlements in the Jewish press and the high cost of the ocean voyage from Europe to South America. These explanations do not seem to be adequate; bad reports about the settlements should not have deterred emigrants from going to Argentina's cities, where the bulk of the country's Jewish population was located and, in general, doing well. JCA's reports, even when, like Aronstein's, they may have been less than enthusiastic about the state of agriculture, did not fail to point out how many of the descendants of the early arrivals were doctors, lawyers or university professors, or active in many businesses, such as the export of grain, the retailing of jewellery, cloth, furniture or motor car accessories. Nor could the Argentine Jewish community be blamed. In 1923, with JCA's help, it set up Soprotimis, an acronym for an organisation devoted to helping newcomers by, among other things, providing guidance and shelter, legal help, vocational training and instruction in Spanish.

The reasons for the comparative paucity of Jewish immigration must be sought elsewhere, and in truth lie with the Argentine government. 'The Russian Revolution [of 1917] increased the government's fear of similar revolutionary activity in Argentina. Since the Jews were generally identified as "Russians", anti-revolutionary fervour developed into overt anti-Semitism.'[16] There was an outbreak of extreme violence and pillage against the Jews in Buenos Aires in January 1919, following on a general strike which the authorities had portrayed as a Bolshevik revolution during which a Jewish 'dictator-president' would attempt to seize control of the country. It was not surprising that a regime that lent itself to such nonsense would create administrative difficulties for Jewish immigrants in subsequent years. After 1930, when power had passed into the hands of reactionaries as the result of a coup, the new government put into force severe limitations on immigration, allowing in only 'authentic' farmers and close relatives of citizens. In this respect it followed the same line as Canada and Brazil during the Depression. Barriers were put up just when ease of access was most needed, on the eve of Hitler's coming to power. JCA, which was accepted as a certifying agent for farming immigrants, was especially careful as to whom it certified, because

129

it needed to retain this status in order to help such Jews as were in this category.

Thus, Jewish immigration fell to less than 2,000 annually in the first half of the 1930s; immigration, to which Aronstein had looked to invigorate the colonies, was a hope that was destroyed almost as soon as it was uttered. Indeed, in 1934, coincident with his report, the Jewish population in the colonies showed a decline. We have seen that in 1930 the figure was 29,606; by 1934 it had fallen to 25,796, but it recovered somewhat to 26,110 in 1937, the last year before the Second World War for which a record is available. Despite the multitude of Jewish organisations offering entertainment and culture by way of films and lectures, and the many others that gave the farmers the opportunity to use their time for good works or religious practices, the social pull of urban centres and the economic pull of urban incomes, at which JCA had so often looked askance, were too strong, and the farm population began to drift away.

Also, it must be confessed that JCA's figures of the Jewish farm population were somewhat inflated. It counted among the colonists all the émancipés; and an émancipé family, especially after the three-year 'buy-back' period had ended, was free to live anywhere. When there were only a few such families, just after the First World War, this statistical practice did not mean very much, but by 1937, about half the colonists had achieved their independence. We know that 40–45 per cent of the émancipés had left the farms during the 1930s, so that by the end of the decade JCA was including in its figures some thousands of settlers who had moved away.

Aronstein in 1934–5 could not name more than three families living in the colonies who had come from Germany. Fortunately, with the passage of time JCA was able to enlarge this utterly negligible figure. It prepared a new colony, Avigdor, in the province of Entre-Rios, for the reception of German immigrants, though by no means all such newcomers went there. To make sure that they would know what to expect, JCA had one member of the family come to Argentina and spend at first a year (later only three months) on a colonist's farm, learning about life and work in that milieu. JCA also gave candidates agricultural training, both in Argentina and in Germany. Twenty-two German families were placed in 1936 and 77 more in 1937. Altogether, 430 families from Germany were placed in the colonies during the Nazi period.[17] Not a large number, considering the circumstances, but the beginning at least of a measurable movement.

Into the war years

In the years that followed, up to the outbreak of the Second World War, there was no basic change in the position of the JCA colonies. There was virtually no immigration. The old issues persisted – of JCA versus the Fraternidad; of the co-operatives and the settlers trying to secure more loans from JCA and on better terms; of what to do about sons who wanted to become farmers. These conflicts did, however, ease considerably, perhaps because both parties were tired of them and because they had found co-operation possible during the dark Depression years. JCA in fact showed itself more willing to accept the farmers' viewpoint, a tendency that culminated in the London Conference of 1950 which will be described in a later chapter. In the meantime, the Association acted to conciliate the colonists by reducing or cancelling large portions of their debts to it. In 1935 interest charges were reduced, as also were land prices to buyers who would pay cash immediately on transfer of title.

The new settlement of Avigdor, which at one time had housed more than 400 families of German refugees, had by 1940 only 119 remaining. In common with all JCA settlers on new lands, those in Avigdor were plagued by locusts and poor weather conditions. However, with typical German discipline they worked hard to make a start, helped by JCA instruction. Not only did they carry out their farming tasks but they installed all the facilities that an isolated village would need – a synagogue, a school, a library, a social hall, a co-operative, even a fortnightly periodical; they organised an orchestra, dramatics and sports. But these activities were not able to restrain a terrible quarrelsomeness which afflicted the colony and necessitated the establishment of an arbitration council to decide on the location and division of water from the wells, property lines, etc. Even more disturbing, as far as JCA was concerned, was the pull of opportunity to do technical or professional work elsewhere; this caused a further decline in the population, which by 1945 had fallen to 104 families.[18]

JCA for its part, after the war began, continued its policy of leniency to its farmer-debtors. For the period April 1941–March 1943 it reduced the interest charge to 3 per cent and cancelled all interest in the case of colonies founded after 1 January 1936 – which meant Avigdor principally. It also extended to eleven years from eight the period allowed a settler to repay his installation costs, with the first three years free of interest. All these concessions were intended to make it easier for the settlers to become owners. And indeed, by 1941 half of the 3435 JCA farmers (who with their families totalled 17,415 people) had title.[19]

As the old problems began to recede, the JCA management was increasingly concerned with the tendency of the Jewish farmers to leave agriculture and occupy themselves in business or the professions. From the perspective of the 1980s, it is easy to say that this movement was only natural, as agriculture became more highly mechanised and fewer people were needed to maintain or even exceed the previous level of output. If the worried staff of JCA had cast their eyes to the north they might have found some consolation. In the United States the farm population reached its highest level in 1910, when there were over 30 million people, a third of the country's population, earning their livelihood chiefly from the soil. Since then there has been a continuous decline, until today when there are perhaps 2 million farmers and their families living on the land in the United States. Yet, as is well known, the output of American agriculture has increased enormously even as the number of producers has declined. But the JCA management, believing firmly in the importance of the existence of a Jewish farming class, could only deplore its decline within the Jewish population of Argentina.

All JCA's yieldings and favours were of little ultimate effect, as Jews continued to leave the farms; and this was a trend that JCA could hardly expect to reverse. As Judith Elkin puts it, the Jewish farm movement was romantic – 'Jewish farmers were bringing to a close the epoch of belief in the possibility of auto-emancipation through self-labour.'[20]

Map 4   Eastern Europe between the wars

CHAPTER 8

The Situation in Russia

Russia in 1920–1

By 1921 the various attempts to overthrow the Bolshevik government had been suppressed, and the war between Poland and Russia was over. When peace was made, it left the borders more or less as they had been defined by the Treaties of Brest-Litovsk and Versailles. A measure of order had been restored to Russia, but to a Russia reduced from its 1914 limits, for on its western border there was a whole set of new countries – Finland, Esthonia, Latvia, Lithuania and Poland – which had been carved principally out of what had been the czarist empire; also, Bessarabia, formerly Russia's southwesterly province, with a population of 800,000 Jews, was now part of Romania. In the Ukraine and White Russia, the principal areas of Jewish habitation, the destruction and devastation wrought by the war had been great, but the brutal civil wars that followed brought even more death and damage, especially to the Jews, who were marked out as special victims by many of the right-wing 'armies' – or, as a large proportion of these were in fact, roving bands of raiders and pogromists. No less than 1,520 pogroms were counted in the period 1918–20, in which, out of about 3 million Jews, some 200,000 were killed and 300,000 orphaned. The most tragic victims of the civil war were these lost and abandoned children, the *bezprizonie*, great numbers of whom wandered the roads and byways of south Russia, stealing and scavenging what they could.

By 1921 however there was one development that held out some hope for the future. Over this scene of death and devastation there was one unquestioned ruler – the Bolshevik government, headed by Lenin in Moscow, which was able to impose a very considerable measure of authority and order. Once this was accomplished, one of the government's chief tasks was to accumulate a supply of foreign exchange so that goods could be purchased from the outside world. In pre-war czarist times wheat had been Russia's premier export and the principal source of foreign exchange. Now the government would have to revive wheat exports or devise other methods of acquiring *valuta*, foreign money. It was this problem and its attempted solution that involved the Jewish agencies: ORT; the American Jewish Joint Distribution Committee (JDC), a new giant in the field which was created in 1916; and the old giant, JCA, which was now somewhat overshadowed by its rich New World colleague.

ORT and JCA

ORT was founded in 1880 with the name *Obshchestvo Rasprostraneniya Truda sredi Yevreyev*, meaning Society for the Promotion of Trades and Agriculture among Jews. (The initials were later adapted in English to stand for Organisation for Rehabilitation through Training.) It was one Jewish organisation that seemed to have been able to keep at least a skeleton staff in existence in Russia throughout the First World War. Perhaps this was because it was an indigenous agency, with its activities confined to Russia (until 1921, when World ORT Union was established in Berlin). One of ORT's founding fathers, Leon Bramson, was prominent enough in Russia's Jewish community to be selected as one of the members of JCA's St Petersburg Committee under Baron de Guenzburg. The two organisations were obviously well-known to each other – and still are.[1]

ORT in 1921 called the attention of JCA to the terrible plight of the Jews in southern Russia. Here, it will be remembered, at the beginning of the nineteenth century, Jewish farm colonies had been set up. By the end of the century, these colonies were in poor shape because of antiquated methods of cultivation, a lack of capital and the inability to acquire more land. In 1916 there had been 39,000 Jewish colonists, according to JCA's count. This figure had been reduced by 40 per cent at the height of the postwar troubles, and then had recovered somewhat to 29,500 by 1922. But the colonists were in terrible straits, for many had sold off or slaughtered their cattle and draft animals in order to survive – that is, those who were lucky: the unlucky ones had lost their animals, if not their lives, to the Red or White bandits who ravaged the countryside. And if some of them did have animals for ploughing, they had no seed to plant. So as a first step, in 1921, through the mediation of ORT, JCA managed to get some seed to them.

In the next year, conditions were more settled. More important, this was the year when Lenin took a giant step backward, instituting the New Economic Policy (NEP), under which individual small entrepreneurs were allowed a certain measure of freedom, albeit under close supervision. (Some observers thought the NEP marked the beginning of the end of Communism.) JCA was now prepared to mount a comprehensive effort. A veteran member of the pre-war staff, A. Sachs, was put in charge, and he obtained permission from the authorities to open an office in Kiev, capital of the Ukraine, from which to set up a full programme. This was to include work with the Jewish farmers in the old colonies, the establishment of loan kassas to lend money to artisans and *koustars* (artisans who worked from their homes), and assistance in building up vocational schools in southern and western Russia. JCA also again sent some seed grain into the country, through the intermediary of the Nansen Committee, an international aid organisation operating under the aegis of the League of Nations.

By 1923 and 1924 JCA's programme was in full swing. The major efforts were devoted to helping the inhabitants of the old farm colonies, who by 1924 had built their number up to nearly 37,000, not far below the pre-war total, as some old members returned and new ones joined. Only 20 per cent of the newcomers had been farmers; the rest had been artisans or petty traders. Eighteen new co-operatives were created to serve the 36 farm colonies in the *gubernias* (governments) of Kiev and Ekaterinoslav, in the Ukraine. JCA employed agronomists to instruct the farmers in modern methods, and through the co-operatives provided money for the purchase of seed, implements, forage, horses and cattle. It also encouraged the farmers to set up cheese factories, and helped finance no less than twenty-two of these. Vocational schools were started in the White Russian cities of Minsk, Homel, Mohilev and Vitebsk, often with the participation of JDC. The kassa system, which had been liquidated, was reinstituted through the efforts of JCA's old staff, and 120 kassas were initiated or reactivated. They would not have been able to get started without outside aid because the poverty-stricken Jewish population had absolutely no money to deposit; it was JCA and JDC (which had operated in Russia in 1921 under the wing of Herbert Hoover's Relief Administration) that together furnished the initial capital. By 1924 the Ukraine State Bank had also provided some funds; and JCA's share in the assets of these institutions had fallen to 20 per cent and JDC's to 12 per cent. By then JCA had had contact with 159 kassas and had made loans to 107; these had an average membership of nearly 400, so that the kassas receiving this help represented about 40,000 families.

By 1925 JCA had in three short years built up a considerable operation in Russia, especially in the Ukraine. It was helping the farmers through the medium of 23 co-operatives with 8,500 members; it was making more effective the teaching methods in

17 vocational schools with some 2,000 pupils; and it was assisting over 100 kassas which were buying and selling for their members as well as lending them money. But as the government and state banks increased their contributions to the kassas' capital, JCA's and JDC's participation declined.

At this juncture JCA decided to send A. Schmoll of its Paris staff to make a survey of its operations in the USSR. Schmoll went to Moscow, where JCA had now established its Russian headquarters, and then travelled through the Ukraine and White Russia, the field of JCA's operations. He was very pleased with what he saw. Though mindful of the terrible recent past, he felt that under the Bolshevik regime anti-Semitism would never return, and as further evidence of his confidence in the future he stated his conviction that JCA would be repaid the money it had lent the kassas and co-operatives, and moreover that it would be able to repatriate the money.[2] He noted that the currency was stable, more important that the government was efficient, and that the Jews were able to function reasonably well under the NEP.

In his survey of the vocational schools, Schmoll was delighted to discover that many staff members were the old teachers who had survived the war, and that Yiddish was the language of instruction. The directors were usually young Communists but they did not, Schmoll noted optimistically, interfere too much with operations. The chief trades taught were those of electrical installation, metalworking, construction work and carpentry. JDC had supplied the equipment, while JCA had financed 'special instruction', which meant teaching in Yiddish. Schmoll recommended that the JCA subventions continue, in order to promote instruction in Yiddish; otherwise non-Jewish peasants would get preference in admission.

JCA had helped the Jewish farmers in Ekaterinoslav and Kherson *gubernias* before 1914; now, after they had been ruined by the war and lost all their animals, the Association was assisting them to make a fresh start, adding something new – creameries, which numbered 24. Thirty-six colonies with 37,000 inhabitants were now recipients of JCA and JDC advances; these had been made through the agricultural co-operatives, 38 per cent of whose assets came from JCA, 22 per cent from JDC. The co-operatives, like the loan kassas in the towns, also provided medical services.

As regards the loan kassas, one of the main branches of JCA and JDC activity in Russia, Schmoll reported that 231 were registered, of which 114 had received JCA credits. JCA's proportion of their capital by now was down to 11 per cent and JDC's to 5 per cent. The kassas served individual artisans, collectives of artisans and petty merchants. Their loans totalled 1,750,000 roubles (about £175,000) but were limited to 100 roubles (£10) per borrower, a limit that Scholl thought was too restrictive.

JDC and Agro-Joint[3]

Schmoll of course saw something of what the American JDC had been doing in the USSR – which was a great deal. When the American Relief Administration ceased working in Russia in 1921, JDC made it clear that it was planning an expanded programme there. It sent out Dr Joseph Rosen, a well-known agronomist who was born in Russia. Rosen had been educated in the United States, where he had made a considerable reputation by developing 'Rosen Rye', a quickly ripening variety of rye that could be harvested in cold climates before the frosts set in. Rosen arranged the importation of seed corn and, more important for the Russians, tractors.

Rosen felt that the NEP would give Jews a chance to improve their economic status, not in the villages and little towns, but by transplanting themselves to farms. The dreams that had inspired the Baron de Hirsch and many others in the nineteenth century obviously still endured in the twentieth. But more than a dream inspired Rosen. Hundreds of thousands of Jews who had been peddlers or petty traders, or who had no defined occupation (*luftmenschen* – living on 'thin air') under the old regime, were now classed as *lishentsy* – 'declassed', without status – which also meant that they were deprived of civil rights, such as the right to sue, the right to vote and the right of their children to an education. Making farmers out of them would not only give them an occupation whereby they could earn their daily bread, but would also allow them to reacquire their civil status.

Not only was JDC eager to do something for the *lishentsy* and other poor Jews; but the Soviet government was eager for foreign goods, like the tractors that JDC could bring in, and for increased food supplies, which the Jewish farmers could produce. A marriage between JDC and the Soviet government therefore seemed made in Heaven, and it was consummated in 1924, the parties to the ceremony being the American Jewish Joint Agricultural Corporation (Agro-Joint), formed by JDC in 1924 with Rosen as President, and Comzet, the government-sponsored 'Committee for the Settlement of Jews on the Land'.

Many people of Zionist persuasion firmly believed that JDC was merely bent upon showing the world Jewish community that it was helping poor Jews, even though it was not doing it in

Palestine. It is true that many of JDC's leading spirits were strongly opposed to Zionism, including Julius Rosenwald, who became a major contributor to the Agro-Joint scheme. Maurice Hexter, who knew many of the donors well, asserts, however, that they were moved only by a desire to help the Russian Jews where they lived. Even some of the pro-Zionists in the early 1920s were certain that Palestine could not absorb great masses of Russian Jews, whom in any case the Soviet regime was not going to release.[4]

A factor that made raising money for the venture relatively easy was the charismatic personality of Dr Rosen. A sum of $8 million was pledged from private sources, chiefly by Mr Rosenwald. With great enthusiasm, Agro-Joint attacked the task of settling Jews on land provided by the government in the Ukraine and the Crimea, and in the years between 1924 and 1928 settled 5,646 families thereon. In addition, JDC spent $1,760,000 in Russia during 1923–33 on other activities, including the financing of loan kassas, the supply of equipment for vocational schools and the provision of medical aid and child care.

When the arrangement was first made between Agro-Joint and Comzet, JCA was asked to join it, but the Association was generally more cautious than its brash young American cousin. (Schmoll had urged that JCA personnel in the field be empowered to make decisions on expenditure their own responsibility, as the JDC staff had authority to do, and not be required to refer all questions to Paris Headquarters.) So JCA held back, maybe because it had premonitions of a darker future; but it did embark on a programme similar to that of Agro-Joint, though on a smaller scale.

Before looking at that programme we should say something about the activity of ORT, the third international Jewish agency at work in Russia. Its contribution was smaller than that of the others, but still significant for the welfare of the Jews in the Ukraine and White Russia. ORT set up some new farm settlements in 1921, and then came to an agreement with the Soviet authorities to spend $5,000 a month in the USSR, carrying this out by providing seed and equipment to the colonies. In 1923 ORT sent in $100,000 worth of goods (half of this money was actually supplied by JDC) and also gave assistance to twenty-nine vocational schools, a form of activity that declined later. A new agreement was concluded for ORT to expend $75,000 in the year 1925–6 to help support Jews in agriculture, and also, in 1928, to import machinery for artisans. ORT supplied instructors in the use of this machinery and thereby helped some Jews to get out of the *lishentsy* class;[5] the organisation also supported evening vocational courses and made grants for instructional equipment and libraries.

JCA's new settlements

In 1926 JCA continued its activities along the lines previously followed. Aid to vocational schools was reduced somewhat as local institutions and the government increased their participation. Metalworkers were still the principal category of students, accounting for about 60 per cent of the total of nearly 2,000. Builders and woodworkers accounted for 10 per cent each. JCA's financing of loan kassas was also reduced, though, as before, emphasis was placed on aid to smaller, out-of-the-way establishments: 135 kassas reported to JCA, which had furnished 76 per cent of their capital; loans averaged 100–120 roubles – £10–£12.

The population of the old farm colonies had grown to 35,000. JCA arranged for a good deal of equipment to be imported and advanced 40 per cent of the cost. One new feature was the introduction of a number of cattle-breeding stations, for which JCA loans provided 90 per cent of the funds required. As before, the Association was not only a source of funds but also supplied instruction and advice on methods of operation through its five agronomists.

The notable innovation of the year 1926, however, was an agreement between JCA and Comzet whereby land in the Ekaterinoslav[6] *gubernia* in the Ukraine, in the vicinity of two villages, Goulay-Polé and Nikopol, was to be put at the disposal of JCA, which was to finance the settlement of new farmers thereon. These new settlers, who had some modest – very modest – means of their own, were chosen by Comzet and numbered 254 families. They came from various districts in the Ukraine, many from Kamenetz-Podolsk. Having been chiefly artisans or petty tradesmen, they were completely lacking in agricultural experience. JCA provided equipment for them, including six tractors which were shared, as these new farmers had formed collectives.

In 1927 the new settlement work of JCA made greater headway; 570 families were settled, more than double the previous year's figure. The majority were able to contribute a horse, or even a horse and cart, to the venture, but about a third of the newcomers were virtually penniless. In every case JCA furnished sufficient equipment to get an agricultural undertaking started. The area assigned for JCA-assisted settlements was 24,000 hectares (about 60,000 acres), each family on average receiving 16½ hectares. JCA gave each settler a credit of 500 roubles towards the construction of a house, and the families did much of the building work themselves. By the end of 1927, 92 per cent of the houses for the 1926 group and 68 per cent of those for the 1927 group were completed. One of the first tasks was to clear the soil, and this was done largely by the tractors supplied by JCA which now numbered about 16. Most of the land cleared was put to wheat. Satisfied with what it had done, as presumably also were the Russian authorities, JCA agreed to take in hand another 1,800 or 1,900 families in the Nikopol area.

Besides its labours in getting the new families established, JCA continued its work in the old colonies, the population of which seems to have stabilised at about 35,000 (7,607 families). As before, JCA financed the acquisition of animals, equipment and houses, helped the cheese factories and encouraged the establishment of a new industry – grape-growing for wine.

The next year, 1928, was one of maximum effort by JCA to settle new farmers. About 2,400 families were established, many more than had been promised. This had strained JCA's human as well as financial resources, for its staff was reduced to three agronomists and one instructor who gave lectures on agriculture. In addition to supplying animals and equipment, JCA saw to it that schools and communal facilities were built.

The Association's support of the vocational school system had by now dwindled to ten schools, where as usual it provided for teaching in Yiddish and where JDC supplied electrical equipment imported from America. These ten schools, three of them in Odessa, had 1,600 pupils, of whom two-thirds were classed as locksmiths (which really meant metalworkers), electricians and woodworkers. By 1929 the number of vocational schools supported by JCA was down to nine; in fact, all foreign agencies' participation in financing them was reduced. JCA's share was 5 per cent, JDC's 3 per cent and ORT's a mere 0.2 per cent.

The number of kassas connected with JCA in 1927 was 185, with 86,518 members, out of a total of 330 functioning. In the next year JCA was concerned with 196 kassas, which had deposits of 2 million roubles. (This is in interesting contrast to 1914, when JCA was involved with 300 kassas in the same area with deposits of 15 million roubles.) In 1929 the kassas made no fewer than 168,460 loans. The *koustars*, the self-employed artisans, who were among their most important borrowers, had begun to join *artels*, or producers' co-operatives.[7] Artels as such became borrowers from the kassas, but if their members were to be counted separately as belonging to the kassas they brought the total to 90,000 individuals. In addition to making loans, the kassas acted as buyers and sellers for their members, who were mostly shoemakers, hatmakers and tailors.

Suddenly, in the midst of all this encouraging activity, something happened: something ominous and, one could say, quite typical of the Soviet regime. The lending operations of the kassas were abruptly ended on 1 October 1929. No explanation was given, no justification – just a decree.

It may be that at some time in the future, when the Soviet archives are opened for public inspection, an antiquarian interested in the history of the vanished Jewish farm settlements in southern Russia during the third decade of the twentieth century may unearth the rationale for this action. Rather than wait for this most unlikely and certainly far-off event, we might attempt to speculate as to its motivation. While JDC and JCA were busily engaged in placing Jews on farms, the NEP period with its comparative freedom for small entrepreneurs had come to an end in 1927, and the first five-year plan, for 1927–32, was instituted, with its strict control imposed over all forms of economic activity. There was no place in the Plan for the independent Jewish tailor or shoemaker: for him it was back to the ranks of the *lishentsy* – cold comfort indeed.

So sudden and wrenching a change in the economic climate could not but have a shattering effect also on the structure of agriculture which was so important a part of Russia's productive system. What happened was described by Joseph Mirkin, a vice-director in the Paris head office of JCA, who was dispatched to the USSR on a mission of inquiry at the beginning of 1930.[8]

Mirkin's report

Mirkin began with a general overview of the Russian situation. The object of the Soviet regime, he said, was to make of Russia an industrial power, and for this purpose it must obtain modern machinery abroad, which required an ample supply of foreign exchange. To secure foreign currency, the country must export; and cereals, especially wheat, were at that time the only feasible export. In order to obtain the quantity required, the peasant had to be squeezed to surrender all his surplus grain to the government (the concept of 'surplus' being very generously interpreted in favour of the regime). However, as long as the peasant operated as an individual, he could contrive to hold back a good deal of grain for his own purposes. The government therefore forced the peasants to group into immense collective or co-operative farms – called *sovhozy* or *kolkhozy* – which cultivated large tracts in common, sometimes as much as 70,000 hectares (175,000 acres). These *sovhozy* were not co-operatives in the sense that we know them in Europe, but rather were instruments for exploiting the peasants by controlling both production and consumption. The result was that the peasants became worse off than they were before the war; in particular they had less to eat, for in the collective they were subject to the same limits in this respect as the rest of the population.

Stalin, by this time the supreme dictator, wrote that collectivisation always accompanies socialisation, and in this connection he considered the possibility of liquidating the *kulaks*. The *kulaks* were the more successful peasants; though labelled 'exploiters', they rarely employed help, but were merely better and harder workers than the others. They naturally were the ones most strongly opposed to the collectivisation policy, as they had the most to lose from it. The *kulaks* were mercilessly liquidated. Mirkin describes the process graphically. Groups of young Communists from a nearby city would descend upon a village and call a meeting from which the *kulaks* were excluded. Hatred against them was whipped up, and at five in the morning – invariably at five – the by-now frenzied peasants would descend on the *kulaks'* houses and, regardless of the wails of children or the feeble protests of the old, would drive the hapless inhabitants into the open, often during the depth of the Russian winter, with no possessions but the clothing on their backs; everything else they owned was confiscated. Students of Russian history have estimated that millions, if not tens of millions, died in consequence of the drive for collectivisation.

In the Jewish areas, 6–8 per cent of the farmers fell into the *kulak* class. The rest, reported Mirkin, were now working harder. (One would have thought the opposite would be the case, since it was working harder that earned the *kulak* label.) Collectivisation was well advanced, being complete in the Goulay-Polé district and having already reached 50 per cent in Nikopol. In the cities individuals were punished for having operated businesses that were perfectly legal during the NEP period; at the least, taxes were imposed on the basis of their past business which had been liquidated, and any current attempt at business activity was characterised as economic sabotage.

A minor outrage committed in the collectivisation drive was the closing of all the cheese factories that JCA had so proudly initiated. This was done because the government wanted to control all the milk produced, as milk can be turned into butter, which was an export commodity.

Mirkin concluded his section on collectivisation with the observation that the Bolshevik revolution was now entering its acute phase, putting into practical effect an economic theory held by only a few. Nevertheless, in his estimation there was no chance of a successful revolt. He then took up some pages in what we now know was a purely academic discussion of JCA's prospects of securing repayment of past and future loans; in the process he revealed that 20–30 per cent of the newly settled farmers had absconded with their cattle and equipment, which meant that JCA would never be repaid for the loans made to these individuals. However, as the sequel showed, this loss proved to be unimportant.

Mirkin's concluding section was entitled, 'What is JCA to do?' It is certain, he says, that we (JCA) will have to become the agent of an enterprise that we condemn. For it is quite possible that the Bolsheviks may destroy the average peasant to benefit the poorest, as they have destroyed the *kulaks*. Therefore JCA has no choice but to withdraw from Russia. Having reached this firm and clear conclusion, Mirkin in true Jewish fashion proceeds to modify if not to contradict it. If we withdraw, he points out, it will deal a grave psychological blow to the 2 million Russian Jews. They will feel that one of their few friends, one of their chief connections with the outside world, has deserted them. Furthermore, if we break relations with the Soviets, they may believe that our Russian staff were responsible and harm may come to them. So in the end Mirkin left it to the Council of JCA to take action on his revelations – or not.

Clearly, the Russia that Mirkin saw on his 1930 visit was very different from the one Schmoll had visited five years earlier. Schmoll had come in the middle of the NEP period, when JCA and JDC were welcomed or even importuned to operate in Russia. Mirkin arrived at a time when the Soviets, reversing the NEP, were attempting to force collective methods of farming on the class most strongly attached to the concept of private property, namely the peasants, and when the government began to feel confident of its ability to handle even the most severe problems.

By this time JCA's activities had become much more comprehensively documented. Not only were the proceedings of the Council reported fully in the minutes, but the minutes were supplemented by hundreds of pages of notes and copies of documents bearing on the subjects discussed. Nevertheless, in all this material covering the six Council meetings held in 1930 and 1931, Mirkin's report is not once mentioned, although relations with the Soviets were discussed at length. It would seem that in 1930, when JCA stamped a document as confidential it was really meant to be such. Although Mirkin's report is never mentioned, nor is the choice of alternatives as set forth by him, it is clear, from the discussions and the decisions taken, which course the Council decided to follow: that was to stay in Russia, despite the difficulties caused by the attitude and policies of the Soviets. The Council did adopt a firm position that JCA would not invest any fresh money in the USSR but would draw on balances already built up there to pay for any new agricultural settlement work, and it re-emphasised its right to take money out of the country. The Council also decided to re-examine JCA's entire Russian programme at the end of 1931.

Mirkin's report must have been made available to JDC, for a number of conferences were held in 1930 and 1931 between representatives of the two organisations at which their Russian programmes were discussed. In any case, JDC's agents had the same sources of information as Mirkin. The interesting question that arises is why two groups of wealthy capitalists, the JCA Council and JDC's officers (headed by Felix Warburg, of Kuhn Loeb & Company), continued to support an activity that was contributing to the building up of the Communist Soviet state. The answer to the question is compounded of several elements, of which anti-Zionism is one. Furthermore, and rather surprisingly, the hard-bitten capitalists who ran JDC were affected by what Bauer calls a Rousseauian and romantic tradition, as Baron de Hirsch had been – that old physiocratic philosophy that living on and by the soil was somehow the most honourable way of making a living, closest to nature. There was probably also an element of inertia. Both JCA (in its reports) and JDC had congratulated themselves on their successes in Russia and were reluctant to leave the scene, even if conditions had changed radically.[9] Doubtless, too, Mirkin's point concerning the maintenance of morale among Jews in Russia by keeping a connection with the outside world and the desire to protect the staff of both agencies influenced their decision to continue.

ORT was confronted with the same dilemma. In the 1930s the ORT office in Russia was forced to amalgamate with OZET, the 'voluntary' Soviet Agency for Jewish Agricultural Settlement. Leon Shapiro, the historian of ORT, believes that the decision to accept this amalgamation was correct, for it permitted ORT to continue to help Soviet Jews, albeit within severe limits.[10]

End of the line

So JCA, ORT and JDC continued to work in Russia. In 1930 JCA contributed to the establishment and maintenance of seven machinery and tractor stations in the 'old' colonies. Tractors did about one-third of the planting and harvesting and most of the clearing in these areas, where by now 72 per cent of the population was grouped in *kolkhozy*. *Kolkhozy* were attractive because the government ensured that they were served by the tractor and machinery stations. JCA agronomists were still free to work, and they gave courses in tree and vine culture that were attended by representatives of twenty-two *kolkhozy*. In what were habitually called the 'new' districts, i.e. Goulay-Polé and Nikopol, there were now 2,275 families, numbering 10,000 people. There, too, most of the planting and harvesting was done by the tractor depots, more than half of which were financed by JCA, as were the seed purchases.

The loans to kassas, as we have seen, were stopped entirely, and the number of vocational schools connected with JCA was reduced to five. The equipment for the schools was still supplied by JDC.

By the following year, 1931, the number of people in the 'new' settlements had risen to over 14,000, living in houses that JCA had financed. The *kolkhozy* by now controlled almost all the available land, but JCA provided them with loans and sometimes materials for building repairs, stables, silos and schools. While crops were harvested collectively, and the revenues derived therefrom, such as they were, were shared collectively, cows could still be individually owned, and JCA made loans for their purchase.

In the next two years matters changed little. JCA paid for buildings, provided vine-grafts and helped support tractor stations; and the agronomists travelled around, teaching the farmers how to grow grapes and other fruit. The 1933 report reviewed the entire situation in Russia. It stated that JCA had helped, in both the old and the new colonies, a total of 4,231 families. It also stated that, as more than 2,000 houses had been constructed in the new colonies, the problem of living accommodation could be considered more or less resolved. Together, the old and new colonies farmed 75,000 hectares (187,500 acres), about half planted to wheat.

JCA's annual reports for the years 1934 and 1935 are very significant as far as the Association's activities in the USSR are concerned. While in the volumes for the previous years the Russian section consists of many pages of narrative and statistical tables, in the 1934 and 1935 reports we find just two short paragraphs in each, announcing that JCA was interested in about 4,500 families occupying 75,000 hectares and would in 1936 and 1937 help to provide credits for the increase of livestock and other improvements. For 1936 there is a little more – to the effect that

JCA was continuing to help the agricultural centres in the Ukraine; that its agronomists were inculcating modern methods of cultivation; that not only were tractors and other machinery being operated by the members of the *kolkhozy*, but even in the more primitive places oxen were no longer used for motive power, having been replaced by horses. In the 1937 report nothing at all is said about the Russian programme. This silence was eloquent.

As far as ORT was concerned, its work in the 1930s shifted from agriculture to industry, which was beginning to absorb Jewish labour. ORT helped support 60 producer-co-operatives and 246 artels, thus assisting in all some 30,000–35,000 workers out of a total Jewish labour force of 1.1 million.[11] ORT also continued to help a number of *kolkhozy* containing 4,000 families.

JDC's work in Russia experienced the same process of attrition as that of JCA and ORT. By the end of 1930, 12,000 Jewish families had been placed by Agro-Joint in the Ukraine and Crimea. In 1931 another 1,800 families were settled. Rosen obtained the land for them in exchange for importing 300 tractors.[12] Thus Agro-Joint, from the beginning of its activity in 1924, had been responsible for placing a total of nearly 14,000 Jewish families on farms in southern Russia. But the writing was soon to appear on the wall. Agro-Joint was told that its work in the Ukraine was finished and its offices were to be liquidated. From 1932 to 1934 its activities were confined to tractor stations in the Crimea and there is no mention of new settlement. Agro-Joint was in fact involved in 1935 and 1936 in a series of complicated proposals for a programme in Biro-Bidjan, but it did no actual work in that unsuccessful Soviet attempt to set up an autonomous Jewish republic in far-off Siberia.

We have seen how the farm settlement efforts of JCA, ORT and Agro-Joint were beginning to run down in the 1930s. In the latter part of the decade the developments that took place in the USSR had a more profound effect on them. One of these developments was the expanding industrialisation, which absorbed Jews and others into the labour force, so that they did not have to look to agriculture for employment. Factory and other jobs in industry began to attract Jews away from the collectives.[13] In addition, Russia's need for foreign exchange was no longer as acute as it had been.

Finally, more for internal than external reasons, the Soviet attitude towards foreigners became highly suspicious; this was the time of the great purge trials, by which means Stalin eliminated rivals and enemies, real or imagined, and the Russian news media were full of stories about meetings (which never took place) between foreign agents and those whom Stalin wished to eliminate. In 1938 the members of the Agro-Joint staff were arrested and disappeared, and some may have been executed. Exactly the same thing happened with JCA. Its offices were closed without warning and the staff arrested. Their subsequent fate is unknown. Sachs, in charge of JCA's work in Russia, was lucky enough, or had foresight enough, to be in France at the time, and he did not return. Tregelnitski, the chief of the ORT office in Russia, who was also a Russian citizen, was not so lucky. Comzet informed ORT that there would be no more agreements, and shortly afterwards Tregelnitski was sent to a labour camp and disappeared. In this outburst of liquidation Comzet itself was also wound up – because, the Soviet authorities blandly declared, the Jewish problem in Russia had been solved.

One problem, however, was only partially solved, at least from the point of view of the Jewish organisations. That was the question of repayment. ORT's modest demand for $264,000 never received even the courtesy of a reply from the Soviet authorities.[14] Agro-Joint had spent a total of upwards of $10 million including the expenditures for other than agricultural work. After many complex exchanges of securities with the Soviets, it received new Russian bonds in the amount of $2,430,000 which were indeed redeemed. JCA had spent a total of $4,136,000 in Russia, and its agreements with Comzet had divided this expenditure into repayable and non-repayable amounts. Under one of these agreements JCA was able to withdraw $225,000 until its office was closed in 1938. All requests for information after the closure remained unanswered.

In the Second World War the invading German armies rampaged through the areas of the Ukraine and Crimea where the Jewish farm colonies had been located and did their Devil's work so thoroughly that apparently there were no survivors of the Agro-Joint settlements and the JCA villages.[15] There may have been as many as 120,000 Jews in these places before the war.[16]

A Daniel come to judgment

How shall we, with the dubious wisdom of hindsight, judge this great Jewish adventure in Russia during the period between the wars? Leon Shapiro says that ORT's activity should not be judged by its inglorious ending.[17] There is no question that, when the Jewish organisations began their labours in Russia in the early 1920s, they were very helpful to their beleaguered co-religionists in Russia, who under the Bolshevik regime had no way of earning their daily bread. Yehuda Bauer declares that Agro-Joint was successful in restoring civil rights to half the *lishentsy*. But he also goes on to say that 'evaluation of the Agro-Joint work presents a very complicated problem' and, later, 'In the long run Agro-Joint work in Russia brought few results.'[18]

We would probably agree to apply this by no means gentle judgment to the work of JCA as well, and we cannot refrain from speculating upon how much the development and absorptive capacity of Palestine – and tiny Palestine in the 1920s was taking in more European Jews than any other country – would have been increased if some of the millions spent in Russia had been diverted there, especially after Mirkin's warning. In plain words, the anti-Zionism of Rosenwald and others still rankles. But in justice, one cannot have expected them to foresee Hitler and the creation of the Jewish state.

Epilogue

One day in 1949, the JCA office in London was surprised by the receipt of a statement of account from the Bank for Foreign Trade of the USSR in Moscow showing a credit balance of 224,445 roubles. How this credit had arisen the JCA people had no idea, although they surmised that it was a consequence of the agreement concluded with the Soviet government in 1932, which provided that JCA could transfer abroad 'sums arising from the repayment by the colonists of loans made to them'. We have seen that JCA did withdraw $225,000 under this agreement. The JCA staff guessed that the credit represented sums collected under the agreement from 1938, when the Moscow office was closed, until the outbreak of the war between Russia and Germany in 1941.

Once apprised of this credit, JCA embarked on a veritable campaign in trying to collect it – letters, cables, memoranda and representations were sent to the Soviet Embassy in London. These methods were employed for 14 years without result. Finally, the Association decided to send an emissary to Moscow. The man chosen was Georges Aronstein. In 1949 Louis Oungre retired and was succeeded by a joint directorate consisting of Victor Girmounsky and Aronstein. The latter resigned shortly afterwards to resume the practice of law in his native Brussels, leaving Girmounsky as sole Director-General. Now Aronstein was asked by JCA to go to Moscow because of his familiarity with JCA's affairs and especially those in Russia.

Aronstein went there in June 1963. In the course of his trip he paid a visit to the old JCA headquarters and found, not surprisingly, that it was occupied by some government bureau and that not the slightest trace remained of JCA's presence there 25 years before. Aronstein spent some days negotiating – if that is the proper word – with the officials of the Bank for Foreign Trade, who displayed the whole panoply of Russian obfuscatory tactics. If the Association did have a claim to these roubles, they said, that was doubtless counterbalanced by debits that must have accumulated elsewhere; alternatively, the money could be recovered if JCA would be willing to spend it in the Soviet Union. After a few days, seeing that further talk was futile, Aronstein returned home, having been told to submit additional documents to support the claim.[19] He and JCA wrote more letters and memoranda recapitulating the history of the affair; this process continued into 1964 when, *mirabile dictu*, the Russians, perhaps tired of 15 years of wrangling over such a paltry sum, suddenly gave in. But the 224,445 roubles, which in 1949 were worth £15,000, produced for JCA only some £9,000 owing to the devaluation of the rouble *vis-à-vis* the pound sterling which had taken place in the intervening years.

And so, 44 years after it began, did JCA's venture into Soviet Russia end with a small, if soul-satisfying, victory.

CHAPTER 9

Palestine and the Near East

Palestine

The number of Jews living in Palestine declined during the First World War, from 80,000 in 1914 to 58,000 in 1919. Economic stagnation, Turkish attempts to conscript citizens into its army, drastic measures against non-citizens[1] and the fighting that took place in Palestine in 1917 and 1918 – all were contributory causes of the decline. As for the Jewish agricultural settlements, by 1919 their fields and orchards, especially those on the coastal plain, which were the biggest and most important, were in poor condition because of the lack of care and shortage of fertiliser.

For the first two or three years after the war an abnormally low rainfall retarded the recovery of agriculture, but through the 1920s and into the 1930s Jewish immigration, and concomitantly population, increased. This was due to a number of factors: the Balfour Declaration by the British government in 1917, which held out the hope that a self-governing Jewish entity of some sort could be established in Palestine; the US immigration acts of 1923 and 1924, which enforced a sharp reduction in the number of immigrants entering that country from Eastern Europe; the simultaneous restrictions enacted by Canada, followed by the severe limitations imposed by Argentina and Brazil on all immigration at the beginning of the Great Depression, which cut these countries' intake of Jews to a small trickle. All these exclusions left Palestine as the only place willing and able to accept substantial numbers. Hitler's accession to power in 1933, with the consequent emigration of half the German Jewish population (about 500,000 people), added to the pressure on the receiving countries. By this time the doors to Palestine had been more than half closed by the British who, under the influence of the waves of Arab riots in 1929 and 1935–6, restricted and finally proposed to put an end to the movement of Jews into the country.

On the positive side, immigration into Palestine was stimulated by a more active Zionist organisation. The World Zionist Organisation had opened its first Palestine office in 1908 but had remained a relatively small factor on the scene through the First World War. Afterwards, under the impetus of the Balfour Declaration and the pressure of hundreds of thousands of Jewish refugees from Russia and other Eastern European countries, it raised more money and founded many colonies in the Holy Land on a scale equalling, by the late 1930s, that of JCA and Baron Rothschild.

As far as the latter were concerned, there were some important developments. The export trade in wine was seriously reduced by the closing of its two major markets: the United States, because of the Prohibition amendment effective in 1919; and Russia, where the lack of foreign exchange made it almost impossible to buy anything abroad, let alone a semi-luxury, and of religious import at that.

But if wine exports fell to almost nil, another export – oranges – flourished. Amid the usually rather glum JCA reports of the early 1920s, we find remarks like: 'in 1921 Nes Ziona did well with its orange crop'; 'in 1922 the almonds and grapes of Rishon-le-Zion did poorly, but the return was good for the oranges at Petach-Tikva'; 'in 1923, while its other products did not do well, Rehovot's oranges were successful, as again were those of Nes Ziona'. This last in JCA's view was the pre-eminent orange centre in Palestine, for again and again the reports mention its successful orange crops. The success of oranges here and elsewhere inspired farmers in the coastal plain to begin growing another kind of citrus – grapefruit – in 1922.

While the JCA settlements in general do not seem to have suffered much damage in the 1919 outbreak of Arab rioting, the isolated outpost of Metulla, at the northernmost edge of Palestine, was sacked by neighbouring tribes of Bedouin in 1920. JCA, following its usual custom of alleviating the plight of its colonies in distress, made loans to the inhabitants for the rehabilitation of their ruined houses, only to see the Bedouin return the next year, this time to destroy the villagers' crops.

PICA

It will be remembered that back in 1900 the Baron Edmond de Rothschild, weakened by ill-health and wearied by the immense losses suffered by the Palestinian colonies he was supporting, turned the administration of his venture over to JCA. Rothschild, however, as chairman and financier of the Commission Palestinienne, which was the formal instrument through which the new arrangement operated, retained great influence. By 1924, when his health had been restored (he was then 79 years old) and by which time he had a mature and able son, James, who was ready

5a Beer Tuvia, Israel. Farmer's house before the 1929 disturbances

5b Beer Tuvia, Israel, 1930. The settlement in ruins

6a Beer Tuvia, Israel. The settlement after reconstruction

6b Israel, 1937. Surveying the Huleh swamps

to participate actively in the work in Palestine, the Baron apparently decided to step once more into the foreground. Another motive may have been his intention to go beyond agriculture and participate in the industrial development of Palestine. JCA had already initiated activity of this kind in 1923 by investing in a flour mill in Haifa and starting salt works at Atlit, south of Haifa. In 1924 a new company, the Palestine Jewish Colonization Association (PICA), was registered. It took over from JCA the management of all the settlements that JCA had supervised, including not only colonies originally under Rothschild's care, such as Petach Tikvah and Rishon-le-Zion, but also places that JCA had taken under its wing in 1896 or subsequently, like Rehovoth and Ness Ziona, or had itself founded, like Hedera and Sedjera. All of JCA's staff seconded to the Commission Palestinienne was transferred to PICA, and James de Rothschild was put in active charge.

In 1925 Baron Edmond made his last – and triumphant – tour of Palestine. He was given a tumultuous welcome in the colonies he had sustained and was greeted as 'Hanadiv', the benefactor. His visit coincided with the completion of the reclamation of the Kabbarah, a marshy region south of Haifa covering 5000 dunams, which was turned into productive land while at the same time the threat of malaria was eliminated. This great task had been initiated nine years before, and its conclusion was a fitting tribute to Edmond's work in Palestine. He lived another nine years, dying in 1934 at the age of 89.

The work of PICA continued under the leadership of Baron James. Its participation in industrial development was greatly increased by investments in cement plants, a brewery and the King David Hotel in Jerusalem. Most important was its contribution to the financing of the Palestine Electric Company. The growing general availability of electric power throughout the country could be said to have been a prime factor in making Israel the first modern country in the Near East. Nor did PICA forget that it had its origins in the role of a protector of Palestinian agricultural colonies; after the Second World War, and after Israel had become an independent nation, settlements were established on all the land remaining in PICA's hands.

The pressure of outside events brought two former opponents together. The Arab troubles of 1935–6 caused PICA and the Zionist settlements to co-ordinate defence plans, and this action was a pointer to the future. When the Jewish state was created and the world-wide United Jewish Appeal experienced its great post-war growth, part of PICA's reason for existence evaporated. Well financed though it had been by Rothschild, there was now an even better financed agency in the field prepared to carry out the work of settling Jews on farms in the Holy Land, and prepared to do it in a communal fashion which never quite fitted in with the concepts of PICA, or for that matter of JCA, both of which organisations were attuned to dealing with individual farmers owning their own plots. The kibbutzim, with their communal structure, wherein there was no individual ownership of the land and the means of production, seemed a fitting expression of the Zionist spirit; they involved not only the development of farming by Jews, but doing it in such a way that the individual worker was directly part of a larger entity than himself and his family. And, of course, the acquisition of land, which was so important a part of the activity of the Baron de Rothschild, JCA and PICA, was now of less relevance, with the state of Israel coming into possession of very extensive stretches of government land and also exercising a measure of control over the areas acquired by the Keren Kayemet (Jewish National Fund), the Zionist land-buying agency.

Also, there was the question of personality. When James de Rothschild died in 1957, at the age of seventy-nine, there was no heir available to carry on the direction of the enterprise that had been so important a part of the lives of his father and himself. Therefore, in accordance with arrangements made by James before he died (he had written to Prime Minister Ben-Gurion that all the suitable land that PICA owned had been colonised, so that 'today there is no cultivable land left to PICA for further colonisation'), all remaining PICA land, about 150,000 dunams, was transferred to organs of the state, as were the 'factories and utilities owned by PICA'.[2] In addition, James promised a donation of 6 million Israel pounds (£1.2 million sterling) for the construction of the Knesset (Parliament) building in Jerusalem. This was implemented on his death.

JCA

With the transfer of the managment of all its Palestine colonies and its staff to PICA, JCA was left with no active function in that country. But it did not discontinue its reports on the affairs of the colonies, in which, after all, it still owned land and was owed considerable amounts of money. The tenor of these reports was chiefly to the effect that Ness Ziona, wholly devoted to oranges, was doing very well, and Rehovoth and Hedera, which were by now also largely devoted to oranges, were doing quite well; while other colonies, such as Sedjera and Mishmar Hayarden, which were without oranges, were not doing well at all. Another matter on which JCA reported in detail was population. In 1922 there had been 2,465 inhabitants in the six JCA colonies, of which Rehovoth, Ness Ziona and Hedera were the most important. Ten years later, in 1932, these same six settlements had a population of 6,568, demonstrating the effect of reasonable economic conditions and the fact that Palestine had been open to Jewish immigration in the intervening years.

Despite JCA's non-involvement in activities in Palestine, Louis Oungre, the Association's Director-General, visited the country from October to December 1932 and, as was his usual custom, wrote a comprehensive report on it. This visit was by no means due to a spontaneous desire on Oungre's part to travel; it was preceded and stimulated by a series of interesting and important conferences between JCA and Zionist officials and among JCA's own Council members and its Director-General.

Palestine Emergency Fund

Before discussing these meetings it is necessary to say a word about the Palestine Emergency Fund, the existence of which provided part of the *raison d'être* of these conferences.

In 1929 there had been a serious outbreak of Arab rioting and assaults on Jewish lives and property in Palestine. The Jewish community at Hebron was attacked, 70 of its members were killed and the remainder fled to Jerusalem; 18 Jews in Safed were massacred and the town's Jewish quarter was sacked; many villages were destroyed, including Beer Tuvia, situated about 10 kilometres east of Ashdod, of which we shall hear more later. In order to bring relief to the victims of these attacks and to rebuild their houses, a fund of £2 million was raised. Two-thirds of this came from the United States, a fifth from England, the remainder from other countries. Well-known Jewish personalities including Felix Warburg and Bernard Flexner in the United States and James de Rothschild, Simon Marks, Lord Reading and Sir Osmond d'Avigdor Goldsmid in England constituted the governing committee.[3] The Fund's activities in Palestine, directed by a very energetic and innovative American social worker, Maurice B. Hexter, were completely independent of those of all other organisations. By the summer of 1932, when the work of relief and reconstruction was essentially completed, there remained at the disposal of the Fund the considerable sum of £192,000 in cash with more to come in the form of repayment of loans.[4]

Sir Leonard Cohen, the President of JCA, had taken part in a long discussion with Chaim Weizmann, the President of the World Zionist Organisation, and Simon Marks, in which his

attention had been called to the parlous state of the finances of
the newly founded Jewish Agency, which had been established
to bring Zionists and non-Zionists together to work for the
upbuilding of the Jewish community in Palestine. At the same
time, representatives of a number of Palestinian organisations
had approached JCA's Director-General in the same spirit: their
resources were running out and they needed help. Lastly, and
most important, because he was not asking for money but actually
controlled a supply of it, Maurice Hexter had submitted to Sir
Leonard and Louis Oungre proposals for the Emergency Fund to
join with JCA for the purpose of establishing settlement projects
or irrigation works in Palestine. To consider these requests and
suggestions, Sir Leonard, Sir Osmond and Mr Oungre met in
London late in August 1932. The former two gentlemen raised
the question of how proper it would be for JCA to interest
itself in Palestinian affairs. They answered their own inquiry by
concurring that at this time, when the great majority of the Jewish
world was concerned with Palestine, it was not right for JCA to
'persist in the attitude of abstention which it had observed up to
this time'.[5]

This attitude, Cohen and Goldsmid felt, had caused pain in
certain responsible circles (*milieux sérieux*), and the Jewish world
would not be ignorant of the fact that in this time of crisis JCA
remained financially the most powerful Jewish organisation in the
world, especially after what they conceived to be the impoverishment of American Jewry as a result of the Great Depression. (This
was a somewhat more pessimistic conclusion than was justified
by the facts, but unquestionably American Jews had suffered
huge losses[6] while JCA's assests on 31 December 1932 were still
substantial.) 'In the moral interest of JCA and to preserve its
reputation in the eyes of world Jewry', it was decided that the
organisation should respond to the proposals it had already on
hand and would receive in the future by undertaking constructive
activity in Palestine.

The world moves, and JCA perforce moves with it, if somewhat belatedly. This declaration of concern for the opinion of
world Jewry and the indication of interest in activity in Palestine
would have rung very curiously, if they could have heard it, in
the ears of those critics who so often had accused JCA of being
utterly unconcerned with public opinion. And certainly, the positive attitude towards Palestine was a far cry from the outlook of
Meyerson, Oungre's predecessor as Director-General.

Having concurred on the taking of constructive steps in
Palestine, the three gentlemen agreed that the cost of these steps,
whatever direction they might take, should be kept within JCA's

ordinary revenues and not impinge on its capital. It was felt that there was sufficient excess of income over expenditure to provide ample funds for work in Palestine.

Of all the suggestions made by Palestinian organisations, those of Maurice Hexter were the most appealing to the JCA officials, not only because he proffered considerable financing but because the idea of working with much the same group of Americans as were on the Board of the 'Foundation' (see p. 173) was very agreeable; these Americans had the proper standing in the community, and the Foundation had operated with little friction and considerable success for the last eight years. Also, despite this change of heart, it was felt that for JCA to work alone in Palestine would be to expose it to all kinds of criticisms and pressures from the opposite, if minority, side of world Jewry; some, indeed, possibly from within its own membership (for example, Leonard G. Montefiore, a member of the Council and President from 1940 to 1947), were opposed to the idea of a Jewish state, and might well have not been enthusiastic about activity in Palestine.

It was concluded that, before further steps were taken to advance these arrangements, the Director-General should proceed to Palestine to look over the terrain of proposed action and confer with Dr Hexter.[7] It was clear that no details of the projected enterprise could be sketched in until an inspection had been made and discussions held with the prospective partner. Nevertheless, one basic rule of action was decided on: namely that all investments by the new enterprise should be made on the principle of recoverability and that no money be used for non-remunerative projects like schools, hospitals, synagogues or outright charity. In other words, JCA was prepared to re-commit itself in Palestine, but not without reservations.

Oungre's report

So in September 1932 Louis Oungre went to Palestine. But his visit was motivated by more than an intention to explore the new agency suggested by Maurice Hexter, participation in which would indicate that the Association had joined the majority of the Jewish world in supporting the Zionist enterprise in Palestine. JCA, whether it consciously perceived the situation or not, had little alternative if it wished to continue activity on a significant scale: where else but in Palestine was it possible to continue JCA's mission of moving Jews out of Eastern Europe and settling them in new and more accommodating circumstances? Oungre himself had said that the Argentine enterprise was in danger of stagnating unless there was a big influx of new settlers, but the Argentine government's regulations had reduced Jewish immigration to near zero; likewise, in Brazil and Canada further growth of JCA's colonies was inhibited by strict quotas, which affected all would-be immigrants and Jews in particular. Palestine, therefore, appeared to be the only place where the Jewish farm population could grow. The JCA colonies there, now managed by PICA, had two-and-a-half times as many residents as ten years before.

Oungre doubtless had some half-formed conclusions in his mind before he set out for Palestine, inasmuch as the idea of the conference with Sir Leonard Cohen and Sir Osmond d'Avigdor Goldsmid had been at least already agreed upon by Oungre and Hexter. As co-Director of the Foundation, Oungre often visited the Foundation offices in Berlin, where the European headquarters of JDC were located; and Hexter came to Berlin occasionally on missions for JDC. Thus the two men had become acquainted, and they had exchanged views on the possibility of the resumption by JCA of work in Palestine. More than this, they had worked out the nature of the relationship that would exist between them if JCA did come back to Palestine.[8]

Despite this agreement on basic principles, when Oungre started his visit to Palestine his mind was still not fully made up. Certainly he put hard and searching questions to Hexter, who believes that what finally convinced Oungre was the opportunity presented by the drainage of the Huleh (which will be discussed below) and the eager interest shown by the settlers' children in their fathers' farm work.[9]

In his report, Oungre not only recommended JCA's acceptance of Hexter's proposal, but took the opportunity of setting down what he considered vital principles concerning agricultural settlement. He reiterated the doctrine of mixed farming (the Argentine colonists, for example, might have ridden out depressions better if they had diversified more) and proposed the same restrictive rules as in Argentina for the sons of settlers, especially the placing of the sons' farms at a specified distance from the fathers', forgetting that this could have inhibiting effects on the number of settlers.

He devoted the last chapter of his report to the possibilities of the drainage and reclamation of the Huleh area, north of Lake Galilee. There the soil was rich but unusable, because it was marshy and malarial. Oungre was impressed by the prospects it offered of being converted to productive farmland. He was also impressed by, but did not report on, two other aspects of Jewish farm life in Palestine. One we have mentioned – the interest that young people and even children took in it, in contrast to the lukewarm attitude of Jewish youth in Argentina; the second was the excellent repayment record of the settlers, which again contrasted with the difficulties JCA experienced in this regard with its South American settlers.[10]

Regardless of Oungre's opinions on polyculture or the proper distance between farms owned by fathers and sons, his object in coming to Palestine was fulfilled. Indeed, he was perhaps more favourably affected by Palestine and its Jewish farmers than he had expected to be. Not surprisingly, since he and Hexter had agreed on much in advance, he came down roundly in favour of the suggestion that JCA should form an organisation in conjunction with the Palestine Emergency Fund for setting up new colonies.

The Emica Association

Oungre hurried back to Paris to present this matter at the JCA Council meeting of 22 December 1932. On the motion of the President, Sir Leonard Cohen, it was formally decided to enter into an accord with the trustees of the Emergency Fund for the establishment of an agency for economic development in Palestine, to be called the Emica Association. Each partner would contribute £25,000 for each of the first three years. The new organisation would buy enough land to settle 150 families or more during this period, at the end of which the project would be re-examined.[11]

As Kurt Grunwald, Hirsch's biographer, remarked in a review of Avni's book on JCA in Argentina, *The Promised Land*, the Baron's rebuff to Theodor Herzl has caused Jewish chroniclers to deny him 'his proper place in the history of the modern Jewish renaissance'.[12] And this denial has extended to his creation, the Jewish Colonization Association. However, the leading Zionist of the time, Chaim Weizmann, was quick to recognise the importance of Emica and to applaud its establishment. On 20 February 1933 he wrote the following letter to Sir Leonard:

> I was delighted to learn from Mr Goldsmid, on my return
> yesterday after an absence of some ten days on the Continent,
> that the agreement between the ICA and the Emergency Fund
> has now been signed. I believe it is a great piece of work
> that you have done in the negotiation of this agreement, and
> one that is bound to have great and far-reaching
> consequences for Palestine, and to redound to the credit of
> those responsible for it. I should like, if I may, to
> congratulate you very warmly on this happy conclusion of
> the discussions.

Emica, which was incorporated in England in July 1933 and registered by the mandatory Government of Palestine in January 1934, immediately planned to found three settlements. It made valiant efforts to buy land but found this next to impossible because of Arab hostility. Therefore it took over 2,000 dunams (500 acres) from the Jewish National Fund located around the village of Beer Tuvia, where the Emergency Fund had already started restoration work. Emica proposed to settle 60 families there, including 15 from Germany. By 1935 the houses had been constructed and irrigation works put in, and before the end of that year some cultivation had been begun. True to Oungre's principles, it was planned that the settlers practise mixed farming, with dairy cattle as the base. Each settler had cows provided by Emica and a 35-dunam plot for growing vegetables and forage. The eight artisan families who were there to perform necessary services like machinery repair each received 3 dunams on which to grow vegetables. Emica gave the new colony a communal building. By 1936 the place was completely settled, but because of the Arab disturbances of that year it was necessary to post guards around the clock. By 1937 Beer Tuvia had grown to 125 families comprising 496 people.

Emica was making plans for further development despite the difficulty of acquiring land. In fact, Emica, in conjunction with JCA and the American Refugee Economic Corporation, had for some years been eyeing the Huleh in which Louis Oungre had displayed so much interest. The three partners had investigated some 36,000 dunams there and concluded, on the basis of a report commissioned from the prominent English firm of civil engineers, Rendel, Palmer and Tritton, that drainage was possible and if successful would add materially to the country's stock of arable soil. The (British mandatory) government was persuaded to survey the area, and its preliminary appraisal was favourable. Therefore, an important part of Emica's planning in 1937 was in connection with the development of the Huleh, in which it hoped to draw in as a partner the Jewish National Fund with its large resources.

All this time, while it was going through its third incarnation in Palestine in the form of the Emica Association, JCA was reporting on the development of its 'old' colonies in the country, now managed by PICA. As before, Ness Ziona, Rehovoth, Hedera, etc., continued to grow in population, though they suffered a setback in 1936 when rains at the wrong time ruined the orange crop. As for Sedjera, it too was damaged in that year, not by the vagaries of nature but by Arab raids.

On the eve of the Second World War Emica was poised to

create other colonies in the style of Beer Tuvia and was preparing another venture on a grander scale: namely, participation in the drainage of the Huleh. The coming of the war put off for a time the accomplishment of these plans, the outcome of which will be described later.

Appraisal

Up to this enforced interruption, what had this series of agencies – the original Rothschild enterprise, JCA, the Commission Palestinienne, PICA and Emica – accomplished in the 58 years from 1881, when Baron Edmond started making grants to some of the struggling Jewish colonies in Palestine, to 1939? First, there was the provision of a home for some of those Jews who wanted to live elsewhere than in Russia or Poland. A great many of these also felt the positive stimulus of wishing to build up a National Home. By 1937 there were 40,000 persons living in the PICA settlements. Not only for these, but for tens of thousands of earlier immigrants, the Rothschild and JCA villages and towns had provided the preferred alternative of life outside Eastern Europe. Second, these settlements, though they had first been sponsored without political intention, turned out to have enormous political importance; because, when the time came for the mandatory power, Great Britain, to consider partition as a solution to the problem of sovereignty in Palestine, the land owned by PICA and JCA and by the settlers they had assisted constituted a large part of the various versions of the Jewish state mapped by the British Royal Commissions and a significant segment of the state that finally emerged from the War of Independence in 1948.

A Swiss scholar, Doris Angst, has devoted a doctoral thesis to the role of JCA in building up Jewish holdings in Palestine.[13] She points out that JCA was responsible for establishing forty-five new settlements in the twenty-four years it had the stewardship of the Rothschild operations, and that by 1941 the JCA and Rothschild settlements together held 41 per cent of the land in private Jewish hands, accommodating 50 per cent of the farm population. In a general way she makes the same claim as has been set forth earlier in this book, that the land occupied by the JCA and Rothschild settlements was the basis for the area putatively awarded to the Jewish state by the British partition plans. The non-Zionist JCA was therefore, she asserts, an important factor in the building of the Jewish state, by providing it with a base of both land and people. It should also be remembered that much of the JCA and Rothschild land had not been in the inventory of arable soil in Palestine before these agencies undertook the reclamation of large areas from swamp, marsh and desert. In other words, the settlers helped by JCA and Rothschild added significantly to Palestine's total stock of usable land.

Miss Angst also calls attention to the importance of the vast monetary outlays of the Baron de Rothschild, who agreed to cover the deficits of the Commission Palestinienne up to a total of 15 million francs, which amount was reached in six years after the JCA takeover of the administration in 1900. This figure does not include the millions that the non-Zionist Baron de Rothschild expended before 1900 and the amount spent by the non-political JCA after that date.

Third, both the Baron de Rothschild and JCA contributed in a major way to the economic development of Palestine and Israel, with special reference to agriculture. Miss Angst makes the sweeping statement that JCA, consequent upon its aim of establishing independent farmers, was reponsible for the modernisation of Palestine's agriculture.[14] This may be an overstatement, but unquestionably JCA, with its insistence that its protégés practise agriculture rationally, and its introduction of items like powerful American-made pumps that could bring water up from hitherto untapped levels, advanced farming technology materially. In contrast to the waste of a good deal of time and money by the Rothschild regime in futile experiments with such things as silk-worm culture and growing flowers for perfume, the Commission Palestinienne improved citrus growing by sending experts to California to become acquainted with the latest techniques, and by helping to introduce the production of grapefruit. And as we have seen, apart from agriculture, JCA invested in saltworks and flour mills, while PICA helped establish the cement industry and made an important investment in the Palestine Electric Company. And on the eve of the Second World War JCA, in its newest incarnation as Emica, was launching a new settlement programme and approaching the initiation of a great drainage effort in the north-eastern corner of Palestine.

From the point of view of JCA, its return to Palestine in 1933 was important in giving the Association an ongoing mission. Its colonization work in the New World was stagnating; and while it was performing Herculean labours of relief in Eastern Europe, its work there – and its beneficiaries – were to be blotted out in a few years by the Second World War and the Holocaust. Palestine and then Israel were the only fields left in which it could take significant constructive action.

Cyprus

By 1912 the JCA administration had decided that its programme on Cyprus was not viable. The place was oppressively hot in summer; persons not native to the island were susceptible to malaria; not enough Jews were attracted there to constitute an organised community, although a school that taught Hebrew among other subjects was maintained with JCA help; finally and most significantly, Palestine, with all it lacked, certainly had a plethora of organised Jewish life and was only a few hours away by sea. Palestine therefore exercised an irresistible attraction for Jewish settlers on Cyprus, who after being on the island for a year or two left it in a steady stream for the Holy Land.

JCA apparently felt that a decent interval should elapse between a decision that a project was not worth-while and action on such a decision. Therefore the two years between the decision to abandon Cyprus and the outbreak of war in 1914 did not provide enough time to do anything about selling the land; and the war years were no time for a land sale either. So 1919 found JCA still ensconced on its three estates, with a population of 169. Crops had been poor and continued so in the following years, and the population continued to decline. It was 1923 before JCA, deciding that its losses in Cyprus had reached an intolerable level, withdrew its administrator, declaring that the *émancipés* were able to take care of themselves. This act, accompanied by the cessation of the subsidies to which the settlers had been accustomed, led more families to leave for Palestine, and by 1927 the population was down to 43. The following year the Association took the final step of liquidating its holdings in Cyprus, which appears no more in its annals. JCA perhaps judged the settlers rather harshly in remarking that they had not had the patience or the energy to make a success of their life in Cyprus; certainly the absence of an organised Jewish community had been one discouragement for them.

Turkey

The reports on the JCA settlements in Turkey during and after the First World War read less like a sober account of farm settlement than a set of fragments extracted from a review of the Turko-Greek War of 1920–2 interspersed with pages from a monograph on the sociology of the Turks in confrontation with aliens. JCA had four colonies in the country, one, Fethy-Keuy, in European Turkey, and three in Anatolia – Or Yehuda, the biggest, which had been both agricultural school and farm colony, Messila-Hadacha and Tikfour Tchiflik.

During the Great War the settlers at Fethy-Keuy, because they were Russians and therefore enemy aliens, had been put into concentration camps, and their premises had been ravaged by the Turks. In spite of these tribulations a few of them managed somehow to remain *in situ* and even did some farm work. Others who were able to return to Russia after the war were detained by the Bolsheviks. After the war, as a measure of protection, JCA as a British company succeeded in getting the place declared British property; this did not however deter the Greek army, who in 1921 destroyed it. Fethy-Keuy was finally wholly abandoned by its Jewish farmers.

In 1920 Or Yehuda was in the path of the fighting between the Turkish and the Greek armies, but some tenants stayed on (the agricultural school had been closed in 1914), some new settlers arrived from Russia, and the inhabitants managed to raise enough food to live on. The Greek army stole all the horses, but the ever-optimistic JCA replaced them with a tractor. Then came Turkish irregulars, followed by the regular Turkish army, who put the buildings to its own use as a school and hospital. As soon as the Turkish troops left, JCA, undaunted, reopened the agricultural school. By 1923 the Association thought the colony's future sufficiently hopeful for modern methods of cultivation to be introduced, but the fifty or so occupants resisted, preferring to produce their grapes and tobacco in the same way as they had done for years past. Meanwhile the attitude of the Turks living nearby became so menacing that many of the settlers left. The attempt to revive the agricultural school had proved unsuccessful and the farm operation was losing money, so JCA decided to dispose of Or Yehuda. It was sold in 1926, and some of the remaining families emigrated to Argentina and Brazil.

Messila-Hadacha, founded by Russian Jews in 1911, was twice despoiled by the Turks and its inhabitants fled to Istambul; but by 1920 some had returned and JCA replaced the lost animals and proceeded to reorganise the colony. When the Turko-Greek War came to an end there was talk of putting in new families, but action was held in abeyance because of the xenophobic attitude of the Turkish neighbours whose patriotic and indeed chauvinistic feelings had been stirred up by the conflict with the Greeks and confrontations with the British and Italian governments. The result was that most of the settlers moved to Palestine; the few who remained eked out a living selling milk and eggs in Istambul.

As for Tikfour-Tchiflik, situated near Or Yehuda, it had been ruined by the fighting, and the half dozen remaining settlers stayed only as long as they still hoped to receive compensation for war damage.

By 1926 Fethy-Keuy had been taken over by Turkish farmers (who paid rent to the government, not to JCA, the proper owner); in Tikfour-Tchiflik three families were left who were sufficiently successful to pay both taxes and the sums due to JCA, as well as purchase two tractors; at Messilah-Hadacha also there were only three families left, but here part of JCA's land was seized by the government on the pretext of non-utilisation. JCA eventually recovered its title to this land after a lengthy but successful legal action.

In its 1927 and 1928 reports JCA stated that its decision to leave Turkey – which country it had entered to help farmers already there (this was not altogether correct; JCA had purchased Or Yehuda on its own initiative) – was justified by the political unrest and the antagonism against non-Muslims. It was not until 1931 that JCA was able to complete the liquidation of its interests in Turkey. Its ventures there had at least provided, during the quarter century of their existence, a temporary refuge for some hundreds of families, mostly of Russian Jews.

CHAPTER 10

Poland and Eastern Europe

Polish Jewry between the wars

The situation of Poland's sizeable Jewish minority between the world wars has to be seen in the context of the social, economic and political conditions that prevailed in the new nation during that period. Jews made up about 10 per cent of a total Polish population of 30 million. Although Poland was primarily an agricultural country, most Jews were urban dwellers. Thus one-third of Warsaw's population was Jewish, and indeed in some towns Jews were in the majority.

The state of the Polish economy between 1918 and 1939 can only be described as wretched. Much of the country had been turned into a battlefield by the First World War, and not long after the Armistice of 1918 had come the Russo-Polish War, lasting from May 1920 to March 1921 and wreaking yet more havoc upon an already devastated land. Recovery was bound to be slow, and the task of rebuilding a nation out of three regions separated from one another for over a century was in any case far from easy, especially in the economic sphere, where each had formerly benefited from access to the large market afforded by a great empire.

By 1926, though still a long way from prosperity,[1] Poland began to experience something of an economic recovery. This trend was boosted by the English coal strike of that year, which redounded to the advantage of Poland, a leading exporter of coal, and more generally by the world-wide prosperity of the mid-1920s. This revival was short-lived, however, for soon the world was plunged into the Great Depression. Among the prices that fell first and furthest were those for agricultural products, a fact particularly critical for Poland, whose welfare, 'because of the preponderance of agriculture', depended 'upon the world prices of agricultural products to a far greater degree than the prosperity of the United States or even of France'.[2] By 1934 Polish agricultural prices were at one-third of their 1928 levels, and the country sank into a slump, with concomitant massive unemployment from which it had not fully recovered by the time of the Nazi invasion in 1939.

This is not the place to explain (if indeed it is possible to do so) why the Poland created by the Treaty of Versailles was so virulently anti-Semitic. The right-wing 'Camp of National Unity', the ruling body after Marshal Pilsudski's *coup d'état* of 1926, made no bones about their hatred of Jews. It is true that Pilsudski restrained his followers inasmuch as he opposed the infliction of actual physical harm upon Jews; after his death in 1935 there was no check on the Camp. The central aim of its policy for Jews was to exclude them from participation in the social and economic life of the nation. This aim entered the popular consciousness via the incitement to Poles to 'engage in economic and cultural self-defence against the Jews'.[3]

The impact of such a policy on the situation of the Jews is not hard to picture. The Jewish 10 per cent of the population paid 35 to 40 per cent of the taxes, but only 1 per cent of the funds distributed to religious bodies by the government went to Jewish organisations. In schools and universities Jews were under-represented, and Jews who had received a professional education outside the country were not permitted to qualify in Poland; any who somehow surmounted this formidable obstacle would still find themselves barred from membership of doctors' or lawyers' associations. There were practically no Jews in the civil service. Boycotts and mass picketing of Jewish stores became everyday occurrences.[4]

These measures had the expected and desired effect of driving almost the entire Jewish community into penury. Dr Bernard Kahn, head of JDC in Europe, reported in 1931 that half of Poland's Jews were unemployed, that one-quarter were on the verge of starvation, and that 70,000 Jewish merchants and 12,000 industrialists had closed the doors of such businesses as they had. In 1937, 40 per cent of the Jewish population applied for Passover relief.

This economic picture was matched in grimness by the social one. The government that came into power after Pilsudski's death in 1935 was controlled by a clique of army officers and aristocratic politicians who, to win popularity, tended to become increasingly anti-Semitic. To the boycott of Jewish shops were added almost daily attacks on Jews, punctuated by occasional pogroms. It has been estimated that between 1935 and 1939, 350 Jews were killed and 500 wounded in anti-Semitic incidents. According to another tally 118 Jews were killed and 1,350 wounded between 1935 and 1937 in 348 'violent mass assaults on Jews'.[5]

The only positive idea proposed by the Camp on Poland's

'Jewish problem' was that this hated minority should emigrate. Unfortunately, no country was prepared to take them except Palestine, and although Palestine could receive some tens of thousands, it could not accept the much greater numbers who were every bit as eager to leave Poland as that country's ruling body was to see them go.

JCA in Poland, 1919–22

Before the Treaty of Versailles Poland's Jewish population made up somewhat more than half the Jews living under the Czar's rule. Thus, a large part of JCA's activity in pre-war Russia had been carried out in an area that was now the major portion of the new Poland. A country that had been the scene of such intense JCA activity was bound to receive the maximum possible attention from the organisation once communications could be reopened. This happened, if incompletely, in 1919, and the JCA report for 1920 has a full section on efforts in Poland. These efforts amounted to a full-scale build-up of JCA's operations, interrupted by the Russo-Polish War of 1920–21 but quickly resumed with the end of hostilities.

When JCA's Paris office re-established contact with Poland, it found somewhat to its surprise that some JCA interests there had survived the war. Chief among these were the vocational schools in Warsaw, Vilna, Czenstoniev and Czestochowa. The Da'ath Society of Warsaw was still running four elementary schools. Communication being what it was, Paris was unable to find out whether the farm school in Czenstoniev was operating or not. Word was received, however, that another farm school at Slobodka-Lesna in Galicia had been severely damaged. As for the fate of the kassas, here too no information could be obtained but JCA was already seeking to have a survey made and a reorganisation plan set up.

JCA's operations recommenced in a rather scattered fashion, and this unevenness was exacerbated by the upheavals of the Russo-Polish War. Thus, on Grysbowski Street in Warsaw workshops belonging to a JCA vocational school were occupied by the military, whereas another school on Stawski Street was unaffected. With help from JCA, the Da'ath organisation continued operating its four Warsaw primary schools, while also paying for the tuition of bright students at higher schools. The Lodz vocational school was taken over by the Polish army but was returned in November 1920 to JCA, which planned reconstruction. The Vilna school was in good shape, and the pupils it trained were apparently able to find jobs. This school had been aided by the Vilna kassa during the First World War, but now the kassa was wholly without funds. Vilna, it will be recalled, was the site of two fair-rent blocks of flats erected by JCA before the war; now these buildings were in deplorable condition and the community wanted to convert them into an orphanage. The town of Piotrkov had an active kassa which JCA planned to expand to a membership of 2,000. Many of the Galician kassas had been destroyed, and some survived only to perish during the Russo-Polish conflict; in many cases the furniture and even the buildings themselves had disappeared. However, a handful had escaped major damage, and by 1920 the Cracow institution was back in business.

Before the war JCA had owned three agricultural estates in what was now Poland, using them as farm schools, land for tenant farmers or farms worked by paid labourers with a view to a financial return. At Czestochowa, in addition to the vocational institution, there had been a gardening school; this was now rehabilitated and its buildings repaired. The Czenstoniev farm, it was found, was closed. Its machinery had been badly damaged and, for the time being, it was not being worked because agricultural wages were high and prices low. Slobodka-Lesna, site not only of the farm school but also of a large property producing enough potatoes to supply the needs of a profitable alcohol distillery, had suffered severely but by 1921 its wells had been cleared, new livestock purchased, the buildings largely restored and 75 per cent of the pre-war acreage resown.

Although Russian Poland had been occupied by Germany in 1915, ORT committees had continued to function there, as in Russia proper, throughout the war. In the early post-war period, JCA, having no infrastructure in the country, worked through ORT in supplying artisans with tools and materials. A large consignment of United States army surplus was purchased in France at favourable prices and sent to Poland, where ORT took care of distribution. The Organisation was further able, on its own, to make some farm machinery available in the Vilna and Minsk areas, and to make loans to individual Jewish farmers and co-operatives in the vicinity of Grodno and in the Vilna region.

Poland at peace

The year 1921 found Poland finally at peace after more than six years of almost uninterrupted war. Peace, however, was the only blessing the country could count. As the JCA report for that year noted, the population was in misery, industry was at a standstill, the rate of exchange was extraordinarily low and interest therefore extraordinarily high, sometimes as much as 300 per cent per annum. Such were the circumstances dictating the orientation of JCA's efforts to sustain Poland's Jews.

Activities were to be organised under three main heads: (1) aid to Jewish farmers, (2) aid to vocational schools, and (3) provision of credit, chiefly through loan kassas. Under the first head, 1921 saw the completion of rebuilding at the Slobodka-Lesna estate, where, thanks to a loan from the Agricultural Bank of Lvov, top-quality seed had been obtained and planted, although the crop was reduced somewhat by the effects of hot weather and drought; also, a wooded area neglected during the war was cleaned up and new trees were planted. At Czestochowa, by contrast, rehabilitation had not yet reached a point where the school could be reopened. In the major activity of making loans to farmers the Association was still using ORT as an intermediary in the Vilna area. In this way advances were made to 747 families and five co-operatives for the purchase of seed and implements. JCA on its own made no fewer than 1,535 loans in the region around Grodno and Pinsk – loans that were to all intents and purposes gifts.

In its approach to vocational education, JCA's aim was to turn out what it called *artisans d'élite* – people so qualified that their capacities would be generally acknowledged and their employment assured. As the later record shows, this goal was largely attained; for, when the Polish government imposed the testing of various skills as a prerequisite to undertaking paid work, 95 to 99 per cent of the graduates of JCA training schools passed. Even in the very depressed years of the 1930s these young people were usually able to find employment, although for the most part, it must be said, in Jewish establishments.

In carrying out this part of its programme JCA in 1921 helped to pay the expenses of seven schools – in Warsaw, Lodz and Vilna among other places – and was preparing to support six more. The main occupations taught for boys were metalworking, electro-mechanics, tailoring, housepainting and lithography; and for girls, dressmaking, embroidery and the sewing of lingerie. JCA's report stressed that many of the schools were still badly in need of rehabilitation.

In an interesting sideline to its activities in the vocational field, JCA gave financial assistance to a newly established rabbinical seminary in Warsaw. Its curriculum, in addition to religious instruction, included Polish language and history as well as Latin, German, geography and the natural sciences. It was hoped that graduates, as 'modern' rabbis, would be able more effectively to represent the community than the more traditional ones, whose education was strictly limited to Talmud and Torah.

Since the interest rate on such credit as was available was still around 250 per cent, JCA was naturally anxious to re-establish the kassas as soon as possible. The system was in complete disarray and had to be reconstructed and supplied with credit, there being no deposits for the kassas to draw on since the local population had no funds with which to make them. By the end of 1922, 30 kassas were operational in the central region and 21 in Galicia. To the north, in the Vilna region, 36 resurgent kassas were able to borrow from an institution called the Popular Bank of Vilna, established by a group of co-operative societies, credit co-operatives and consumers' and producers' organisations. The kassas charged their members from 12 to 18 per cent on loans – a far cry indeed from the ruling rate. Taken together, the three areas had 87 active kassas, with 57,000 members.

The importance and efficiency of the institution of the kassa had very much impressed JCA's Director-General, Emile Meyerson, who made two visits of inspection to Poland in 1921. He wrote:

> I cannot tell you how heartening an impression I carried away. These are truly little nuclei full of life. It is certain that this form of relief is the most prompt and most direct; it is also that form which the interested parties best know and best appreciate.[6]

It is worth noting that the typical loan offered through this form of relief was amazingly small: the largest ran to some 50,000 Polish marks, equivalent at the time to $30, or between £6 and £7 sterling.

One other sphere of JCA activity that deserves mention is housing. During the war years many houses near the front had been burnt or ripped apart for beams to shore up trenches. Yet the inhabitants had in many cases returned and were trying to reconstruct their former homes. Thus it was that JCA, in conjunction with an organisation called EKOPO (Jewish Committee for the Relief of War Victims), which received financing from American groups, made loans to 150 families to rebuild houses in towns near Vilna. In 1922 JCA greatly increased its aid to EKOPO, enabling this organisation to make construction loans to 900 families, comprising about 5,000 people, in 51 localities.

In another development in the area of housing, JCA decided to renovate the two former fair-rent blocks of flats in Vilna, one as an orphanage, as the community had requested, and the other as dwellings for white-collar workers.

171

JCA and JDC

As in the USSR, JCA was not working alone in Poland in the post-war period, for JDC was also active there. Though agreed on the goal – the rehabilitation of Poland's Jews – the two organisations differed both in the way they were financed and in their philosophies. JDC was supported by annual fund-raising drives and thus did not have the obligation that JCA felt to husband the capital of a fixed endowment. Consequently, JDC could more easily afford to take a 'charity' view of its expenditures than JCA and could enter such 'unremunerative' areas as health and child care, including, for example, sending some 100,000 Polish Jewish children to summer camp. And, as we shall see, JDC's flexibility also allowed it to make interest-free credit available to the most distressed sector of Polish Jewry. Despite this difference of emphasis, however, the two organisations were sufficiently mature to collaborate effectively in some fields, to take separate paths in others, and successfully to avoid fruitless duplication of effort.

In the vocational area, for instance, JCA by the end of 1922 had under its wing nineteen schools with a total attendance of 1,500. Since JDC was likewise interested in vocational training the two organisations agreed to divide the work. JCA undertook to cover deficits in the schools' operating expenses, while JDC would supply all needed machinery and teaching equipment – no small burden, in view of the special needs of vocational schools.

JCA and JDC also decided to collaborate in another sphere of great concern to both, namely the provision of credit for the hard-pressed Jewish small traders and artisans through the medium of loan kassas. In June 1922 a joint committee was formed, staffed by representatives of both agencies, whose task was to inspect each applicant institution and pass on its findings to its principals. At this time the kassas were grouped into four geographical districts, a measure necessitated by the great increase in their numbers, and hence in the number of loans made. For example, in the Old Kingdom 61,766 loans were made in 1922 as compared with 9,599 in 1921; and in Galicia, 8,817 as against 3,608.

JCA's activity in Poland was now almost back to its pre-war level. Together with JDC, it was supporting a comprehensive system of vocational education and was supervising and financing a network of about 200 kassas. JCA had assumed full responsibility for the programme of aid to Jewish farmers and was planning to extend this work. The rehabilitation of the farm schools was virtually complete: at Slobodka-Lesna the burned distillery had been replaced; Czestochowa was operating with 30 students

172

and was fully supplied with animals and tools; Czenstoniev, though far from completely restored, had livestock and produced crops, and on the site was a school with 58 students; lastly, the Stanislavov school had opened its doors to 40 orphans.

Apprenticeships

A new direction taken by JCA in 1922 was the launching, against opposition from both parents and unions, of a successful apprenticeship programme. Under this scheme boys and girls learned a wide range of skills while at the same time attending night school in order to acquire the rudiments of a general education. JCA paid the employers for the provision of the training, as well as remunerating parents, presumably for the loss of the child's services. Starting out with 300 apprentices in four cities, the programme had expanded by 1928 to eight cities and over 1,600 apprentices.

The 'Foundation'

All was not smooth sailing in these years, however. The Polish mark underwent drastic depreciation and was replaced in 1924 by the zloty, which had a nominal value of 1 gold franc ($0.20). This rate held firm for a time, making it possible for JCA and JDC to continue financing the kassas after loans in marks had become impossible because they would lose all value between the signing of the documents and delivery of the funds. The kassas staggered under the strain of first devaluation and then revaluation, but the monetary support and the supervision supplied by JCA and JDC preserved the system as a whole, albeit in a weakened state. Surveyed in 1924, 109 kassas were declared to be in a satisfactory situation, 55 were put under further observation and 50 were deemed incapable of continuing. Membership declined very substantially, from 104,500 in 1923 to 62,000 a year later.

In May 1924 JCA and JDC, having decided to place their collaboration as lenders on a more formal footing, established the American Joint Reconstruction Foundation (generally referred to as 'the Foundation') as a loan and inspection agency for the kassas. $3 million of its capital came from JDC, $2 million from JCA. As time went on, the Foundation extended its operations to as many as 15 European countries, but the main focus of its attention was always Poland.

The Foundation's co-directors were Bernard Kahn of JDC and Louis Oungre of JCA. It was governed by a Board drawn from JCA and JDC plus representatives of the Jews in Poland, Lithuania and Bessarabia. These 'outsiders' were supposed to include labour and business nominees, as well as an Orthodox Jew and a Zionist, although the last two never attended board meetings. In the 1930s the labour representatives clashed with JCA and JDC, more particularly the latter, ostensibly over the question of loan policy. In reality, the conflict arose from personality differences and power rivalries. The arguments ended when the labour representatives resigned.[7]

The period between 1925 and the onset of the Great Depression, though characterised in the main by improving economic conditions, began with a down-turn. The revaluation of the zloty was a mixed blessing, for it caused a rise in the cost of living. This was aggravated by a poor harvest. The resulting crisis and unemployment hit Jews especially hard.

These economic vicissitudes were naturally reflected in each of the three principal spheres of JCA activity – aid to farmers, vocational education and the kassa credit system.

Aid to farmers

By this time JCA's programme of aid to farmers was well established in the central provinces of Bialystok and Polesie and expanding fast in the Vilna area, where 1,300 Jewish families were in dire need of help. In 1925, 764 farmers in that region received JCA aid in the form of loans for seed, livestock, tools, trees and fencing; and professional advice on modern methods of using machinery and fertiliser was provided for the backward farmers by a corps of roving JCA agronomists. These efforts continued as the economic picture improved. Thus, in 1927 JCA made 1,535 loans to farmers and in the following year, 2,000 loans. In addition, the Association donated agricultural machinery to some farmers, and an agricultural library was even established to further the modernisation efforts.

Vocational schools

For the JCA–JDC vocational schools, this period opened with a critical situation, as local contributions began to decline with the fall of the newly created zloty, obliging JCA to increase its contributions. Likewise, takings of the sales *ateliers* operated by some of the schools fell, so here also JCA had to step into the breach. Attendance at the vocational schools in 1925 started out at 2,156, but 23 per cent of the pupils dropped out because they lacked the means to pay even the partial fees asked of them. Half of these drop-outs were however able to find jobs in their trades.

174

From the standpoint of the Jewish population, a significant event of 1926 was the passage of legislation requiring artisans to obtain certificates attesting to their skills and general knowledge before being allowed to continue to ply their trade. This seemingly innocent regulation wreaked cruel havoc among older Jewish craftsmen: a lifelong cobbler, for instance, had to pass a test requiring knowledge of Polish history and the Polish language before he could mend a pair of boots.[8] For the young, the best way of obtaining certification of this kind was to attend a vocational school.

With the turning economic tide, JCA was able by 1927–8 to reduce its share of operating costs to 31 per cent, and this trend continued as municipal and state authorities increased their subsidies.

The teaching in the vocational schools concentrated on 'real work' and the production of goods for sale. The output was remarkably varied: the metalwork classes, for instance, turned out hammers, saws, axes and safes, while the woodworkers sold tables, beds and wardrobes. The flexibility of the system is shown by the fact that, even in 1925, amid financial crisis, new courses were started in motor mechanics and driving.

The kassa system

In 1925 the Foundation was making twice-yearly inspections of 197 kassas. As many as 200,000 loans were made that year, principally to artisans and small tradesmen. These loans were still very small, averaging 130 zlotys, or about £5 or £6. The figures for the next year (295 kassas, 258,000 loans) reflect both the incipient general economic turn-around and the Foundation's resolve to expand the kassa system as quickly as possible since Jewish tradesmen and artisans had virtually no other sources of credit. The Foundation did not normally lend directly to the kassas but rather through intermediaries such as the Popular Bank of Vilna or the Co-operative Bank of Warsaw.

The expansion continued, and even accelerated, in 1927, in which year some 150 new loan institutions opened their doors (see Table 10.3 for figures on the kassa system).

Other activities

With its procedure for supervising the kassas well established, the Foundation branched out in two directions: financial assistance for what it called 'middle-sized' businesses on the one hand, and the establishment of artisans' co-operatives on the other. As

175

regards the former, the Foundation set up 'banks' designed to make loans to people who operated on a larger scale than kassa borrowers. Table 10.1 gives some data on the growth of this system. Gradually, as these banks were able to obtain credit from the Polish State Bank, their calls on the Foundation decreased.

Table 10.1   Banks for middle-sized businesses

Year	Number of banks	Membership
1925	17	4,099
1927	30	9,911
1929	56	19,308
1931	48	16,000
1933	20	5,900
1935	34	9,423
1937	41	11,500

Source: relevant JCA Annual Reports.

As for the co-operatives set up by the Foundation, the first of these, established around 1925, were in Warsaw; they comprised 18 consumer co-operatives, 5 producers' co-operatives, and 4 printing and publishing co-operatives. Their aggregate membership was 7,000. A year or two later the Foundation financed a 355-member umbrella organisation which bought raw materials for the co-operatives and also offered them credit, legal advice and general supervision. By this time the movement as a whole embraced 33 co-operatives with over 10,000 members; it had spread from Warsaw to many other cities and included 33 *cuisines populaires* (presumably restaurants for working people) and five bakeries. Since no further record of these eating places exists, we may assume that they did not survive very long.

Free Loan Societies

While the 'average' artisan was being served by the kassas and the middle-sized businessman by the Foundation's special banks, there still remained a mass of Jewish workers and tradespeople, numbering in the hundreds of thousands, who were too poor even to scrape together the $5 or so minimum deposit for joining a kassa. The Foundation, working on the principle that loans should be handled, at least ostensibly, in a businesslike manner, could not see its way clear to assisting this poorer class. The JCA position was similar. JDC, however, with its greater freedom of manoeuvre, and bolstered by a particularly successful fund-raising campaign, accepted the challenge by setting up in 1926 the first in a chain of Free Loan Societies (Hebrew: *Gemilluth Chassodim*),

176

which lent money either without interest or at purely nominal rates. This was in fact a traditional way of helping the poor in the Jewish world. In 1938 these societies made 221,000 loans. Assuming that each borrower took three loans per year (which we know to be true of kassa borrowers in the early 1920s), we arrive at the rough-and-ready estimate that some 75,000 Jewish families in Poland benefited from this programme in that last year before the German invasion.

Onset of the Great Depression, 1929–30

Post-war Poland was not destined to enjoy even semi-prosperity for long. As a nation she was liable to suffer disproportionately from any decline in world agricultural prices, and one of the first indicators heralding the Great Depression was the fall in farm prices. With the reduction in their income, Polish peasants restricted their purchases. This in turn hit their traditional suppliers, Jewish artisans and small tradesmen, whose lack of business added them to the ranks of the unemployed in the midst of an already general economic slow-down. A very cold winter in 1929–30 did nothing to help matters: the temperature was so low that many cows died, dairy farmers could not produce milk, and potatoes, vegetables and grain could not be harvested. JCA naturally resolved to help farmers in the most seriously affected areas. It made 1,970 loans in 36 localities in central Poland, while its agronomists tried to encourage farmers to save their trees, to revive the dairy industry, and to use manure and fertilisers to improve their crops' chances of survival.

In 1929, 94 per cent of vocational school graduates passed their public examinations, and despite the hard times most of them were able to find jobs in Jewish firms. By now there were 2,512 students in these schools. But income generated locally by the schools was quickly affected by the Depression, so that once again the larger part of the expenses had to be assumed by JCA. The Association's other vocational endeavour, the apprenticeship programme, was meanwhile extended to one more city, bringing the total to nine and the number of participants to 1,046 boys and 147 girls.

The Jews' main sources of credit were the banks for middle-sized businesses, the kassas and the Free Loan Societies. The kassas themselves depended on the Foundation for about four-fifths of their borrowing and on local sources like the state banks for the remainder. In 1929 the Jewish kassas numbered 450, with 180,000 members and outstanding loans totalling 233 million zloty, or

177

about £5 million.[9] In view of the parlous state of business and the danger of losing membership, the kassas began to make loans against borrowers' accounts due.

The co-operatives sponsored by the Foundation did not fare as well as the network of banks for middle-sized businesses, and some were forced into liquidation. The co-operative movement received a not altogether welcome boost when a law requiring that dough be kneaded mechanically prompted bakers to form associations and come to the Foundation for financing.

The next year, 1930, saw the beginning of JCA's long-planned expansion of its farm aid programme into southern Poland. The Association's agronomists had been in the Lvov, Stanislavov and Tarnopol areas since the year before, gathering information. According to their count there were still 4,500 Jewish farmers in Galicia (as compared with some 8,000 before the Great War, military action having driven many from the region). JCA now set up its programme around Lvov and Stanislavov, planning to tackle the rest of Galicia later. In the central provinces, meanwhile, the Association was trying to establish dairy co-operatives and was donating equipment in an attempt to introduce apiculture.

The graduates of the vocational schools continued to do well in the public examinations despite the obstacles placed in the way of Jewish applicants. As anticipated, older artisans had difficulty in passing those of the tests dealing with design technology and legal matters, as well as with Polish history and geography. To help such people JCA subsidised special courses at vocational schools which drew 120 students.

The kassa system continued to grow: in 1930, 488 kassas made 346,000 loans. If we assume (as we did in evaluating the contribution of the Free Loan Societies) that the average member took three loans in the course of a year, 115,000 Jewish families would have obtained credit from the kassas during the year; this means that the system served more than one-fifth of Polish Jewry. A large portion of the remainder obtained credit from the Free Loan Societies, while a relatively small number were able to deal with the businessmen's banks. And of course, farmers also received loans under JCA's farm aid programmes. In all, 40 to 50 per cent of Polish Jewish families were benefiting at this point – possibly the highest point reached – from the credit networks established by JCA and JDC and by their offspring, the Foundation.

But this large extension of credit, and especially the acceptance by the kassas of accounts due as security for loans, caused strains between the Foundation's Western-minded officials and the Polish beneficiaries of what the Westerners looked upon as their largesse. It was felt that the Central Bank for Co-operatives through which the Foundation operated had been too easygoing in its supervision of the individual kassas in allowing them to assume responsibility for their borrowers' accounts due, and, further, that it charged too high an interest rate to its kassa members. In the early 1930s, therefore, the Foundation forced the dissolution of this bank and prohibited the kassas from lending money against uncollected accounts.[10]

A holding action

The next years saw no lessening of the economic crisis. For Jews the effects of the crisis were everywhere aggravated by official and unofficial anti-Semitism, so widespread and deep-seated that JCA and the Foundation never really had any prospect of effecting more than a holding action. These organisations had it within their power to alleviate symptoms – and they did so valiantly – but such were the social and economic forces arrayed against them that cure was quite beyond their capability.

Paradoxically, because of discrimination, the government's steps to offset the effects of the Depression often affected Jews adversely. Thus, the granting of moratoria on debts owed by peasants hurt the Jewish artisans and tradesmen, who could not collect money due to them but still had to meet their own obligations. Similarly, the government's encouragement of the development of co-operatives while excluding Jews from them created competition that was harmful to Jewish traders. The government's attitude towards shopkeepers, tradesmen and middlemen in general was curiously ambivalent. According to its aristocratic and retrograde ideology, middlemen served no useful economic purpose. But this did not prevent the authorities from giving displaced peasants posts in its co-operatives or in the state alcohol and tobacco monopolies, where the hiring of Jews was in principle prohibited. In practice, these job-holders unofficially subcontracted their responsibilities to Jews, who, given the unemployment situation, were happy to work for much less than the official wage, the difference going to their 'benefactors'.[11]

The attempt to create a non-Jewish middle class by transplanting surplus agricultural population to urban centres was another blow to the Jewish tradesmen. In JCA's rather desperate search to find some solution to the problem, it conceived the notion of placing some of the tradesmen on farms – not that a farmer's life was very rewarding in Poland during the Depression, but at least he usually had enough to eat. Furthermore this idea was consistent with the Baron de Hirsch's beliefs. Accordingly, in the early 1930s JCA organised lectures on the rudiments of farming for some hundreds of city dwellers. Many applied for places as farmers and some did become such in a small way. But obviously, only a very small number were able to take this way out. By 1936 JCA was still thinking along the same lines, increasing its staff of agronomists and enlarging its agricultural loan programme in order to help people to use the plots around their houses for growing vegetables, starting small orchards or keeping bees.

Dr Bernard Kahn of JDC had the more ambitious idea of 'industrialising' Polish Jewry by setting up factories under Jewish control where Jews could find employment. Unfortunately, Dr Kahn never found the funds to get this project off the drawing board, for the Depression's effect on JDC, dependent as ever on fund-raising, was to cut its receipts from $3.5 million in 1928 to $385,000 in 1932, and its expenditure was reduced accordingly.

In the circumstances, there was nothing for the two big relief organisations to do but soldier on. They simply did not have the resources to effect any major change in the lives of 3 million Polish Jews. Nor was there any place, now that the British were closing the door to Palestine, whither large numbers might emigrate. (In 1936 only 1,200 Polish Jews reached Palestine. It is doubtful in any case whether Palestine would have been able to absorb any significant fraction of Polish Jewry.)

Aid to farmers

JCA's agronomists continued their work, making loans, giving instruction in modern farming methods, promoting apiculture, and helping to organise groups for teaching purposes as well as to facilitate collective representation in dealing with the authorities. By 1931 this work was well under way in the Stanislavov area, where the Jewish farm population was about 7,500. Conditions for some of them seemed not to have changed since the days of serfdom, while others were quite well acquainted with modern agricultural practices. In any event, JCA, through the media of farm co-operatives and eight kassas, made 691 loans to farmers in Galicia in 1931.

The perversely hard winters of the early 1930s added to the woes caused by low farm prices. JCA sought to combat these conditions by developing co-operatives among Jewish farmers, who were excluded from government-sponsored co-operatives. Some indication of its success may be found in the fact that in 1937 JCA was working, in the Lvov area alone, with eleven dairy and eight agricultural co-operatives. The Association was particularly proud of a dairymen's co-operative known as Chema, which set up a casein factory and – its main achievement – operated six successful dairy stores, four of them in the city of Lodz. This co-operative survived the hard Depression years and was still functioning, though encountering distribution difficulties, in 1937.

In the sphere of farmers' aid programmes, JCA not only pursued its traditional forms of activity throughout these years but considerably intensified its efforts. Table 10.2 gives an idea of JCA's activities from 1922 to 1937 for the benefit of the Jewish farmers, of whom there were about 7,500 in Poland.

Table 10.2 *JCA farm loan and vocational work in Poland*

Year	Number of farm loans		Attendance at JCA vocational schools*	Number of apprenticeships
	Poland	*Galicia*		
1923	145		2,361	450
1925	764		2,156	922
1927	1,535		†	798
1929	1,910		1,959	1,193
1931	1,518	692	1,669	1,225
1933	952	599	1,607	1,156
1935	967	167	2,206	1,920
1937	1,254	228	2,165	1,778
1938	†	†	†	3,102

* In 1927 JCA contributed 31 per cent of operating costs (1,240,007 zloty) to the vocational schools; in 1937 it contributed 33 per cent (756,367 zloty).
† Figure not available.
Source: relevant JCA Annual Reports.

This is perhaps an appropriate place to note that by 1937 no mention is to be found in JCA's annual report of the four farm schools of which so much was made in the early 1920s. We assume that most of these estates had by this time been sold off or otherwise disposed of. We know however from post-war records that Slobodka-Lesna, at least, survived until it was overrun during the Second World War. It was located within the territory annexed by the USSR, and JCA was able to establish a claim through the Foreign Compensation Commission in London and secure restitution of a part of the value of the assets lost.

Vocational education

As local contributions to the vocational schools dwindled, JCA's contributions increased. These and a devoted teaching staff kept the schools going during the 1930s. It was now noticeable that

181

those attending vocational schools often included holders of college degrees, or graduates of *lycées*, who were learning a trade so as to have at least a chance of finding a job. Throughout this decade, as in earlier years, nearly all graduating pupils passed their public qualifying examinations and were generally able to secure employment in their chosen trade. But this fortunate outcome awaited a few hundred people per year at the very most.

Like the farm aid programmes, JCA-sponsored vocational education continued to expand throughout the decade, in spite of financial problems. By 1937 fourteen schools with a total enrolment of 2,165 were assisted by JCA, which underwrote one-third of their budget. In that year, in a departure from its normal practice, the Association also paid for repairs to buildings, the improvement of workshops or the purchase of new machines for seven of the schools in the system.

JCA's apprenticeship programme also expanded throughout the 1930s, so that by 1938 the number of participants reached 3,102, including students attending night courses. This activity, which had initially met with opposition from some unions, was now organised with their help, together with that of community and educational organisations. Again, however, it should be borne in mind that, even had every one of these apprentices succeeded in obtaining a job, it would still have constituted a mere drop in the enormous bucket of unemployment among Polish Jews.

Table 10.2 gives attendance figures for both the vocational schools and the apprenticeship programme throughout the years of their existence. It should be added that, beginning in 1934, JCA subsidised 45 short courses at its vocational schools designed to help young Jews wishing to become artisans. By 1936–7 these courses had 580 students and were offered in ten cities.

Decline of the kassas

Whereas JCA's farm and vocational work weathered the Depression with some success, the period had a disastrous impact on the kassas; 1929 and 1930 turned out to be the years of maximum extent of the kassa system (see Table 10.3). This high point of kassa lending already contained the seeds of decline, for many of these loans would not be repaid on time, if ever.

In 1936 and 1937 world farm prices at last began to creep upwards, and Polish farm prices followed suit. The country was embarked on a semi-recovery, and this is reflected in the slight improvement in the situation of the Polish kassa system in 1937, the last year for which JCA printed a full report on the subject.

In this, our last glimpse of the Polish kassas as a working machine, we find the Foundation operating through a new organisation which it had helped to create, the Central Credit Co-operative. Apart from the Foundation-sponsored kassa network, 87 active kassas belonged to the Agudah Organisation in Poland. Although these were technically outside the Foundation's ambit, the Foundation inspected a number of them in 1937, and some received loans from the Central Credit Co-operative. Another 45 Jewish kassas were unaffiliated with any national organisation.

Table 10.3   *The Polish kassas*

Year	Number of kassas	Kassa membership	Deposits (zloty)	Number of loans	Kassa borrowing from Foundation (zloty)	JCA agricultural loans (zloty)
1923	218	101,514	†	177,949	†	†
1925	197	67,446	1,612,866	205,998	†	†
1927	342	138,205	14,092,937	†	†	†
1929	455	179,597	38,982,124	†	9,126,969	341,956
1931	496	177,502	33,960,017	305,374	7,884,799	401,207
1933	440	131,998	21,390,509	113,000	5,765,396	746,659
1935	322	87,279	16,763,888	103,190	2,083,841	754,598
1937	371	85,260	19,015,632	100,000*	3,034,077	1,433,238

* Approximate figure.
† Figure not available.
Source: relevant JCA Annual Reports.

Businessmen's banks

The fortunes of the Foundation's banks for middle-sized businesses during the 1930s mirrored those of the kassas, except that these banks had significantly recovered from the effects of the Depression by 1937 (see Table 10.1). The Depression's first effect had been to increase the banks' business: deposits in 1930 increased by 14 per cent. But repayment on loans was slow, and before long the Foundation had to determine which banks were in a position to continue operations. Twelve went bankrupt in 1931 (though three others opened their doors for the first time). In the years 1930–3 the effects of the economic crisis were dramatic: membership fell from 20,000 to 6,000. Thereafter, however, the banks began to make slow but steady headway. By 1937 loans had reached the respectable total of 118.5 million zlotys (about $22 million), much more than total kassa loans to small tradesmen and artisans. It should be borne in mind that by far the largest part of the funds borrowed by these agencies came from the Bank of Poland and private banks; in 1934, for example, only one-tenth of borrowing was from the Foundation.

In justice, it should be recorded that by 1939 the government had eased its anti-Semitic campaign in order to curry favour with its Western European protectors, but this welcome change came too late. Also too late was a general upswing in the economy resulting from an enlarged public works programme.

We cannot leave the subject of Polish Jewry without recalling the 'statistic' that overshadows all others, and puts all the aid that we have been discussing into a very different context: this is the fact that, according to one well-known estimate, only 240,000 Polish Jews survived the Second World War out of a pre-war total of 3.3 million.[12]

We have seen how at least half the Jewish population of Poland was helped in one way or another between 1920 and 1939 by JCA, JDC and the Foundation. We shall now offer a brief account of the operations of these agencies in other countries in Eastern Europe.

The Baltic countries

Activities in the Baltic states fell into two categories: vocational education and loan kassas. In the former sphere, JCA learned in 1922 that the Jewish community in Riga, Latvia, wanted to reopen its vocational school. By the end of that year, thanks to JCA aid and JDC grants for the purchase of machinery, these wishes were realised. Similarly, in Dvinsk (Daugovpils), also in Latvia, where the Jewish vocational school had been used as a hospital during the war, JDC assistance made reopening possible in 1920, and by 1922 JCA was also contributing.

Both these schools continued to receive JCA subventions until the outbreak of the Second World War, and both were quite successful. Such was the reputation of the Riga school that almost 50 of its 100 students came from outside the country, from Estonia and Lithuania. During the 1930s the school built and sold a variety of complex machines and supplied equipment to the government post, telephone and telegraph departments, as well as to other national and municipal government entities. The Dvinsk school, which had been founded in 1887, won a gold medal in 1936 for the excellence of its farm implements. These schools played an important part in the life of Latvia's 90,000 Jews, and

7a Kishinev, Bessarabia, 1920s. Trade school

7b Poland, 1925. Trade school

8a Petrovka, Bessarabia, 1920s. Jewish farmer and son

8b Petrovka, Bessarabia, 1924. Wine-making

flourished despite an official anti-Semitism nearly as virulent as Poland's.

In Lithuania JCA's vocational activity centred on a school in Kovno (Kaunas) which received aid from ORT in 1921 and direct assistance from JCA from 1922 onwards. In that year the school had 58 pupils. In addition, JCA financial aid had enabled ORT to set up an apprenticeship programme with 65 participants, the boys in tailoring and shoemaking and the girls in dressmaking.

When the Foundation commenced operations in 1924, apart from Poland's vast network of kassas and the many small loan agencies in Bessarabia, there were 83 kassas in Lithuania, with a combined membership of 24,000. These were financed by the Central Bank of Kovno. Latvia had 16 kassas with 8,373 members. Estonia had one small kassa at Narva.

The size of the Lithuanian kassa movement is surprising when one considers the country's comparatively small Jewish minority of about 153,000 people, 7.5 per cent of the total population; but perhaps the community's unusually high level of education and sophistication had something to do with it. In any event, when the Central Bank of Kovno, because of difficulties in meeting its own obligations, was obliged in 1926 to begin calling in its loans to the kassas, the Foundation came to their rescue. The finance thus provided enabled the kassas to weather the crisis, and by 1930 they presented an almost rosy picture; in that year 88 active institutions made 68,000 loans totalling $5,552,117.

The Depression had serious effects in the Baltic states, as elsewhere. In Latvia, where in 1931 23 kassas made 57,000 loans totalling $2 million, there was a panic run on the banks, kassas included. The Foundation felt obliged to keep the system afloat in view of its importance to the Jewish community (which numbered 95,000 out of a total national population of 1.6 million). And in this aim it succeeded, although it considered it necessary to prohibit kassa loans unbacked by equivalent funds in deposits. The Lithuanian agencies also ran into trouble at this time, though for extrinsic reasons: the banking system in Lithuania was closely involved with that of Germany, and when German banks got into difficulties in 1930–1 the Lithuanians also lost money. But things did not degenerate to the point of panic, and the Foundation protected itself by dealing only with kassas that adhered strictly to its prudential rules.

As the Depression gradually passed, the situation of the Baltic kassas improved, and they continued in operation, rather uneventfully, until the Hitler–Stalin Pact led to the absorption of the little Baltic states into the USSR in 1939–40.

The Foundation and the kassa system, 1924–39

While the two parent organisations were equally responsible for both the direction and the financing of the Foundation, its head-quarters were at JDC's offices in Berlin. Apart from the commendable desire to eliminate needless duplication of effort, JDC probably had another motive when it agreed to the setting up of the Foundation in 1924; for JDC's New York principals had long cherished the hope that, once the immediate post-war relief needs of European Jewry had been met, the situation might become stable enough, and the Jewish communities independent enough, for JDC simply to close down. In all likelihood it was felt in 1924 that the projected Foundation, together with JCA, might safely be left, once that moment arrived, to 'clean up' after JDC's dissolution. (These were no more than dreams, of course: JDC was fully occupied during the entire inter-war period; it mounted a tremendous relief effort after the Second World War; and, so far from closing down, it is at the time of writing (1981) deeply involved in Eastern Europe, Morocco and above all Israel.)

The Foundation inherited the task of supervising and financing the kassa networks not only of Poland and the Baltic countries, but also of Turkey, Romania (including Bessarabia) and several other countries. In 1925, a year after its establishment, the new organisation was busy putting the kassa system in the Old Kingdom of Romania on to a solid footing by opening agencies in Jassy, Bucharest and three other cities. In the same year the Czechoslovakian kassas were brought under the Foundation umbrella. (The kassas in these two countries will be discussed in a later chapter.) Another adherent to the Foundation in the early years was Austria's sole kassa, in Vienna, which in 1924, its first year of operations, recruited 734 members and made about 600 loans. In 1927 yet another country came under the Foundation's aegis with the establishment of a kassa in Sofia, Bulgaria. This institution grew rapidly: by 1929 it had 1,030 members and made loans totalling $24,383. Kassas were also set up before long in two smaller Bulgarian cities.

Thus, hundreds of kassas dealt with the Foundation, either directly or through a central institution. During the relatively prosperous late 1920s this whole web of operations continued to expand, experiencing only 'normal' ups and downs. By 1929 JCA was able to contemplate the Foundation's achievements with some degree of pride: it recorded that on 1 October 1929 749 kassas in 13 different countries or provinces, with a combined membership of 323,640, were being sustained and regulated by the Foundation.

The effects of the Depression, as we saw in the case of Poland, were not immediately felt by the kassas. Thus, although the Great Crash of 1929 is generally regarded as marking the beginning of the Depression, 1930 was actually a good year for the Foundation, which reported that in October of that year it had under its wing 760 kassas with a membership of about 325,000. The Foundation could find added reason for satisfaction in the fact that these results had been attained in countries where the Jewish population suffered great hardship because of discriminatory policies. In Poland, Romania and Latvia the drive to force Jews out of their trades or businesses by means of boycotts or through competition from state monopolies was relentless. For those whose businesses were destroyed, as for those who managed to hang on, the Foundation was the major source of credit.

The kassas began to feel the Depression's bite in 1931. Although membership fell only a little in that year, deposits were greatly reduced. The figures given in Table 10.4, compiled from the relevant JCA Annual Reports, tell their own story.

Table 10.4   *The decline of the kassas, 1929–33*

	Number of kassas	Total membership	Deposits ('000)	Loans outstanding ('000)
October 1929	749	323,640	$10,720	$15,661
October 1930	760	325,000	$11,755	$16,126
October 1931	756	315,000	$ 9,800	$13,720
October 1932	694	264,782	$ 7,650	$ 9,861
October 1933	711	248,908	$ 5,896	$ 8,335

By 1933 the bottom had been reached, and JCA felt able to sound an optimistic note in its Annual Report for that year (which was written in mid-1934). The Association congratulated itself – and the Foundation – on the fact that prior to their activity co-operative efforts had been quite unknown in Bulgaria, Greece, Romania (excluding Bessarabia) and Turkey. The establishment of Jewish financial co-operatives on a sound basis in these nations was wholly due, JCA pointed out, to the stimulus provided by the Foundation. In Poland, Latvia and Bessarabia, where JCA had been responsible for building up 'important networks of co-operatives' before the First World War, the Foundation could take credit for their continuing development and expansion. JCA's confidence was not altogether misplaced, for the next few years saw a general revival of the fortunes of the kassa system.

Germany and German refugees

In 1932 the Foundation offered its support to a German organisation the corporate members of which resembled kassas in their
functioning. This was the Zentrale für Jüdische Darlehnkassen,
set up by Jewish communities because of the great difficulty
encountered by Jewish artisans and tradesmen in search of credit.
In 1935 58 German kassas made 1,948 loans totalling $407,165.
The number of kassas in the country rose to 68 in 1936 but
dropped to 45 the following year. In 1937, in the face of the
ever worsening position of Jews in Germany, the Foundation
undertook the liquidation of the kassas there as well as the one
in Austria.

Other activities

The Foundation was active in 16 countries; its 700 member organisations included one in Salonika, Greece, and one in Abo,
Finland, which had a Jewish community of 300. The scope of the
operations of the kassa system was truly astonishing, justifying
JCA's faith in the value of this type of institution. In 1937 300,000
loans were made, amounting to $56,377,650, and $15,000,000
was outstanding in the hands of the borrowers at the year's end.
Not content to work only in Eastern Europe and Germany, the
Foundation began to provide financial assistance to the refugees
from Hitler who were by now reaching Western Europe and the
Americas: by the end of 1936 it had opened agencies in London
(where refugee doctors formed a large proportion of the clients),
Paris, Amsterdam and Zagreb. In Palestine the Foundation lent
funds to the Central Co-operative Bank so that it could in turn
lend to German Jews. The Foundation also acted to make loans
to refugees available in New York through the good offices of
the Hebrew Free Loan Society there. Meanwhile, as we shall see
in Chapter 12, HICEM, the umbrella organisation which united
JCA and a number of migration agencies including HIAS, had
encouraged the creation of kassas in South America with the same
end in view.

The long-cherished dream of many JDC leaders of some day
being able to dissolve their organisation was still harboured by
some as late as 1939, on the very eve of the Second World War,
when JDC began setting up a committee in Poland which was
intended to take over all its operations in that country. It was
formally constituted on 2 September 1939, just one day after the
beginning of the Nazi invasion of Poland. On this note of unreal-
ity JDC's work in Europe came to a halt for six years – hardly

in the manner desired or contemplated by the organisation's leadership. Having said this, we must not forget the valiant efforts of JDC workers in Marseilles and Lisbon for refugees extricated through unoccupied France and the financial help provided to many Jews in Europe, especially through the efforts of Sali Meyer, JDC's agent in Switzerland, during the war.[13]

A considerably more realistic assessment of the situation had been put forward by JCA's President in his address to the Association's Annual General Meeting of 15 October 1938, which took place just when the Munich Peace Pact was being negotiated. Against this backdrop of illusory hopes, Sir Osmond d'Avigdor Goldsmid summed up the situation of European Jewry after 20 years of backbreaking work by JCA, JDC and many other relief agencies as follows:

> For many years now, the addresses which I have delivered to you on the occasion of our Annual General Meetings have been, like this one, brimful of the disquiet evoked in us by the ever-growing distress of masses of Jews. But never yet has the situation of our co-religionists appeared to me more full of anguish than it does today, nor their despair more profound. Last year I painted for you, Gentlemen, a picture of the many, many thousands of families who, as victims of racial discrimination, were forced to leave their native lands and cross the earth in search of work and bread. Since then other victims have swollen the ranks of those deprived of their homelands. New injustices have been piled upon the heads of our unhappy brothers. Several countries, often without even the excuse of economic reasons, are trying to make of Jews second-class human beings, to 'denationalise' them, to drive them from the positions they occupy in commerce, industry or the liberal professions, and to deprive them of all means of existence.[14]

CHAPTER 11

Romania and Czechoslovakia

Romania

Between the wars

Before the First World War Romania was a small Balkan kingdom consisting of the provinces of Moldavia and Wallachia – often afterwards referred to as the Old Kingdom – with an oppressed Jewish minority of 230,000, concentrated in the principal cities of Bucharest and Jassy. Although Romania contributed little to the Allied war effort, it was rewarded at Versailles with the addition of three large provinces: Bessarabia on the east, which had been Russian, and Transylvania and Bukovina on the west, taken from the Austro-Hungarian Empire. Bessarabia had a Jewish population of about 250,000, and Transylvania and Bukovina together contained over 300,000 Jews, living in primitive conditions and in extreme poverty.

The story of Romania between the wars bears a considerable resemblance to that of its northern neighbour, Poland. The economy, which in general functioned on a low level, reached a state of near collapse during the Great Depression. As for the Romanian Jews, greatly increased in number by the accretion of Bessarabia and the other provinces, they suffered from the economic malaise like the other Romanians but more intensely, because they were the objects of discrimination, of governmentally inspired competition and, especially after the Nazis came to power in Germany in 1933, of boycotts, demonstrations and attacks stirred up by semi-fascist or fascist governments.

The immediate post-war period

It seems that JCA was not able to communicate with Romania in any meaningful way in 1919. The Association's Annual Report for 1920, however, indicates that by then JCA was receiving information and taking action. Ever since the country became independent in the middle of the nineteenth century, Jewish chil-

dren had experienced great difficulty in obtaining entry to the
state school system, and this situation did not change after the
First World War, when the government schools were short of
both space and funds. The Jewish community therefore set up
and maintained its own elementary schools, which in 1919
numbered 44. JCA, now that it was in touch, contributed to the
support of 24 of them. There was also a vocational school in
Bucharest which JCA had helped before 1914 and which reopened, but with only 46 pupils. Another quite well-known and
comparatively elderly institution, the vocational school for girls
in Kishinev, the capital of Bessarabia (and scene of the pogrom
of 1903), was operating with 260 pupils in 1920 and 320 the
next year, most learning dressmaking. Another establishment in
Bessarabia, the *pépinière* (tree nursery) at Soroki, which had been
the object of much solicitude on the part of JCA and was an
important source of young trees for the Jewish farmers before
1914, had been utterly destroyed, so that restoration did not seem
feasible.

The Jews of Romania, like those elsewhere in Eastern Europe,
were desperately anxious to emigrate, but many destinations were
barred to them by immigration restrictions. However, by 1921
one of JCA's chief activities in Romania had become helping some
hundreds of people to emigrate to Argentina; 260 settled in its
colonies there.

The year 1922 brought no great change in the situation faced
by JCA in Romania. The regime still would not assist the Jewish
schools, and JCA felt itself obliged to continue its support of
those maintained by the communities. For a time at least the
communities were able to do something to help themselves; while
JCA assisted 32 schools in 1920–1, by the beginning of the 1923–4
school year the number of JCA-supported schools had been
reduced to 18. At the vocational school in Kishinev JCA saw to
the repair of the old building and the construction of a new one,
which allowed departments to be added for teaching marquetry
and dental mechanics.

Loan kassas

As in Poland and elsewhere in Eastern Europe, the financing and
supervision of the loan kassas in Romania was taken over by the
Foundation in 1924. The Foundation proceeded to extend the
system to parts of the country not hitherto covered. Kassas were
established in Bucharest and Jassy, and five more were planned
to be opened in other cities of the Old Kingdom. In one of the
new Romanian provinces, Transylvania, the Foundation proposed

191

the establishment of 11 kassas in towns with sizeable Jewish populations, particularly in the poverty-stricken Marmorosch area.
The local bureaucracy put obstacles in the way, but by 1926 there
were nevertheless four kassas in operation in the province, with
4,000 members, half of whom were businessmen, nearly a quarter
artisans, and the rest in various occupations including farming.
The kassas made 1,128 loans in that year totalling about $47,470.

The weather, depression and prices

From 1924 to 1929 the weather in Romania was very poor indeed.
In the winter of 1925 there was no snow, thus no protection for
winter wheat or other crops planted in the autumn; in the spring
no rain fell, and the summer was hot and abnormally dry. The
result was a year of misery and famine. Nor did the passage of
time afford relief; in 1926 weather conditions were about average,
but grain prices were low and in 1927 the cycle of bad weather
returned.

The year 1929 saw decent weather at last, and decent crops.
This good crop year, however, marked the beginning of the Great
Depression, when the Romanian economy, largely dependent on
exports, was materially weakened. The trade in cereals, in which
Jews played a large part, suffered a serious decline. Prices fell so
low that costs were not covered. The export trade in timber,
another field in which many Jews were engaged, came nearly to
a halt. Banks suffered losses, as did the Jewish kassas, which
were forced at best to grant their debtors extensions of time for
repayment and at worst to give up hope of collection on many
loans. Things became so bad that in 1931 the government granted
farmers a moratorium on the payment of debts, while industry
was paralysed.

Throughout this period JCA and the Foundation continued
and developed their wide range of activities in the provinces of
Bessarabia, Bukovina and Transylvania.

Bessarabia

As far back as 1899 JCA had worked with Jewish farmers in
Bessarabia, helping to improve methods of growing tobacco, to
develop grande culture, to improve animal stocks and to replace
grape vines which, in common with most in Europe, had been
destroyed by the phylloxera disease. All this work had been halted
by the war. Soon after JCA had resumed its activities, the government of the new Romania passed an agrarian law which put into
the hands of 3,000 rural Jewish families in Bessarabia small lots

of 2–6 hectares each. Curiously, considering that ordinarily JCA responded to cries of distress from Jewish farmers like a fire brigade to a sudden conflagration, the American JDC was the first relief organisation to come to the help of these people. JCA, however, was not far behind. In September 1922 it sent an emissary to survey the situation, and by 1923 had a credit programme in operation through the medium of local co-operatives, the financing of which was shared with JDC. JCA deployed a group of agronomists in the field, supplied farmers with loans, and in conjunction with 11 loan kassas in the province set up stations alongside each for the purpose of supplying farmers with machinery on the basis of long-term advances.

JCA may have been a little slow in starting its agricultural programme in Bessarabia, but once under way this progressed rapidly. By 1924 its facilities had been extended to 2,972 farms in 23 localities, involving a population of about 15,000. The services offered were many and varied. For example, the number of stations supplying long-term loans for equipment increased to 16; the agronomists were providing much-needed instruction; there were numerous demonstration plots; breeding stations were established where the local cows and horses could be mated with superior stock; high-grade animals were also purchased for the farmers; a special effort was made to revive fruit growing, which had been completely neglected during the war, and JCA tried to rebuild a few orchards as examples; the farmers were likewise encouraged to produce seed – a successful effort, for their product was sold throughout Bessarabia.

In 1928 Bessarabia had the worst weather on record. The Jewish farmers were reduced to such penury that some had to rely on the foreign agencies for food. JCA considered that dairy farming offered the best defence against drought, so it encouraged the building up of dairy herds and the development of three butter co-operatives. The situation was still so bad, however, that JCA was called upon to transmit money collected from Bessarabian Jews in Argentina to their fellows in the 'old country'.

JCA and the Foundation continued to do what they could to improve the situation of the farmers so bludgeoned by fate. The network of kassas in Bessarabia was expanded. The agronomists, with some success, got farmers to grow drought-resistant crops; indeed, the grape vine grafts distributed by JCA stood up well to the dry weather. Seed was scarce, and JCA supplied the farmers with this vital necessity, especially for cereals. As might be expected in such cruel climatic conditions, many of the farmers would have been unable to maintain payments to creditors for land purchased had not JCA and JDC lent them money to do so. For once a

Romanian law helped the Jews. Legislation was passed breaking up large holdings, and the small farmers were able to add to their plots. In the case of the Jews however 73 per cent of their farms were still under 6 hectares in extent. The smallholders who did all their own work were able to survive the terrible years of the 1920s better than the larger operators who had to hire labour.

Bad weather did not prevent JCA from going forward with its programme of demonstration farms and its attempts to modernise the agricultural practices of Bessarabia's Jewish farmers. In 1927 the Association provided the first tractor, which was used to work the land of the poorest and newest cultivators. JCA and JDC made advances not only for the improvement and enlargement of Jewish farms but also to enable farmers to hold back their crops in times of low prices. By 1930 the Association had managed to assemble in its ownership an area of 700 hectares in southern Bessarabia. The Jewish farmers in the district took cheer when they learned of this acquisition, and many applied to settle. JCA decided to select 35 families and allotted to each a plot of 20 hectares of which 1 hectare was to be devoted to grapes; 100,000 grafts were obtained from French nurseries, to be planted in 1931. In addition to grapes, the farmers planted barley, sorghum, maize and sunflowers, and each kept at least one cow; 550 sheep supplied by JCA were raised on a co-operative basis. Each family had a full complement of agricultural machinery. The construction of houses began in 1931. The families were given long-term loans of 300,000 lei (approximately $1,900) each for the purchase of the land, house and equipment.

The village was named Ungrovka, in honour of JCA's Director-General, Louis Oungre, and soon developed into an exemplary settlement not only for the Jewish farmers but for the Gentiles also. It even became a summer resort for Jewish tourists. In addition, 30 pioneers were trained there for agricultural settlement in Palestine. So widespread was the good feeling of the settlers towards their settlement and towards the JCA administration that not a single resident moved away. Indeed, in the course of time Ungrovka grew by 18 families and 200 hectares.

After the conclusion of the Hitler–Stalin pact in 1939, Romania agreed to re-cede Bessarabia to Russia, but Ungrovka was apparently unaffected by the change in sovereignty. However, when the German army, accompanied by the Romanian, invaded Bessarabia in July 1942 in the course of the Nazi attack on Russia, the situation altered; but the 53 families then living in the village had time to pack up and migrate to central Asia. After the war most of them reached Israel.[1]

Before commencing the development of Ungrovka, JCA had

become involved in the formation of a colony called Serbeschti in northern Bessarabia. Beginning in 1922, some Jewish farmers began to drift in and establish themselves there, but they found it impossible to operate successfully, especially because they were plagued with malaria. JCA stepped in, had houses built and wells dug, provided cattle and tools, set up a breeding station, and formed a dairy co-operative. By 1934, when Serbeschti was quite well established, with 35 families cultivating a total of 284 hectares, JCA set up a number of demonstration plots which were useful for all the farmers in the area. These not only displayed the most rational and modern manner of working the soil, taking account of the peculiarities of the region and the conformation of the land, but they also, in JCA's words, served as a practical school where the farmers learnt the use of up-to-date machinery and equipment as well as other skills, for example how to combat weeds and parasites.

The Serbeschti settlement was chiefly devoted to milk production, and in consequence had fields of alfalfa (lucerne) capable of two and even three crops a year. It was equipped with a dairy and a creamery, which produced butter and cheese to be sold in a nearby city. In addition, barley, oats, maize and sunflower were grown. Unfortunately, because of the dry weather that so often prevailed in Bessarabia during the inter-war period, these crops sometimes failed after the first planting and had to be seeded again. By 1938 the settlement had the same 35 families but had increased its area slightly to 300 hectares.

Bukovina and Transylvania

JCA had not worked in these two provinces before 1930, except in so far as the Foundation had rebuilt or created their kassa systems. As in so many countries in Eastern Europe, the kassas were of the greatest importance, because in these provinces also Jewish petty traders and artisans found it next to impossible to obtain credit from other sources. By 1930 the kassas operating around Czernowitz in Bukovina had 8,867 members. Loans issued numbered 4,887, for a total of £76,000. In Transylvania there were now 12 active kassas which made 20,000 loans totalling £187,000.

In 1930 JCA decided to extend help to the Jewish farmers in these regions. Before the war there had been 2,000 in Bukovina, and those in the southern part of the province were fairly advanced. Their properties had been ravaged during the conflict, however, and afterwards anti-Semitic persecution had forced many to sell out very cheaply. By 1930 there were only 500 left, mostly in the northern part of the area, impoverished and in no position to obtain credit. JCA determined to help at least the poorest families, and in order to work more effectively put them into groups of five to ten and sent its agronomists to teach them milk production and how to raise potatoes and forage. Two demonstration farms were also set up, one for Leghorn chickens, which are specialised egg-layers, and the other for Rhode Island Reds, which are dual egg and meat producers. Later, farmers in the area were provided with flocks of these fowl and with modern tools. Another crop that some of the Jewish farmers were able to raise successfully was sugarbeet, and JCA helped 50 to 100 farmers to obtain contracts to supply the local sugar refinery. The resulting income, however, was not up to expectation because bad weather reduced the yield.

In Transylvania JCA counted about 1,800 Jewish families living on farms or in rural areas, most of them in the Marmorosch in the northern part of the territory, which is quite mountainous, as it lies in the foothills of the Carpathians. Here again the rural Jews were sunk in poverty. Even those who had prospered through the trade in salt and timber had been rendered destitute by the collapse of exports in the Depression and by Hungary's prohibition of imports from Transylvania, which before 1918 had been part of Hungary. JCA's efforts here centred largely on attempts to establish dairy farming. Every year, beginning with 1932, it put about 100 cows on Jewish farms in the Marmorosch. The cows, JCA said, were a blessing for these extremely poor people, as their milk or its products brought in cash. JCA also sent a cheese expert who helped to form dairy co-operatives, so that families who formerly had no income to speak of were now able to begin to earn. To supplement the cows, JCA introduced flocks of sheep, small orchards and colonies of bee-hives, which helped more than half the Jewish farm families.

All through this period, the Foundation continued working with the kassas in these two provinces. In Bukovina as elsewhere the Jews felt the Depression keenly because of the almost total cessation of the export of wood and cereals. Another blow fell in 1931, when a large commercial bank in which a great many kept accounts failed to the tune of about 150 million lei – nearly $1 million. The kassas were affected by these developments, but the supervision (with special emphasis on preventing the growth of arrears) and the credit provided by the Foundation kept the system viable, though with fewer members and a smaller turnover than in 1929 or 1930. The fact that these kassas were newly established and had had no opportunity to accumulate capital compounded the difficulties. It was found necessary for the Czernovitz kassa to set aside part of its capital to cover doubtful accounts. The

Foundation also cancelled part of the debt owed to it, which eased the pressure on this institution. In 1934 there were 10 kassas in Bukovina, with 8,318 members, which issued loans totalling $368,612. As the indebtedness of these kassas to the Foundation amounted to $316,850, this meant that in effect the Foundation was providing almost all the money they were able to lend. In Transylvania there were now 12 kassas, which issued 5,470 loans amounting to $375,000; this was a tremendous reduction from the 1930 figures.

The 1930s

As in most of the decade of the 1920s, Romania suffered again from bad weather in the 1930s. Throughout that period JCA carried on with its various programmes. As the decade neared its end, JCA's main effort in Romania, though at a lower level than in 1930 because of the effect of the Depression, was devoted to assisting the country's 5,000 or so Jewish farmers (most in Bessarabia), granting credits for the purchase of animals, tools and seed, making collective loans for the purchase of expensive machinery like threshers, and providing other items that were not recoverable from the farmers, such as demonstration fields, grain-judging stations and nurseries. In Bukovina, where JCA had started on the improvement of farming methods by providing good animals and modern tools, the Association was now encouraging intensive cultivation of wheat and sugarbeet. In 1938, the last year of peace, nature finally smiled, and the crops turned out well. In the Transylvanian Marmorosch, where JCA had laid emphasis on dairy-farming, this activity supported 900 families, more than half the Jewish rural population; their equipment had been modernised, and their products enjoyed a favourable reputation. Sheep-rearing had also been encouraged, and the caracul breed had been introduced to upgrade the local stock. Another branch of agriculture important in the Marmorosch was fruit, and JCA had helped hundreds of families to plant apple trees.

Finis in Romania

'Growing social and political tensions in Romania in the 1920s and 1930s led to a constant increase in anti-Semitism and in the violence which accompanied it.' Thus stated the *Encyclopaedia Judaica*, which mentions a number of specific anti-Semitic incidents and even pogroms (organised by the Ministry of the Interior) that took place in the 1920s. To quote the *Encyclopaedia* again, 'After Hitler came to power in Germany the large

197

Romanian parties also adopted anti-Semitic programs.'[2] In consequence, the latter half of the 1930s was marked by a spate of anti-
Semitic decrees, regulations and legislation. In 1935 the National
Bank refused credit to non-Romanians and decrees were promulgated limiting the employment of persons so classified. These
measures struck at the Jews, many of whom had not acquired
citizenship or, if they had, had lost it. Commissions were busy
examining the status of Jews and by 1938 had deprived of their
citizenship 150,000 who were thus unable to find work. In 1935
and 1936 no Jews were admitted to the Bar or to medical school.
In fact, there was a widespread movement to revoke the licences
of Jewish lawyers who were already members of the Bar and to
prevent Jews from attending universities altogether. Heavy taxes
were imposed on Jewish businesses with the object of ruining
them. In 1938 a decree was issued calling for the liquidation of
the Jewish kassa system, but the Court of Cassation abrogated
this regulation in regard to some.[3] 'Germany financed a series of
publications – aimed at fastening an alliance between the two
countries and removing Jews from all branches of the professions
and the economy.'[4] As Germany penetrated into Eastern Europe
with the Austrian Anschluss, the annexation of Czechoslovakia
and the conquest of Poland, Romania fell even more completely
under German influence, becoming in effect a satellite of the
Reich, with consequences for its Jews that can readily be imagined. It must be said, however, that since 57 per cent of the Jewish
population under Romanian rule during the war survived the
Holocaust,[5] the destruction of Romanian Jewry, horrible as it was,
was not carried so far as the annihilation of their co-religionists in
Poland.

Czechoslovakia

Czechoslovakia, incorporating the provinces of Bohemia,
Moravia, Slovakia and Russian Sub-Carpathia, all of which had
been part of the Austro-Hungarian Empire, was established as an
independent country by the Treaty of Versailles. JCA instituted
programmes only in the easternmost province, Russian Sub-
Carpathia, which was a largely agricultural and forested area,
much poorer and more primitive than the industrialised and
comparatively affluent western sections. There were about
100,000 Jews in this province, constituting one-tenth of the total
population. In contrast to the succession states that took over parts
of Russia, Czechoslovakia was not afflicted by governmentally
provoked anti-Semitism until the Munich Pact in 1938 ceded the

Sudetenland of Bohemia and Moravia to Germany, and Slovakia declared its independence in 1939.

Russian Sub-Carpathia was sometimes called the Hungarian Marmorosch, because it had been part of Hungary before 1914; it was separated from the Romanian Marmorosch (northern Bukovina) only by the Thiess (Tisza) River and had the same kind of rough and hilly landscape. To compound the geographical confusion, after the Second World War Russian Sub-Carpathia was awarded to the USSR, as was the northern part of Bukovina, so that both banks of the Thiess River are again under a common sovereignty.

There were no events of note in this remote area after 1918 until the Great Depression struck, when its remoteness proved to be no protection against the world-wide economic slump. JCA described the condition of the Jews in 1931 simply and effectively – it was one of '*détresse féroce*'. By 1932 conditions were so bad that the government felt obliged to distribute food to the starving inhabitants.

JCA's programme

In 1933, when JCA mounted a campaign to help the Jewish farmers in the Romanian Marmorosch, it decided to do the same on the other side of the Thiess River, where there were about 800 or 900 Jewish families who could be considered agriculturists. JCA started operations in the rugged western section and, as in the Romanian part, brought in cows, whose milk was turned into butter and sold in the towns. JCA wanted the farmers to form dairy co-operatives. This turned out to be difficult to accomplish because they lived in scattered and inaccessible places, but the agronomists sought them out and put seven organisations together which successfully produced and sold cheese. Attached to each was a machinery station and a breeding station. JCA reckoned that if a family owned three cows it could make a living. The Association also provided instruction in fruit-growing, distributing 4,000 trees among 40 farmers. It was estimated that, in addition to the Jewish agricultural families proper, there were 2,500 more that did some farming, and a large proportion of these also benefited from the activities described. In 1935 another 5,000 fruit trees were distributed, as JCA was hoping to develop fruit production on the basis of home gardens.

The Association understood, of course, that all this good work had a very tenuous base, because of the darkening political trend as Nazi power increased. If this trend were to be reversed, JCA felt that the Jewish rural population could support itself; but this was a vain hope.

Beyond farming, JCA was planning to start apprenticeship courses. Such a plan was carried out in 1937, but curiously not in the rural area of eastern Czechoslovakia. Apprentice *'foyers'* – offices – were established in the western Czechoslovakian cities of Prague, Brünn and Moravka-Ostrava, apparently on the supposition that students from Russian Sub-Carpathia and Slovakia would apply to them. It was felt that openings for artisans were so few in the eastern part of the country that it made more sense for these facilities to be placed in the industrial, heavily populated and more prosperous western section which offered much greater opportunity.

Loan kassas

In 1925 the Jewish kassa system in Czechoslovakia joined the Foundation. In Russian Sub-Carpathia there were ten kassas affiliated to the Union of Jewish Co-operatives of Mukacevo, the chief city of the region, and there were four more in Slovakia. The kassas had a total membership of 9,259, of whom 25 per cent were small businessmen, 23 per cent petty traders, 17 per cent artisans and 17 per cent agriculturists. The average loan was about £20.

These comparatively minor operations of JCA and the Foundation in Czechoslovakia were rudely terminated when, after the Munich Pact in 1938, the Sudetenland was transferred to Germany, and Slovakia broke away to become an independent – and violently anti-Semitic – country.

CHAPTER 12

Migration

The post-war situation of Jews in Eastern Europe

If, after the November 1918 Armistice, the greatest, most immediate task facing the organised world Jewish community was the
economic rehabilitation of the impoverished Jewish masses of
Eastern Europe and Russia, the second most urgent priority was
dealing with the problem of the hundreds of thousands of refugees
from Russia who had fled that country during the civil wars that
followed the Communist revolution. Others who feared the rule
of the government imposed on Russia by that revolution also
made their way across the frontiers. The newly created states
bordering on Russia were flooded with people who were just as
anxious to escape from Europe to the United States or other
American countries as their unwilling hosts in Poland, Romania,
Turkey or the Baltic states were to see them go.

Unfortunately – and this became more true as the 1920s wore
on – countries that had been open to immigrants progressively
raised bars to the intake of newcomers, especially those from
Eastern Europe. For all that, some of the fugitives succeeded in
leaving Europe before the doors of the United States began to
close with the passage of the 'Quota' Act of May 1921 and were
almost slammed shut, as far as Eastern Europeans were concerned,
with the Johnson Act of 1924. The plight of the migrants
distracted attention for a time from the larger and unceasing
problem of the Jews who lived in the succession states. Later,
Nazism came to power in Germany, swallowed up Austria and
Czechoslovakia and influenced neighbouring states to follow its
violently anti-Semitic example. What JCA did to meet this
continuing crisis is the subject of this chapter.

1919–21

In 1919 JCA recorded with regret that Jews emigrating to the
West did not have the benefit of the advice and protection of the

Association's pre-war information bureaux in Russia and what was now Poland. Hence, wrote Louis Oungre, there was a mad flight, an unregulated tempestuous attempt to save their lives by people 'fleeing persecution, invasion and ruin'. In contrast to the time before the war, when the emigrants had largely come from the poorer segment of the population, this was a flight of all classes, 'who, left to themselves without guidance or counselling, fell into the hands of unscrupulous dealers who cheated them out of all their possessions'.[1]

Unable to take any action in Poland where the Russo-Polish War was going on, JCA had perforce to limit its operations to helping the Ezra Committee in Antwerp and the Montefiore Committee in Rotterdam. The majority of Jewish emigrants did in fact pass through the former city – about 38,000 from June 1920, when emigration began, to the end of that year. Of these, 8,600 had recourse to Ezra and 1,800 of them received monetary aid. The others needed help in obtaining passports or buying tickets. Montefiore in Rotterdam also helped Jews in transit by procuring passports and visas for those who lacked them, and many were lodged in a splendid building provided by the municipality of Rotterdam. But the numbers involved were only about 600.

Altogether, 1920 was a year of considerable movement: 60,000 Jews left Poland, 25,000 left Bessarabia and 5,000 departed from Russia and Bulgaria. Their destinations were as follows:

United States	65,000
Palestine	8,000
Canada	8,000
Argentina	4,000
Mexico and elsewhere	5,000
	90,000

The American countries, alarmed by this influx, began to impose restrictions on entry. The United States required visas issued by the American consuls in the country of origin, a condition that was difficult for the fugitives to fulfil. Canada enforced its law confining entry to farmers – who also had to have $250 in their possession. And the South American countries in the course of the following year, 1921, also adopted restrictive measures.

In 1921 JCA re-established connections with many transit committees in Berlin, Cologne (where the amazing number of 52,000 Jews spent some time *en route* in 1920–1), Genoa, London, Liverpool, etc. The Association also succeeded in setting up a committee to help would-be emigrants in Warsaw (this was the nucleus of the JEAS, the Jewish emigration agency in Poland) and in communicating with the migrants' committees in Kishinev, Bessarabia, where earlier (in March 1920) the American immigrant aid organisation, HIAS, had opened an office. No less than 35,000 Jews entered the free city of Danzig in 1920; as the influx continued into the next year, the local authorities placed some 12,000 new arrivals in internment camps, where conditions were primitive – they had originally been built for prisoners of war. Charles Netter, a member of the JCA Council, went to Danzig and was able to get conditions improved. As the authorities began to restrict entry to those with valid passports and onward tickets, the incoming migrants were able to leave after a stay of only a few days, which eased the work of the hard-pressed committee in that city.

In order to help the Russian Jewish refugees in Romania, JCA sent Lucien Wolf, a well-known British publicist, to ask the League of Nations High Commissioner for Refugees to urge the Romanian government to defer an expulsion order against these refugees. This action was successful. Later Wolf was appointed to the High Commissioner's Consultative Committee.

JCA convened a conference of parties interested in migration in Brussels in June 1921, followed by a second one the next month in Paris. At these meetings the Association stressed the importance and advantages of unity among the various Jewish agencies; but, fearing that unification on JCA's terms would reduce them to instruments of JCA, the agencies refused to take any action. One positive result, however, partly attributable to the Paris conference, was the creation of a Commissariat for Refugees by the League of Nations.

Transit committees

Despite the lack of agreement in Paris, many of the Jewish agencies concerned with the refugee problem did in fact unite to set up an organisation called Emigdirect (United Committee for Jewish Migration) which was initiated at a conference in Prague in October 1921. This meeting had been convened by HIAS and a union of Jewish welfare associations in Europe and overseas called the World Jewish Relief Conference. Emigdirect, largely financed by HIAS, organised committees in many Eastern European countries, as well as France, England and the Far East.[2] Although JCA was not a member of Emigdirect, it co-operated with many of its branches, some of which adopted methods of operation advocated by JCA and even asked JCA to undertake the responsibility of co-ordinating their activities.

Since the work of the local groups, often called 'transit commit-tees', was of great importance in the 1920s, it deserves a brief description (based on information in the JCA 1922 Annual Report). These committees provided shelter for the travellers waiting to embark, helped them with problems of foreign exchange or the transfer of funds to or from relatives, assisted them in obtaining steamship tickets, supported them in disputes with the shipping companies, helped them to secure passports or other necessary documents, and when necessary provided them with new, clean clothes (as Louis Oungre observed, fresh linen made a strong impression on medical examiners, and medical tests had an important place in the migration process). The committees also provided medical care for the migrants. While they were not intended primarily to supply cash for the travellers, they did give money to the needy, especially when these were held up in port for long periods. In some cases where the travellers stayed long enough, the illiterate among them were offered lessons in reading Hebrew or Yiddish.

Reception committees

JCA was also active in the countries receiving immigrants. In 1920 a reception committee had been set up by JCA in Buenos Aires, with sub-committees in other Argentine cities and the JCA colonies. JCA's own office in Buenos Aires investigated possibilities for immigration into Chile and Bolivia. Despite the difficulties posed by Argentine regulations, which allowed in only agricultural workers, 3,660 Jewish immigrants disembarked at Buenos Aires in 1921, of whom 722 were helped by the JCA committee. This organisation developed into the agency called SOPROTIMIS, an acronym for the Spanish title of an association to help Jewish immigrants, with membership drawn from Argen-tina's Jewish community in general.

As we have seen in an earlier chapter, the JCA committee in Montreal gave support to the Jewish Immigrant Aid Society of Canada. Because of the 1920–1 economic slump and consequent high unemployment, Canada imposed restrictions on immi-gration, but 10,500 Jews nevertheless succeeded in entering the country in 1921.

JCA had financed a mission to Mexico, organised by the Indus-trial Removal Office of New York, and had inspired the establish-ment of reception groups in Mexico City, Tampico and Monterey; and a small number of Jews did manage to enter Mexico.

The United States, because of its size and its history of admitting large numbers of Eastern European Jews, was the area of greatest concern, especially when Congress passed the restrictive Quota Act in May 1921. This had been prompted by the post-war depression and the consequent trade union opposition to immigration, plus the xenophobia that every now and then mani-fests itself in the country, stimulated at this time by false but widely disseminated racial theories adumbrated by Madison Grant, H. S. Chamberlin and others.[3] The Act restricted the immigration from any European country to 3 per cent of the number of natives of that country residing in the United States in 1910. The object was to limit the intake of immigrants from southern and eastern Europe as against those from the western and northern parts of the continent. This militated against Jews from Poland or Romania who, though regarded and treated as different from true natives by their own governments, were included by the United States in the totals of those originating from these countries. In May 1924 the Quota Act was succeeded by the even more restrictive Johnson Act. The immediate effect was to reduce immigration from Europe to an annual total of 167,000 in contrast with the peak of 1.2 million reached in 1913, 805,000 in 1921, and even the 310,000 who gained entry in 1922 under the Quota Act. The figure of 167,000 was arrived at by taking 2 per cent of the number of residents in the United States in 1890 originating from the various European countries. As this base-date was before the big immigration from Italy and Russia that subsequently took place, the regulation effectively limited the intake from these two countries. However, 167,000 was not to be the permanent limit, which was to be fixed in 1927 at 150,000.

By 1921 JCA's activities in regard to migration had assumed a certain geographic logic. Help was being given to committees in the countries whither the Russian refugees had first fled, such as Poland, Romania, Danzig and, later, Turkey. Also, in Poland and Romania there were plenty of native Jews who wanted to leave and could use the advice and information provided by the committees. JCA further had ties with and gave support to committees in the countries of transit, which essentially were the Western European nations. Lastly, the Association was working with groups in the Western Hemisphere which provided reception services, for example HIAS in the United States, JIAS in Canada and Soprotimis in Argentina. The last two were recipients of JCA subventions.

JCA supported reception work not only in the countries mentioned; it was also actively engaged in seeking out possible new areas where European Jews could settle, such as Mexico,

Chile, Cuba and even Bolivia. This search was made necessary by the stringent limits on immigration adopted by the United States, Canada, Argentina and Brazil, which had been the principal destinations of Jews from Eastern Europe before the war. Of these, the United States was by far the most important, and its restrictions were a tremendous and frustrating obstacle in the way of the efforts of JCA and other agencies to find havens for the refugees.

1922–4

While the Jewish migration agencies had been unwilling to join an organisation that they feared would be dominated by JCA, in the event they were perfectly agreeable to have JCA's office in Paris act as co-ordinator of their actions. The immediate problem was the continuing presence of tens of thousands of Russian refugees who were left principally in Poland and Romania, even after the large exodus already described. A few figures will illustrate the extent of the problem and the success of the agencies' and the migrants' own efforts to overcome it. In March 1922 there were an estimated 45,000 such persons in Romania; by the end of the year only 11,000 were left. In 1921 there had been 150,000 refugees in Poland; at the end of 1923 the number was 11,000.

Although many of these people relied on their own devices, the Warsaw Committee assisted 4,500 with grants of money and helped about 5,000 more to obtain Argentine visas; 40,000 migrants passed through Cologne, where the local committee helped most of them over the German frontier; about 11,000 embarked from Hamburg and Bremen, in the latter city helped by the Hilfsverein der Deutscher Juden; another 7,000 went through the Low Countries assisted by Ezra and Montefiore. Many were helped by English transit committees; Liverpool had been a big embarkation centre in 1921 when 15,000 passed through, but in 1922 the number was down to 2,500 as the focus shifted to Southampton and continental ports.

A new trouble spot was Constantinople, where about 3,000 Russians had arrived and could not find work. JCA despatched an agent to that city where he found that one-third of the refugees required financial assistance. The measures taken to move these people from Turkey will be discussed below.

Even while Argentine visas were still obtainable, the multitude of bureaucratic formalities made the process very difficult; this was especially so for Russians, because the Argentine government did not recognise USSR passports. As the result of intercession by JCA, the government was induced to be satisfied with fewer documents. It was because of the large movement of Jews to Argentina in 1923 (in addition to the 5,000 Poles, 3,000 came from elsewhere) that JCA helped to create Soprotimis. This organisation performed port services, found the newcomers lodging and jobs, helped artisans with loans to set up in business, and kept its eye out for white-slavers, a breed of pest long endemic in Buenos Aires.

Whatever virtues the post-war Polish and Romanian governments possessed, patience and tolerance were not among them. They threatened constantly to expel the Russian Jews who had sought refuge within their boundaries, and the Poles did force some out. Anti-semitic to begin with, these governments were all the more reluctant to suffer the presence of thousands of undocumented foreigners, a great many of whom had no money. For the Association this was an even greater problem. Where were the unfortunates to go? To arrange for destinations for them needed time. JCA therefore intervened with both governments. The deadline for expulsion from Romania, already deferred, was put off to 15 February 1923 and again to 31 December 1923. In Poland the intercession of the Nansen Committee of the League of Nations and promises by JCA and other Jewish organisations that the refugees would be moved out persuaded the government in April 1923 to put an end to forcible repatriation to Russia. However, by October of that year the Russian quota to the United States was filled, and about 1,000 people from Poland who had intended to go there had to be repatriated to Russia. The Soviet authorities would not at first re-admit those who had fled the country without passports, but they finally relented. It was clear that the collaboration of all the Jewish organisations would be necessary, and the American agencies, the London War Victims' Fund and the Alliance Israélite in France asked JCA to act for them in dealing with the Polish regime.

Thus JCA was now actor as well as co-ordinator in assisting the refugees. By the end of May 1923 some 5,000 of the refugees who had left Poland had received advice from JCA and 3,500 had had money. The Warsaw Committee helped 10,000 to obtain visas and/or cheap tickets and provided 850 with cash. In addition to the Russian Jews there was an even larger number of native Polish Jews leaving the country – 30,000 in 1922, 42,000 in 1923. Unable to secure admission to the United States, they went to Canada, Argentina, Brazil, Cuba and Palestine.

Meanwhile, the number of refugees going through Danzig was increasing. The two movements may have been connected, as some of those who had fled to Poland, afraid of deportation, went on to Danzig. To its considerable cost, JCA had undertaken the supervision of the refugees in Danzig, but on the positive side it was able to persuade the authorities to ease the conditions. English classes were also organised, a workshop for the sale of dresses was opened, a reading room was prepared, gymnastic instruction was given and, perhaps most important, milk was provided for children and nursing mothers.

In Romania, where the refugees were supported by JDC, JCA opened offices in Bucharest, Kishinev and southern Bessarabia. Their main functions were to determine the refugees' destinations, send them out in groups so that they did not have to travel in isolation, arrange for medical examinations and passports, obtain tickets at reduced prices, and keep the transit committees in Germany informed as to coming movements (60,000 emigrants passed through Germany in 1923). JCA headquarters in Paris also informed the reception agencies in the United States, Argentina and Canada what to expect. In all, 7,500 refugees left Romania in 1923, of whom 4,700 were helped by JCA.

In addition to the large number of emigrants passing through Germany that year, about 4,000 left via Liverpool and 1,700 via Rotterdam, while Ezra in Antwerp helped no fewer than 14,000 of whom 2,000 had to stay an appreciable time in that city. This group included a substantial number of children, so an elementary school was set up for them which taught Yiddish and English, the latter being the language which it was expected they would need at their destination.

Argentina admitted over 13,000 Jews in 1923 (two-thirds from Poland), by far the largest number in any year between the wars. Perhaps this was because Argentine consuls for part of the year were willing to accept 'certificates of morality' from JCA, a privilege that was later withdrawn. Since about 5,000 of the immigrants needed special assistance, Soprotimis was kept busy. Many of the new arrivals were placed outside Buenos Aires with the help of local sub-committees and about 1,000 were sent to the JCA colonies. Some worked on the railroads, as had their precursors in Canada in earlier years. Loans were made to artisans for the purchase of tools, and a regular loan kassa for that purpose was planned for the next year. JCA helped to create a showroom for dresses, which provided both instruction for beginners and work for those who had skill, thus obviating the 'danger to which the impossibility of obtaining gainful employment exposed isolated young women'.

Rabbi Isaiah Raffalovich, who had performed similar tasks before, was sent by JCA to Brazil to initiate reception committees in Porto Alegre and other cities in the southern state of Rio Grande do Sul. In Porto Alegre alone there were loan kassas, two synagogues, a Jewish school and a library. JCA observed that the immigrants here followed the course familiar in so many places to which Jews have moved. They started as itinerant pedlars; as time went on they opened retail shops, progressed to wholesaling, and sometimes even to manufacturing. In Rio de Janeiro a local committee took care of the new arrivals with the help of a placement office established by JCA.

While Canadian immigration regulations made entry from Eastern Europe almost impossible, the government was persuaded to admit 5,000 Russian refugees from Romania at the rate of 100 per week. As we have noted previously, only about 3,000 were able to take advantage of this arrangement. JCA's Canadian Committee and JIAS were occupied in receiving these arrivals and finding employment for them, with the aid of sub-committees throughout the country. Ninety per cent of the immigrants under this scheme received financial help from JCA.

The next year, 1924, was marked by the coming into force of the Johnson Act in the United States. Its shattering effect, both psychologically and practically, can be judged by JCA's remark (in the Report for 1924) that the impact of this law was comparable to the expulsion of the Jews from Spain in 1492. Like that action 432 years before, the Johnson Act left thousands of Jews with nowhere to go. At the end of 1923, 8,000 were stranded in European ports, their plight exacerbated because the other New World countries were following the lead of the United States in closing their gates. The number of immigrants from Russia and Poland admitted to the United States in 1924 was only 7,148. The one place accepting significantly larger numbers of Jews was Palestine, where nearly 13,000 were received in 1924, as against 7,000–8,000 in previous post-war years.

As we have seen, almost all the Russian refugees had left Poland by the end of 1923; and in spite of great difficulties about 11,000 left Romania in 1923 and 1924, of whom 69 per cent had help from JCA. Likewise, by the end of 1924 almost all the migrating Jews had moved out of Danzig and JCA was able to terminate its activities there. It also closed its Romanian offices. Activity still continued in Antwerp, however, where Ezra dealt with 10,000 people; and in 1924 only 19,000 registered with the Hilfsverein and passed through Germany.

Argentina, concerned about the influx of Polish Jews, cut its intake of all Jews to 7,800 in 1924, much below the record of the year before. It was a small compensation that the reception of Jews by Uruguay increased to 833 from 463 the previous year.

Soprotimis took care of them also. Brazil was helpful in instructing its consuls to respect JCA's recommendations, and 2,000 Jews were able to enter, 400 of whom were assisted by the local Jewish Beneficent Society. In Canada JIAS and JCA were still occupied with those arriving under the 100-a-week arrangement.

1925–6

By 1925, despite the bars to immigration imposed by various countries, the vast majority of Russian Jewish refugees, who had numbered 250,000 or more after the Armistice, had succeeded in leaving Europe, only 6,000–8,000 remaining. These were located mostly in port cities, for example 1,300 in Constantinople and 2,100 in Constanza, Romania, with smaller numbers in Antwerp, Riga and Libau in Latvia. As might be expected, most of these were the old and the disabled.

At this juncture the agencies comprising Emigdirect, perhaps because their task was largely completed, overcame their previous reluctance to join with JCA. They did so at a meeting in Paris in July 1925, together with the New York Emergency Committee for Refugees. Out of this conference emerged a new entity, the United Evacuation Committee, which embraced all the major Jewish migration agencies including those in the countries of origin, transit and reception, as well as the executive of the Zionist Organisation in Jerusalem. Louis Oungre was one of the three co-directors of this new association. Its initiation was marked by the need to face a further closing of the gates to immigration. The Johnson Act was now fully operative in the United States, the South American countries were admitting only qualified farmers, and Argentina was even excluding relatives of residents and was requiring very extensive documentation that few refugees were able to complete.

The action of clearing the remaining refugees from the ports was not accomplished without a certain amount of tension and suspense. In Constantinople, for example, the number was down to 1,307 at the beginning of 1926. Careful examination revealed that 132 had no right to protection by the United Evacuation Committee, presumably because they were not Jewish or had told false stories. This left 1,175 without means of earning a living and unable to leave the city. Worse, many were threatened with expulsion and, as the 1926 JCA report remarks, even if this threat was finally not carried out, the persons affected nevertheless suffered extreme anxiety. By dint of great effort, and at a cost of $30,000, partly provided by JDC, destinations were found in the course of the year for 758 persons, 326 going to Palestine, 200 to South America and small numbers to France, Canada, the United States and Russia. Not only visas were obtained for them, but medical certificates as well. Arrangements were made for their embarkation, a matter, the 1926 report reminds us, that was always very delicate and complex to achieve in Constantinople. It was found that 280 more could go to Canada in 1927, some with the aid of money from friends. This left 132, mostly elderly or widows with young children. The Committee made a grant of $6,500 to the loan kassa in the city so that it could lend money to some of the refugees to go into business; 67 did, successfully. Small grants were made to local Jewish institutions, including the hospitals, which were willing to care for the others. By October 1926 the United Evacuation Committee decided that its object was accomplished, not only in Constantinople but also in the other ports, and the organisation was disbanded.

Despite the success in organising the departure from Europe of the last remaining refugees in transit in 1926, the basic problem confronting the Jewish world remained as intractable and insoluble as ever: in 1926 only 40,000 Jews were able to move out of Eastern Europe, about half the previous year's figure and an even smaller fraction of the numbers in the years before that. An added handicap to immigration was now imposed, a 250 per cent increase in the steamship fare from Europe to South America, from £6 to £21 per person.

The difficulties in getting to the Americas had been responsible for a tremendous upswing in migration to Palestine in 1924 and even more so in 1925; but, as Palestine became engulfed in an economic depression, immigration there declined to negligible figures in 1927 and 1928.

HICEM, 1927–9

The Jewish organisations had learnt from the experience of the United Evacuation Committee the extent to which unified action facilitated migration work; it was obviously helpful, for instance, if the agencies in the countries of reception and transit could know in advance how many persons were due to arrive and when. Therefore, no sooner had the United Evacuation Committee been discontinued than JCA, HIAS and the migration organisations that constituted Emigdirect started a series of conferences out of which a new broadly-based migration agency emerged. This was called HICEM (HIAS, ICA, Emigdirect), and it began operating early in 1927. All local migration branches of the three associations and the European transit committees became branches of HICEM, which was sometimes known as HIAS–JCA because these two organisations played the leading role. HIAS was to supply 60 per cent and JCA 40 per cent of the expenses of HICEM; local groups were to pay their own expenses as heretofore, but in the event HIAS, JCA and JDC paid much of these also. A number of JCA staff members were seconded to HICEM. Louis Oungre became one of the two managing directors, and Sir Leonard Cohen, Sir Osmond d'Avigdor Goldsmid and Leonard Montefiore of the JCA Council became members of its board.

At its inception it had offices in Poland, Danzig, Latvia, Lithuania, Romania, Turkey, England, Belgium, France, Holland, Portugal, Argentina, Brazil, Uruguay and China. This last was opened because a number of Jews fleeing Russia during the post-revolutionary turbulence had reached Harbin in Manchuria via the Trans-Siberian Railway. The Harbin office was called the Far Eastern Jewish Central Information Bureau for Emigrants, which through the mysteries of Russian orthography was shortened to Daljevcib. This bureau remained active for two decades. In 1927 and 1928, 1,727 people passed through it to be helped on their way not only to China and the Philippines but to the United States, India, Australia, Palestine, Latin America and Western Europe.[4] Daljevcib continued to operate until the Japanese took control of Manchuria in 1937–8. It then moved to Shanghai (where there were 17,000 Jews).

The creation of HICEM did not mean the complete cessation by JCA of certain migration activities of its own. Notably, in 1928 it opened emigration information bureaux in a number of Russian cities. In that year 7,500 Jews left Russia, following on the 5,000 of the year before. A complicating factor was the absence of any US consuls in the USSR, a country that the United States did not then recognise, so that consular matters had to be handled from Riga in Latvia. After 1928 Jewish emigration from Russia declined rapidly and virtually ceased.[5]

With some justification, JCA looked on HICEM's work very much as if it was still a function of the Association and devoted full chapters in its annual reports to accounts of HICEM's activities (see Tables 12.1 and 12.2).

With the departure of nearly all the Russian refugees from Europe and the establishment of HICEM, the process of moving Jews out of Eastern Europe assumed something of a regularised aspect. At least the emergencies, the threatened expulsions of travellers *en route*, were experienced no more, and the migration agencies could work in a 'normal' fashion. Sadly, they did not have enough work to do because of the restrictions on intake so

Table 12.1 Jewish immigration, 1921–39

	United States	Palestine	Argentina	Brazil	Canada	South Africa	Western Europe and overseas	Total
1921	119,036	8,517	4,095	*	2,763	781	1,500	135,982
1922	53,524	7,844	7,198	*	8,404	367	1,500	78,837
1923	49,989	7,421	13,701	*	2,793	773	2,000	76,677
1924	10,292	12,856	7,799	2,025	4,255	773	6,000	43,990
1925	10,267	33,801	6,920	2,624	4,459	1,353	4,500	63,924
1926	11,483	13,801	7,534	3,901	4,014	1,479	3,500	45,712
1927	11,639	2,713	5,584	4,167	4,863	1,752	4,500	35,218
1928	11,639	2,178	6,812	3,193	4,768	2,293	7,650	38,533
1929	12,479	5,249	5,986	5,610	3,848	2,788	9,000	44,960
1930	11,526	4,944	7,805	3,558	4,164	1,881	8,500	42,738
1931	5,692	4,075	3,553	1,985	3,421	885	6,000†	25,511
1932	2,755	9,553	1,801	2,044	649	676	4,000†	21,463
1933	2,372	30,327	1,962	3,317	772	754	3,500†	43,004
1934	4,134	42,359	2,215	3,794	943	1,123	4,500†	59,068
1935	6,252	61,854	3,159	1,758	624	1,078	9,500†	84,225
1936	6,252	29,727	4,261	3,418	880	3,348	4,000†	51,885
1937	11,352	10,536	4,178	2,003	619	954	4,400†	34,042
1938	19,736	12,868	1,050	530	584	526	5,000†	40,294
1939	43,450	27,561	4,300	4,601	890	300	3,500†	84,602

* Exact information unavailable: probably a few hundred each year.
† Estimated.
Sources: M. Wischnitzer, To Dwell in Safety, Philadelphia, 1948, pp. 288–93, and relevant JCA Annual Reports.[6]

Table 12.2   *HICEM activity, 1927 and 1928*

	Year	Poland	Romania	Lithuania	Latvia
Jewish emigrants who	1927	18,211	2,869	*	*
left	1928	18,074	3,288	2,700	*
Emigrants who came	1927	30,876	2,655	2,240	3,818
to HICEM committees	1928	34,519	6,725	6,752	4,380
Interventions with	1927	7,685	1,400⎱	3,075	2,356
consulates	1928	11,877	3,300⎰		
Advances guaranteed	1927	$10,000	$ 6,130	$23,850	$ 548
for voyage expenses	1928	$50,346	$11,745	$20,000	$3,470

* Exact figures not known.
Source: JCA Annual Report, 1928, p. 262.

often mentioned herein, which were tightened as the worldwide economic depression rapidly made its malign influence felt everywhere.

HICEM's work fell into predictable patterns. In the countries of emigration and transit it informed would-be emigrants as comprehensively as possible of conditions prevailing in countries of reception; helped travellers in approaching consular offices to facilitate the obtaining of necessary documents, especially visas; offered transit and port services, including legal protection against abuses; and gave assistance in securing steamship and railway tickets, often at reduced prices. Before the migrants left, HICEM tried to prepare them for the conditions they would meet by giving language and vocational courses. (All the emigrants wanted to learn English; apparently it was difficult to make them believe that in South America Spanish was more useful.) In the countries of reception HICEM offered port services and shelter and tried to establish the immigrants economically by creating employment bureaus and providing language and vocational instruction and sometimes credit through a loan kassa.

HICEM also undertook to pay special attention to young women and girls travelling alone, and in South America appointed agents for this purpose. Even before HICEM was officially in operation some of its constituent agencies, for instance Ezra in Antwerp, had emphasised their concern in this area, and the Transmigrants Aid Committee in Liverpool made a point of working with the Jewish Association for the Protection of Girls and Women in London, an organisation that had long been subsidised by JCA. The efforts in this connection were not always successful, for the 1929 Report complains that some who arrived in Buenos Aires in that year fell into white slavery.

In 1928 there was a rather unexpected addition to the roll of receiving countries. France permitted the entry of a few hundred

Jews who came in as manual labourers. By 1931 the number so admitted rose to 888, of whom 56 were engaged in agriculture.

In 1929 Romania came in for attention because the number of Jews able to leave in that year rose to 4,500, the highest annual figure for some time. This was interesting inasmuch as, of all countries dealt with by HICEM, Romania was perhaps the most difficult: many documents could be obtained only in Bucharest, whereas most of the Jews were in Bessarabia, hundreds of miles away. Even worse, there were many unscrupulous characters there who tried to turn a dishonest *leu* by preying on gullible would-be emigrants.

Another HICEM office that had a higher level of activity in 1929 than previously was in Harbin. This dealt with 7,000 consultations, gave aid to 1,350 individuals and sent 900 on to distant destinations, 421 of them to China and Mongolia and the rest to the four corners of the earth. In promoting this movement the Harbin office spent about $56,000.

1930

The next year, 1930, saw immigration rules tightened still further in Australia, South Africa, Canada, the United States, Argentina and Brazil. South Africa now proposed that all immigrants be required to make a deposit before arrival so that they would not become public charges. JCA put up money for passages to South Africa quickly, before this new regulation was enforced. Likewise, in Canada it was feared that a decree halting immigration entirely was about to be imposed, so visa holders had to hurry to get into that country. The fares to South America were due to rise on 1 January 1931; therefore the Warsaw office of HICEM hastened to obtain 400 Argentine visas between 1 and 15 December 1930. No fewer than 67,400 people came to this Warsaw office in 1930 and 15,700 cases received help, constituting a substantial proportion of the 17,000 Jews who left Poland in that year (4,800 went to Argentina, 3,200 to the United States, 3,000 to Canada and 2,400 to Palestine). The work of the transit committees, though they had fewer cases to handle than in the 1920s, was greater because so many more documents were required and there were more regulations to satisfy.

In Argentina bad crops, low prices and unemployment led the government to ask Soprotimis and JCA to stop helping immigrants. Nevertheless, 7,800 Jews succeeded in entering the country in 1930, about the average number for the post-war decade. The presence of a large and influential Jewish community and the philanthropic help made available to newcomers made this immigration possible. Soprotimis also assisted the 1,100 or so Jews who arrived at Montevideo in Uruguay, where the local community found employment and provided evening classes. In Brazil political upheavals and economic troubles limited the intake to 3,558; HICEM found jobs for 759, while its committees were operating three loan kassas in the country. To complete the story of HICEM's activities in South America in 1930, it should be stated that it also investigated Chile for settlement possibilities, and found it favourable.

Although Canada restricted immigration to close relatives only, 4,000 Jews managed to enter in 1930. The United States, in addition to the quotas set by law, reduced immigration further by instructing its consuls abroad to grant visas only to wives and children of residents. In spite of this rule, over 11,000 Jews squeezed their way in. The last important country of reception was Palestine, where that year some 5,000 Jews entered.

1931–2

In 1931 and 1932 there was a further decline in the work of the migration agencies because of the worsening economic situation and the further tightening of immigration controls. In Argentina economic conditions were so bad that 1932 saw for the first time more people leaving (43,400) than entering (31,300). Among the entrants were only 1,800 Jews as against 3,600 in 1931 and 7,800 in 1930. One reason for the decline was the imposition of a tax on immigrants as a result of pressure from the trade unions prompted by high unemployment. Because the immigrants now were all related to residents, Soprotimis ended its vocational and language programmes. In Brazil more stringent requirements cut total entries in 1932 to 38,473, which was 7,000 less than in the previous year; but the number of Jews coming in remained at about 2,000. By this time not only were the kassas in Rio de Janeiro, São Paulo and Porto Alegre making hundreds of loans, but two new ones in Belo Horizonte and Campinos opened their doors. The Rio Women's Committee was much concerned with the care of female travellers; 119 ships were inspected on arrival and help was given to 279 women and girls and 209 children. A kassa was initiated in Santiago de Chile, though emigration to that country in 1932 was only 124, in contrast to 174 in the previous year, when HICEM opened its office there. In Cuba 165 Jews entered, but 136 left on account of the poor economic

9a Petrovka, Bessarabia, 1924. Milking sheep and goats

9b Lvov, Galicia, 1924. Separating cream

10a Colony Clara, Argentina, 1948. Grain elevator

10b Colony Clara, Argentina, 1964. Vegetable oil extraction plant

conditions, and some had to be helped by the local committee with their passage money.

In these two years only about 14,500 Jews left Poland for overseas. Of these, 30 per cent went to Palestine, 26 per cent to Argentina and 11 per cent each to the United States and Brazil. We have noted that France had become a country of immigration in a modest way; in 1932 2,500–3,000 Jews were able to enter from Eastern Europe.

The Great Depression, which reduced JDC's fund-raising, affected HIAS in the same way. In 1932 the agreed proportional contributions to HICEM were reversed; HIAS contributed $40,000 and JCA $65,000.[7] Emigdirect had even worse financial trouble. Two years later it had to withdraw from HICEM because it could no longer make contributions.

HICEM, 1933–41

1933–4

Bad as these money problems were, they were as nothing compared with the task that Hitler's accession to control of Germany in February 1933 thrust upon the Jewish migration organisations. The most serious situation they had had to deal with previously had been when comparatively few Jews were able to leave Poland or other Eastern European states and millions were obliged to continue to live, impoverished, some on charity, in a country that had made it clear that Jews had no place in it. This was bad enough, but it was not comparable to the position in Hitler's Germany, particularly in the latter part of the decade. Then the question of emigration became quite simply a matter of life and death. This put the agencies involved into an agonising dilemma because, with the regulations then prevailing in the countries of reception, there was virtually no place where many German Jews could take refuge.

The pressure to emigrate was felt immediately on Hitler's becoming Chancellor. In the seven weeks from the middle of March to the middle of May 1933, the French Central Committee for Assisting Jewish Emigrants added the names of 2,300 German refugees to its lists. However, the immediate fears of the German Jews subsided a little; the pace slowed, and only 1,438 more were registered by the Committee in the remainder of that year. Altogether, in that first year of Hitler, HICEM in France helped 2440 persons get themselves repatriated, go overseas or settle in the country. Another 3,197 refugees were helped by groups in

Strasbourg, Marseilles and Lille. HICEM's work was notably supplemented by that of the National Committee of Help to German Refugees which was founded in Paris when the German crisis began. JCA calls attention to its vast and important work in obtaining documents to help professionals of all kinds get established in countries where they could start on new careers. Very careful and extensive research was carried out to find possibilities for young German refugees to continue their studies.

Other migration agencies that were in a position to do so also responded to the needs of the commencing exodus. Ezra in Antwerp and Montefiore in Rotterdam between them helped 3,500 fugitives from Germany. Even the JEAS office in Poland dealt with some hundreds of people from Germany, most of them Polish repatriates. The big task of JEAS, however, was to handle the emigration from Poland to Palestine, for 10,344 individuals travelled this route in 1933 compared with 2,875 in the previous year. The year also saw an improvement in Jewish migration to Brazil. The development there of kassas for immigrants was notable, 2,000 loans being made to newcomers, for many of whom also employment was found.

So desperate was HICEM to find a place – any place – whither to send refugees from Germany that it considered it worth-while to explore some rather unlikely possibilities. Representatives were sent to Spain to look into opportunities for Jewish settlement in Spanish Morocco, to Yugoslavia, to Greece, Turkey, Bulgaria, Italy and the Italian colonies in Africa. That such places from which little could be expected were examined was a measure of the extremity in which HICEM felt itself to be.

The expedition to Spain, however, turned out not to be a waste. During the First World War a few Jews drifted into Spain, the first to settle in that country since the Expulsion in 1492. They formed a handful of small and poor communities. The largest, in Barcelona, appealed to JCA for help in 1923–4. Because they maintained a school for 30–40 pupils and helped immigrants, JCA provided the (rather exiguous) sum of 3,000 pesetas. In 1934 there was a revolution against the monarchy which installed a democratic government in Madrid, sympathetic to the refugees. After Hitler came to power, Republican Spain proved to be a refuge for about 4,000–6,000 Jews from Germany. This brought JCA and HIAS, through HICEM, to extend systematic aid to refugees in Spain. Immigrant aid societies, named EZRA, were established in Madrid and Barcelona, and 3,000 Germans were enabled to enter the country, most of them going to Barcelona. Spain appeared so promising as a haven for German Jews that JCA sent a representative there in 1935 on an exploratory mission.

He recommended, in spite of the country's blatant anti-Semitism, that 50–100 families of artisans should be helped to enter Spain, and 60 heads of families were actually sent there. But these small beginnings, and all hope of Spain as a refuge for Jews fleeing from German fascism, were abruptly brought to an end by the outbreak of Franco's revolt against the Republican government in July 1936. In fact, the Jews who had recently gained admittance had to leave.

HICEM was working with 17 rescue organisations and operating in 25 countries. In 1934 it helped 5,000 Jews leave Germany and 4,600 leave Eastern Europe. A total of 19,000 left Poland, of whom 12,719 went to Palestine, 1,470 to Argentina and about the same number to Brazil. The Polish JEAS had a very busy time supplying documents to people who had lost them during the First World War. It made 9,000 applications to the consulates of countries of destination. It also performed location services, finding relatives overseas, especially for women whose husbands had preceded them and in some cases had contrived to forget that they had left a wife and children behind. JEAS located many of these amnesiac husbands and brought about family reunions which perhaps were not always entirely welcome. Of 1,100 Jews who left Lithuania, 646 reached Palestine and 263 went to South Africa, a country that over the years had attracted a large number of Lithuanian Jews. Although only 275 Jews left Romania with the help of the HICEM committee, the organisation nevertheless won a notable victory there: it persuaded the government to reduce the number of documents required of an emigrant from 18 to 4. Also, the requisite fees were reduced. The many loan kassas in Romania associated with JCA and the Foundation acted as agents of HICEM.

In Istanbul, where 550 Russian Jews were registered and 1,500 more were to be found unregistered, JCA persuaded the Jewish Agency, which controlled the entry certificates to Palestine, to issue more to the HICEM committee. This partially solved the problem of the Russians. But a new one arose: some 700 refugees from Persia who came into the city could not obtain permits for residence in Turkey. Here, too, Palestine proved to be the haven: 473 of the Persians were sent to the Holy Land.

In spite of continuing economic troubles in Argentina, marked particularly by heavy unemployment, there was a small increase, to 2,215, in the number of Jews entering. Soprotimis found employment for about 300, and its efforts were supplemented by a newly created Aid Association of German-speaking Jews, founded in 1933, which also placed close to 300 people.

Brazil had already confined entry to persons having employment contracts or relatives in the country and who possessed at least $200. In June 1934 it required a resident to guarantee that the immigrant would not become a public charge for five years, and it still reserved the right to exclude the newcomer if the number of persons originating in his country exceeded a certain quota. JCA persuaded the government to delay the enforcement of this regulation for some months. The loan kassas were very active, distributing 2,571 loans. About 500 Jews, almost all from Poland and almost all relatives of residents, entered Uruguay with the help of Soprotimis. To complete the Latin-American story, 612 Jews arrived in Cuba in 1935 but 550 left, some to other American countries.

1935–6

The JCA annual report for 1935 cast a backward glance at developments in the field of migration since 1933, when Hitler came to power. It quoted with approval the pithy description of the Jewish position in many European countries given by one of the HICEM committees – 'stabilised misery', they called it. Alas, in 1935 it became misery unstabilised, for that was the year in which the Nazis promulgated the anti-Semitic Nuremberg laws, greatly worsening the position of the Jews in Germany. The report went on to elaborate the reasons why Jews found it almost impossible to escape their misery:

> Emigration has not ceased to be one of the saddest and most
> severe problems of Jewish life. The situation of many
> hundreds of thousands of men and women living under
> intolerable conditions cannot be solved otherwise than by
> emigration; but that is hindered by nearly impossible barriers
> against newcomers raised by the countries of destination.
> The result is a veritable tragedy for tens of thousands of our
> co-religionists who are forced to abandon any hope for a
> normal life. [translated from the 1935 report, p.159]

In the period May 1933–December 1935 HICEM helped out of Germany 13,428 refugees, of whom Palestine took in 3,371.[8] The JCA report reminds us that the figures quoted – and this includes others later in this chapter – refer only to those who travelled under HICEM auspices and therefore understate the numbers who actually left Germany. Many more did so with resources of their own or were helped by other organisations. The cost of moving these people over the two-and-a-half-year period came to 9,621,000 French francs, contributed by JCA, JDC, the Central British Fund and other organisations. (This sum did not include

the expenditures of the committees in the countries of reception.)
A step forward in handling the movement of Jews from Germany
was taken by concentrating all organised activity relating thereto
under the Hilfsverein.

In 1935 the pace of departures from Germany quickened. The
Nuremberg laws convinced many German Jews that they had no
future there, and the improved operations of the migration agencies may also have helped. At any rate, the number who left in
1935 with the assistance of the agencies was 10,600.

Polish Jewish emigration in 1935 also increased, to nearly
31,000, as Jews found themselves in general being excluded from
the country's economic life and losing their customers because of
the impoverishment of the peasants. The large movement from
Poland caused great activity in the JEAS office in Warsaw, finding
replacements for lost birth and marriage records and other
documents.

As far as Russian Jews were concerned, despite the recognition
of the USSR by the United States in 1933, Riga still had the only
consulate available for those who wanted to go to America, and
if there were visa problems transit was further delayed.

In Turkey there was both triumph and disaster in 1935. The
HICEM delegate there managed to obtain Turkish nationality for
500 refugees from Russia, but in May the government put an end
to all JCA and HICEM activity in the country.

At the other end of Asia, in Manchuria, many Jews who had
settled there fled, following changes in the political situation
arising from the advance of the Japanese army and the evacuation
of the Russian staff of the Eastern Chinese Railway. Daljevcib
became very active, helping 1,071 persons to leave Harbin and
rendering other services to thousands more. About 500 refugees
from Germany had been assisted by this agency to settle in this
distant location between 1933 and 1935.

The transit agencies in Europe and reception agencies in South
America continued to perform their customary functions. Soprotimis placed 500 entrants in jobs in Montevideo and helped 100
German Jews enter Paraguay, where there were openings for
artisans. In Brazil 1,400 new arrivals were provided with financial
aid as well as documents, railway tickets and information. Cuba
accepted 400 Jews, who received help from the Centro Israelita,
and the local branch of HICEM set up a loan kassa for the
immigrants and a school for their children. Back in Germany, the
Hilfsverein started a farm school, which began modestly with 11
students. The idea was to prepare candidates for entry to many
American states which were willing to admit bona fide farmers.

The transcendent fact is that, despite all the hindrances and obstacles repeatedly stressed in this narrative, 81,500 Jews were able to leave Eastern Europe and Germany in 1935; this number exceeded the 60,250 of the previous year and was almost double the 46,000 of 1933. The Polish government was so eager to get Jews out that it covered the deficit of JEAS. The main reason for the achievement of these figures was that Palestine was prosperous enough to admit 75 per cent of the total numbers leaving Europe. When entry into Palestine was restricted in 1936 and only 30,000 were admitted, Jewish emigration from Europe to all destinations was reduced to 54,000. Another calamity that befell Jews in flight was the outbreak of the rising in Spain, where a few thousand had taken refuge, at a time when the Latin-American nations had placed fresh restrictions on Jewish immigration. Nevertheless, Argentina and Brazil together admitted 7,700 in 1936, which was in fact an increase over the previous year and included 2,500 from Germany; and Chile admitted 600 German Jews. In contrast, Paraguay decreed the expulsion of all new arrivals who were not farmers. But if some of the South American countries made difficulties, South Africa became somewhat more encouraging, admitting 3,300 Jews in 1936.

The financing of HICEM had changed considerably since its inception. In 1936, out of a total of £50,000, most came from JCA – £30,000; JDC gave £5,000 and the British Council for German Jewry £14,000.

1937–9

In 1937 South Africa, Brazil and Uruguay stiffened their restrictions against immigration, and Mexico and Cuba made it impossible for Jews to enter. But the United States made things easier, and the figure for Colombia went up to 500. The position in Palestine worsened, the number allowed in being only 10,500. The net result was that no more than 37,000 Jews were able to escape from Europe. Emigration from Poland was especially affected; only 8,500 Jews left that country, half the 1936 figure. HICEM's committees now numbered 51, in 23 countries, including such comparatively far-off places as the Philippines, South Africa and Australia.

As Nazi pressure increased outside Germany's borders, the Jews remaining in places like Danzig tried their best to get out, with HICEM helping, as always, in every way possible. Of 7,000 Jews who were in Danzig in 1937, only 1,666 remained in August 1939, on the eve of the outbreak of war. The Austrian Anschluss in 1938, the Munich Pact of September 1938 and the seizure of Czechoslovakia by the Germans in March 1939 brought another

325,000 Jews under direct German control. What they could expect was made clear by the infamous Kristallnacht pogrom of November 1938. They were desperate to flee under any conditions.

Early in 1939 two ships with 290 Jewish passengers sailed from Germany for the British West Indies, but the refugees could not disembark because their visas were invalid. By dint of extreme effort HICEM placed these people in Venezuela and Ecuador. Similar pressures needed to be employed in Uruguay, where Jews were finally permitted to land on the understanding that they would go on to Paraguay and Chile. The most notorious of the happenings of this kind involved the liner *St Louis*. In May 1939 it left Bremen with 900 Jews aboard who had valid visas for Cuba, but the emigrants were refused permission to land when they reached Havana because the government had just cancelled the permits that it had previously issued.[9] After the ship had spent agonising days wandering the ocean, Belgium, on the appeal to its government of Max Gottschalk (a member of the boards of both JCA and HICEM), allowed 300 to land; the French government was persuaded by Baron Robert de Rothschild to admit a further 300; and Britain and Holland took in the remainder. At the other end of the world there was trouble also; as the Japanese army moved into Manchuria, many Jews left Harbin and HICEM moved its offices to Shanghai.

The United States, to make up, as it were, for the niggardliness of its immigration policy at the beginning of the decade, took the positive step of instructing its consuls to give special consideration to visa applications from German and Austrian Jews, with the result that Jewish immigration from Germany and elsewhere to the USA increased to 43,450 in 1939, compared with 19,736 the year before.

A conference called by HICEM in Paris in August 1939 was given the figures for the period March 1933–August 1939. Of 880,000 Jews living in Germany, Austria and Czechoslovakia, 380,000 had fled, but only half had left Europe – the other half had gone mostly to England and France. While the meeting was taking place the Hitler–Stalin Pact was signed, followed by the outbreak of the war on 1 September 1939. This sealed the fate of the half million Jews left in those three countries, as well as most of those who had sought refuge in France.

One of the many crises HICEM now faced was financial. With the outbreak of the war, JCA, as a British corporation, was prevented from transferring funds abroad. However, HIAS, domiciled in the United States, which was still a neutral country, was able to do so, and it was thus that HICEM could help some hundreds of Czech and German refugees through France to America. A thousand Jews were plucked from French internment camps. HICEM was also able to provide service to Jews in the Baltic states and eastern Poland; for the Soviets, on taking control of these areas at the end of 1939 allowed more than a year for Jews to leave if they were able to. With HICEM's help, 2,000 of them were able to reach Palestine or the United States; another 4,400 went in the other direction, through Kobe, Japan, 1,300 of them settling in Shanghai and the others proceeding to a variety of places overseas.

1940–1

In June 1940, with the fall of France imminent, HICEM opened an office in Lisbon. The tiny Jewish community there had already assisted many Jews fleeing Europe. In the remainder of 1940 this office helped 1,550 depart from Portugal. The HICEM staff in Paris left the city together with JCA's personnel as the Germans advanced. They went first to Bordeaux and then to Marseilles in unoccupied France, where they set up operations in October 1940. This office was recognised by the Vichy regime as the Jewish emigration agency for unoccupied France, and it succeeded in getting a few thousand Jews to the United States. Even after American consulates in all parts of Europe controlled by the Germans were closed on 15 July 1941, HICEM was able to persuade the Vichy government to honour visas for Jews in the area under its jurisdiction, and also prevailed on the Spanish government to permit visa-holders to pass through *en route* to ports in Morocco.

Though these actions are treated summarily here, it must be emphasised that securing the release of inmates of Vichy camps or passage through Spain required skilled, persistent and tension-filled effort by HICEM personnel. All in all, between July 1940 and December 1941, when Pearl Harbour brought the United States into the war, HICEM and HIAS helped no fewer than 25,000 people to journey overseas from European and North African ports, about 10,000 of whom required financial assistance.

1942–5

Early in 1942 the Vichy government dissolved HICEM and made it part of the general Jewish organisation for occupied France, UGIF. The German take-over shortly thereafter forced the staff to leave Marseilles and move to a small town called Brive, and its functioning was effectively halted. However, after the fall of France a number of the leading members of the JCA and HICEM staff succeeded in reaching the United States or South America. Louis Oungre was already in New York, having secured passage on the last ship to leave Toulon in 1940. Maurice Hexter had interceded with Judge Samuel Rosenman, President Roosevelt's assistant, to provide Oungre with the highly important visa.[10]

Oungre and officials of HIAS incorporated the HIAS–JCA Emigrant Association in New York on 30 June 1942 and became members of its board. Edouard Oungre, Louis's brother, who was a vice-director of JCA, was named one of the co-directors of the revived migration agency, heading its operations in South America. Between 1942 and 1944 this organisation was able to get thousands of Jewish refugees out of Spain and Portugal and to place most of them in various Latin-American countries – not without difficulty, as these latter had broken relations with the Axis powers and were inclined to treat German Jews as enemy aliens. Offices were opened in Chile and Colombia, and the Shanghai bureau also maintained a high level of activity. In 1944 and 1945, as the Germans fell back, HIAS–JCA opened offices in France, Italy, North Africa, Romania and elsewhere in Europe. JCA, however, was still unable to transfer funds outside the sterling area. Therefore, at a conference held in London in October 1945 it was decided to wind up the affairs of HIAS–JCA as such and transfer its remaining assets to HIAS.

HICEM, its predecessor organisations and its successor, HIAS–JCA, had operated for nearly twenty years in a Europe terribly troubled and financially devastated by depression, extreme nationalism, fascism, anti-Semitism and lastly, to cap this litany of ill-fortune, the Second World War. On the other side of the Atlantic, the traditional receiving countries for immigrants had made entry progressively more difficult. That the Jewish migration agencies were able to move some hundreds of thousands of migrants and refugees out of Europe was a tribute to the skill, devotion and courage of their staff, a number of whom themselves perished in the war or in concentration camps. That more Jews were lost than successfully escaped from Europe in the years from 1930 to 1945 does not detract from HICEM's achievements. It did not have enough money, time and, most important, places of refuge to save more.

FROM THE SECOND WORLD WAR TO THE PRESENT

Towards the end of the last chapter we saw that in the summer of 1940 the JCA staff, together with that of HICEM, left Paris. As the Germans advanced into France the Central Administration of JCA was in a state of almost constant movement. Its operation was further inhibited by the fact that the registered official address of the Association was always in London (at the office of its solicitors), and France under Nazi occupation was according to British regulations an enemy country to which British citizens or corporations could not address communications or transfer money. JCA's administrative officers were mostly in the Americas: Louis Oungre had been preceded to New York by Max Gottschalk of Brussels, Vice-President of the Association, and was joined there by Messrs. Calius and Cherniak of the Paris staff. Edouard Oungre went to Buenos Aires; Victor Girmounsky, a Vice-Director of JCA, made his way to Brazil; and a third Vice-Director, Georges Aronstein, was in London as a member of the Free Belgian Army.[1] It was arranged that the JCA offices in Canada, Brazil and Argentina would thenceforth report to Mr Oungre in New York. Emica, JCA's subsidiary in Palestine, was not covered by these arrangements; this left Charles Passman, its director, free to act on his own.

After the war was over, JCA decided to transfer its headquarters to London, and this was done in 1949. The Annual Reports, hitherto printed in French and in the 1920s often running to more than 200 pages, were now in English, mimeographed, and a dozen pages long. This shrinkage of the reports did not at first reflect a geographical shrinkage in the operations; for in the years following the war the Association remained active in the Western Hemisphere as well as in Palestine (soon to become Israel) and proceeded to extend its interests to Morocco, Tunisia, Kenya, Ethiopia, France and Australia. By 1980, however, JCA had found it expedient to bring its work in nearly all these countries to an end, so that the chief focus of its activity today is almost exclusively Israel, where there now exists a self-sufficient and capable farming fraternity to whose welfare and advancement JCA has been a large contributor. In this respect the Baron de Hirsch's dream has been brought to fruition.

CHAPTER 13

End in Argentina

Perón's pricing policy

The most important political event in Argentina during the Second World War was a governmental overturn. We have seen that in 1930 a military coup had installed General Uruburu as President. He was followed by other dictators. But in 1943 Juan Perón, a military man (he was a colonel when he took power) who openly appealed to and depended on the popular mandate, seized control of the government and had that control ratified by being elected President in 1946.

The authoritarian military governments of the 1930s had favoured urban workers at the expense of the farmers. In this one respect at least Perón continued the policy of the previous regime and indeed intensified it. He set up an organisation called Instituto Argentino de Promoción del Intercambio (IAPI – Argentine Institution for the Promotion of Trade), a highly capitalised commercial enterprise which dealt with farm crops. IAPI fixed the prices paid to farmers for their products below world levels but sold them at the prevailing international rates. The margin provided a source of income to the government. An example of this policy was the fixing of the price paid to farmers for wheat at 25 pesos per quintal in 1948, when the world price was 60 pesos. As the farmers had difficulty in covering their costs, this pricing system gave rise first to loud complaints and then to action in the shape of abandonment of farming.

For the Jewish farmers in the JCA colonies this caused a special problem. The young women were the first to move away from rural areas, and their departure made it difficult for young men to find suitable mates; so they also started to move to where the ladies were. This was a concern outside JCA's customary frame of reference, but the Association rose to the occasion and encouraged the colonies to institute 'events' which it hoped would help persuade young people to stay on the farms. As part of this effort JCA prompted the creation of *salles de fêtes*, where such things as lectures and theatrical performances could take place (and which

229

were used in 1946 for commemorations of the fiftieth anniversary of the founder's death). More influential than any of these, one suspects, but not influential enough to counteract the tendency to move to urban centres, was the opening of the first cinema in the colonies, at Montefiore. This example was soon to be followed in many of the other colonies.

The London Conference

As far as JCA was concerned, one notable aspect that was missing from the post-war picture was the interminable quarrel with the Fraternidad Agraria. We have seen that the question of the contracts had lost its acuteness because most of the colonists had obtained title to their lands. They were now able to do so by paying 20 per cent of the purchase price and giving a mortgage for the balance. JCA, at long last abandoning its policy of maintaining huge land reserves for the benefit of new settlers who obviously were never going to arrive, also made it possible for the colonists to enlarge their holdings to a 'reasonable size' and dropped the restrictions it had set on the acquisition of its lands by sons and sons-in-law. These changes were put into effect with the help of some prodding by Max Gottschalk, the Belgian member of the JCA Council, who went to Argentina on a visit of inspection in 1949. The Council, indeed, so recognised the maturity of its Argentine protégés (two generations had passed since the first JCA settlements in 1891) that it was willing to establish a consultative committee in Buenos Aires, in conjunction with the Fraternidad, to deliberate on questions of policy.

The changes were formalised by the resolutions adopted at a conference held in London in June 1950 between the Council and a delegation from the Fraternidad consisting of its president and vice-president. It was agreed that JCA should try to bring all farm holdings up to a basic level of 150 hectares. In the Montefiore colony, where the soil was poor, 350 hectares would be the standard. (As late as 1963, however, at Baron Hirsch colony holdings were still much smaller than the average.[1]) The price charged by JCA for land would be 30–40 per cent below commercial levels, but sales would be made only to authentic colonists working their land personally. If a colonist who had purchased JCA land wished to sell it, JCA would be willing to help with its repurchase, so as to keep it in Jewish hands. Sons of colonists would be helped to buy land and all previous restrictive conditions in such cases were dispensed with. Lastly, JCA agreed formally to the establishment of the Consultative Committee in Buenos Aires.

The next year, as a further sign of JCA's belated recognition of the maturity of the Argentine settlements, it elected to membership of its Council Dr Ricardo Dubrovsky, a leader of the Buenos Aires Jewish community and prominent in both medical and political circles. This appointment was received by the colonists with acclaim. The untimely death of Dr Dubrovsky in 1954, however, seemed to some an indication that the colonies had not only achieved maturity but had gone into decline. For by now JCA could not deceive itself with dreams of a revival of Jewish colonization in Argentina.

First, in contrast with the pre-war situation, the great pool of potential immigrants in Eastern Europe had been all but wiped out by the Holocaust, and Israel now existed as an alternative destination for those who survived. Second, the political and economic upheavals in Argentina, plus the numerous anti-Semitic incidents that have sullied the Argentine scene to the present day,[2] made the country completely unattractive to new Jewish settlers, even if the regime had been willing to admit them. Jewish immigration having thus for all practical purposes ceased, the JCA Council concluded in 1958 that the Association's mission in Argentina was approaching its end.

Exodus from the countryside

The influences towards urbanisation that affected the Jews in rural areas continued in full force. We see a steady decline in the count of Jewish farmers in the JCA annual reports, from 3,435 colonist families in 1941 to 2,066 in 1957. A majority of those still actively engaged in farming had moved to the nearby villages and towns, obviously preferring to live in more gregarious surroundings than in the comparative isolation of the pampas, even if they continued to work there. In 1956, for example, less than 40 per cent of the number of colonists recorded in the Annual Report were living on their farms.

A major preoccupation of JCA was to stem this tide by trying to bring such amenities to life in the countryside as would induce the Jewish farmers to remain there. In the 1948 Report we read that JCA was encouraging the colonies to improve their facilities for education and entertainment. But this same Report states that land values had started to rise appreciably and that many farmers were taking advantage of the trend. The Report goes on to wonder whether it would ever be possible for JCA to reawaken interest in Jewish farm settlement and answers its own question, realistically, in the negative. It did indeed seem that without an infusion of new blood the outlook for the Argentine colonies was bleak.

But JCA was not yet ready to abandon its aim of helping Jews to stay on the land. In 1949 and 1950 the Association made loans either directly or through the medium of the co-operatives to enable farmers to buy land, seed and cattle and to erect fencing. In each of these years it also lent a total of about 400,000 pesos (£13,000) to the co-operatives to enable them to make grants to schools, libraries, youth clubs and cinemas and to assist farmers to purchase agricultural machinery. Nor did the Association neglect public relations. In these years and after, it donated land to state and municipal governments for schools, hospitals and other public institutions.

In 1951 a meeting of the Consultative Committee was held in Buenos Aires to consider methods of countering the movement away from the land by the extension and improvement of individual holdings and the further development of rural cultural and social life. In that year 226 farms were enlarged and 36 new farmers installed. Much of this was accomplished with the aid of loans from JCA; 238,000 pesos were advanced to purchasers of vacated land. JCA emphasised its support for Hebrew classes and, in addition to its usual grants to charitable and social organisations, made a grant to ORT to help it set up a school for vocational training in Dominguez, Entre-Rios.

The trend towards colonist ownership, which had been well established even before the war, continued; now, 90 per cent of occupiers owned their farms. But notwithstanding all this effort and expenditure of money, the 1951 Report ruefully states that, of 17,000 Jews living in the colonies, in that year 500 moved away. How eager the farmers themselves were to receive newcomers was demonstrated by the great welcome given to a mere 11 families who arrived from Europe in 1953.

Changes in the Council

The year 1951 happened to be one of important changes in the JCA Council. The Marquess of Reading, who had been President for three years, was appointed to the British government as Under-Secretary of State for Foreign Affairs and resigned from the Council. Sir Henry d'Avigdor Goldsmid, who was destined to have an influence on JCA affairs second only to that of the

Baron himself, became President in Reading's place. Leonard Montefiore also resigned in that year. Dr Ricardo Dubrovsky was elected to the Council, not only to the great acclaim of Argentina's Jewish community, but with favourable notice in the general Argentine press as well. And finally, Sir Keith Joseph, eminent in English business, economic and political circles, became a member. (The following year, it should be noted, Maurice B. Hexter, the American who had been so instrumental in reawakening JCA's interest in Israel, was also elected to the Council.)

JCA goes on

The next years saw no important changes in JCA policy. The Association continued to make loans for the repurchase of vacated Jewish farms and for farm extension or improvement, and saw the percentage of farmers owning their land increase a little each year. JCA continued its role of mother hen, guarding and helping her sometimes errant children when they got into difficulties. In 1957 there was a drought in Entre-Rios province, the area with the highest concentration of Jewish farmers in the country. JCA, with its customary solicitude, hastened to make loans to the worst affected colonists.

That year was one of considerable unrest and unsettlement in Argentina. Juan Perón had been ousted and exiled in 1956, and the controlling junta had set elections for 1957. Not only the political scene was confused, but, after Perón's mismanagement, also the economic. But JCA went about its business, making emergency drought loans, helping the appropriate committees arrange social and cultural events in the colonies and providing advances to the co-operatives and other community institutions.

Rather surprising, in view of the cessation of Jewish immigration, was the Association's purchase in 1957 of an estate of 150 hectares in the province of Rio Negro, south west of Buenos Aires. The estate was wholly devoted to fruit and grapes, principally grapes, and contained its own winery. The chief object of the purchase was as a hedge against devaluation of funds surplus to requirements, which could not be withdrawn from Argentina. Some of the land might be used for the settlement of a few families (under fruit, 10 hectares or less would constitute an economic unit), but in the event no suitable candidates were forthcoming. Also noteworthy in this year was the fact that, after many years of effort, JCA was finally able to win a tax exemption in Entre-Rios province as a charitable organisation. The Association's philanthropic character had been recognised by the federal government long before, but this had not protected JCA against taxes imposed by the provinces on absentee landowners. Now at last Entre-Rios was persuaded to rescind its levy, and later other provinces followed its lead.

The following year, 1958, saw the number of colonists further reduced, and even among those still farming more were not living on their land. There were 2,045 Jewish farms and, with family members counted, 6,300 people making a living from agriculture. By now 95 per cent of the farms were owned by the colonists and 85 per cent were free of mortgage. The JCA staff was involved in making arrangements for social and cultural programmes, and the Association continued its support for religious education. JCA was still making loans to co-operatives and individuals, on four criteria: (1) the repurchase of vacated land, (2) installation of sons of colonists, (3) extension of mechanisation (though this doubtless contributed to the exodus from agriculture which JCA so deplored), and (4) relief in cases of special hardship, as happened when drought struck Entre-Rios the year before, or when in 1955 colony Avigdor had suffered economic difficulties brought on by its isolation and JCA restored equilibrium with special credits.

JCA was also indulging in ventures on its own account, producing fruit and wine on the estate in Rio Negro and raising cattle on some of the land in the old colonies which it was still holding in reserve. This latter enterprise was proceeding satisfactorily, but the Rio Negro undertaking began rather badly as the crop was injured by frost in 1959. The next year was in almost all respects a repetition; JCA earned 1 million pesos on its cattle-raising efforts – in less spectacular terms, £4,300 sterling – and lost money on fruit and vine growing. By 1962 there was a reversal in the performance of these direct farming ventures as the cattle enterprise had suffered from the effects of two years of drought while the fruit and wine estate, which depended more on irrigation than on rainfall and had also benefited from patient work of improvement carried out over several years, showed markedly better results. The number of Jewish farming families in the colonies was down to 1,984, comprising 5,907 persons.

Through the eyes of a third party

Towards the end of 1958, A. Alperin, who wrote for the New York Yiddish newspaper, *Der Tog-Morgen Journal*, paid a visit to many of the JCA colonies in Argentina and produced a series of articles on the subject.[3] He wrote that one-third of the Jews then living in Argentina were connected with the colonies in one way or another: 'one may have been born on a farm – another may have lived . . . there for a time, another may be drawing absentee income from a farm that he has turned over to a neighbour to work.' He remarks that 'the JCA colonies are the basis of all Jewish life in Argentina. The flourishing Jewish community of Buenos Aires . . . is the direct outgrowth of the agricultural colonies.' In the older colonies in Entre-Rios province he met second-, third- and even fourth-generation Jewish settlers. He talked about 'authentic Jewish gauchos' who had never even been to one of the big cities. Alperin quickly perceived that one of the great problems of the colonies was the preservation of their Jewishness. Like so many other visitors, he was impressed that the pupils of the schools in the colonies came many miles on horseback to attend. 'Every pupil from the eight-year-olds and older rides to school . . . to get a Jewish education, to learn Hebrew prayers. I watched them riding off home, heads up, happy little riders. If only their parents displayed the same degree of enthusiasm about their children's Jewish education!' He noted with sadness that, when he was asked to give a lecture in Domín-guez, in the centre of the Jewish settlements in Entre-Rios, and was promised a plenteous audience in the 'large auditorium', there were only about 'fifty or sixty middle-aged listeners'; and the chairman of the evening in introducing him said, 'Had you been here fifteen years ago your reception would have been quite different and you would have had a larger audience.' When Alperin visited colony Avigdor, one of the settlers who conducted synagogue services on the High Holydays told him that he 'doubted there was one person in the congregation who under-stands a single word'. And yet he tells of meeting a colonist who boasted that he and his neighbours 'observe the Sabbath and do no work on their fields that day', and besides 'read Yiddish books and newspapers'. Alperin met a number of Yiddish-speaking young people, and he opined that this was still the mother-tongue of more than 30 per cent of the colonists.

A question of perhaps greater concern to JCA was whether the colonists would remain on the farms. On this point Alperin's evidence bore out what we have already remarked: that young women were the first to leave, and that their leaving was a stimulus to young men to do the same, particularly in the more isolated villages where there was a lack of suitable marriage partners.

Near the end of his account Alperin says 'that the seed of Jewish culture planted six and seven decades ago in the soil of Argentina still bears fruit', but he has already made it clear in his description of his lecture and the Holyday services that this fruit is not very plentiful. Alperin then remarks that 'the trend from the farm to the city applies not only to the Jewish colonies [but] it is more evident in the Jewish colonies'; so he saw that, even though some Jews had become 'authentic gauchos', fully acclimatised to rural life, their children would not be.

Further retrenchment

Although JCA was in some ways slow to respond to the perception that its mission in Argentina was over, it needed no persuasion that the diminution in the number of Jewish farmers and the increasing independence of those who remained called for a gradual dismantling of its extensive administrative machinery. This began with the reduction of its field staff in the northern part of its area of operation, i.e. the provinces of Entre-Rios and Santa Fe, where the majority of the JCA colonists were located. The process continued until, eventually, what . administrative work was necessary was done from the headquarters in Buenos Aires. This meant that JCA's direct participation in local social and cultural activities was no longer possible, but it did not prevent the Association from continuing to make its usual grants to social, cultural and religious institutions.

The co-operatives

An unpromising sign in 1962 was the descent of many of the co-operatives into financial difficulties. These were in effect bankers for the producers, advancing to them the value of the crops before their sale. Now, because of inflation (creditors in general do badly in inflationary times) and slow payment by the purchasers, the co-operatives' own capital position began to be impaired. Nevertheless, they felt sufficiently emboldened to sponsor the erection of a linseed oil mill in Entre-Rios, with financial help from JCA and the provincial government. At its beginning this mill operated profitably. Unfortunately, in the next year it was out of operation for three months because of a fire, but again JCA and the provincial government came forward with credits to enable it to be repaired and reopened.

The next years saw no major change. About 2,000 families continued to earn their living from the land 'or in related occupations' (a phrase occurring regularly in the Association's Annual Reports at this time, which clearly meant that the number of true farmers was smaller). The co-operatives continued to struggle against the effects of inflation and slow payment. JCA made its usual grants, including some for vocational training, and made credits available for the purchase of equipment, repurchase of land and to help growers affected by drought in Entre-Rios. In 1964 there was a seventy-fifth anniversary celebration of the beginning of Jewish farm settlement in Argentina, with events being staged in Buenos Aires and Moisesville. (It will be remembered that the ill-fated 'Podolians', later rescued by Löwenthal and the Baron, landed in 1889.)

JCA's staff was again reduced, paralleling a reduction in the number of farmers they served. By 1966 the count of families earning a living from the soil or related occupations was 1,620.

Land holdings

The farmers remaining, comprising nine major groups, occupied about 375,000 hectares (937,500 acres), of which half was under cultivation and half was carrying 300,000 head of cattle. By 1969 the land in the hands of Jewish farmers was down to 300,000 hectares. Unfortunately, there are no very accurate and definitive figures available on the ownership and disposition of the land holdings, in part because of the great reduction in the staff, which made impossible the compilation of as comprehensive and exhaustive statistics as formerly. However, some earlier figures contained in the records of JCA are of interest in this connection. In 1948 an analysis of the occupancy of the 617,666 hectares originally owned by JCA was as follows:

Occupied by colonist owners	202,031	
Rented by colonist owners to Jews	17,546	
Sold by colonist owners to Jews	63,405	
Occupied by other colonists (tenants)	88,973	
JCA reserve land rented to Jews	79,927	
Total no. of hectares occupied by Jews		451,882
Rented to non-Jews	81,690	
Sold to non-Jews	44,605	
Sold, not suitable for colonization	39,489	
Total occupied by non-Jews or not farmed		165,784
Grand total		617,666

By 1972, when JCA was ready to put an end to its Argentine operations, the amount of farm land it still owned was minuscule.

The closing process

The JCA Annual Report for 1971 acknowledged publicly what had been patently obvious for a long time to the Council: that the Jewish farmers in Argentina, now a well-established group, almost without exception the sons or grandsons of the original immigrants, hardly needed the assistance of a 'colonising agency'. The Association therefore finally decided to withdraw from Argentina. The decision had in fact been made long before, but little action to implement it was taken until the Fraternidad Agraria proposed in 1969 that the co-operatives should handle JCA's closing affairs. In the end they did not, but their proposal seems to have sparked off the final closing process.

The termination of the Association's activities in Argentina was not accomplished without heartaches, bureaucratic obstacles and delays. The JCA Council had for some time been considering the creation of a foundation in Argentina to take over and/or realise the Association's assets there and to act as a successor organisation in respect of any work remaining to be done after its departure. Progress in carrying out this proposal 'was slow and hampered by successive political and economic crises and natural disasters in the colonies such as droughts and floods'.[4] By 1965 the staff had been reduced to ten, and in 1966 it was reduced further to three, in one office in Buenos Aires. After the President, Sir Henry d'Avigdor Goldsmid, visited Buenos Aires in 1967, it was concluded that the proposed liquidating foundation might well cost more than it could collect, especially in view of the unstable economic conditions in the country.

Because of this rather uncertain state of affairs no action was taken until the end of 1969, when the Fraternidad Agraria put forward the idea that an entity with a membership drawn from the co-operatives should handle JCA's affairs – the assets were now estimated at £140,000 – after its withdrawal. Such an organisation, called the Asociación Barón Hirsch, was accordingly established, with statutes approved by the tax authorities. The necessary tax exemption registration, however, was not forthcoming, despite repeated requests over a period of years. It was presumed that the reason for this delay, apart from 'the perennial difficulty of dealing with Argentine officialdom', was the country's 'state of political instability and uncertainty' when no official cared to make a decision, 'especially in a case such as this, *sui generis*'. When the tax exemption began to seem impossible to obtain and other fiscal difficulties had arisen, the idea of a successor organisation was abandoned.

An alternative plan of action, formulated by Mr Joseph Neville following his visit to Argentina in October 1973, was adopted by the Council. The plan called for the outstanding debts, amounting to 544,000 pesos (the exchange rate was then 24 pesos to the pound sterling), to be transferred to tax-exempt charitable institutions. The farm land still owned by JCA, a mere 500 hectares – less than 0.1 per cent of the 600,000 or more that JCA possessed at its apogee, and now in the hands of tenants – would be sold to the co-operatives; 'suburban' lots would be sold at auction; and plots of 'urban' land would be given as gifts to municipalities for public purposes. The archives were to be transferred to the Hebrew University in Jerusalem. It was expected that the Buenos Aires office would close on 31 January 1974, and the building be sold. The official liquidation for technical reasons would not commence until 1975. JCA's cash resources in Buenos Aires, it was estimated, would be sufficient to cover the cost of all the above actions. Any surplus, together with debts remaining uncollected, would be donated to charitable institutions. The 1974 Annual Report declared that the final disposal of JCA's assets in Argentina had taken place 'as a preliminary to the official liquidation which was to be put in hand later'.

After JCA

At present, the active Jewish farmers in Argentina and the remaining landmarks of the great JCA colonies are relatively few. However, the old co-operatives – Fondo Comunal of Clara, Sociedad Agrícola of Lucienville, Mutua Agrícola of Moisesville and others – were still in operation in 1980. Their overhead organisation, the Fraternidad Agraria, was very much alive, publishing El Colono Cooperador, then in its sixty-fourth year, holding meetings and conferences to assess the agricultural situation and proposing ameliorative legislation to the government. The Fraternidad was affiliated to Coninagro (Confederación Intercooperativa Agropecuaria), which is the overall representative body of the co-operatives that makes recommendations to the government for projects of interest and concern to the agriculturists of Argentina.[5] The names of the directors and staff of the individual co-operatives and of the Fraternidad were redolent of their Russian-Jewish origin – Salomon Halperin, Samuel Jarovsky, Joaquim Pollacq, Enrico Freidemberg, Arturo Melamed . . .

Conclusion

So, 83 years after it began to buy land and settle Russian Jews in Argentina, JCA put an end to its activities in that country. These activities had been the major focus of its interest before the First World War and an area of great concern during the inter-war period. After the Second World War, when the Argentine colonies entered a period of declining population, the Association put its resources to work in Israel, where the prospects for the consolidation and improvement of Jewish farming activity and future expansion were excellent. This was also the recommendation of Sir Keith Joseph, at present Secretary of State for Education in the British Cabinet. From 1951 to 1960 and again from 1967 to 1970 he had been a member of the JCA Council. In 1958 he conducted a survey of JCA's activities and arrived at the conclusion that Israel was the most promising location for the exercise of the Association's efforts. He also offered the opinion that JCA's day in Argentina was done.[6]

Georges Aronstein had had some perception of this as early as 1934, when he talked about stagnation in the colonies in the absence of further immigration, and made it evident that he saw no great prospects for immigration. The doughty Louis Oungre had had at least a glimpse of this dull future as far back as 1921, when he too had uttered the word 'stagnation'. But between the first glimpse, full perception and action based on that perception there were many long intervals. Set minds change slowly, and it is hard to move from an accustomed and comfortable groove; JCA had not hurried to do so.

Long before the end, it was obvious that the Baron de Hirsch's massive strategy – to move vast numbers of Jews out of oppression in Russia and create from them a great class of independent Jewish farmers in South America – was far from attainable by JCA. And indeed, his parallel object of defusing anti-Semitic canards by demonstrating that Jews could be successful tillers of the soil was not attained, least of all in Argentina, which is among the most anti-Semitic of countries. Shall we, then, mark the Baron and his creation, JCA, as failures, responsible for a waste of vast effort and, in current terms, millions of pounds sterling?

If JCA did not move millions of Jews from Russia, it moved thousands: in place of a life of misery with no prospects, they and their children were offered a life of opportunity. JCA is to be credited not only with improving the lot of the thousands of families it moved to Argentina, but also for its vital role in opening that and other countries in South America as destinations for Jewish emigrants in their hundreds of thousands, eager to flee

Eastern Europe for safe havens overseas. In Argentina itself, not only did the JCA immigration and the wider influx to which it led add a vibrant, capable and useful element to the country's mix of peoples, but specifically the JCA colonists made notable contributions to the development of Argentine agriculture. They introduced co-operatives and the benefits thereof to the country; as late as 1972 it was estimated that half the Argentine farm co-operatives were operated mainly by Jews. Jews were among the first, if not the first, in the country to practise rational crop diversification. They introduced important crops like alfalfa, sudan grass, sunflowers and groundnuts, and were among the first fruit producers.[7] Poultry rearing was largely a Jewish occupation. The first large grain elevator in the country was erected by a Jewish co-operative, Fondo Comunal, in Colony Clara; the first creameries were also started by Jewish co-operatives. When after the Second World War the Argentine government founded an Institute for Colonization and an Agrarian National Council, they largely borrowed their plans and programmes from the JCA colonies and their organisations. And quantitatively, Jews still play a part in Argentine agriculture. According to Judith Elkin, 'Independent Jewish farmers and cattlemen in Argentina presently own some eight hundred thousand hectares [2 million acres] including land within the original colonies.'[8]

Few would question that it is better to be alive in Argentina than dead in Poland or the Ukraine, and death would have been the fate of thousands of Jewish families if they had not been able to leave Europe for Argentina in the years before the Second World War. To quote Judith Elkin again,

> As European Jewry entered the Holocaust Kingdom, each individual who found his way to the Dominican Republic or to Bolivia represents a triumph. Jewish farmers of Argentina (and the paradigm will serve Brazil and Uruguay as well) found not only secure homes, but also time and space in which to orient themselves to their new environment linguistically, ecologically, behaviorally.[9]

What fate now holds in store for them in the present (December 1983) state of the Argentine polity is unpredictable, the country having just enjoyed its first democratic election in years. It would seem that the days of military dictatorships which were blemished by the suspension of civil liberties and the disappearance without trace and without trial of thousands of citizens, amidst a strong aura of anti-Semitism, are over and done with. There are therefore grounds for at least muted hope for the future.

CHAPTER 14

JCA World-wide

This chapter may have something of a patchwork appearance, for it wanders all over the map, from East Africa to North Africa, from Canada to South America, and even to Australia. Furthermore, the programmes in the countries dealt with have little in common; for example the long-established farm settlement efforts in Brazil and Canada do not share much common ground with the loan schemes for housing and tuition intended for North African immigrants in Paris. The actions discussed, however, do have a common time frame, i.e. the period from 1945 to the present. And they also have a common theme – the withdrawal of JCA from either a long sustained or a more recently initiated activity, a withdrawal dictated by the cessation of Jewish immigration to the area of interest or, as in Tunisia and Morocco, by the large-scale departure of the Jewish population from the country.

Brazil

Towards the end of the Second World War a notable event in Brazil from JCA's point of view was a fire at Quatro-Irmãos, which was a heavily wooded area. The fire raged for several months, and when it finally died out JCA found itself with a vast amount of partly burnt timber on its hands which it tried to sell off as best it could. To the surprise of Isidore Eisenberg, the JCA administrator, the price obtainable was very good; this led him to recommend, and JCA to adopt, a policy of selling its timber, which for the next few years became a major preoccupation of the management – all the more so since further Jewish settlement in the colony had virtually ceased.[1] So the JCA staff occupied themselves mainly in negotiating with buyers and operating JCA's 18 kilometre railway, which was connected to the main Brazilian system and was used chiefly to transport the timber.

But this is not to say that things were quiet. In 1948 Quatro-Irmãos was invaded by intruders who squatted on sections of

242

JCA's land. The local police were not overly interested in protecting the possessions of a foreign corporation and made no attempt to expel the uninvited visitors. In the next year, however, the government took a hand in the affair and arranged a settlement, of which JCA bore the brunt. Those intruders who had the wherewithal were allowed to retain the land they had seized, provided they could pay something to JCA. Those who could not make any payment were moved from Quatro-Irmãos and given plots of government land elsewhere – with JCA contributing to the cost of moving them.

In Rezende, where before the war JCA had also purchased some land on which it hoped to settle refugees from Europe (who in the event were not allowed into Brazil), JCA had relocated some Jewish families already in the country. But now the government started taking steps to expropriate this land, claiming to need it for a military academy. JCA decided to do whatever was necessary to protect the interest of the settlers. However, realising also that discretion was the better part of valour, the Association began in 1948 to sell some of the land, keeping only a building and part of the acreage to be used as a holiday camp for children from Rio de Janeiro.

Despite its difficulties with invaders at Quatro-Irmãos, JCA had new sawmills installed, as the price of timber continued favourable. For the same reason it maintained the railroad in good operating condition and was also able to sell plots to sawyers. Meanwhile some sons of settlers were persuaded to remain at Quatro-Irmãos, and in 1951 and 1952 25 sons of previous settlers were installed there. At first, at least, they were quite successful and they helped to maintain the Jewish population, which in 1954 was 299, consisting of 94 families.

In this same year a large number of Jews were brought to the country by HIAS. JCA, in collaboration also with JDC, set up loan kassas in Rio de Janeiro and São Paulo to help them. This in effect constituted a revival of the kassa movement in these cities, which had helped thousands of immigrants before the war. The São Paulo kassa was especially active, in 1955 making 152 loans, totalling 2.5 million cruzeiros (£12,500), to help immigrants establish small businesses and integrate themselves into the country's economy. In Rio only 29 loans were made, for 650,000 cruzeiros. The kassa in São Paulo, however, proved so successful that when in 1956 large groups of Jews began to arrive from Egypt in consequence of the Israeli campaign in the Sinai, and from Hungary following the quickly crushed anti-Soviet insurrection there, another kassa was opened in that city to help these latest refugees; it made 100 loans amounting to 1.8 million cruzeiros. Another new venture in which JCA joined because of its longstanding interest in vocational education was the establishment of an ORT school in Rio de Janeiro.

Meanwhile, at Quatro-Irmãos, timber sales continued at remunerative prices and the railway covered its expenses. The Jewish population was still holding up fairly well, at 284. But though sales of timber went on for a year or two longer, the end was now in sight; by 1958 it was believed that almost all the marketable wood had been sold. By 1959 the railway had become so little used that JCA started to sell off the rolling stock, consisting of 2 engines and 33 freight cars. With the timber all but gone, JCA also resolved to dispose of the land remaining in its hands and sold 8,000 hectares in 1959 and 1960. With the end of JCA activity imminent, the Jewish population of Quatro-Irmãos declined to 33 families in 1961. It turned out, however, that the price of timber in Brazil rose so high that it became worth-while for JCA to garner the wood of poorer quality that was still left and sell it. Continuing to divest itself of the rest of what it owned there, JCA in 1961 and 1962 disposed of a few remaining pieces of railway equipment as well as another 2,000 hectares of land. There were by now only 20 Jewish families at Quatro-Irmãos. Despite this relinquishment of its property in Rio Grande do Sul, JCA continued to make contributions to cultural and religious institutions in the Brazilian cities.

The story of JCA in Brazil was not yet quite finished. Some land remained in its ownership, but the sale of another 4,000 hectares in 1963 reduced its possession to a few scattered parcels. Jewish immigration had dwindled, and the loan programme was therefore terminated in 1964. In its ten years of activity the loan scheme had been responsible for 1,850 loans to a total of 91 million cruzeiros (£90,000) to help newcomers get started in small businesses. A year later a housing loan operation in which HIAS had participated was also terminated, having granted 845 advances in the years 1962–5 totalling 39 million cruzeiros (£11,000). The collection of the amounts remaining due was handed over to the São Paulo Jewish Welfare Board. By now JCA retained no interest in any part of Brazil, except that for many years it continued to make contributions to a sheltered workshop for the elderly and physically handicapped in São Paulo and to the ORT school and the Hospital Israelita in Rio de Janeiro.

The sale of land and timber brought in approximately £600,000. Of this sum, after the grants to the institutions named above and a few other minor annual donations, most of the rest was invested in two buildings in Rio de Janeiro, as the money could not be transferred from Brazil.[2] The Association continued to help support these local agencies until, finally, it decided to realise its remaining assets in Brazil.

What was the result of JCA's years of effort in Brazil? The final assessment depends on one's point of view. That the Jewish settlers had left Quatro-Irmãos – a colony, it must be emphasised, buried in an inhospitable forest – Isidore Eisenberg regarded as a sign of his and JCA's failure, and one not compensated for by the fact that the individuals concerned had gone on to prosper in such places as the city of Porto Alegre. Eisenberg was a fervent adherent to the idea of the creation of an agricultural class among Jews; but to one who does not hold such firm views, the fact that many Jews entered Brazil as would-be farmers but achieved prosperity in some other occupation would not seem to be a matter unduly to be deplored. If JCA, challenging economic and sociological realities, did not create a substantial Jewish agricultural class in Brazil, it did accomplish there – to a lesser degree, to be sure – what it achieved in Argentina. It helped to make the country a locus of Jewish immigration, opening it up for thousands of immigrants from Eastern Europe, many of whom it aided directly, not only by way of agricultural settlement but through the loan programmes run in partnership with JDC and HIAS. Through JCA's help to Jewish institutions like schools and synagogues, its encouragement of translations of Hebrew religious texts into Portuguese and its support of the visits to Brazil of Rabbi Raffalovich in the 1920s, it made a significant contribution to the raising of the consciousness and the revitalisation of the Jewish community, which today, considering its size – 150,000 – is an influential element in the life of the country.

This concludes the story of JCA in South America, but to complete the tally of the Association's involvement in that continent and to make clear the geographical extent of its interests we must note that in the 1950s JCA participated with JDC in establishing small lending agencies in Santiago, Chile, and Montevideo, Uruguay. The Santiago office was closed in 1963 because of the near-cessation of Jewish immigration; the one in Montevideo was kept open for another year. And one final good work must be mentioned. In 1960 JCA, together with JDC and the Jewish community of Santiago, made a grant to help victims of an earthquake in Chile.

Canada

After the Second World War JCA did not attempt to place new settlers in western Canada, but it did what it could to maintain the existing ones there. It also placed immigrants on farms in the provinces of Quebec and Ontario, particularly the latter, although, as compared with the scale of the Association's colonization work in the past, relatively few individuals were involved. JCA's major post-war settlement exercise in Canada took place in the Niagara Peninsula in Ontario, where farms suitable for growing fruit or producing milk were purchased in 1948 for $220,000, with the idea of settling 25 families recruited in the Displaced Persons camps in Europe. Buildings were erected, land was prepared for cultivation and a central machine station was set up. Sixteen families were installed in 1949 and a few more arrived later. The usual loans were granted to meet the various needs of the farmers, and by 1952 JCA found it possible to discontinue the operation of the central machine station and sell the equipment to the settlers. In that year also JCA hired a Hebrew teacher for the children. In the course of the next few years the newcomers were successful in making their way in the New World. By 1955 six of them had progressed to the point of acquiring ownership of their farms with the help of mortgages, and six more did so the following year. By then there were 19 families in the group.

In 1954 JCA embarked on a new scheme, that of making loans to individual Jewish farmers who had settled in the provinces of Quebec and Ontario independently or with the help of the Canadian Jewish Congress – a programme similar to that of the Jewish Agricultural Society in the United States. By 1960 32 such loans had been made, for a total of $59,600, and there were now 31 families in the area living on farms originally purchased by JCA or, in the case of the beneficiaries of the loan scheme, purchased or developed with the help of JCA.

In 1959 a new project was commenced; a loan kassa for newcomers was set up in Toronto in conjunction with Canadian Jewish Congress, in response to the increased immigration from Hungary and Egypt. In the fourth quarter of 1956 1,500 Jewish immigrants from Hungary entered Canada. Then Israel's attack on and capture of the Sinai, concerted in 1956 with the British and French assault on the Suez Canal, triggered an exodus of Jews from Egypt. In 1957 6,000 more Jews arrived in Canada, three-quarters of them from Hungary. From the inception of the Toronto kassa in 1959 to the end of 1965, 105 loans were made for a total of $154,000. In 1965 the kassa's activity increased significantly as immigrants from Morocco began to arrive in substantial numbers following the removal of restrictions on departures from that country. They came to Canada because as French speakers they expected to feel more at home there (those who ended up in Toronto were, so to speak, an 'overflow' from the francophone areas).

As these Jewish immigrants were not the pioneering type who had populated the settlements in the western provinces, JCA took no active steps to add to those settlements. The Jewish farming fraternity there began to disperse, shrinking from 116 families (337 people) in 1950 to 76 families (201 souls) in 1957. The next year the area was afflicted by an intense drought, and the Jewish farm population was further reduced in consequence, notwithstanding the 'dried-out bonus', as the government grants to the drought victims were called. But if drought came, so did liquid relief, of an interesting sort. There began to be rumours that the area of Jewish settlement in Saskatchewan might overlay oil-bearing strata, and by 1960 oil companies were doing exploratory work in Sonnenfeld colony. However, the Jewish farm population continued to decline, falling to 39 families (112 people) in 1960.

The loan programme for scattered individual families in Ontario and Quebec also contracted, as larger and larger sums, more than JCA or the settlers wanted to risk, began to be required for the purchase or development of a farm. In 1964 only 5 individual loans were made, and in 1965 only 4. In that year 44 families were living on farms in eastern Canada purchased or improved with JCA finance.

In the west the oil prospectors had commenced drilling on land where JCA had been astute enough to retain the mineral rights even when it sold the land; in 1967, the Association received oil royalties of $7800.

In that same year, with JCA's help, the Lincoln County Baron de Hirsch Congregation and Community Centre was completed. Lincoln is in eastern Ontario, near Niagara Falls, conveniently located for the majority of the Jewish farmers, who used the Centre as a synagogue, a Hebrew school and a meeting place for social activities. The Toronto kassa continued at its previous level, making 24 advances. The repayment record of the small immigrant businessmen, chiefly from Morocco, who became the predominant borrowers was excellent.

For the next decade the pattern of JCA's activity in Canada remained much the same, except that the loans made to individual farmers continued to dwindle because, on the one hand, of the decrease in the number of applicants qualifying for such assistance and, on the other, of the constant rise in the price of land and equipment. In 1974 JCA reported that this loan progamme had been responsible for 115 loans totalling $531,000, of which by that time only $110,000 was still outstanding. The number of families still living on farms purchased or developed with JCA credit under this programme had actually risen somewhat, to 60, but this figure represented less than half the total number of farms – about 140 – for which JCA had made loans in eastern Canada. In addition, there were in the two provinces about 60 Jewish farmers who had had no connection with JCA. The Niagara group was doing well with fruit, dairy and poultry production and the raising of cattle and pigs (obviously, they were not Orthodox Jews). The Lincoln Centre continued to be lively and well attended. In the west, 38 families remained, and the oil royalties continued to flow into the JCA treasury, albeit on a comparatively modest scale; the prospects were still favourable, for the oil companies were agreeable to renegotiating the leases.

At bottom, however, it was clear that there was no longer any point in considering Canada as a possibility for settling Jews as farmers. Land prices were too high, and Jewish immigrants in any case were attracted to vocations other than farming, of which on the whole they had no experience. The same trend was observable in the United States, where the Jewish Agricultural Society had its period of greatest settlement activity in the years 1945–50, when the Displaced Persons Act permitted about 65,000 refugees from central Europe to enter the United States and about 7 per cent of these became farmers. But as Jewish immigration fell to a trickle thereafter and the cost of starting a farm increased, the Society found itself making ever fewer loans, until in 1970 it went out of existence altogether, being merged into the Baron de Hirsch Fund.

The one JCA activity in Canada that continued at a steady level was the Toronto loan kassa. In addition to immigrants from Morocco, some began to arrive from the USSR; and because of this last group of newcomers the kassa was more active in 1976 than ever before: it made 53 loans for $118,000, contributing to a total of 410 loans for $670,000 since inception of this agency in 1954.

Apart from this, however, JCA's interests in Canada had by now diminished to a point where it was no longer worth-while to maintain an office there, and by 1977 winding-up plans had been worked out with JCA's Canadian Board. The sale of the farmland in Saskatchewan begun in 1976 was completed, most of the buyers being the existing tenants. Most of the other assets and the income therefrom were transferred to the Jewish Community Foundation of Greater Montreal, which proposed to employ them as far as possible for purposes similar to those of JCA. The

11a Quatro-Irmãos, Brazil, 1930. JCA's railway

11b Rezende, Brazil, 1939. Colonist's house

12a Quatro-Irmãos, Brazil, 1950. 'Reception day' at the administrator's office

12b Quatro-Irmãos, Brazil, 1952. Extracting the timber

13a Niagara Peninsula, Ontario, Canada, 1953. M. Gottschalk, JCA Vice-President, and V. Girmounsky, Director General, visiting a farmer settled by JCA

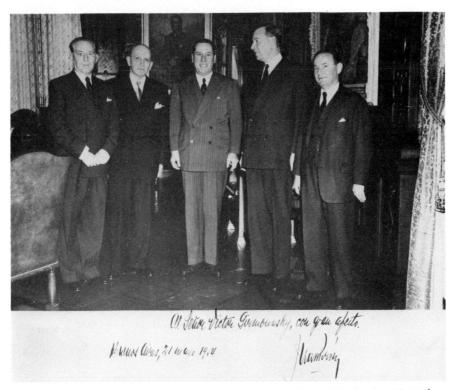

13b Buenos Aires, 1954. JCA representatives received by General Perón, President of Argentina. (L. to r. J. Calius, JCA's Argentine manager, V. Girmounsky, Director General, General Perón, Sir H. d'Avigdor Goldsmid, JCA President, Dr R. Dubrovsky, Council member)

14a Casablanca, Morocco, 1953. Jewish artisans in the mellah

14b Casablanca, Morocco, 1953. The loan kassa manager interviewing clients.

supervision of the funds that JCA had provided for the Toronto kassa was also transferred to the Foundation. In 1978, with its affairs thus disposed of, JCA was able to close its Montreal office.

As in South America, JCA's settling of some thousand or more farmers in western Canada helped to open the country to Jewish immigration and achieved whatever good is achieved by proving that Jews can be successful farmers under difficult conditions. Perhaps more important, JCA worked with the Baron de Hirsch Institute in assisting tens of thousands of the immigrants who came to Canada in the years before the First World War by receiving them in the ports, finding jobs for them, organising classes in English and other subjects, and at times undertaking legal action to enforce their right of entry. After the war, too, JCA and JIAS, which JCA helped to establish, made possible the immigration to Canada of thousands who, but for the activities of JCA, JIAS, HICEM and the Canadian Jewish Congress, would not have been able to enter. This was notably so in the case of the 3,000 Russian-Jewish refugees from Romania who under arrangements made by JCA reached Canada in 1923–4.

North Africa

JCA had long been aware of the economic plight of the Jews of Morocco, which seemed to cry out for aid from their brethren of the Western World. Various measures of constructive assistance had been contemplated, but it was not until 1950 that JCA, in consultation with the Alliance Israélite Universelle, which maintained a longstanding and extensive educational programme in North Africa, decided on a concrete course of action: this was to train young men in agricultural skills and, if the training project was successful, place them on farms. In 1951 JCA and the Alliance, which provided 10 per cent of the initial capital, established the Société Agricole pour les Israélites Marocains (SAIM). A property of 96 hectares was purchased at a place called Fkih-ben-Salah on which a combined training and settlement scheme was to be carried out.

A generation later, it is hard to discern the nature of JCA's motives in attempting to establish agricultural training and farm settlement for Jews in Morocco. It was not likely that many candidates would be available for this sort of venture. Further, what kind of permanent settlement could be made in this Muslim, Arab country? Anti-Israel, anti-Jewish feeling was not, in the early 1950s, as strong as it later became, after four wars between Israel and the Arab states and 33 years of violent hostility and frequent bloodshed, but such feelings did exist and were strong enough. Also, the Association might have remembered its experiences in Turkey, where long before the creation of Israel the anti-Jewish feelings of the Muslim Turks made it impossible for the JCA colonies to continue.

Despite such considerations, JCA and the Alliance, impelled by the desire to help a community so badly in need of support from the Jewish world outside, decided not to leave even an unlikely stone unturned in developing what alternatives they could for the deprived Jews of Morocco. At this time the possibilities offered by migration to Israel, France or Canada had not yet taken shape.

SAIM began by recruiting 12 young men, all graduates of Alliance schools in Morocco, to study farm management and practices. The next year, their studies completed, this group was replaced by another 12 young men, also from the Alliance schools at Marrakesh and Meknes. At the same time, houses for the first four settlers were constructed and four families with some pretensions to an aptitude for farming were installed and furnished with animals and implements. The training centre managed to produce a crop worth 4 million francs (£2,800). In the next year four more houses were constructed, but the land needed by the settlers reduced the amount available to the training centre, which produced crops to the value of only 1.77 million francs. This reduction was also due in part to poor weather and low prices. So far, most of the young men having completed the course at Fkih-ben-Salah had been found some sort of work in agriculture, and the eight families settled were able by 1956 to repay to SAIM 4 million of the 7 million francs advanced to them. But Morocco had just received its independence from France, and tension was mounting. Despite the tensions, and also the strains on Arab–Israeli relations arising from the Suez War, the centre continued in operation, and by 1958 27 young men had completed the training course. There was practically no crop that year, however, owing first to excessive rainfall and then to a drought. The next year saw a considerable improvement in climatic conditions, and the settlers, who were chiefly occupied in raising cattle, found this sufficiently profitable to permit them to discharge their entire short-term indebtedness to SAIM.

But all was not well at Fkih-ben-Salah. With an increasing uneasiness spreading among the Jews of Morocco, it was becoming more and more difficult to find young men willing to enlist for agricultural training, especially in a spot so far removed from the main areas of Jewish population. It was therefore decided to discontinue this activity, and in 1960 the training centre was closed. The small group of settlers, too few in number for full viability, not over-endowed with farming skills and now without the training centre on which they had depended for various agricultural and other services, could not be expected to achieve the object originally conceived. So the farm settlement scheme was also terminated, and the families found means of making a livelihood elsewhere in Morocco. The whole property was then sold and the Société Agricole pour les Israélites Marocains liquidated.

At the same time as JCA was working with the Alliance to establish an agricultural settlement and training centre, it was collaborating with the Joint Distribution Committee to set up a system of loan kassas in the cities to supply Moroccan Jewish artisans with a source of credit for the purchase of tools, materials, etc. In 1950 there were about 200,000 Jews in Morocco, and the first loan kassa was opened in Casablanca in 1953; by the time their activity came to an end concomitantly with a great decrease in the Jewish population, the Moroccan kassas had provided a service to several thousand borrowers.

And not only in Morocco, for JCA and JDC decided to extend the scheme to Tunisia (where there were 71,000 Jews in 1946). A loan kassa commenced operations in Tunis in 1953, and in 1954 a branch office was opened in Sfax. In 1955 these two kassas made 276 loans, totalling about 15 million francs (£3,000), of which 13.5 million was repaid within the year; in addition, 149 members received 4.5 million francs in bank loans guaranteed by the kassa.

The Casablanca establishment lent 11.5 million francs (£2,300) in that year, of which nearly half had been repaid by the year's end. The next year new kassas were opened in Marrakesh and Fez (serving also Sefrou and Meknes), while the business of the one in Casablanca, the location of the country's largest Jewish community, increased to 362 loans totalling 16.5 million francs. In Tunisia also there was an increase in activity, the two agencies there distributing 506 loans for 24 million francs (£4,800).

The kassas supplied not only credit but also technical assistance, to encourage their borrowers, who were chiefly shopkeepers, shoemakers and workers in leather, metal, wood and textiles, to learn modern methods and the use of modern tools. In 1957 the Casablanca office was even busier, as its services were extended to Jews from the hinterland: 480 loans were distributed that year. In the same year the office in Marrakesh made 320 loans, Fez 250 and Rabat, another new kassa, 127. In Tunis 300 loans were granted and a number of bank loans were again guaranteed.

In 1958 the Moroccan government, under various administrative pretexts, suspended the operation of the kassas in Casablanca and Rabat for five months; the others were apparently not affected. Despite this action, the programme of technical aid, especially for shoemakers, went on without interruption. In Tunis also a five-month hiatus was imposed on the kassa on the pretext that its legal status was not in order.

In a review by JCA in 1959 of the work of the kassas in Morocco since their inception in 1953 (half the financing was provided by JDC, it will be remembered), it was stated that 203 million francs (£40,600) had been lent, that the average loan was about 600,000 francs (£125), and that 152 million francs had been repaid. About three-quarters of the borrowers in Casablanca were artisans, the rest small tradespeople. In the other Moroccan towns the proportion of shopkeepers was higher. In Tunisia the loans had totalled 120,000 dinars (£100,000) and repayments 97,000 dinars. The borrowers were almost entirely artisans except for 28 victims of a flood disaster in the town of Gabes who were the recipients of credit.

The activities of the North African kassas increased, if anything, in 1960 but they were checked in both countries in 1961. In Tunisia the cause was the aftermath of the 'Bizerta incident' in July, when a sizeable flight of Jews from the country took place.[3] The effect of the emigration from Tunisia showed up clearly in the loan figures: 474 loans, for 34,000 dinars, in 1960, 292 for 21,400 dinars in 1962. In Morocco, in October 1961 the government decreed that Jews could leave the country. A great many rushed to take advantage of the opportunity, and the kassas' scale of lending dropped abruptly.

By 1963 business in the Rabat and Marrakesh offices had fallen so far that they were closed and the remnants of their activities transferred to Casablanca. The demand in Fez was still enough to justify maintaining that kassa. Since inception the Moroccan kassas had made 6,851 loans totalling £261,000,[4] of which over 90 per cent was repaid. In Tunisia, the hard times being experienced by the Jewish artisans and shopkeepers because of the deteriorating economic conditions resulted in the level of operations being reduced still further. Here, since inception 3,465 loans had been granted, almost exactly half the number in Morocco, totalling £195,000; repayments, again, were close to 90 per cent.

In 1964 the emigration fever among Moroccan Jews had spread to Fez, but the fewer loans made were offset by the raising of the loan limit, so that owners of workshops and small retail businesses still found it worth their while to borrow from the kassa. In the next two years the wave of Jewish emigration began to abate. The outbreak of the Six-Day War in Israel in 1967 brought about increased emigration again from the two countries and consequent reductions in kassa activity. The flight reduced Jewish population by 1969 to only 40,000 in Morocco and 10,000 in Tunisia. Despite anti-Jewish political attitudes, the borrowers remaining in both countries were able to do well enough to maintain a satisfactory repayment record. Two years later the Jewish populations were reduced still further – to 35,000 in Morocco, where the Fez office had been closed, leaving only the one in Casablanca, and to 8,500 in Tunisia, where the kassa ceased operations at the end of 1971. In Casablanca the kassa remained active and started to guarantee letters of credit, as had been done in Tunis many years before.

The departure of Jews from both countries continued through the following years, accelerating in Morocco in 1972 because of an attempted *coup d'état* against the King; this frightened many Jews, who felt that the monarchy was their sole defence against the generally chauvinist, anti-Semitic feelings of most of the population. The Yom Kippur War in Israel in 1973 increased the rate of Jewish departures again, and the greatly reduced demand and the uncertain political situation resulted in the closure of the Casablanca office in 1974.

In the course of their existence the kassas in North Africa made more than 14,000 loans totalling over £1 million. Their help to artisans and tradespeople in the purchase of materials, tools and equipment kept thousands of small businessmen out of the clutches of money-lenders and rapacious wholesalers. Most important, they introduced a new concept into the area: that of constructive rehabilitation for people in distress rather than the demeaning almsgiving which had been the only form of assistance they had previously known.

France

A large proportion of the Jews who left Morocco and Tunisia went to France (many of them held French nationality), and the influx from North Africa increased further after the revolutionary insurrection in Algeria which preceded the attainment of independence by that country in 1962 – almost all of Algeria's 140,000 Jews fled. Already by 1956 the Caisse Israélite de Démarrage Economique (CIDE – the Jewish Fund for Economic Renewal), a loan agency of France's Jewish community, was overwhelmed by the demands from Jews from North Africa, and turned to JCA for help. This was forthcoming in the shape of a credit to be used for the issue of loans for business purposes to immigrants from North Africa. For years thereafter JCA continued to provide finance for CIDE to this end. In 1958, for example, CIDE made 449 such loans from the money advanced by JCA; in 1959, 317 loans and in 1960, 281. In 1960 CIDE made 1,532 loans altogether, so that the loans to North Africans made with JCA money were about one-fifth of the Fund's total operations.

In November 1961 JCA, JDC, the Central British Fund and the Fonds Social Juif Unifié (FSJU) together set up an agency to make housing loans to immigrants. By the end of 1962, 521 such loans had been issued for 1.5 million francs (£109,000). By 1964 the capital of the Housing Fund amounted to £180,000, JCA's contribution thereto being £57,000. The CIDE loans to immigrant North Africans were still being made to the number of 100 or more each year.

The two loan activities in Paris continued steadily for the next few years, until 1967 when the Six-Day War in Israel gave a further stimulus to migration from across the Mediterranean. The Housing Fund was particularly affected; it made 479 loans in 1967 and 334 in 1968. By 1970 the pace of CIDE and Housing Fund lending to North Africans was slowing down, but now refugees from Poland and Egypt were added to the borrowers. In this year, moreover, the Housing Fund, with matching sums from FSJU, began to finance a Students' Revolving Fund, to make loans, repayable after graduation, to immigrants attending college who for reasons of nationality were ineligible for state aid; in 1970 and 1971 332 such loans were granted, mainly to young people from Morocco and Tunisia.

The Yom Kippur War in Israel, like the Six-Day War, stimulated further immigration to France, bringing an increase in activity to both the Housing Fund and the Student Fund. In 1973 the Housing Fund made 132 loans for the equivalent of £49,000 and the Student Fund, 177 for £23,300. For the next two years these two funds continued working at a high level, but by 1976 the number of advances made by the Housing Fund fell sharply. From its inception in 1961, it had made 3,799 loans for over 13 million francs which helped to provide housing for some 21,000 individuals. The loan activities in France are still being carried on, but at a much lower level of activity than in the years of big immigration.

Australia

In 1953 Mr Leslie Prince, the member of JCA's Council who more than any other undertook long journeys on its behalf (he also carried out missions in Kenya, Canada and Ethiopia at various times), visited Australia. His assignment, on behalf of JCA and JDC, its partner in this as in so many other projects, was to consult with the Australian Jewish authorities on the situation of

Jewish immigrants from Europe, the possibility of further numbers being absorbed and the advisability of setting up a lending agency to facilitate this. It was concluded that an institution similar to a loan kassa would be very useful, and on Mr Prince's recommendation JCA and JDC proceeded accordingly in 1954. They jointly advanced £20,000 to the Jewish welfare societies in the states of New South Wales and Victoria to finance immigrants who wished to start or carry on small business enterprises. In the first year A£6,500 was lent (A£5 = £4 sterling). In 1955, when the activity had got into full momentum and JCA and JDC had doubled their contribution, 63 loans, for A£29,650, were made. After 2,500 Jews, a large number by Australian terms, entered the country in 1957, 80 per cent of them from Hungary, the operation reached a new level: 86 loans were granted in 1958. By then repayments were coming in at a good rate and there were no defaults.

At the same time, because housing was in short supply, JCA and JDC financed a plan to assist immigrants to buy dwellings. Instead of making loans to individuals, the welfare societies deposited the money provided by JCA and JDC in banks to constitute a guarantee fund for housing loans advanced by the banks. In this way the respectable total of 219 such loans was guaranteed in 1957. By the end of 1959 the number had reached 533.

In 1962 yet another scheme in the housing field was initiated. JCA, on its own this time, provided capital of A£100,000 for the creation of a co-operative building society in Sydney. This amount was absorbed by 34 mortgage loans to applicants selected by the Welfare Society.

The loan programmes in Australia progressed steadily. By the end of 1965, 665 business loans and 1,286 housing loans had been made. There were now three co-operative building societies financed by JCA; by 1969 there were five. In May 1972 JCA's investment in Australian loan activities stood as follows:

Original loan programme		£ 33,422
Housing loan funds		44,734
Co-operative building societies:		
Advanced	£327,103	
Repaid	148,388	
Outstanding		178,715
Total		£256,871

In the next few years Jewish immigration to Australia came nearly to a halt and the business loan programme, which was intended for newcomers, wound down accordingly. The demand for housing loans also slackened. In accordance with the terms on which the finance had been supplied by the sponsoring organisations, the welfare societies began to repay to them such of the money as could no longer be used for the purposes for which it had been provided. By 1977 the Melbourne Welfare Society had repaid the whole, and the Sydney Society a substantial part, of the JCA and JDC funds that had been under their control.

Altogether, the loan activities in Australia in which JCA had been concerned were responsible for distributing about 1,000 business loans, 1,620 housing loans and over 150 more housing loans through the five Sydney co-operative societies, a total of approximately 2,800 separate loans. There was, no doubt, some overlapping between business and housing loans, and some individuals may have received more than one business loan; but after making allowance for this we estimate that at least 2,000 immigrant families received JCA-connected loans. This is an impressive figure, for there are only 70,000 Jews in Australia, constituting about 17,500 families, of whom two-thirds, or 11,600, are immigrants who arrived after the Second World War.[5] Therefore nearly one-fifth of these recent arrivals benefited from the loan activities sponsored by JCA and its associates.

Kenya

As part of the Jewish organisations' wide-ranging search for any possible haven for refugees from Germany during the 1930s, the Central British Fund and the Council for German Jewry took the step of incorporating the Plough Settlements Association Ltd in London in August 1938. Its object was to settle German Jews in Kenya. The company had an authorised capital of £25,000, of which JCA agreed to subscribe £5,000. Two members of JCA's Council, Leslie Prince and Leonard Montefiore, were among its directors.

In November 1938 a committee sent to Germany selected 28 candidates, consisting of 20 young bachelors and 4 married couples. Some of these people were from farming backgrounds and others had received agricultural training. An advisory committee was formed in Nairobi, where 19 of the would-be settlers arrived early in 1939. Most were placed with local farmers for training, but before all could be taken care of, the war had begun. Nine thereupon joined the Kenya African Rifles Regiment; 10 others, who were acting as managers of farms, were for that reason considered not available for military service. Because of the war all action regarding permanent settlement was deferred.

With the war over and those who had joined the Army discharged, the settlement project was revived. JCA made a loan to Plough of £25,500 to provide the necessary capital. Seven farms of from 400 to 960 acres in size were bought in Kenya and occupied by ten of the settlers (there were three partnerships). The settlers were granted ownership subject to mortgages to Plough. The remainder of those who had originally come to Kenya left the country or were able to take care of themselves. By 1948 JCA had moved into the position not only of financing the company, but of controlling it, Leslie Prince having been its chairman since 1943. In 1948 Prince and Georges Aronstein of the JCA staff visited Kenya and reported that the ten settlers were making good progress. The Kenya government, however, made it very clear that they considered the Plough effort concluded.

By 1950 some of the settlers gave weight to the report made two years earlier by Prince and Aronstein by making sufficient repayment to enable two additional farms to be purchased by Plough, and two new settlers were installed as tenants with the prospect of ultimate purchase. But the Mau-Mau troubles which began in 1952 eventually made living and working in Kenya very difficult for the white farmers. This led the Plough settlers to dispose of their farms over the period 1955–63. The money invested and lent by JCA was fully repaid, and in 1965 the company was placed in liquidation.[6]

Ethiopia

The Falashas are a group of black Jews in Ethiopia numbering (in 1978) about 25,000; they are scattered in over 400 villages around the city of Gondar, about 200 miles north of Addis Ababa, and about 3,000 are in the province of Tigre, northeast of Gondar. Their legend connects them with the Queen of Sheba, but modern scholarship opines that they are descended from tribes in the area of Yemen and Aden who were converted by the many Jews living in that region 1,500 or more years ago and then crossed the Red Sea to Ethiopia. It is said that by the fifteenth century there were no fewer than 500,000 living in their own kingdom, but wars and conversion to Christianity reduced their numbers to a small fraction of what they had been. Their existence was largely unknown to the European world until the beginning of the twentieth century, when they were visited by Jacques Faitlovitch, a French sociologist and orientalist. He brought out a small group, had them educated in Europe and brought them to the attention of Jewish communities in Western Europe and America. In 1907

JCA showed interest in the establishment of a school for Falashas in Eritrea, but the expected financial participation of the Alliance Israélite did not materialise.

The Falashas are in effect a class of inferior status in Ethiopia ('Falasha' is a term of denigration), cultivating with medieval methods plots of land they have not been permitted to own. Through all their tribulations they have maintained a Jewish ritual of a pre-Talmudic cast, including the practice of circumcision and observance of dietary laws, the Sabbath, and certain Holydays. Whether or not they should be recognised as authentic Jews was long treated as a debatable point. In more recent years the presence of visitors has given them the opportunity to express their consuming desire to migrate to Israel. However, during the reign of Haile Selassie, the last Emperor, deposed in 1974, and under the communist regime that succeeded him, no one was permitted to emigrate. Nevertheless, by 1979 a couple of hundred Falashas succeeded in reaching Israel. In 1980 and 1981 they were followed by about 1,500 more, who walked hundreds of miles on foot and spent months in refugee camps *en route*. In Israel, where they have now been recognised officially as Jews, they have effected the transition from their almost medieval situation to modern life very well.

In 1965 JCA, under the urging of some important members of England's Jewish community who were interested in the Falashas, began to pay for the sending of Israeli instructors to the area around Gondar, to teach young Falashas Hebrew and Jewish history. This action was repeated thereafter. The JCA Annual Report for 1971 (p. 11) describes the Falasha community as 'enduring great poverty and exposed to the dangers of proselytism and extinction'. JCA was by then paying the salaries of 18 of the teachers in 13 village schools with about 800 pupils and giving grants for construction and repair work and for furniture, books and equipment. In 1973, by which time the number of pupils involved had risen to 950, it was agreed with the American Joint Distribution Committee and the Central British Fund that all help to the Falashas, which now included welfare and medical services (provided mainly by 'dressers', though one or two Israeli doctors paid occasional visits), should be channelled through the Falasha Welfare Association. Based in London, this body was constituted by a number of organisations and individuals who had hitherto been working together on a consultative basis. Unfortunately, political unrest in the country was mounting, making the teaching and relief work very difficult.

In 1976 a census was undertaken by the Falasha Welfare Association and 28,000 Falashas were counted. Since then their numbers have probably declined, as a result of both emigration and outright slaughter, carried out by wandering groups of bandits, anti-government guerilla groups and possibly by 'regular' troops.

The World ORT Union took over the assistance programme in 1977; but, on account of disturbed conditions and fighting in the Gondar area and the anti-Semitic attitude of the local provincial governor, ORT found it impossible to continue, and was obliged to suspend its activity in Ethiopia in 1981.

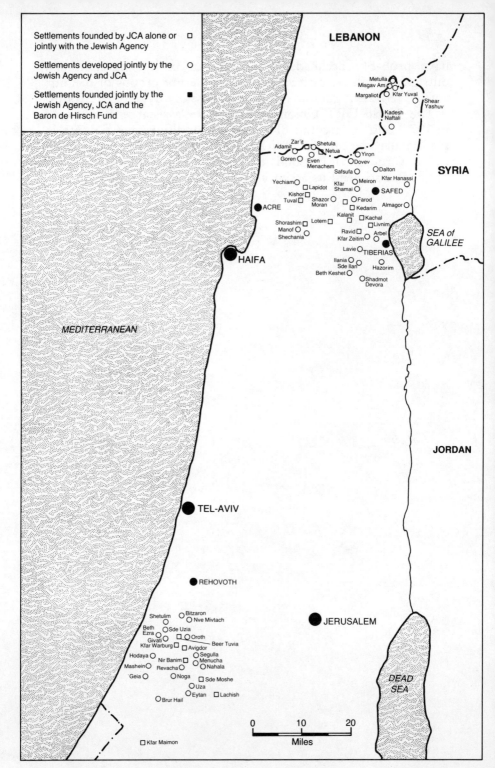

Map 5   Israel: Settlements associated with JCA, 1934–83 (continued on facing page)

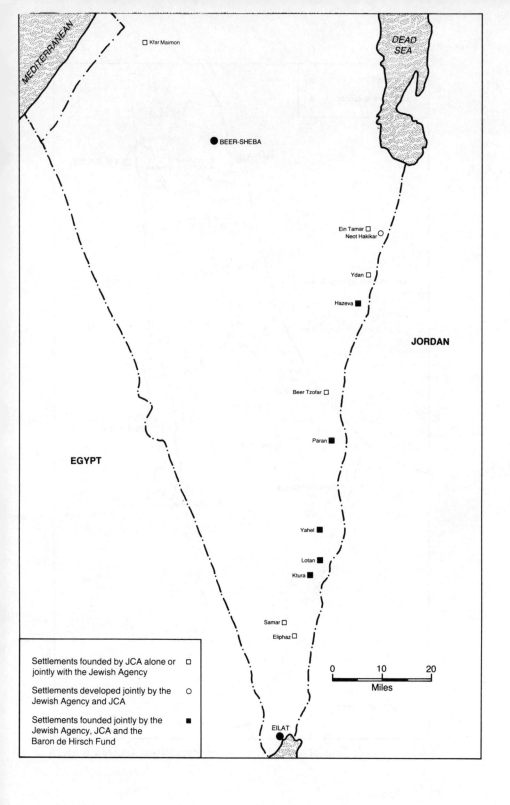

MEDITERRANEAN

☐ Kfar Maimon

DEAD
SEA

● BEER-SHEBA

JORDAN

Ein Tamar ☐
Neot Hakikar ○

Ydan ☐

Hazeva ■

Beer Tzofar ☐

Paran ■

EGYPT

Yahel ■

Lotan ■
Ktura ■

Samar ☐
Eliphaz ☐

Settlements founded by JCA alone or   ☐
jointly with the Jewish Agency

Settlements developed jointly by the   ○
Jewish Agency and JCA

Settlements founded jointly by the   ■
Jewish Agency, JCA and the
Baron de Hirsch Fund

0   10   20
Miles

EILAT ●

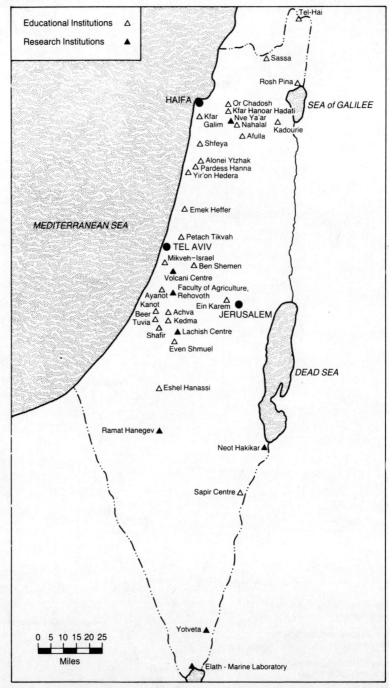

Map 6   Israel: Educational and research institutions assisted by JCA

CHAPTER 15

Israel

The work of Emica

Emica had time before the Second World War to establish two
colonies, Beer Tuvia and Kfar Warburg,[1] about 15 kilometres
southeast of Ashdod in the Lachish area. Their agricultural practice at the beginning was based on mixed farming, with dairying
as the core. All through the war these two villages expanded; for
Palestine was a major supplier of produce to the British forces in
the Middle East. By 1947 Beer Tuvia had a population of 697
and Kfar Warburg, the younger of the two, 248.

With the effects of the war behind it, and Israel from 1948 an
independent nation, Emica by 1949 was ready to expand its two
settlements. But now it had a new partner. This potent new
participant – to the extent of 50 per cent – was the Jewish Agency,
the organ created in 1929 by the Zionists in conjunction with
prominent non-Zionists like Felix Warburg. The Agency was
established in accordance with that section of the League of
Nations Mandate for Palestine which called for an 'appropriate
Jewish Agency, . . . for the purpose of advising and co-operating
with the administration of Palestine in such economic, social and
other matters as may affect the establishment of the Jewish
National Home and the interests of the Jewish population in
Palestine'. From 1929 until the establishment of the State of Israel,
the Agency 'played the principal role in the relations between
the National Home and world Jewry on the one hand and the
Mandatory and other powers on the other'.[2] As matters turned
out, after Israel became independent the Jewish Agency became
the main recipient of the funds raised by the United Israel Appeal.
Among the most important of its many functions, then and now,
is land settlement and the reception of immigrants.

Under the arrangement between Emica and the Agency, work
was begun in 1950 on adding 35 houses and related farm buildings
to the two colonies. While this development went forward Emica
decided to transfer its great project, the draining of the Huleh, to
the Keren Kayemet (Jewish National Fund), the land purchase

and conservation fund of the Zionist Organisation. The Keren Kayemet carried out the plans commissioned by Emica, completing the task by 1958. The drainage of the Huleh added 80,000 dunams (20,000 acres) of fertile soil to Israel's land resources, increased the supply of water entering the national water carrier, and eliminated the plague of malaria from the north-eastern section of the country. While some thought had been given to a drainage project at the turn of the century, under the Turkish regime, much of the credit for this bold, imaginative and successful undertaking must go to Maurice Hexter and Louis Oungre who, as far back as 1932, had had a concept of what could be done in the Huleh, and under whose initiative the critically important surveys were carried out and plans drawn up.

In 1951 Sir Henry d'Avigdor Goldsmid, the son of Sir Osmond (who had been JCA's President from 1934 until his untimely death in 1940), himself became President of the Association. He lost no time in paying a visit to Israel, the first JCA President to do so on behalf of the Association. This visit, the first of the 15 or so he made between that time and his death in 1976, was indicative of his deep interest in Israel. As Sir Keith Joseph had pointed out in 1958, Israel was now the most favourable location for a JCA agricultural settlement programme; but there is a world of difference between undertaking a project only because there is no other choice and embracing it with enthusiasm even if it *is* the only one feasible.

However, the great expansion of JCA's work in Israel lay some years in the future. For the time being Emica contented itself with enlarging its settlement programme by adding a third village, Avigdor, and beginning to plan for a fourth, Nir Banim, both in the same Lachish area where the first two were situated. The growth of the settlements continued without interruption, not only in population but also materially and financially. By 1954 the milk cattle, now numbering 1,350 in Beer Tuvia and 1,100 in Kfar Warburg, were giving excellent yields, and in consequence the settlers were ahead in meeting their repayment schedules. They enjoyed a high standard of living in Israeli terms, meaning that they had electric power and the advantages of household appliances like refrigerators. Beer Tuvia had a medical clinic and a general store, Kfar Warburg a communal centre. The residents of the two newer settlements, Avigdor and Nir Banim, who had been carefully selected not only for their innate qualities but also for how well they would fit in with the others, lived on a scale not far below that of the older communities.

15a Avigdor, Israel, 1955

15b Kfar Warburg, Israel, 1960. Farmer's house

16a Beer Tuvia, Israel. The school

16b Nir Banim, Israel. The communal hall

JCA gets into its stride

In 1955 there took place a change seemingly of slight practical importance but of considerable symbolic significance. Emica, for whose management and finances JCA had already for some time been wholly responsible, became formally a subsidiary company of JCA and its name was changed to 'Jewish Colonization Association (ICA) in Israel'.

Nir Banim had enjoyed a successful first year, and the construction of 15 additional houses was begun. Plans were made for the establishment of a fifth village, and by the end of 1956 65 houses, a store and a communal meeting house were well on their way to completion there. In the next year this newest settlement, given the name of Sdeh Moshe to commemorate the Baron de Hirsch, was in full operation, had produced a crop, and had added a school and kindergarten to its facilities. The five JCA settlements in the Lachish area were now peopled by 362 families, 1,843 individuals; they cultivated 25,000 dunams, of which about half were irrigated; their principal products were milk and its derivatives, poultry and vegetables.

Growth, in both population and crop returns, continued into 1958, and JCA began to plan for a sixth settlement. This was to be devoted chiefly to industrial crops such as groundnuts and cotton, although it would also have poultry, vegetables and citrus. An experiment in growing bananas was initiated at Sdeh Moshe. An important new departure in 1958 was JCA's decision to set up a revolving loan fund of IL1 million[3] for the purchase of fodder by the colonies. This was the first of a number of similar pools of credit which JCA established over the subsequent years to make various kinds of loans to the settlements.

Ten years after Israel's independence, the pace of JCA's work in the country began to quicken. Planning started for a seventh settlement, and an eighth was discussed. The area at the disposal of all the JCA villages had increased to 57,000 dunams, of which 16,000 were irrigated. The basic activity was still milk production (in fact, in 1961 4.6 per cent of all Israel's milk came from the JCA settlements), but poultry, eggs and beef were also important products, citrus planting was being started in some of the settlements, and in the newer ones industrial crops like sugarbeet, cotton and groundnuts were grown. Vegetable growing was restricted to what the limited allocation of irrigation water would allow. The IL1 million loan fund was working effectively (IL5.04 at this time equalled £1 sterling); and with its aid the colonies were able to buy fodder and fertiliser at relatively favourable prices. They continued to prosper, their receipts in 1960 being 23 per cent more than in the previous year. Other aspects of life were not forgotten, as plans for a big cultural centre in the Beer Tuvia–Kfar Warburg district bear witness. The population of the seven JCA settlements at the end of 1960 was 2,119.

The moshav

The JCA settlements were all *moshavim*, a form of organisation responsible for about half of Israel's agricultural output. A moshav essentially is composed of families who own and operate their farms individually, making their own decisions as to planting, cultivation, crop protection, harvesting, etc., albeit in consultation with the other farmers in the village, with a view to achieving the best results. The moshav does, however, have a number of communal characteristics. For one thing, at the initial stage, before the land is fully prepared and houses and other structures built, the members may cultivate in common the area assigned to the group, although they settle in their own houses and on their own plots as soon as these are ready. Afterwards, the moshav as a community will perform certain services for each member, such as selling his produce co-operatively or hiring big and specialised machinery for a particular task, and will provide amenities, such as a retail store, that are the customary functions of a village organisation. Members producing the same crop may band together in a co-operative for buying, selling, cultivating or harvesting it. But in the end the individual owner is responsible for his own fields or barns or greenhouses, and is free to dispose of his holding or to buy and add to it.

JCA by tradition was intended to help create a self-sufficient class of Jewish farmers; therefore, in the settlement work that it undertook in Israel it was inclined to be favourably disposed toward the moshav type of organisation. This did not, however, prevent the Association at a later stage from working wholeheartedly with *kibbutzim*, the collective type of farm settlement which makes up the other half of Israel's agricultural scene and which is perhaps better known to the outside world than the moshav.

The consolidation plan

In the period after Israel attained independence there was a great flood of immigrants into the country. They came from all corners of the earth – Holocaust survivors and displaced persons from Europe; from the internment camps of Cyprus; from the Arab

266

countries of North Africa and southwest Asia, where many had been treated as second-class citizens; from India; from Persia. A million Jews came into a country that at the end of 1948 had a population of only 750,000, and most of the newcomers arrived in the first four years of independence. This enormous intake put great pressure on the Israel government and the Jewish Agency to find permanent homes and jobs for the immigrants, tens of thousands of whom had to live in poor, temporary quarters (*Ma'abarot*) like tent cities for several months and sometimes longer. It was no wonder, then, that when the authorities of the Agency had time to draw breath they found that many of the hastily assembled agricultural villages to which they had sent recent arrivals from Yemen, Iraq or Morocco were poorly planned, too small, or not well enough equipped to provide a decent living for their inhabitants – who, in addition, may not have known very much about modern farming. No wonder, too, that the hard-pressed Agency turned for help to JCA, which had demonstrated considerable expertise in developing agricultural settlements.

Consultations between the Agency and JCA resulted in 1960 in the formulation of what was called a consolidation plan, to benefit some 20 under-developed villages populated by recent immigrants. A fund of IL12 million, over one-third supplied by JCA, was to provide loans to ameliorate the condition of these sub-standard settlements and put their inhabitants on the road to self-reliance. Most of the villages in the plan were in the south, not far from the Lachish area where JCA had been working.

'Consolidation' required a variety of tactics, such as increasing the number of farm units, extending and improving irrigation systems, buying good cows from Holland and other countries, installing equipment for poultry raising, acquiring machinery and providing additional working capital for the purchase of fertiliser and other supplies. Transport and communication were improved by laying down internal roads. The organisation of the villages was rendered more cohesive by the construction of communal buildings. By 1964 work on the scheme was completed. Twenty-one settlements, containing approximately 1,650 families numbering 8,500 persons, had been affected. Their income in aggregate had risen in three years from IL11.5 million to IL20 million, an average increase of 74 per cent; some of them had doubled their income.

The start in Galilee

The favourable outcome of this enterprise encouraged JCA to undertake another, again in collaboration with the Jewish Agency. This concerned agricultural and economic development in Galilee, in the north of the country, far from the Lachish area to the south where JCA's previous settlement activities had been concentrated. Before 1964 was over, preliminary work on this scheme was begun. It was to start by establishing two new settlements of 60 families each near the Lebanese border. In 1966 the first families arrived and it was decided that JCA and the Jewish Agency should build a third settlement in the area. JCA's work in Galilee was broadened further to include an existing kibbutz, Kfar Hanassi, to the south of the three new villages, about 12 kilometres from the border. The plan here was to enlarge and improve the means of agricultural production. This was the first kibbutz to become part of the JCA 'family' and one, incidentally, where the settlers came mostly from English-speaking countries.

Further progress at Lachish

In 1964 Kfar Maimon and Moshav Lachish, the sixth and seventh of the Association's 'own' colonies, were completed and were in operation. Milk and beef continued to be the chief sources of income, but an expansion of poultry production enabled the returns from this branch almost to equal those from milk and meat. Following a decision of the Ministry of Agriculture that industrial crops should play a greater part in the crop rotation, the area under sugarbeet and cotton was tripled.

An interesting new development was that JCA started making loans for the acquisition of farms by the sons of some of its original settlers. In order to widen the outlets for the products of the villages, JCA supported ventures for further processing – a cattle and poultry slaughterhouse and an oil-extraction plant that produced cattle feed. As usual, the Association's interest went beyond the economic; the building of a social and recreational centre was now begun in the Beer Tuvia–Kfar Warburg sector, to commemorate (a little belatedly, although it had actually been planned at the proper time, 1961) the seventieth anniversary of JCA's founding. Assistance was given for the erection of community centres in other places also.

The population of the seven settlements had reached 2,300 and the area controlled had risen to 67,000 dunams, of which 37,000 were arable and 21,300 irrigated. Income from poultry was now on a par with that from beef and milk, and the industrial crops had also become important sources of revenue, as was citrus expected to be in the future, for plantings of this crop were greatly expanded. As its colonies grew, JCA enlarged its credit services by offering short-term loans for carrying crops till marketed and medium-term loans of three to eight years for construction purposes.

The Six-Day War and after

One of the most astonishing aspects of the Six-Day War of June 1967 was how little it disturbed Israel's economic rhythm. In fact, it can be said to have given the county's economy, which had been somewhat in the doldrums, a considerable jolt.

> There was a growth of production due to deferred accumulated demand, defence orders and the need to replace dwindling military and civilian stocks. Some demand for Israeli goods for the population of occupied territories and a revival of foreign tourism were additional stimuli. In the agricultural sector, basic development projects such as land amelioration, irrigation and afforestation continued and production rose by 13 per cent compared with 2 per cent and 3 per cent respectively during the two previous years. The successful agricultural year is the more remarkable in the light of the war and the period of mobilisation when almost the entire farming generation was in the armed forces and the work was carried out by women, children and the elderly.

Thus said the JCA Annual Report for 1967.

In the light of the above, it is not surprising to learn that most of the projects JCA had planned for that year went forward almost without interruption and some new developments took place. Thus, Beer Tuvia and Kfar Warburg were able to export dairy cattle, which was a real tribute to the skill and assiduity of the Israeli producers. Some of the earlier JCA settlements began to build greenhouses for growing flowers – mainly roses but some carnations also – to supply European demand for off-season fresh blooms before the end of winter. This trade, which has since grown to enormous proportions, was made possible by a very efficient computerised system whereby the Israeli grower, informed by telephone of up-to-the-moment demands, picked and transported the flowers immediately to Lod airport, where they were instantly loaded and flown to cities like Rome or

Hamburg for delivery the next day. As the sources of capital – government, Jewish Agency and farm co-operatives – would provide only 70 per cent of the cost of erecting greenhouses, JCA made supplementary loans to farmers who were able to invest only a small part of the cost. For the rest, the Lachish settlements did well in this war year when crops, especially cereals, were exceptionally good because of unusually heavy rainfall.

Expansion in Galilee

In Galilee the two new villages completed in 1966 were settled in many cases by children of farmers who went to the region shortly after 1948. In the next year construction of the third settlement was finished, but the people had not yet moved in.

JCA continued to expand its interests in this area by taking five more settlements under its wing. These had been founded in the 1950s by immigrants from North Africa, Hungary, Czechoslovakia and Latin America. Galilee is a quite mountainous territory, which to this day has been a problem for the Israeli authorities because its Jewish population is smaller than that of Arabs. It is also a problem from the agricultural point of view because of its rocky terrain and because its topography prohibits extensive fields. In consequence the chief branches of agriculture practised have been orchards, for which level land is not indispensable, and poultry, which requires little land. Another difficulty was that some of the settlements near the Lebanese border had been located there more for security than agricultural reasons; they had little cultivable land, and sometimes that was situated at a considerable distance from the houses.

The problem was how to increase the income of the settlements under such difficult circumstances. Certain steps were comparatively simple – the enlargement and intensification of poultry and fruit production, and, in aid of this, an inquiry into improving methods of coop construction and orchard planting, two subjects on which JCA supported research for many years. Other steps were, as in the south, to bolster the settlements' organisational structure by improving the internal roads and communal facilities. Discovering new crops that could do well in Galilee's tough environment was an obvious tactic and JCA tried to encourage some of the settlers to grow avocado pears and to construct greenhouses for flowers. Alternative sources of income included industrial and resort development, and some of the villages already had small factories for making irrigation equipment. JCA encouraged further moves in this direction such as the building

270

of guest houses and the creation of facilities for meat-processing and the manufacture of ceramic insulators.

To complete the story for 1967, in addition to its work with its 'own' villages and with about eight more in Galilee, JCA undertook a programme of enlargement and extension at Brur Hail, a kibbutz in the Negev.

More consolidation

The year 1968 saw JCA's return to the south, where it was now to do further work with 15 of the 21 settlements it had assisted under the big consolidation programme of 1960. Selected farmers were to be helped to intensify their operations and their houses and poultry coops were to be improved; also, roads in the villages were to be paved. Some help was still needed by certain farmers in JCA's original seven settlements; the more progressive ones needed credit for the construction of greenhouses and the install-ation of systems for growing vegetables under plastic for export to replace dairy and egg production. This enabled more traditional operators still producing milk and poultry to obtain larger quotas within the limited total allowed and made their farms more efficient and more profitable, a very important consideration for the moshav as a whole, for the members were bound by the principle of mutual guarantees. The fact that some members of the well established, generally prosperous moshavim were heavily in debt was therefore a source of concern to all, and this means of increasing their income lightened the burden for the settlement as a whole.

In Galilee JCA took on four additional villages. These were peopled by a diversity of immigrants from Hungary, Britain, Brazil and Argentina (some the grandchildren of JCA settlers in those countries) and by the second generation from older settle-ments in Israel itself. The plans were for enlargement by the provision of additional farm units or the extension of existing ones, and in many instances short-term debts were refinanced by longer-term credits.

By this time JCA had engaged in financial and advisory rela-tions with no fewer than 41 settlements, containing 15,000 inhabi-tants. With the Jewish Agency it had initiated seven settlements in the Lachish area and two in Galilee and had worked to 'consolidate' – to use the term it preferred – more than 20 already established villages in the south and about 10 in Galilee. As time went on it became apparent that a programme of initiating or consolidating settlements tended to be open-ended; there was no very definite limit, no borderline that marked completion. If, as in the case of the old original settlements, they were well towards having paid off the loans made to them at the beginning, new techniques and opportunities created a need for fresh credit. Having an established relationship with JCA, they turned to it as a further lender, the more so as the Association, in pursuit of its mission of helping Jewish farmers, was willing to make credit available at something less than the prevailing commercial or even government rates.

The management of JCA was quite conscious of the fact that 'its' villages had advantages, that the 'JCA connection' meant that these places could and would attain higher levels of development than the general run. Others, it was hoped and expected, would eventually reach the same level, albeit later and with more difficulty. Such matters as these are hard to quantify, but at a rough estimate the JCA settlements, which constituted about one-tenth of the 400 or so established after Independence, were two or three years ahead of the others. In one sense this might be thought to give certain fortunate settlers an unfair advantage; but in defence of JCA and its partner, the Agency, it should be pointed out that the resources of both were limited. To try to spread JCA financing over hundreds of settlements would have meant that each recipient would have obtained a pointlessly small amount. Therefore it was necessary to limit the number to be helped, and the ones chosen were those suffering from special handicaps, like living in the difficult terrain of Galilee, or having had little education and a limited cultural background, for example some of the immigrants from North Africa or Kurdistan.[4]

JCA's loan programme

Now that JCA was making loans in such a large number of settlements, its system of providing credit had been, as it were, institutionalised. Its loan programme had a four-pronged structure.

In the case of a new community, JCA and the Jewish Agency would come to an agreement that a total investment of, say, IL2 million would be required to prepare the land, install irrigation works, build roads and provide the buildings and equipment and other facilities needed according to the type of farming to be engaged in. JCA would supply a substantial proportion – usually half – of the capital in the form of a loan in pounds sterling to the Agency, which would supply the other half and carry out the work of preparation and construction within a specified time limit, usually three years. The JCA loan to the Agency would be at a concessionary rate of interest and repayable over a 15-year period. The whole sum for the founding of the village would be represented by an indebtedness of the settlers to the Agency on a long-term basis in Israel pounds. Other agencies, when necessary, would be called upon to do specific parts of the work; for example, the Ministry of Housing would erect dwellings, the Jewish National Fund would carry out land reclamation.

Similar to the financial procedures described above were the programmes for the consolidation and extension of existing settlements in need of help to improve or attain full economic and/or agricultural viability. JCA's first big effort in this direction, involving 21 villages in the south, as already described, lasted from 1960 to 1965. Then in 1967 a similar programme for six settlements in Galilee was undertaken and planned to be completed by 1969. In the meantime, another four Galilean settlements were included in a scheme begun in 1968, and yet another four, also in Galilee, in a programme that commenced in 1969. The details of this last, as described in the Annual Report for 1969, provide a good illustration of what was meant by 'consolidation' and how JCA went about it:

> Even Menachem (population 360), situated in Western Galilee, was founded in 1960 with settlers of North African origin. The main branches of farming engaged in are fruit and poultry. Although the community is socially sound, its income is low. The new programme provides for additional fruit plantations, the enlargement of the irrigation network, the introduction of irrigated fieldcrops and the extension of livestock branches (poultry and sheep). Additional farm buildings and cold storage space for fruit will also be provided.
>
> Dalton (population 615), in Upper Galilee, was established in 1952 by religious immigrants, mostly from Libya. The farming embraces fruit, poultry, beef cattle and sheep. The development plan is intended to raise the income of the farmers by increasing the area under fruit, enlarging the irrigation network and improving farm buildings and equipment.
>
> Metulla, one of the oldest moshavoth in Israel, was founded in 1896 by Baron Edmond de Rothschild. The settlers, of Russian origin, were joined in 1958 by other immigrants from Eastern Europe, and the total population is now about 300. The development programme has as its main purpose the creation of 24 new farm units for sons of settlers and the

273

consolidation of the farms established in 1958. The population will then be over 400.

Kibbutz Farod, in Upper Galilee, has a population of 270. Founded in 1948 by Hungarian refugees, it was one of the first settlements in this mountain area then largely occupied by Arabs. The kibbutz has a high social and cultural level. The consolidation plan is intended to raise the settlement's income substantially by adapting new land for fruit growing in the mountains, installing new irrigation on land allocated to the settlement in the coastal plain of Galilee, and developing livestock branches. This will enable the kibbutz to double its agricultural resources and allow for the absorption of a substantial number of new members.

In 1969 JCA invested £170,000 in consolidation and extension schemes of this nature.

Once a village was established and the farmers and their families had moved in, JCA stood ready to provide direct credit to the settlement or individual settlers. Medium-term loans, repayable over a period of three to five years, would be given for a variety of productive or communal purposes, while short-term loans (one to six months) would be used for day-to-day farming needs or for bridging purposes (for example, a temporary loan for constructing a farm building pending the arrangement of permanent financing), or to provide revolving capital to carry crops until they could be sold favourably. Continuing with 1969 as our typical year, we see that medium-term loans to a total of IL1.6 million (£190,000) were provided in 27 settlements and short-term loans to a total of IL3 million (£357,000) in 30 settlements. Under a joint scheme with the Agricultural Bank (Bank Yaad), 65 loans for IL2,125,000 (£254,000) were made to settlement co-operatives and individuals.

The variety of purposes for which the medium-term loans might be used is well illustrated in the percentage breakdown for 1969:

Productive purposes	(%)	(%)
Farm buildings and hothouses	13.2	
Water supply and irrigation	8.1	
Fruit plantations	.3	
Livestock	25.2	
Machinery, equipment, fishponds	14.5	
Industry, crafts, services	5.0	
Total		66.3

Other purposes	(%)	(%)
Housing	10.9	
Communal buildings	1.6	
Shelters, etc.	11.6	
Public services, roads, electricity, sewage	4.4	
Miscellaneous	5.2	
Total		33.7
		100.0

Geographically JCA's programmes for the settlements it was assisting at the end of the 1960s can be divided into four regional groups:

1 old moshavim in the south;
2 immigrant moshavim in the south, many inhabited by people from North Africa;
3 moshavim in Galilee;
4 kibbutzim, mostly in Galilee, though later a few in the Arava.

Educational work

JCA's work, especially with people from Arab countries who had been educationally deprived and sometimes did not appreciate the value of education for their own children, roused the Association to the need for including educational activities in its programme. Another factor in this situation was the perception that there were two Israels, which might be quickly, if too simply, classified as the Ashkenazic and Sephardic, roughly equal in numbers but not otherwise. Generally speaking, the first group, of European origin and with European attitudes and values, was the class from which government servants, business people and academics were drawn. They expected their children to succeed them in such callings. The Sephardim, whose style and philosophy of life had been conditioned by their birth and upbringing in Arab, Middle Eastern countries, were in general the hewers of wood and drawers of water, their occupational opportunities constricted by their lack of training and education. Their patriarchal traditions dictated that the father should be the dominant figure in the family, but inadequate housing and 'foreign' examples of freedom undermined the parents' control. As the numbers of such families grew and the clash of cultures became more evident, the alienation of the children found expression in movements like the 'Black Panthers', fomented by the existence of large numbers of school drop-outs – perhaps as many as 25,000 in the mid-1970s – who wandered the streets without having access to any kind of job or organised activity, a fertile ground for the growth of crime or hooliganism. JCA, aware of the need for agricultural education to elevate the capabilities of the country's future farmers, also saw in agricultural boarding schools, where children freed from over-crowded city dwellings could be given an education and training in a fresh, country atmosphere, a means to fulfil two ends with the same instrument. The whole Israeli nation eventually awakened to the importance of providing specialised educational opportunities for the underprivileged children, but JCA could point with justified pride to its having been a pioneer in this regard.

In the 1950s JCA had begun to make grants to the Youth Aliyah agricultural training centre at Beit Dagan near Tel-Aviv and to the Mikveh-Israel agricultural school, also on the border of Tel-Aviv. Mikveh-Israel is a place of historical interest. Founded in 1870 as an early part of the Alliance Israélite school network in the Middle East, it was in a sense the first organised step taken in Palestine by modern Jewry, 25 years before the founding of what can be called the official Zionist movement (although the Alliance was far from being a proto-Zionist organis-ation). JCA made grants to Mikveh-Israel continuously for many years and in 1970 undertook to pay for the rehabilitation of three of its ancient dormitory buildings. In 1972 the Association moved on to participate in the construction of a new dormitory at the Pardess Hanna agricultural boarding school, and in the next year it bore part of the cost of building new kitchens and dining halls at schools at Kanot and Kfar Hanoar Hadati.

JCA was aware that in all probability agriculture would not expand enough to provide employment for all the youth from a farming background. They would therefore need instruction not only in agriculture but in other vocations, so as to be able to take advantage of other openings. At the same time, many of the farm children in the settlements associated with JCA came from the same kind of underprivileged Sephardic families as their city coun-terparts. Guided by such considerations, JCA in 1972 made a grant for building vocational departments in regional secondary schools in Beer Tuvia and Shafir in the south. The plans were worked out in conjunction with ORT-Israel, which operates the largest vocational training programme in the country. The Messing Foundation granted an interest-free loan, and the govern-ment and the regional authorities provided the remainder of the funds needed. In 1973 a similar scheme was initiated for the regional school at Kfar Blum in the north.

JCA not only contributed facilities to these schools but also provided scholarships to help poor boys and girls attend them.

The Yom Kippur War

Although the Yom Kippur War of 1973 imposed a very severe strain on the country, which suffered thousands of casualties, including the deaths of 39 men from JCA-associated settlements, and saw the mobilisation of 45 per cent of the male working force, the amount of immediate economic disruption was remarkably small, physical damage was minimal and recovery was rapid. What happened later, in consequence of the raging inflation that developed after the war and the defence measures inspired by it, is another story.

JCA's President, Sir Henry d'Avigdor Goldsmid, paid a visit to Israel immediately after the war's end, and the Council at his urging adopted an expanded programme, although the objectives were on the same lines as before. JCA's investment programme in 1973 covered 17 settlements including Shear Yashuv, a border village whose development had been hindered by Syrian artillery barrages. The plan was to expand the moshav by increasing the number of farm units. Most of the other settlements included in the programme were in Galilee, many of them inhabited by oriental Jews with large families, and here, as before, the emphasis was on poultry raising and fruit growing; but there was much else. In some of the places cold storage and meat and fruit packing facilities were introduced; fish ponds were dug; a metal factory was enlarged; and regional services for processing and storing the area's agricultural produce were aided. In the south the dairy enterprises, turkey rearing and greenhouses for flowers and vegetables were developed.

In addition to this investment programme, 42 settlements received medium-term loans totalling £245,000 for such things as housing and public services, and 44 obtained short-term loans totalling £1,135,000 for day-to-day farming needs or bridging purposes. Nor was this the whole story, for 40 settlements received 18-month credits for revolving capital from the joint fund operated by JCA and the Bank of Agriculture.

The Arava

The Arava is the extreme eastern part of the Negev, lying along the Jordan border south of the Dead Sea. Ten years ago it was almost completely uninhabited, with only two or three villages along the 250-kilometre stretch from the Dead Sea to Eilat. Because of the long unguarded border, the government was eager to see communities planted in the Arava, though that particular area had been quiet since 1948 and indeed has remained so to this day. There were, however, very obvious drawbacks to engaging in agriculture in the Arava. The region is part of the Great Rift Valley, which runs from Turkey to the middle of Africa; it is largely below sea level and is extremely hot, with temperatures reaching 50° or 60°C in the summer, so that work then is impossible except in the early morning. The whole area is extremely dry, the average rainfall being only three or four inches per annum. The soil is very poor, a typical desert formation, both rocky and sandy.

There were, however, certain countervailing factors present which convinced the Israel government and the Jewish Agency that it was worth trying to put some agricultural villages in this unpromising area. A kibbutz, Yotvata, which had been operating there successfully for some 15 years, had demonstrated that dairy cows could do well in the hot, dry Arava (there was also an experimental station at Yotvata). Furthermore, the Arava was a natural hothouse, and if crops could be grown there they could be ready for consumption in the European winter. Another positive factor was the presence of a considerable amount of underground water in buried aquifers; but this water is often brackish and sometimes contains a heavy concentration of minerals. However, largely on the basis of work done at the Yotvata experimental station, Israeli scientists have developed trickle irrigation, a system of feeding each plant very precise amounts of water and dissolved fertilisers; and it has been shown that many plants, for example tomatoes, cucumbers and melons, as well as fruit trees, are able to tolerate brackish water if it is supplied to them by this method. Such crops could therefore be grown in the Arava, even though the area does not have access to the national water-carrier.

JCA and the Jewish Agency had for some time been discussing the Arava as a possible new locus for agricultural settlement, although JCA took the position that it could not, early in the 1970s, make large sums available for investment there in addition to the money it was already putting into its consolidation and loan programmes. However (as has not happened often enough in Jewish history), according to the old adage, 'God provided an answer'. Since 1970 the Baron de Hirsch Fund of New York had been contributing to various institutions in Israel, among them ORT-Israel and the Agricultural Faculty of the Hebrew University. JCA, offering to act as the Fund's agent in Israel, persuaded its trustees to lend $500,000 to the Jewish Agency, to enlarge an existing moshav in the Arava and start a new one.

When the Baron created the Fund he directed that its work

should be confined to the United States. Like the Pope in 1506, who declared that the Line of Demarcation he drew was to divide the world into Spanish and Portuguese spheres, so the Baron also divided the world into two parts, the United States, which was to be the field of the Fund, and the rest, where JCA was to function. The constitution of the Fund therefore limited its activities to the United States. In 1970 however an amendment was effected whereby this geographical limitation was abolished, enabling the Fund to operate in Israel and elsewhere. In 1973 it entered into a loan agreement with the Jewish Agency, similar to those between JCA and the Agency, and later into further agreements of the same type, for the setting up of new moshavim and kibbutzim in the Arava. JCA continued to act as agent for its cousin organisation, supervising the carrying out by the Agency of its agreement with the Fund. Subsequently JCA made investments of its own in the Arava.

Wider activities

We have seen how JCA's activity with a few new settlements in the south broadened until it was dealing with over 40 settlements and engaging in a wide variety of lending and consolidating operations to expand and alter the practices and output of 'its' colonies so that they could keep up with the times and increase their income. So, also, did the Association's programme for assisting schools and organisations that taught, supplemented or otherwise aided Israeli agriculture broaden and deepen. For many years JCA had made grants to the Agricultural Faculty of the Hebrew University (beginning in 1942), to Mikveh-Israel (1897), and the Youth Aliyah organisation (also 1942). In 1958 the Weizmann Institute was added to the list, for research purposes. By the 1970s JCA was concerned with a wide range of educational, social and research activities, most of them connected with agriculture. For example, in 1974 JCA was involved in the rehabilitation of a number of agricultural boarding schools by means of both grants and loans: with the help of the Association a kitchen and dining hall were finished in one, similar facilities began to be added in another, dormitory rooms were completed in a third. We have already mentioned the agro-mechanics departments at the Beer Tuvia and Shafir schools. In Rehovoth, on the campus of the Agricultural Faculty of the Hebrew University, a large multi-purpose building with classrooms and laboratories was being erected with the aid of a grant for that year of IL400,000 from JCA; the government, the university itself and a private donor paid the rest of the cost. JCA provided scholarships for pupils at agricultural schools through the Harzfeld Memorial Fund and directly for students of farm management at the Agricultural Faculty and for students of social and community services at Haifa University. A number of farm experts recommended by the Ministry of Agriculture were sent on brief study tours of their specialities to Europe. JCA was also instrumental in persuading the Baron de Hirsch Fund to help finance a building for teaching motor mechanics and electrical installation at Merom Hagalil in the north. In the south, again at JCA's suggestion, the Fund also helped to finance an experimental addition to a comprehensive regional school at Even-Shmuel with the aim of providing vocational instruction for children below the secondary school level and thus giving them an incentive to continue at school, which might not have been the case if they had followed the conventional curriculum.

Besides all this work in the educational field, JCA was subsidising a number of research projects including, at Yotvata, the construction of a laboratory to study water salinity and, at the Volcani Institute, the breeding of turkeys, the cross-breeding of the local Awasi sheep with Finnish and Merino varieties to increase fertility and meat production, and the improvement of irrigation methods on hill farms. These last three projects had obvious application to Galilee.

More often than not, JCA used its contributions to research or educational projects as a lever to stimulate the participation of other bodies such as the Ministries of Agriculture or Education when such participation might not otherwise be forthcoming, or forthcoming so readily. JCA's usual procedure therefore was to cover up to one-half of the expenditure and further to divide this contribution into two usually equal parts, one in the form of a loan and the other as an outright grant.

JCA in the Arava

In 1974 the Baron de Hirsch Fund made a second $500,000 loan to the Jewish Agency for further work at Hazeva and for initiating a kibbutz, Ktura, in the southern part of the area (the general development plan for the Arava was for kibbutzim to be established in the southern sector, and moshavim in the northern). For its part, JCA decided to join the Agency in a development programme for moshav Paran. The Association also interested itself in another activity in the Arava. As the number of settlements in the area approached 15 with a population of upwards of

2,500, the need arose for centres to be built as focal points for communal affairs. One was decided on near Hazeva for the northern moshav group and another near Yotvata for the southern kibbutz group. At this juncture JCA was able to make use of the Nathan legacy. A rich South African had left some millions of pounds for the betterment of Israel, to be administered by an organisation whose name as given in the will did not correspond exactly to that of any existing entity. JCA was able to establish a claim to at least a part of the legacy and decided to use its share as a contribution to the Sapir Centre, as the northern Arava complex was named in honour of Israel's late Finance Minister. When completed, it was to have schools, food processing and storage plants, community offices and meeting halls – a concentration of structures that would contrast strongly with the bleak landscape of the area.

To a visitor it is a most impressive experience to watch one of the Arava villages growing up. Starting perhaps as a military camp, with a few dilapidated buildings in the moon-landscape, after a year it has a few simple dwellings housing 50 or 100 bright, enthusiastic young men and women and perhaps a rough dining-hall serving also as meeting place and club-house. A well has been dug, delivering brackish water, which can be used for trickle irrigation and even, with suitable treatment, for drinking. As the surrounding land is worked and the biggest boulders are hauled away, an outline of a field appears. By the third year there are more houses, a better community building, turkey sheds; stretches of desert have become fields, planted to peppers, tomatoes and carnations. There is also a young grove of date palms. A nursery may be under construction, for the young families have begun to reproduce. Some of the roads may be paved, and if this is a moshav a few cars may be parked on them. There is talk of a dairy herd, and the next year the cows may have come; the turkey sheds have been stocked, a store is being built, little grass plots are beginning to appear around the houses. There are setbacks; some of the crops may not have turned out well. Curiously, in high spots in the hot Arava (for example Paran, 300 metres above sea level) there can be a few winter nights when the temperature is below freezing, so large propellors are installed to dissipate the cold air. But older Arava villages like Yotvata, 20 years old, or Hazeva, 10 years old, have an air of permanence and prosperity which belies the fact that a few short years ago they looked like raw frontier outposts. The whole of the growth process can be seen in the space of a day or two merely by visiting a number of settlements at various stages of development.

The Council and Israel

In 1976 Sir Henry d'Avigdor Goldsmid, President of JCA for 25 years – longer than any of his predecessors in the office – died at the age of 67. It was largely through his inspiration and action that JCA had come to concentrate its efforts on Israel. Not that he was parochial in his interests; it was during his presidency also that JCA became involved in North Africa, Ethiopia and Australia. But Israel was his abiding concern.[5]

One of the ways in which the JCA Council under Sir Henry's leadership manifested its interest in Israel was its practice from 1961 onwards of holding one of its meetings there every few years.[6] This now gives its members a reasonably frequent opportunity of collectively inspecting some of the Association's work and items proposed for inclusion in its annual budget. Another indication of Israel's place in JCA's outlook is the presence of a number of Israelis on the Council. First to be elected, in 1961, was Eliahu Elath, who was Israel's first Ambassador to the United States and later Ambassador to Great Britain. He was followed by Arthur Lourie, another former Ambassador to Great Britain, who was elected to the Council in 1972. In 1977 they were joined by Gideon Hausner, who as Israel's Attorney-General had received world-wide notice as prosecutor at the trial of the infamous Adolph Eichmann. Lourie died in 1978 and was succeeded on the Council by Walter Eytan, for ten years Israel's Ambassador to France. The tally of Israeli Council members was increased to four by the inclusion in 1979 of Yehiel Admoni of the Jewish Agency.

Adult education

Before Sir Henry's death the regional colleges springing up in Israel had already claimed JCA's attention and the Association had promised IL400,000, part grant and part loan, to such a college at Achva. On Sir Henry's last trip to Israel, in 1975, he had visited and been greatly impressed by Achva. It is situated in the centre of the Beer Tuvia–Lachish area where there were 20 settlements associated with JCA, many of them peopled by families of oriental origin. Its purpose, like that of other such institutions, was to serve adults rather than children, to provide them with the academic training that they had not had at a younger age.

In January 1977 JCA's Israel office proposed that, as a memorial to Sir Henry, JCA should enlarge its agreed participation in the development and rehabilitation of Achva to enable a new wing to be built which would bear his name. The building would contain classrooms, a library and administrative offices. There was also to be a permanent exhibit displaying a pictorial record of JCA's achievements. It was estimated that the Association's contribution to this project would be £130,000. The Council accepted the proposal and the building was erected in time to be dedicated on 1 August 1980. The importance of the college to the local population is shown by the registration figure of 1,160 students for the 1980–1 academic year as compared with 773 three years before.

The other major memorial for Sir Henry established by JCA was the endowment of a chair in agricultural economics in his name at the Agricultural Faculty of the Hebrew University at Rehovoth. The first and present holder of this chair is the renowned economist, Professor Yoav Kislev.

JCA's interest in adult education was also directed to the improvement of the capabilities of those who were already farmers and to the advancement of the educational status of rural adults generally, especially those from oriental backgrounds. A Centre for Agricultural Advisory Services was established by the Ministry of Agriculture in the town of Lachish with JCA support in 1977. It intended, by means of short courses (a customary mode of adult agricultural education in the United States and elsewhere), to raise the level of the farmers' skills to cope with modern sophisticated practices such as growing vegetables under plastic or hydroponically. JCA helped with the establishment of a research and demonstration farm at the Centre and later a demonstration orchard.

Further research

Just as JCA's concern with education widened, so did its involvement in research. Its choice of research projects was governed not only by the intention of helping 'its' settlements but also by the priorities of the national Agricultural Research Authority, so that JCA-sponsored research was co-ordinated with state policy. In the study of uses for the brackish water of the Arava, JCA supported the Yotvata research station's experiments with raising varieties of edible fish. Some of these experiments were conducted in the semi-commercial ponds of kibbutz Eilot, a few kilometres north of Eilat. Two years after the experiments were begun in 1978 it was reported that the break-even point in cost had been attained.

Another aspect of JCA-supported research was concerned with the perennial problem of finding alternative crops for Galilee. Experiments were therefore made to raise flower bulbs in the region for propagation; the bulbs after starting would be transferred to other areas in Israel to produce commercial flower crops. The results of these experiments were encouraging. 'Israel's advantage over Europe in this respect is that bulbs harvested there are ready for planting after a short treatment, while the European bulbs must be stored for an entire year before they can be planted' (Israel report, 1979). In addition, local plants not hitherto raised commercially were studied for their export potential.

In order to tackle the problem of new products in Galilee by financing experiments on a larger scale than in research plots, in 1977 JCA participated with the Agency in such programmes for nine moshavim of the region. An amazing number and variety of innovative products were tried. First, climate-controlled poultry houses were introduced. Second, orchards were enlarged. Then goats were kept for the production of cheese, a product with good export possibilities. Pilot studies were undertaken for the cultivation of flowers, herbs, mushrooms and ornamental house plants under glass. It should be added that research has also been carried out by other agencies, not associated with JCA, to find ways to bring into cultivation substantial tracts of land in Galilee where the soil had been deemed too shallow to grow crops satisfactorily. It now seems that there are technologies, mainly in the field of trickle irrigation and fertilisation, that will make it possible to introduce intensive agricultural crops.

This approach to developing new sources of income caused financial difficulties for some of the moshavim requiring resources needing heavy investment, such as orchards (bananas, avocado pears and mangoes) and greenhouses. JCA and the other financing bodies thereupon took steps to lighten the repayment burden on the moshavim. Incidentally, in expanding the villages ecological considerations were now taken into account and greenhouses, poultry houses and livestock were concentrated in groups outside the residential areas.

1977–80

In 1977 activities in Galilee were disrupted by the Litani operation, the expedition of Israel's defence forces into southern Lebanon to destroy PLO centres from which attacks were being launched against Israel. During the military operations people living in

Galilee had to spend nights in bomb shelters and otherwise alter their mode of living and working.

A notable feature of the economic situation as a result of the recent change in government was the freeing of foreign exchange from control. This precipitated a 43 per cent devaluation of the Israel pound, which in turn favoured an increase in exports and a decrease in imports, but which also helped to bring about an equivalent rise in the cost of living, the first of the great inflationary leaps that Israel has suffered since that time. The continuing and increasing inflation, rising to 100 per cent per year and more, has, not surprisingly, caused considerable disturbance on the Israel financial scene, at times forcing JCA and other lenders to suspend the issue of loans pending a government decision on interest rates and other loan conditions. Also intensified was an already well-developed penchant for calling strikes as groups of workers tried to secure wages aligned with the strongly upward price trend. Interest rates of 80 per cent or more continue to amaze outside observers. The Israeli economy, however, with such measures as the linkage of interest charges and wages to the cost-of-living index, has managed to keep going, as have entities within it such as JCA.

In 1977 loans were issued by JCA to 35 moshavim, 11 kibbutzim and 2 agricultural boarding schools, about the same number as the year before. The money figures in Israeli currency would obviously be higher, if only because of inflation. Interest rates charged by JCA were now up to 18 per cent, but were still low in comparison with bank charges or the rates on government loans. The 1977 report from the Israel office remarks that the balance of the Israel pound loan funds includes 'a very substantial part of interest payments earned (about 45 per cent of the balance)', which went some way to compensate for their loss in value in sterling terms. The concomitant of this loss in value was a shrinkage in terms of purchasing power. To increase the effectiveness of the money it lent, JCA decided to reduce the number of settlements receiving loans in Israel pounds by omitting those which had reached an economic level that no longer 'justified subsidised loans'. The figures nevertheless remained substantial – IL5,516,000 in medium-term loans and IL20,411,000 in short-term loans, all provided for purposes similar to those previously described, as were the loans granted from the joint fund with the Bank of Agriculture which amounted to IL6 million.

All these loans provided supplementary financing that would not be available 'under the official general norm fixed by the authorities. The flexibility and timing of such supplementary assistance has proved to be of great importance for the economic progress of the settlements' (1977 Report).

In the last couple of years, JCA in Israel has continued to act along the lines described in the foregoing pages. This is not to say that its programmes and policies have remained static, for outside forces dictated changes and new ideas were brought to bear on old problems. Thus, through most of 1979 JCA curtailed its lending activity to some extent, awaiting a government decision on credit policy. When this was promulgated it made index-linked loans feasible. In that year, as inflation soared and with it interest rates, JCA's rates on its normal short-term loans rose likewise: 32 per cent from January to July, 50 per cent from August to November and 65 per cent in December. With the introduction of the linkage policy the medium-term loans were linked to the extent of 70 per cent to the cost-of-living index. A difference from past experience was seen in the identity of the borrowers: 16 per cent of the loans went to new moshav settlers including sons of moshavniks, a category that had been minimal in previous years.

Also, a new form of lending was introduced towards the end of the year: namely the issue of dollar-linked loans through the intermediary of the settlement movements[7] at interest rates of 7–10 per cent. This was advantageous to all parties concerned: to JCA because the movements are stronger financially than any single settlement and the repayments would be dollar-linked; to the settlements who would be able to borrow on relatively favourable terms, because the movements, eager to foster the development of their younger and less firmly established affiliated settlements, were willing to subsidise loans to them; and to the movements, because it provided them with a new source of funds.

In Galilee JCA joined in a new plan designed to supplement the income from agriculture. This entailed, for the kibbutzim, that small industries should be established in them, and for moshavim, that some of their members should work outside their villages. One kibbutz formed a building team, which not only built the houses in the settlement but contributed further to its income by construction work in other kibbutzim. In another, a plastics factory provided the main source of income. In kibbutz Moran employment was distributed as follows:

	(%)
Agriculture	25
Industry	30
Salaried outside work	15
Construction team	30

At the end of 1980 a number of new kibbutzim were in the process of formation in Galilee whose prospective members were receiving training at older kibbutzim. Some of the candidates were still serving in the army. Because of the strategic importance of establishing new settlements in the Arava and Galilee, the army was willing to hand over old camp sites in both areas to groups of new settlers and to allow a certain amount of leave to prospective settlers to enable them to learn the rudiments of farming. The new kibbutzim in Galilee were not only to depend on the traditional poultry houses (except that these were to be thoroughly modern, with controlled temperature) but also to try greenhouses and plant nurseries, keep milch goats and grow spices and herbs under the supervision of scientists from the Volcani Institute. They were also to have small factories producing machine parts. A rather unique kibbutz activity, by Yahel in the Arava, was to offer a travel service for trips to Sinai. In the new Galilean moshavim of Kolamit, Lunim and Lapidot, while the houses and farm sites, including avocado orchards, were being prepared, most of the future settlers were employed outside the moshavim.

The most dramatic occurrence in Galilee in 1980 was a Palestinian terrorist attack on kibbutz Misgav Am in the northern sector, on the Lebanese border, which had been associated with JCA for some years. A child, an adult member and a soldier were killed in the incursion. 'After having overcome the first shock, the kibbutz returned to its normal activities and absorbed a few families from other places in Israel who were not deterred by this calamity' (JCA Israel report for 1980). JCA contributed towards the rehabilitation of Misgav Am.

In the Arava, JCA in conjunction with the Jewish Agency was working on development programmes for five settlements. The most notable feature in this area was the continued growth of the two regional centres. At Sapir in the north, in addition to the various administrative and industrial buildings already mentioned, there were now functioning primary and secondary schools and a building for the grading, processing and packing of dates – a sign of the growing importance of this crop, of which the many orchards planted earlier were now coming into bearing. The southern centre at Yotvata also had by this time a date house, a school and an auditorium in addition to the facilities mentioned previously. The growth of these two centres was an obvious indication of the development of the Arava, despite its hostile climate and desert environment and the occasional setbacks that may affect the early stages of any new undertaking. Not only had the Arava settlements, which now numbered over 15, grown steadily, but future growth seemed assured by the existence of a waiting list of candidates for settlement who outnumbered the places available. An interesting discovery was an underground source of hot water at moshav Paran. One use found for it was to heat the ground for planting melons earlier than usual. The progress in the Arava was good for Israel's economy in general, because by 1980 the country had almost reached self-sufficiency in food production, so that if agriculture were to expand it could do so only by developing more and new outlets for export, and the products of the Arava are almost all destined for shipment overseas.

JCA continued in 1980 with its usual loan programmes at what had become, after years of hyperinflation, the customary almost incredible interest rates, albeit still well below commercial levels. Medium- and short-term loans went to 48 settlements, two regional councils and one school and amounted to IL54,563,000; IL9,435,000 was granted from the joint loan fund with the Bank of Agriculture in which JCA had a 46 per cent share. The total amount distributed in loans represented a nominal 89 per cent increase over the 1979 figures, but the cost-of-living index in the same interval had risen by 110 per cent.

The present

In its programmes for 1981, JCA stated that these came under the same three general headings as before: agricultural settlement work, assistance to rural educational and advisory projects, and assistance to agricultural research. There were, of course, some changes in detail. Because of high interest rates and curtailment of government-subsidised credits, settlements reduced their agricultural development programmes, so that there was a smaller demand for loans for this purpose. In the educational field there was to be participation in the building of dormitories in three agricultural boarding schools, in order to absorb more children from disadvantaged backgrounds, as well as the construction of classrooms, a kitchen and a clinic at others.

The core of JCA's activity in Israel remains, as it has been for 90 years, the financing of farmers and providing them with advice and direction. How far this work extends is demonstrated by the fact that in 1981 50 settlements received JCA assistance, while 71 in all had received such assistance since 1933. Out of a total of between 600 and 700 moshavim and kibbutzim in the country, this is a not negligible proportion. In 1981 the moshavim that had been helped by JCA comprised 3,560 farm units, i.e. families;

together with the 18 kibbutzim helped, they represented a population of 24,166. The agricultural population in Israel was 320,700 in 1981, so JCA's help had involved 7.5 per cent of the total.

Thus the immediate future envisaged for JCA in Israel is both a repetition and an outgrowth of the past. As Israel's agriculture has evolved, and become more varied, more complex and more export-orientated, JCA, which started with the comparatively simple aim of just putting settlers on the land, has likewise found its plans and programmes becoming more complex and varied. That it is nevertheless still walking in well-worn paths is not surprising; for it can look back on its efforts in Israel with the satisfaction of having contributed to the establishment of a self-sufficient farming class who have not succumbed to the blandishments of the cities. This fulfilment of the Baron de Hirsch's vision has, incongruously, taken place in a land of whose suitability for the settlement of Jews he was, to say the least, very doubtful, and where probably not in his wildest dreams did he believe it possible that Jews would create a State of their own. Theodor Herzl, who had such dreams and believed in them, had told the Baron this would happen. But the Baron had remained unstirred.

In 1983 JCA maintains a small headquarters in London and a small staff in Israel. This is a far cry from the JCA world of the 1930s, with its extensive agricultural activities in Argentina, Brazil and Canada, its multifarious operations among the Jews of Russia and Eastern Europe and its important functions in the fields of emigration and immigration. But it can look back with pride on what it did, both to improve the quality of life for the Jews living in the countries of anti-Semitic repression and to ensure a secure future for the thousands who fled from such countries. And JCA's work in Palestine and Israel has been of real importance to the development of the State.

This is a tale of historic irony. The Baron de Hirsch, that great practical man of affairs, successful builder of railways in Turkey despite all obstacles, had a vision of transforming Jews into independent and successful tillers of the soil (it is true that Jews had been farmers in Judea 2,000 years before, but they had barely practised the occupation since then). To this end the agencies Hirsch created, JCA and the Baron de Hirsch Fund, settled colonies of Jews in many likely and unlikely places, from all of which they, or more particularly their children, tended to drift away as the economic and social pull of urban occupations, professions and life-styles prevailed over the attraction of life and work in a rural environment. One man, the visionary Herzl, had told Hirsch how to make Jews into farmers – hold a flag before them as an ideal in the service of which they would labour zealously. And Herzl, with his rare gift of successful prophecy, pointed to Palestine as the location for such labour. It was in that very area, which Hirsch avoided because of his distrust of both Turkey and Russia, that his Association and his Fund eventually helped to establish a successful farming class who are remaining on the land, on their own soil, in their own country.

MEMBERS OF THE JCA COUNCIL, 1891–1984

1891–1896	Baron de Hirsch (President, 1891–6)
1891–1896	S. H. Goldschmidt (President, 1896) (France)
1891–1892	Isidore Loeb (France)
1892–1918	Herbert G. Lousada (England)
1894–1932	Salomon Reinach (Acting President, 1917–18; Vice-President, 1930–1931) (France)
1896–1903	Alfred L. Cohen (England)
1896–1905	Zadoc Kahn (France)
1896–1909	Dr E. Lachmann (Germany)
1896–1915	Narcisse Leven (President, 1896–1915) (France)
1896–1921	C. G. Montefiore (Acting President, 1915–16) (England)
1896–1914	Franz Philippson (Vice-President, 1901, 1903, 1910)
1896–1903	Julius Plotke (Germany)
1898–1902	Georges Kohn (Belgium)
1900–1908	Charles Hallgarten (Germany)
1902–1916 1918–1922	Paul Errera (Belgium)
1919–1929	Franz Philippson (President, 1919–29) (Belgium)
1903–1935	Sir Leonard Cohen (Vice-President, 1920–2, 1924; President, 1929–34; Hon. President, 1934, Vice-President, 1935) (England)
1903–1914 1921–1939	Dr Julius Blau (Vice-President, 1934) (Germany)
1906–1935	Arnold Netter (Vice-President, 1933–4) (France)
1908–1909	Isaac Dreyfus (Germany)
1909–1914 1921–1922	Carl Netter (France)
1909–1914 1922–1929	James Simon (Germany)
1916–1934	Professor Albert Wahl (France)
1918–1940	Sir Osmond d'Avigdor Goldsmid (Vice-President, 1933; President, 1934–40) (England)
1921–1951	Leonard G. Montefiore (President, 1940–8) (England)
1923	Colonel Herbert Lehman (USA)
1923–1928	Dr J. Stern (Germany)

1926–1941 1943–1945	Jules Philippson (Vice-President, 1934) (Belgium)
1928–1941	Alfred Klee (Germany)
1929–1934	E. Baerwald (Germany)
1929–1976	Max Gottschalk (Vice-President, 1952–76) (Belgium)
1932–1933	Jacques Sée (France)
1933–1941	Jacques Helbronner (France)
1934–1951	Marquess of Reading (President, 1948–51) (England)
1934	Jacques Lyon (France)
1934–1941	Emil Oettinger (Germany)
1935–1957	Maurice Stern (France)
1936–1941 1946–1971	René Mayer (Vice-President, 1948, 1952–71) (France)
1939–1942	Wilfred Israel (England)
1941–1943	Sir Lionel (afterwards Lord) Cohen (England)
1941–1968	Leonard J. Stein (England)
1943–	Leslie B. Prince (England)
1944–1946	Viscount Bearsted (England)
1946–1976	René Cassin (France)
1946–1976	Sir Henry d'Avigdor Goldsmid (Vice-President, 1948; President, 1951–76) (England)
1946–1978	Paul Philippson (Vice-President, 1977–8) (Belgium)
1947–1956	General E. E. Wiener (Belgium)
1947–1978	Georges Wormser (Vice-President, 1973–4; Président d'Honneur, 1975–8) (France)
1951–1954	Dr Ricardo Dubrovsky (Argentina)
1951–1960 1967–1970	Sir Keith S. Joseph (England)
1952–	Dr Maurice B. Hexter (USA)
1956–1981	Jean Bloch (Belgium)
1956–1967	Marcus J. Sieff (England)
1957–1975	André Goldet (France)
1960–	Dr Eliahu Elath (Vice-President, 1968–) (Israel)
1963–	Hon. L. H. L. Cohen (Vice-President, 1969–76; President, 1976–)(England)
1968–	Michael M. Sacher (Vice-President, 1977–) (England)
1971–	Jules Braunschvig (Vice-President, 1978–) (France)
1972–1978	Arthur Lourie (Israel)
1975–1983	Major-General Sir James d'Avigdor Goldsmid (England)
1975–1983	Hon. Mrs. E. A. Samuel (England)
1975–	André Wormser (France)
1977–	Gideon Hausner (Israel)
1978–1980	James Block (USA)
1978–	Walter Eytan (Israel)
1978–1984	Hubert Heilbronn (France)
1979–	Yehiel Admoni (Israel)
1980–	George Harrison Heyman, Jr (USA)
1981–	Alain M. Philippson (Belgium)

PRESIDENTS OF JCA, 1891–1984

Baron Maurice de Hirsch	1891–1896
S. H. Goldschmidt	1896
Narcisse Leven	1896–1915
C. G. Montefiore (Acting)	1915–1916
S. Reinach (Acting)	1917–1918
F. Philippson	1919–1929
Sir Leonard Cohen	1929–1934
Sir Osmond d'Avigdor Goldsmid	1934–1940
L. G. Montefiore	1940–1948
The Marquess of Reading	1948–1951
Sir Henry d'Avigdor Goldsmid	1951–1976
The Hon L. H. L. Cohen	1977–

JCA's ACCOUNTS

The Jewish Colonization Association was incorporated with a paid-up capital of £2 million, Baron de Hirsch's initial gift to the Association. In his will (he died in 1896) he also left to the Association a bequest of £7,100,602 which the subtraction of death duties of £1,228,498 reduced to £5,872,104. Based on the increase in the cost of living between 1896 and 1982, the current value of the Baron's beneficence to JCA would be set at about £200 million, 25 times as much as the original amount.

JCA's balance sheets and income and expenditure accounts up to 1914 are no longer available; possibly they were lost when the Head Office was moved from Paris in the chaos of the Second World War. And the figures between 1914 and the early 1920s present a distorted picture because of the First World War and its aftermath.

By the middle of the 1920s, however, economic activity had returned to 'normal'. Let us look at the expenditures and receipts for 1924. (In interpreting the figures for this and other years the reader should bear in mind that they are sometimes an amalgam of capital and income items. It should also be borne in mind that over the 90 years covered by this review the systems of accounting, and indeed accountancy practices in general, changed many times. This often makes the comparison of one year with another very difficult, if not impossible.)

Expenditure and Receipts, 1924

	Expenditure	*Receipts*
Colonization	£195,276	£285,362
Communities	72,021	6,506
Emigration	57,738	10,261
Education	59,285	3,171
General expenses	14,170	
	398,490	305,300
Central Administration	17,150	36
Exchange differences	29,101	
Other expenses	48,206	
Investments (purchases and sales)	304,754	204,034
Investment income		160,347
	£797,701	£669,717

Broken down by country of operation:	Expenditure	Receipts
Argentina	£107,766	£246,150
Russia	85,513	10,940
Poland	69,916	6,343
Romania	41,484	12,129
Palestine	18,036	7,559
Canada	15,995	5,253
Lithuania	14,903	
Turkey	10,834	6,407
France	10,749	5
Other	23,294	10,514
	£398,490	£305,300

It is interesting to note from the amount spent on emigration how important this activity had become. Argentina was still the major centre of operations; though large sums were being spent there, repayments were even larger. This fact, combined with the sizeable expenditure in Russia, prompted a bitter attack on JCA by a journalist who asserted that JCA was wasting its income from Argentina by spending it on the Association's Russian activities. In one sense, however, the money was usefully employed: it made life easier, or even procured a living, for thousands of Jewish families, albeit temporarily. On the other hand, the money might indeed have provided a more certain and more long-lasting benefit had it been spent elsewhere, particularly in Palestine.

The balance sheet as at 31 December 1924 shows the net assets at £5,997,456, startlingly depleted from the approximately £8.3 million they had totalled some 30 years before. The reduction was due not only to the loss or reduction in value of German and other European securities as a result of the 1914 war, but also to the writing-off over the period of sums invested in JCA's colonization and other activities that had also been severely affected by the havoc of the war. As will be shown later, opportunities were taken in subsequent years to restore the position.

Balance Sheet as at 31 December 1924

Assets		
Cash and securities		£3,432,021
Sundry debtors		135,723
Real estate		175,701
Colonization: Argentina		1,849,178
Brazil		45,466
Other		245,490
Advances		54,945
Baroness's bequest:		
Cash and securities	£118,261	
Profit and loss account	307,734	
		425,995
	Carried forward	6,364,519

		Brought forward	£6,364,519
Liabilities			
Provisions and reserves		£360,514	
Sundry creditors		6,549	
			367,063
Net assets			£5,997,456
Financed by:			
Share capital			2,000,000
Donated funds:			
Baron de Hirsch		5,872,104	
Baroness de Hirsch		425,995	
Other		298	
			6,298,397
			8,298,397
Net cost of operations and adjustments, 1891–1924			2,300,941
			£5,997,456

Let us now look at the expenditures and receipts for 1928. Clearly, Russia, which accounted for more than half the total expenditure in countries of operation, had become the principal locus of JCA's efforts. For the moment migration work was less important than in previous years, as the refugees from Russia had finally been moved out of Europe. Including various accounting items, the total of the expenditure side in 1928 was £785,536, and with revenues from securities amounting to £371,226 in addition to repayments, receipts, at £768,215, were almost equal to the expenditure. The large amount of the Argentine receipts and the even larger expenditure in the USSR lend further point to the journalist's criticism concering the funnelling into Russia of receipts in South America.

Expenditure and Receipts, 1928

	Expenditure	Receipts
Colonization	£485,805	£364,952
Communities	52,682	30,095
Emigration (including HICEM)	19,119	
Education	39,521	1,942
General expenses	44,600	
	641,727	396,989
Administration	19,839	
Investments	342	200,161
Investment income		171,065
Exchange differences	1,902	
Transfers to reserves, etc.	121,726	
	£785,536	£768,215

Broken down by country of operation:	Expenditure	Receipts
Argentina	£105,911	£300,883
Brazil	28,104	17,222
Canada	21,799	6,615
HICEM (Emigration)	13,745	
Palestine	9,190	13,344
Poland	35,229	15,787
Foundation	6,778	
Romania	28,473	9,733
Russia	372,123	28,870
Other	20,375	4,535
	£641,727	£396,989

In 1929 and again in 1933, the Association's real estate holdings were revalued. In 1934, after allowing for losses on bad debts, increasing reserves for doubtful accounts and for depreciation and writing off losses for past years, the assets in the balance sheet as at 31 December 1934 totalled £6,950,613. Although this was still £1,347,486 less than the total sums received from the Baron and Baroness, the process of restoration referred to above was already beginning to take place. On the basis of these figures, it can be calculated that in its 43 years of activity up to 1934 JCA had 'lost', or spent from its capital funds, about £31,000 per annum.

Expenditure and Receipts, 1938

	Expenditure	Receipts
Colonization	£185,935	£114,304
Communities	56,270	1,888
Emigration	151,731	
Education	20,764	2,472
	414,700	118,664
Administration	50,141	
Investments	213,519	347,622
Investment income		171,770
	£678,360	£638,056

Broken down by country of operation:		
Argentina	£116,839	£83,589
Germany and action for German Jews	98,770	555
Poland	51,313	10,933
Romania	13,611	5,015
Palestine	12,845	685
Brazil	11,258	11,666
Czechoslovakia	6,914	3,173
Canada	5,171	965
USSR	3,609	955
HICEM	51,604	
Foundation	34,907	
Other	7,859	1,128
	£414,700	£118,664

The 1938 receipts and expenditure account is representative of the Association's activities after Hitler had come to power. The report that accompanied the account began with a remark about the unavailability of any information from Russia after the first quarter of the year. Since the JCA staff members in Russia had been arrested or liquidated, the absence of information is not surprising. A country now involving a large expenditure, £98,770, was Germany. The size of this figure (the comparable amount in 1937 was £39,589) shows how important emigration had become to the Association. The HICEM figure of £51,604 also included expenditure for refugees from Germany. The Argentine expenditure of £116,839 attested to that country's continuing prominence in JCA's scheme of things, but with receipts at only £83,589, repayments of capital were no longer what they had been in the 1920s. Only £12,845 was spent in Palestine, compared with £64,514 the year before, reflecting the big decline in immigration. It is to be noted that another country of major expenditure was Poland, £51,313. The total sum disbursed on operations in 1938 was £414,700. Against this, £118,664 was received (over 70 per cent of this from Argentina) in the form of repayments. The difference (in round figures) of £300,000 was made up from investment income of £170,000 and the £130,000 by which sales of securities had exceeded purchases.

During the war period that followed, no general audit was possible. In the preparation of the 1946 accounts the securities in the portfolio were revalued in accordance with then current quotations; ample reserves for holdings in South America were set up; and debts from Hungary, Czechoslovakia, Russia and the Foundation were written down to £1 each. The same was done for debts owed by communities in Argentina. After all these write-offs and revaluations, the total of assets came out to £7,012,717. In real terms, however, the pound sterling had depreciated considerably in the eight years since the previous balance sheet.

Assets in Balance Sheet as at 31 December 1946

Investments	£4,617,945
'Participation' investments	46,787
Cash at banks	144,457
Sundry debtors and current accounts less sundry creditors	166,330
Colonization (after reserves):	
Argentina	1,514,441
Brazil	308,911
Canada	61,265
Palestine	143,567
Other (Turkey, etc.)	9,014
	£7,012,717

The assets in the balance sheet as at 31 December 1946 show that the Argentine colonization figure is not large – even if one takes into account write-offs and depreciation – in relation to what was accomplished: not only the settlement on farms of 15,000 European Jewish families, but the whole Jewish emigration to Argentina, which was largely due to JCA's pioneering efforts. Moreover, the balance sheet figure does not show the very large sums expended on colonies and repaid by the colonists under their contracts.

By 1955 the method of presentation of the income and expenditure account had been changed to show only the net balances of the local income and expenditure accounts in the countries of operation; again, these scarcely reflect the scale of JCA's activities in those countries. Although the Association had arrived at the conclusion that it should wind down its activities in Argentina, that country still showed a comparatively large net expenditure. The explanation probably is that, accustomed as JCA was to treating the Argentine settlements as favoured recipients of aid, the Council were not able in practice to act brusquely in accordance with their intellectual conclusions. Thus, although it had become clear that Israel should be the future focus of the Association's activities, this perception, amply implemented later, was not reflected in the accounts of 1955.

Net Balances of Income and Expenditure, 1955

General expenses		£27,384
Pensions		27,186
Grants		61,880
Operations:		
Excess of expenditure over income:		
Argentina	£31,018	
Canada	6,857	
North Africa	15,597	
Israel	4,000	
	57,472	
Excess of income over expenditure:		
Brazil	43,955	
		13,517
Depreciation of foreign currencies		105,167
Total expenditure		235,134
Investment income		193,779
Net deficit for the year		£41,355

By 1965 the form of presentation of the accounts had been changed again, and the Income and Expenditure Account had been replaced by the Operations Account.

Operations Account, 1965

Investment income	£263,343
Interest on advances and sundries	33,135
Net profit on sales and redemption of investments	111,576
Net surplus on sales of land, etc.	37,661
	£445,715

Operations Account, 1965 (cont)

General expenses		£49,427
Excess of expenditure over income:		
Argentina	£ 7,775	
Brazil	3,072	
Israel	11,904	
Loan activities	5,847	
	28,598	
Excess of income over expenditure:		
Canada	7,547	
		21,051
Grants		172,185
Depreciation of foreign currencies		32,979
Provision for doubtful debts		18,560
Total expenditure		294,202
Net surplus for the year		151,513
		£445,715

Balance Sheet as at 31 December 1965

Assets		
Land, buildings and equipment		£152,637
Stores and livestock		27,598
Loans and debtors		1,667,238
General Investments:		
Quoted securities at cost (market		
value £4,858,250)	£4,148,533	
Other	297,941	
		4,446,474
Baroness de Hirsch estate investments		118,007
Cash		103,372
		6,515,326
Liabilities		
Provisions and reserves	413,462	
Sundry creditors	16,759	
		430,221
Net assets		£6,085,105
Financed by:		
Share capital		£2,000,000
Donated funds:		
Baron de Hirsch	£5,872,104	
Baroness de Hirsch	118,007	
Sundry	7,912	
		5,998,023
		7,998,023
Net cost of operations and adjustments,		
1891–1965		1,912,918
		£6,085,105

Ten years later, at 31 December 1975, the net assets had increased to £7,654,160 as a result of operating surpluses and capital profits on realisation of investments in the intervening years. The accumulated deficit from 1891 had correspondingly decreased to £353,327. Another notable difference between the two balance sheets is in the item 'Loans and debtors' – £1,667,238 in 1965 and £4,433,072 in 1975 – reflecting the expansion in the Association's activities in Israel. A concomitant of this was the substantial reduction in General Investments.

Balance Sheet as at 31 December 1975

Assets		
Land, buildings and equipment		£84,013
General Investments at cost (market		
value £3,757,279)		3,396,175
Baroness de Hirsch estate investments		122,442
Loans and debtors		4,433,072
Cash		175,236
		8,210,938
Liabilities		
Provisions and reserves	£496,174	
Sundry creditors	60,604	
		556,778
Net assets		£7,654,160
Financed by:		
Share capital		£2,000,000
Donated funds:		
Baron de Hirsch	£5,872,104	
Baroness de Hirsch	122,442	
Sundry	12,941	
		6,007,487
		8,007,487
Net cost of operations, 1891–1975		353,327
		£7,654,160

By this time JCA had reached its present mode of operation, that is, to confine its activities almost entirely to Israel, except for making grants to organisations such as World ORT Union, HIAS and the Alliance Israélite, where its support had become, as it were, traditional. The Operations Account for 1975 shows income of £501,073 from loans and investments. Against this, grants were made to the tune of £215,991, and currency exchange losses of £312,394 were sustained, chiefly on investment holdings in the United States; but a surplus of £89,927 on sales of land in Canada and Argentina and profits on sales of investments amounting to £62,605 enabled the year to end with a small net surplus of £1779.

Operations Account, 1975

Investment income			£300,498
Interest on loans and advances			200,575
Surplus on sales of land:			
Canada		£87,445	
Argentina		2,482	89,927
Net profit on sales and			
redemption of investments			62,605
			£653,605
Excess of expenditure over income:			
Israel	£64,895		
Argentina	10,645		
		£75,540	
Excess of income over expenditure:			
Brazil	5,462		
Canada	48,875		
		54,337	
			£21,203
Grants			215,991
General expenses			86,466
Net increase in provisions and			
reserves			15,002
Depreciation of foreign currencies			312,394
Debits applicable to prior years			770
Total expenditure			651,826
Net surplus for the year			1,779
			£653,605

The latest accounts available at the time of writing are those for 1981. The balance sheet is not essentially different from those immediately preceding, although there is one interesting change. The previous item representing losses and expenditures from 1891 to date has been replaced by a surplus amounting to £1,030,650, the accumulated deficit having been exceeded by gains in the intervening years. 'Land, buildings and equipment', which was such a familiar item in previous years, has also disappeared following the winding-up of the Association's interests in Argentina, Brazil and Canada. The comparatively small figure for equipment remaining refers to the Israel office.

Balance Sheet as at 31 December 1981

Assets	
Equipment	£9,141
General Investments at cost (market	
value £5,648,489)	5,037,312
Baroness de Hirsch estate investments	83,107
Loans and debtors	4,054,537
Cash	188,003
Carried forward	£9,372,100

	Brought forward	£9,372,100
Liabilities		
Provisions and reserves	£364,382	
Sundry creditors	21,858	
		386,240
Net Assets		£8,985,860
Financed by:		
Share capital		£2,000,000
Donated funds:		
Baron de Hirsch	£5,872,104	
Baroness de Hirsch	83,106	
		5,955,210
		7,955,210
Net surplus on operations, 1891–1981		1,030,650
		£8,985,860

Operations in 1981 showed an income of £836,109 from investments and interest and a foreign currency surplus of £243,423, largely arising from the appreciation of the US dollar in sterling terms. Total expenditure and provisions came to £354,113, leaving a net surplus for the year of £750,667. This formed a major part of the accumulated surplus from 1891 shown in the balance sheet.

Operations Account, 1981

Investment income		£458,076
Interest on loans, advances and deposits		378,033
Net profit on sales and redemption of investments		21,736
Net surplus on translation of foreign currencies		243,423
Donations		3,512
		£1,104,780
Excess of expenditure over income:		
Israel	£55,159	
Brazil	4,030	
		£59,189
Grants		132,316
General expenses		72,324
Increase in provisions		90,284
		354,113
Net surplus for the year		750,667
		£1,104,780

This review of JCA's finances shows it on 31 December 1981 with assets of nearly £9 million, not very different from the total in 1900, after the deaths of the Baron and the Baroness. But, as stated earlier, the value of the pound now is about 4 per cent of what it was at the turn of the century, so the capital of JCA in real terms is but a small fraction of what it had been when Queen Victoria was still on the British throne.

Whatever one can make of the necessarily summary figures quoted in this Appendix, looking at the picture as a whole, and even allowing for the decline in the purchasing power of the pound sterling, the expenditure depicted for the myriad of good works performed by JCA since 1891 would appear to be relatively modest. In some sense this seems to justify the hopes of the Baron de Hirsch that the farmers whom he established in Argentina, Canada, Brazil and elsewhere would ultimately become self-supporting. In terms of the hundreds of thousands of individuals whom JCA helped, the cost to the Association for each family per year must have been a comparatively negligible amount. Because of the vagaries of inflation, because the balance sheets and other accounts are affected by JCA's operations in the securities markets, because of the unavailability of the accounts for the early years and because the balance sheets do not show the total amount spent on JCA's projects, it is beyond our capacity to put a figure on this total expenditure. What we do know is that for most years the expenditure consumed the whole of the income, which, as we have seen, often amounted to £500,000–£750,000.

RATES OF EXCHANGE[1]

	Unit of currency	1892	1902	1912	1919	10 Oct. 1921	1930[2]
Argentina	Peso (gold)	5.04	5.05	5.04			
	Peso (paper)			11.4	11.6	11.6	11.6
Australia	Pound						
	Dollar						
Austria[6]	Schilling						34
Aust.-Hungary	Florin or gulden	10.2	10.2				
	Crown		24.0	24.0	24.10	7,500	
Belgium	Franc	25.2	25.2	25.2	25.2	53.3	
	Belga (= 5 francs)						35
Brazil	Milreis (gold)	8.9	8.9	8.9			
	Milreis (paper)			15.8	15.5	28.4	40.7
	Cruzeiro						
Canada	Dollar		4.87	4.87	4.87	4.175	4.87
Egypt	Pound	0.985	0.985	0.99			
	Piastre				97.5	97.75	97.5
France	Franc	25.2	25.2	25.2	25.2	52.3	124
Germany	Mark, RM or DM	20.4	20.4	20.4	20.4	469	20.4
Holland	Florin or guilder	12	12	12	12	12	12
Israel	Pound						
	Shekel						
Morocco	Franc						
	Dirham						
Poland	Mark					18,000	
	Zloty						43
Romania	Leu	25.2	25.2	25.2	25.2	437	820–806
Russia/USSR	Rouble	6.3	6.3	9.5	80	12.5	9.5
Switzerland	Franc	25.2	25.2	25.2	25.2	21.3	25.1
Tunisia	Franc						
	Dinar						
Turkey	Piastre	111	111	111	111	1125–1025	
	Pound						
USA	Dollar	4.87	4.87	4.87	4.87	3.80	4.87
Uruguay	Peso	5.04	5.05	4.8	4.8	5.4	6.4–5.2

Notes
1 All quotations: units of foreign currency to £1 sterling.
2 Where two rates are quoted these are the maximum and minimum for the period 1 January–24 October 1930.
3 (a) Gold standard suspended by UK 21 September 1931.
  (b) Where two rates are quoted these are the maximum and minimum for the period 1 January–17 October 1931.

1931[3]	1932[4]	1938[5]	1939	1948	1956	1966	1976	14 Dec. 1981
11.6	11.6	15	19	20	50	606	235	
	1.25	1.25	1.25	1.25	1.25			
						2.50	1.36	1.65
35–28	37–30	26.5		40	72	72	29	30
				177	140	140	62	78
35–26.5	27–24	30–28	26.5					
40.7	61–43	96–80						
			82	75	201	6,168	19	228
4.87	4.28–3.75	5.03–4.78	4.54	4.03	2.72	3.01	1.62	2.23
				0.975	0.975	1.22	0.705	1.5
98–94	98–94	97.5	97.5					
124–96	96–85	179–147	176	1,062	980	13.77	8.20	10.78
22.5–15.8	16–14	12			11.76	11.14	4.04	4.26
12.1–9.5	9.4–8.4	9.0–8.7	8.34	10.69	10.64	10.10	4.26	4.66
				1.00	5.04	8.40	14.05	
								28.50
			176.10	1,062	980			
						14.06	7.12	10.17
43–33	34–30	26	24	403	11	11	34	67
818–635	645–565	670	658	605	17	17	8	
9.5–7.3	7.3–6.5	26	24	21	11	2.5	1.3	1.36
25.3–19.2	19.6–17.2	21.8–20.9	19.9	17.35	12.24	12.08	4.08	3.45
				1,062	980			
						1.45	0.721	0.93
	1030	960–780	622–590	555				
				11.33	7.87	25.31	27.42	246
4.88–3.83	3.80–3.36	5.04–4.71	4.49	4.03	2.80	2.79	1.66	1.87
12.0–6.4	8.3–7.3	8.57	9	9.27	4.25	194	6.50	

Notes

4 Where two rates are quoted these are the maximum and minimum for the period 1 January–15 October 1932.

5 Where two rates are quoted these are the maximum and minimum for the period 1 January–31 October 1938.

6 After the Anschluss the currency in Austria was the German Reichsmark during the war period.

Chapter 1   The Baron de Hirsch and Russian Jewry

1 The Alliance Israélite Universelle, founded in Paris in 1860, was the
first modern international Jewish defence organisation. Its objectives
were to combat anti-Semitism anywhere in the world, to help Jews
everywhere gain civil rights, to assist Jewish emigrants, chiefly from
Russia and Romania, and to establish a network of schools for Jewish
children in North Africa and the Middle East.

2 The Baron lived most of his adult life in France and Belgium and
habitually spoke French. Therefore it seems appropriate to use the
French form of his name, which indeed he himself adopted, though
in later life he did become a citizen of Austria.

3 K. Grunwald, *Türkenhirsch*, Israel Program for Scientific Translations, Jerusalem, 1966, p. 18. The following pages are based on
Chapters IV and V of this book.

4 Ibid., p. 33.

5 Ibid., p. 35.

6 Ibid., p. 41.

7 Ibid., p. 60.

8 In an effort to assess the value in today's terms of the amounts of
money quoted herein the author consulted Raymond Goldsmith,
Yale Professor of Economics Emeritus. The latter expressed the
opinion (in a letter dated 4 November 1980) that, based on a comparison between Britain's gross national product in 1890 and that in
1979, a multiplying factor of 121 should be used. Another calcul-
ation, based on the British cost-of-living index, gives a multiplying
factor of about 25.

9 C. Hibbert, *The Royal Victorians*, Lippincott, Philadelphia, 1976, p.
173.

10 There might also have been some ancestral influence inclining him
to charity. His grandfather established a charitable foundation in his
will, and his father was also open-handed and indeed received many
distinctions therefor, including a barony in 1869. His ancestry may
also have been influential in another important respect. Grunwald
(op. cit., p. 7) remarks: 'A student of this family record is struck by
the unvarying devotion to the land, by a physiocratic philosophy,
which sees in agriculture the source of all wealth, a philosophy
typical of the romantic period.' Maurice de Hirsch turned out to be

both a physiocrat and a philanthropist. In noting parental influence, it should also be mentioned that his father was deeply involved in financing railway construction.

11 S. Adler-Rudel, *Moritz Baron Hirsch, Profile of a Great Philanthropist*, reprint from Year Book VIII of the Leo Baeck Institute, London, 1963, p. 15.

12 Ibid., p. 17.

13 *Encyclopaedia Judaica*, Keter Publishing House, Jerusalem, 1971, vol. 14, p. 446.

14 This was the Beilis case. Beilis was acquitted by an all-Russian jury.

15 S. Joseph, *History of the Baron de Hirsch Fund*, Jewish Publication Society, New York, 1935, p. 11.

16 Baron de Hirsch, in *The Forum*, August 1891.

Chapter 2   The Beginning of the Jewish Colonization Association

1 In the *North American Review*, July 1981.

2 It has at times been asserted that the Baron opted for Jewish settlement in Argentina because the failure of an English financial house, Murietta & Co., made him the owner of land in Argentina and also gave him some claims on a railway there. Grunwald, the Baron's biographer, disputes this strongly, noting that the Murietta failure did not take place until 1892, while the Baron had decided on settlement in Argentina as much as two years before.

3 See n. 8, Ch. 1.

4 The local Jewish community at this time was very small, and the antagonistic minority was composed of some who, it must alas be confessed, had come to Buenos Aires to engage in the white slave trade (R. Weisbrot, *The Jews of Argentina*, Jewish Publication Society, Philadelphia, 1978, pp. 60–1). Needless to say, they were treated with the greatest opprobrium by the community whose good name they besmirched. JCA was very much alive to the problem and lent its support to English and other European organisations occupied with the protection of young women travelling alone. For more on the white slave trade in Argentina and Jews' part therein see article by Nora Glickman in *American Jewish Archives*, vol. xxxiv, no. 2, November 1982, pp. 178–89. See also Judith L. Elkin, *Jews of the Latin American Republics*, University of North Carolina Press, Chapel Hill, 1980, p. 108.

5 M. Alperson, *Dreisig Yar in Argentina*, Jüdischer Literarischer Verlag, Berlin, 1923.

6 Even this led to an incident. One of the husbands wanted to enter the warehouse to see his family; the guard misunderstood his intention, and since there was no common language, the guard and the husband got into a fight and the 'intruder's' nose was bloodied. This led to a great outcry – Jewish blood was being shed. (L. Schallman, 'Historia de la Jewish Colonization Association', pp. 80–1, translated. This is a typed MS. in Spanish, in the JCA office in London, which

appears to date to 1956. Lazaro Schallman was an employee of JCA in Buenos Aires. He wrote many pamphlets on the Jewish community, Jewish immigration and Jewish colonization in Argentina.)

7 C. Avni, 'The Promised Land', English translation in possession of JCA, not yet published, p. 182.

8 *Jewish Chronicle*, London, 23 December 1892.

9 The same edition of the *Jewish Chronicle* as printed JCA's first annual report also carried the following announcement:

A New Hirsch Foundation in Hungary

Baron de Hirsch has created a new foundation of three million florins, the annual income of which, 120,000 florins, is to be divided among Hungarian poor, irrespective of religion. Madame David Bischitz, to whom Baron de Hirsch gave charge of a former munificent foundation for Buda-Pesth, has been entrusted by him with the distribution of the annual amounts. She has organised a Committee which will carry out the object of the trust.

10 Avni, op. cit., p. 258.

11 Ibid., pp. 477 *et seq.*; Schallman, op. cit., pp. 239–78.

12 *Jewish Chronicle*, London, 2 February 1894, p. 7.

13 The peculiar language was Yiddish.

14 Schallman (op. cit., p. 232, translated) says:

Yarcho's abnegation in responding to the calls of the sick was legendary. He defied bad weather, downpours, tempests, the cold and the heat, the bad roads, and the constant danger of bandits who roved the countryside in search of plunder. In a wagon drawn by oxen he would travel 30 to 40 kilometres per day under such conditions.

He calls particular note to the heroic efforts of Yarcho during a typhus epidemic in 1894.

15 S. J. Lee, *Moses of the New World*, Thomas Yosseloff Ltd, New York and London, 1970, p. 263.

16 There is some evidence that Lousada was never called to a meeting. One member of the Council, who presumably was Lousada, was quoted as saying that he never attended a meeting and indeed had never been summoned to one (S. Temkin, typed MS. in JCA records, pp. 27–8).

17 Alperson, op. cit., pp. 391ff.

Chapter 3   Activities in Russia

1 D. Feinberg, 'Historical survey of the colonization of the Russian Jews in Argentina', *Journal of the American Jewish Historical Society*, vol. 43, no. 1, September 1953, translated by Leo Schpall, pp. 63–5.

Chapter 4 JCA in Palestine

1 The President of this organisation was Leon Pinsker, the author of 'Autoemancipation', published in 1882, one of the most influential of the pre-Herzl Zionist tracts.
2 This paragraph is based on Narcisse Leven, *Cinquante Ans d'Histoire*, vol. II, Paris, 1920, pp. 498–510.
3 Grunwald, op. cit., p. 123.
4 M. Lowenthal (ed. and trans.), *The Diaries of Theodor Herzl*, Dial Press, New York, 1956, Chapter II.
5 Ibid., pp. 109–10.
6 S. Schama, *Two Rothschilds and the Land of Israel*, Collins, London, 1978, pp. 110–11.
7 *Encyclopaedia Judaica*, vol. 14, p. 343.
8 Schama, op. cit., p. 135.
9 Ibid., p. 167.
10 Ibid., pp. 236–7.
11 Ibid., p. 170ff.
12 Ibid., p. 181.
13 *Encyclopaedia Judaica*, vol. 10, p. 48.

Chapter 5 Argentine Colonies

1 Schallman, op. cit., p. 420.
2 Ibid., p. 404.
3 Twenty-three people were killed in this incident, which caused immense indignation and an outpouring of condemnation of the czarist regime in Western Europe and the United States.
4 A mitigating note may be sounded. The tens of thousands of Jews who emigrated to Argentina between 1905 and 1913 and settled outside the colonies came because JCA had opened the country to Jewish settlement.
5 Schallman, op. cit., pp. 416–20.
6 This colony, founded in 1903, was located on the 100,000-hectare Leloir purchase, and the site was quite possibly not carefully examined.
7 Schallman, op. cit., pp. 421ff.

Chapter 6 JCA Elsewhere

1 Translation of Mr Eisenberg's version of JCA's history in Brazil. Typescript in JCA office, London, dated May 1960.
2 Ibid.
3 S. Belkin, *Through Narrow Gates*, Canadian Jewish Congress and Jewish Colonization Association, Montreal, 1966, pp. 76–7.
4 C. E. Leonoff, 'Pioneers, ploughs and prayers. The Jewish farmers

of Western Canada', *Jewish Western Bulletin*, 16 September 1982, pp. 9 and 15.

5 Belkin, op. cit., p. 84.

6 Ibid., pp. 211, 216.

7 Ibid., p. 86.

8 Ibid., p. 41.

9 Ibid., p.141.

10 H. Troper and I. Abella, *None is Too Many*, Lester and Orpen Denys, Toronto, 1982.

11 Ibid., p. 151.

12 Ibid., p. 237.

13 *Encyclopaedia Judaica*, vol. 14, p. 389.

14 Ibid., p. 390.

15 A. Gabis (ed.), *Fondo Comunal*, Villa Domínguez, Argentina, 1957, p. 18.

16 The history of Woodbine is described in detail in Joseph, op. cit. It is also outlined in an article by the present author, 'The Baron de Hirsch Fund since 1935', which appeared in I. Trainin, *From the Pages of My Communal Diary*, Commission on Synagogue Relations, Federation of Jewish Philanthropies, New York, 1977.

17 This section is based on the records of JAS and the author's own knowledge of the organisation, of which he was an official from 1950 to 1972.

18 E. Kedourie (ed.), *The Jewish World*, Abrams, New York, 1979, p. 158.

Chapter 7   *Argentina after the First World War*

1 The people who were not classed as colonists were those who, living within the precincts of the colonies, were engaged in occupations other than farming.

2 JCA recognised that this was the organisation's aim and therefore did not view its creation with equanimity (L. Oungre, 'Rapport sur l'Argentine', Paris, 1928, typewritten, in JCA office, London, p. 143.

3 Elkin, op. cit., p. 142.

4 *Fondo Comunal*, Villa Domínguez, Argentina, 1954, p. 32, translated.

5 Elkin, op. cit., p. 142.

6 G. Aronstein, 'Rapport sur l'Oeuvre de la JCA en Argentine', Paris, 1934, in JCA office, London, p. 52, notes that the price of farm land in Buenos Aires province took the following course (prices given in pesos per hectare):

1903	34
1921	257
1928	234
1934	147

Aronstein remarks that, while in 1928 farmers were eager to acquire title, in 1933 they were not. He also observed that not one single colonist ever offered to share with JCA any of the profit he made on the sale of his property.

7 In the 1920s JCA had 80 cases being processed in the Argentine courts and employed 12 lawyers (Oungre, op. cit., p. 154).

8 M. D. Winsberg, *Colonia Baron Hirsch*, University of Florida Monographs, Social Sciences, no. 19, Summer 1963, Gainesville, Florida, 1964, p. 60.

9 Ibid., p. 64.

10 Schallman, op. cit., pp. 445–8.

11 *Fondo Comunal*, 1954, op. cit., pp. 182–8.

12 Two extracts from Oungre's 1928 report illustrate JCA's attitude very nicely. The older contracts of sale had required a 20-year period on the farm before the colonists could become owners, so that they could be moulded into *vrais paysans*. Then, just before the First World War Entre-Rios province imposed a special tax on absentee landlords. This tax could have been avoided if JCA had granted ownership immediately to the colonists holding contracts of sale, but it did not do this because it did not want the settlers to lose the advantage of its tutelage.

13 JCA Annual Report 1930, p. 8.

14 Schallman, op. cit., pp. 475–83.

15 Oungre, op. cit., p. 124.

16 *Encyclopaedia Judaica*, vol. 3, p. 414.

17 *JCA – Su Obra en la Republica Argentina*, Buenos Aires, 1954, pamphlet.

18 Schallman, op. cit., pp. 541, 552 and 557.

19 Ibid., p. 566.

20 Elkin, op. cit., p. 154.

Chapter 8   *The Situation in Russia*

1 For many years JCA has made a substantial annual grant to World ORT Union.

2 A. Schmoll, 'Rapport sur l'Oeuvre de la JCA en Russie', 1925, typed, in JCA office, London.

3 This section is largely based on Y. Bauer, *My Brother's Keeper*, Jewish Publication Society, Philadelphia, 1974, pp. 57–104. This is a history of JDC from 1929 to 1939.

4 Conversation with Dr Hexter.

5 L. Shapiro, *History of ORT*, Schocken Books, New York, 1980, pp. 131–51.

6 Ekaterinoslav is now known as Dnepropetrovsk.

7 Artels were small groups of workers collectively engaged in industrial or agricultural projects.

8 J. Mirkin, 'Rapport sur la situation des Oeuvres de la JCA en Russie', 12 February 1930, confidential report, typewritten, in JCA office, London.

9 H. Agar, *The Saving Remnant*, Compass Books, New York, 1962, p. 49.
10 Shapiro, op. cit., pp. 152–3.
11 Ibid., pp. 153–5.
12 Bauer, op. cit., p. 83.
13 Ibid., pp. 83–104; Shapiro, op. cit., p. 55.
14 Shapiro, op. cit., p. 159.
15 Agar, op. cit., p. 51. Perhaps not absolutely all the Jewish farmers were killed. In May 1981 Professor Altschuler of the Hebrew University told the author that many years previously he had met in Israel a survivor of either the JCA or JDC colonies in the Ukraine who indicated that a few others like him had lived through the war and made their way afterwards to Israel. Even if a tiny number did manage to escape, the main point remains true, for the Einsatzgruppen and other Nazi instrumentalities wiped out hundreds of thousands of the Jews in the farm colonies in southern Russia.
16 Shapiro, op. cit., p. 135.
17 Ibid., p. 160.
18 Bauer, op. cit., pp. 70, 99 and 103.
19 JCA Circular no. 740, 11 July 1963, and enclosures.

Chapter 9   Palestine and the Near East

1 In part perhaps this is due to the uncovering of the British spy ring 'Nili', manned by Palestinian Jews.
2 Schama, op. cit., pp. 295 and 317.
3 Felix Warburg (1871–1937), senior partner of the banking firm Kuhn, Loeb & Co., chairman (*inter alia*) of Joint Distribution Committee;
Bernard Flexner (1865–1945), eminent lawyer and Zionist leader, chairman of Palestine Economic Corporation, member of executive committees of Joint Distribution Committee and Jewish Agency;
James de Rothschild (1878–1957), son and successor of Baron Edmond, head of Commission Palestinienne;
Simon (later Lord) Marks (1888–1964), leading English Zionist, chairman of the great retailing chain Marks and Spencer;
2nd Marquess of Reading (1889–1969), statesman and lawyer, member of JCA Council 1934–51 and President 1948–51.
Sir Osmond d'Avigdor Goldsmid (1877–1940), eminent public servant, member of JCA Council 1918–40 and President 1934–40.
4 Conversation with Dr Maurice Hexter, 24 November 1980.
5 This is translated from a memorandum in French in the JCA records, dated 24 September 1932, unsigned, but presumably written by Louis Oungre. The preceding and following pages are based on this document.
6 The income of the JDC was $3.5 million in 1928 but fell to $380,000 in 1932 (O. Handlin, *A Continuing Task*, New York, 1964, p. 54).
7 Oungre's trip resulted in part at least from a certain amount of direct lobbying on the part of Maurice Hexter, who went to see Sir Leonard

Cohen in the summer of 1932 and urged him to send Oungre on a mission to Palestine. Sir Leonard did not consent until his wife broke in to say, 'Leonard, you can't send this young man home empty-handed' (conversation with Dr Hexter, 14 October 1981).

8 Letter to the author from M. Hexter, 7 October 1980.
9 Oungre was greatly impressed, when he and Hexter were in Beer Tuvia, by a young boy who rushed out to greet the visitors, very anxious to show them a calf, just born on his father's farm; 36 years later this boy became General Tal, the famed tank commander (conversation with M. Hexter, 24 November 1980, and letter, op. cit.).
10 Letter from M. Hexter, op. cit.
11 JCA minutes, 22 December 1932.
12 *Jerusalem Post*, 5 October 1973.
13 D. Angst, *Nichtzionisten in Pälestina*, Universität Zurich, Zurich, 1977.
14 Ibid., p. 70.

Chapter 10   Poland and Eastern Europe

1 S. Segal, *The New Poland and the Jews*, New York, 1938, p. 39.
2 Ibid., p. 99.
3 Ibid., pp. 72–3.
4 Ibid., pp. 137, 143, 147, 180, 197 and 199.
5 Bauer, op. cit., pp. 50 and 184.
6 JCA Annual Report 1922, p. 103 (translated).
7 Bauer, op. cit., pp. 36, 46–7.
8 Ibid., p. 32.
9 The 1929 Report (p. 199) makes the claim: 'Les caisses desservent aujourd'hui presque tous les Israélites.'
10 Bauer, op. cit., p. 43.
11 Segal, op. cit., pp. 149 and 207.
12 L. S. Davidowicz, *The War against the Jews*, Bantam Books, New York, 1976, p. 537.
13 Bauer, op. cit., pp. 296 and 301.
14 JCA Annual Report 1937, p. v.

Chapter 11   Romania and Czechoslovakia

1 Summary of the Chronicle of M. Mariassin, in archives of JCA-Israel, Tel-Aviv.
2 *Encyclopaedia Judaica*, vol. 14, p. 394.
3 Bauer, op. cit., pp. 214–17.
4 *Encyclopaedia Judaica*, vol. 14, p. 396.
5 Ibid., p. 404.

Chapter 12   Migration

1 JCA Annual Report 1919, p. 97.
2 M. Wischnitzer, *Visas to Freedom*, World Publishing Co., Cleveland and New York, 1956, pp. 96, 97 and 121.
3 Article by S. Gould in *Natural History Magazine*, vol. 89, no. 12, December 1980, p. 14.
4 Wischnitzer, op. cit., pp. 123 and 128.
5 Ibid., p. 127.
6 These authorities do not always agree, and a further difficulty is that some of the years referred to are fiscal years, some calendar years. The author, acknowledging the possibilities of error, has done his best with the sources available, and if some of the figures presented lack exactitude they nevertheless reflect clearly enough the general picture and the main tendencies.
7 Wischnitzer, op. cit., p. 131.
8 A German authority – none less than the Gestapo – tells us that in the years 1933–6, HICEM helped 15,846 Jews to get out of Germany at a cost of £175,000; that in November 1939 HICEM opened an office in Brussels; and that between then and March 1940 this office received 7,476,000 Belgian francs, 4,776,000 from JCA and 2,700,000 from JDC. These interesting pieces of information are to be found in a memorandum written by an SS Sturmbahnführer in the Gestapo office in Brussels and dated 12 December 1940. The memorandum found its way after the war into the JCA archives in London. It contains an excellent brief summary of HICEM and JDC activities. It also states that by the time the Second World War broke out HICEM had 41 affiliates for emigration, transit and immigration.
9 Wischnitzer, op. cit., pp. 149–50.
10 Interview with Dr M. Hexter, 13 October 1981.

Part III   From the Second World War to the Present

1 Interviews with Mr V. Girmounsky and Mr J. Rosemblum, retired members of JCA staff, April 1980.

Chapter 13   End in Argentina

1 M. D. Winsberg, *Colonia Baron Hirsch*, University of Florida Press, Gainesville, 1964.
2 'Of 313 anti-Semitic incidents in the world reported in 1967, 142 occurred in Argentina' – *Encyclopaedia Judaica*, vol. 3, p. 416.
3 Reproduced in English translation in JCA Circular no. 586, 15 June 1959.
4 Quotations here are from a report by Mr J. Neville (Director of JCA, 1971–9) in Circular no. 1077, October 1973, in the JCA files.

This account of the termination of JCA's activities in Argentina is based on that report.

5 *El Colono Cooperador*, Buenos Aires, 5 October 1979.

6 JCA Circular no. 541, 22 September 1958.

7 R. Weisbrot, *The Jews of Argentina*, Jewish Publication Society, Philadelphia, 1979, pp. 52 and 176.

8 Elkin, op. cit., p. 152.

9 Ibid., p. 159.

Chapter 14   JCA World-wide

1 Interview with V. Girmounsky, April 1980.

2 Ibid.

3 When France granted Tunisia independence in 1954 it retained control of the naval base at Bizerta. In 1961 certain activities there caused the Tunisians to believe that the French were intending to expand their area of influence and stay permanently. Violent rioting ensued and there were many killed or injured. Tunisian Jews, who were thought to be siding with the French, were attacked. The *American Jewish Yearbook for 1962* (p. 435) remarks that 'the greatest shock to Tunisian Jewry was probably psychological', for Tunisia had always been considered the least anti-Jewish of all the Arab countries, and now it appeared that Jews were not safe there either.

4 Because of the changes in the currencies and rates of exchange after independence, from Moroccan francs to dirhams and from Tunisian francs to dinars, the figures for operations over a period covering both old and new currencies are given in their equivalents in pounds sterling.

5 1980 Annual Report of HIAS, p. 31.

6 Memorandum, 13 May 1965, signed L. B. P(rince), in JCA files.

Chapter 15   Israel

1 Named after the noted American philanthropist, Felix Warburg, who played a large part in the Palestine Emergency Fund (one of the progenitors of Emica) and countless other Jewish charitable organisations in the period between the wars.

2 *Encyclopaedia Judaica*, vol. 10, p. 26.

3 The accepted abbreviation for Israel pounds is IL.

4 Kurdistan is not a separate country, but that name can be applied to the northwestern area of Iraq and the bordering northeastern part of Iran, where the indigenous population is Kurdish, not Arab or Iranian.

5 Sir Henry manifested his concern for Israel outside JCA. For example, he was for many years chairman of the London arm of the Bank Leumi.

6 JCA's administration expenses are closely controlled, and Council

meetings, once more frequent, are now limited to two a year held in London, Paris or (occasionally) Brussels; but a meeting in Israel, preceded by a week of touring JCA projects, is substituted for one of these meetings when occasion requires – recently as often as alternate years.

7 The settlement movements are nationwide central organisations to which the settlements are affiliated according to their character or ideology.

INDEX

INDEX

321